The Contributors

Paul Allen Beck
Lawrence C. Dodd
Charles H. Franklin
James L. Gibson
John E. Jackson
Gerald H. Kramer
Duncan MacRae, Jr.
Gary J. Miller
Terry M. Moe
Richard G. Niemi
Bert A. Rockman
Kenneth A. Shepsle
Herbert F. Weisberg

POLITICAL SCIENCE:
The Science of Politics

Edited by

HERBERT F. WEISBERG
The Ohio State University

Published in cooperation with the
American Political Science Association

AGATHON PRESS, INC.
New York

© 1986 American Political Science Association
1527 New Hampshire Avenue, N.W.
Washington, DC 20036–3669

Library of Congress Cataloging in Publication Data

Main entry under title:

Political Science

   Collection of papers presented at the 1983 Annual
Meeting of the American Political Science Association.
   Includes bibliographies.
   1. Political science—Congresses.   I. Weisberg,
Herbert F.   II. American Political Science Association.
Meeting (1983 : Chicago, Ill.)
JA35 1983   320   85–15082
ISBN 0-87586-066-4 cloth
     0-87586-075-3 paper

Printed in the United States

To William H. Riker,
for helping to redefine
how many of us think
about the science of politics

CONTENTS

III. The Science of Political Behavior

PREFACE

When American Political Science Association President-Elect William H. Riker appointed me Program Chairperson of the 1983 Annual Meeting of the Association, we chose as a theme for the meetings "The Science of Politics." The 1982 Annual Meetings had focused on "The State of the Discipline," leading to Ada W. Finifter's excellent collection of the theme papers from those meetings in the APSA book *Political Science: The State of the Discipline.* For the 1983 meetings we wanted to build on the very successful 1982 experience, while focusing attention more specifically on the scientific elements of the discipline and encouraging reflection on its scientific status.

Not only did papers presented at the 1983 meetings extend the science of politics, but several panels were specifically devoted to assessing the status of science in the study of politics. In particular, the Lasswell Symposium on the second evening of the convention had "The Science of Politics" as its topic, and special "theme panels" were organized for each of the 23 regular sections of the official program on the science of politics as applied to that section of the discipline. The theme papers included in this volume originated at those special sessions.

It seemed desirable to publish the theme papers from the 1983 meetings, given the excellent reception of the Finifter volume cited above. However, the Publications Committee of the Association wanted to further evaluate the success of that volume, so it was decided to seek a commercial publisher for a collection of the 1983 theme papers. Unfortunately, the large number of papers meant that the resulting volume would be too large. Rather than condense the many papers on all the topics into a single book, the decision was made to publish those papers which focus on political institutions and behavior. Thus the important scientific work being done in international relations, comparative politics, public policy, and the study of race, gender, and ethnicity issues cannot be considered here. While we regret that more comprehensive coverage was not possible, the in-depth analysis of the state of science in the areas included helps make up for this loss.

The publication of this volume of papers inevitably owes much to the efforts of many people. As President of the Association, Bill Riker played an important role in the development of the 1983 Annual Meetings, the setting of the theme for the sessions, and the planning of the Lasswell Symposium and the program sections. The program committee found excellent people for writing theme papers on the science of politics in their areas of the discipline. The panel chairs and discussants at the theme panels helped the authors refine their views as presented in these papers, as did a special set of reviewers recruited for giving the authors final advice as to modifications of their papers. Regrettably it is impossible to list these reviewers for public gratitude while maintaining the commitment to anonymity, but at least they know the importance of their contribution to this effort. Tom Mann, Executive Director of the American Political Science Association was a valuable source of advice, solace, and encouragement throughout my service as program chair and my preparation of this volume. Terri Royed has helped prepare the manuscript. And finally, I should extend my own appreciation to the authors of these papers for sharing with us their views of the science of politics. All of these expressions of debt further make the larger point of this book: the study of the science of politics is now a collective enterprise in which a large number of people share the efforts. I hope that it is useful to summarize the status as of 1983 in this volume, fully realizing that this is only a prelude to our continuing development of the science of politics.

Herbert F. Weisberg

About the Contributors

Paul Allen Beck is Professor of Political Science at Florida State University and Chairman of the department. He has written extensively on electoral behavior and public opinion, with recent articles appearing in *The American Political Science Review*, *The Journal of Politics*, and *Political Behavior*. His recent coedited book, *Electoral Change in Advanced Industrial Democracies* (Princeton University Press), focusses on the realignment and dealignment of contemporary electorates. Currently he is conducting research designed to explain the often contradictory attitudes of citizens towards local taxes and spending.

Lawrence C. Dodd is Professor of Political Science at Indiana University. He has written extensively on legislative politics and legislative-executive relations, and is concerned particularly with the conditions that foster institutional change and policy responsiveness. He is the author of *Coalitions in Parliamentary Government*, the coauthor, with Richard Schott, of *Congress and the Administrative State*, and the coeditor, with Bruce Oppenheimer, of *Congress Reconsidered*.

Charles H. Franklin is Assistant Professor of Political Science at Washington University in St. Louis. His research on the dynamics of party identification has appeared in the *American Journal of Political Science* and (with John E. Jackson) the *American Political Science Review*.

James L. Gibson is Associate Professor of Political Science at the University of Houston-University Park. His research interests are generally within American politics, with specific foci on judicial process and behavior, political parties, and public opinion (political tolerance). His articles have appeared in the *American Political Science Review*, the *American Journal of Political Science*, the *Journal of Politics*, *Law and Society Review*, and in several other journals. Recently he coauthored *Party Organizations in American Politics* and *Civil Liberties and Nazis* (both by Praeger). Currently, he is involved in additional research on the role of party organizations in the electoral process, and the implications of political intolerance for freedom, political repression, and democracy.

John E. Jackson is Professor of Political Science, Director of the Program in American Institutions, and a Program Director in the Institute for Social Research at the University of Michigan. His research interests include empirical methodology, political behavior, and political economy and institutions. He is the coauthor, with Eric A. Hanushek, of *Statistical Methods for Social Scientists* and of articles on Congress, public opinion, and political economy. He is currently working on a book on institutions and public policy.

Gerald Kramer received his Ph.D. at the Massachusetts Institute of Technology. He has taught at the California Institute of Technology, the University of Rochester, and Yale University. He has been a Ford Fellow and has been at the Center for Advanced Study in the Social and Behavioral Sciences. He has published extensively on positive political theory, including seminal articles on economics and voting behavior and on equilibrium in multidimensional voting.

Duncan MacRae, Jr. is William Rand Kenan, Jr., Professor of Political Science and Sociology at the University of North Carolina at Chapel Hill. He has written extensively on legislative behavior and on the foundations of public policy analysis. His most recent book is *Policy Indicators: Links between Social Science and Public Debate.*

Gary J. Miller is Associate Professor of Political Science at Michigan State University. His principal research interests are formal theories of bureaucracy and small group experimentation. He is author of *Cities by Contract: The Politics of Municipal Incorporation* and coauthor, with John H. Aldrich, Charles Ostrom, Jr., and David W. Rohde of *American National Government.*

Terry M. Moe is Associate Professor of Political Science at Stanford University and Senior Fellow at the Brookings Institution. His research interests include bureaucratic politics, organization theory, regulatory policy, and interest groups. He is author of *The Organization of Interests* and various articles, the most recent of which are "An Adaptive Model of Bureaucratic Politics" (with Jonathan Bendor) and "Control and Feedback in Economic Regulation: The Case of the NLRB," both in the *American Political Science Review.*

Richard G. Niemi is Professor of Political Science and Distinguished Professor of Graduate Teaching at the University of Rochester. He has written extensively on political socialization, voting behavior, and formal models of voting. He is currently engaged in work in all three areas along with studies of political districting.

Bert A. Rockman is Professor of Political Science at the University of Pittsburgh. His research interests encompass the American presidency and the comparative study of leadership, the comparative analysis of bureaucracy and civil servants, and foreign policy making. Among other works, he is the author of *The Leadership Question: The Presidency and the American System* and the coauthor of *Bureaucrats and Politicians in Western Democracies.*

Kenneth A. Shepsle is a Professor of Political Science and a Fellow in the Center for Political Economy at Washington University, St. Louis. His research interests include positive political theory and American politics, and currently focus on analytical models of political institutions. He is the author of *The Giant Jigsaw Puzzle: Democratic Committee Assignments in the Modern House* and, among his articles, are a series of papers on institutional equilibrium.

Herbert F. Weisberg is Professor of Political Science at The Ohio State University. His research interests include voting behavior, Congress, and research methods. He has served as coeditor of the *American Journal of Political Science* and has coedited *Controversies in Voting Behavior* and *Theory-Building and Data Analysis in the Social Sciences.*

Part I
The Science of Political Science

CHAPTER 1

INTRODUCTION: THE SCIENCE OF POLITICS AND POLITICAL CHANGE

Herbert F. Weisberg

In establishing "The Science of Politics" as the theme of the 1983 Annual Meeting of the American Political Science Association, no attempt was made to define or limit the meaning of the theme. Political science has come so far as a discipline that different schools and scholars have different interpretations of science in the study of politics, and that diversity is important to maintain. As a result, the papers from those meetings included in this collection do not employ any single approach to the study of the science of politics. Indeed, they are interesting as a collection precisely because they illustrate the multiplicity of interpretations that are presently given to the common enterprise. Each author is concerned with science, but each interprets science differently. Our collective notion of science in the study of politics has certainly changed over the decades, but science, like beauty, proves in many ways to be in the mind of the beholder. If at one time we thought that the movement to science would yield unification of the discipline, it is now apparent that there are many roads to science (though some would argue that this is a temporary situation). Still it is important for us to consider yet again what the appropriate goals are for our scientific enterprise. In what follows I muse about these concerns while introducing the essays in this book.

THE SCIENCE OF POLITICAL SCIENCE

When political science began to be "scientific," this generally meant that political scientists were becoming concerned with objective description and generalization. Induction was the dominant mode of theory building, with the goal of explanation being paramount. But we have come far enough along in our scientific endeavor that some would now demand more for the science of political science.

An increasingly common view of science is the deductive approach to theory, as emphasized by Gerald Kramer in chapter 2 of this book. For Kramer, science is theory building. He speaks of prediction and control as "useful byproducts," but the "central object" to him is understanding, by which he means explanation in terms of a simpler set of principles. He finds the formal theory endeavors closest to this approach. While admitting that too much of the early formal work was devoted to impossibility theorems, he is heartened by the current trend toward positive models of processes. The lack of empirical testing is described as in large part due to poor measurement in empirical work, with insufficient attention to error in data and overuse of inadequate measuring instruments. Finally, he expresses his concern that we need less complexity in our theory combined with less simplicity in our measurement.

By contrast, others would consider successful prediction to be the ultimate goal of our scientific inquiry. Duncan MacRae makes this case in chapter 3. Certainly such prediction must be based on theory, but his test of success is prediction. His enjoyable idiom for this test is our inability to predict the next election when asked by friends from the natural sciences at cocktail parties. In part this is like looking at the most recent voting behavior articles and asking "Where's the politics?" After all, what could there be to the study of voting if we can't predict the results of elections? But it is also useful in forcing us to remember the questions of consequences and uses of our work. MacRae is arguing that discovery is not enough in political science, that we must be concerned with the use of our results. Because of the importance of that "practical action," political science to MacRae is more than just a science.

A further criterion for science in political science that goes beyond the debate between Kramer and MacRae is a capability for incorporating notions of political change. If our models are to be truly explanatory, they must be capable of explaining change as well as constancy and must be able to cope with change in the system. After all, change is inherent in politics, so a theory of politics should not be time bound. Ideally a theory of institutions would include a theory of institutional change while a theory of political behavior would incorporate behavioral change. Our first cut at theory development can be static, but as scientific observations accumulate, it becomes more important to be able to understand the over-time changes in those observations. Unfortunately, a science of political change can be even more challenging to construct than is a science of politics.

The existence of this multiplicity of criteria for science aptly points to a dilemma in our current development of science in political science. The pioneers in the scientific treatment of politics expected that the scientific revolution would lead to unity in the understanding of political science. That has not been achieved even if our means of data collection and analysis have become more scientific. In part, this is because we do not agree on what "theory" is. Thus there is still a debate between the "empirical theory," which has become common in some areas of the discipline, and the "formal theory" which Kramer supports, to which we might add the "predictive theory" that MacRae desires and the "dynamic theory" advocated in the preceding paragraph. True believers may see value in only one of these approaches, but many political scientists recognize the contribution of each and do not wish to choose a single road toward science. The dialogue as to the proper criteria for science and the proper role for theory in science is continued in the assessments of the state of science in the study of political institutions and behavior in the later chapters of this book, with different authors advancing the different approaches discussed in this section.

THE SCIENCE OF POLITICAL INSTITUTIONS

The second section of this book examines the familiar topic of political institutions, but often from new perspectives. At times it has seemed more difficult to establish science in the institutional realm than in the behavioral realm, as if there were a discontinuity between science and the study of institutions. These essays show that there has been real progress in developing the science of institutions, even if the enterprise is not completed.

The reexamination of the role of institutions is illustrated in chapter 4 by Kenneth Shepsle, who views institutions as providing an element of equilibrium into a political system where individual preferences might not otherwise lead to equilibria. Shepsle's chapter directly challenges the claim of discontinuity between science and the study of institutions. At one level, he examines the role of institutions in the policy process. Institutions are intermediary between voters and policy, and he focuses attention on that role. At another level, Shepsle considers science in the legislative area, showing how a formal model perspective can be useful in the study of legislative institutions. He is not content with an overly simplistic model of a legislature, but instead tries to incorporate the institutional characteristics that make legislatures special.

Legislatures are also Lawrence Dodd's topic in chapter 5. Dodd suggests a broadbased theory of legislative change which relates change in the legislature to change in the public. The vastness of the area of legislative politics is such that Dodd's essay just covers one of many possible topics; it does not review science in the study of legislative committees, science in the study of voting in legislatures, or science in the study of political representation. The development of science is probably further along in each of these areas, whereas the topic of change (whether in the legislative or other arenas) has proved to be more difficult for scientific study. Dodd finds an absence of theory on legislative change, and so he builds one.

His approach is not mathematical, but it is based on an understanding of the goals of political actors within an institutional setting. The work is exciting in terms of building a theory where one did not previously exist. Dodd does a nice job of integrating diverse strands of insights in the literature, though one can still challenge some of his arguments. For example, his assertion that a policy image for the minority party helps it in elections conflicts with the usual survey finding that voters have limited information about issues in congressional elections. Dodd's theory is explicitly based on an interpretation of recent developments in the electorate and the Congress, though many electoral behavior scholars would disagree with the claim that a realignment occurred around 1964, a claim which is central to the dynamics of Dodd's model. This is not to take away from the excitement of the theory building exercise, for Dodd has found an area where theorizing is necessary, and he has put diverse elements together to begin to develop such a theory.

Moving on to the executive branch, in chapter 6 Bert Rockman provides a valuable review of the science in the study of the presidency. Rockman categorizes the work in the field in terms of whether it focuses on the one (the president and his personality or successfulness), the few (the president with his executive), or the many (the president and the public). His concern is with governability and from a scientific perspective, but he is less concerned with theory. His argument in favor of better science rather than better theory provides a fascinating glimpse of the difficulties that emerge when we really are concerned with explaining the politics of an institution.

By contrast, James Gibson's analysis of the science of judicial politics, chapter 7, demands theory as well as generalization and valid measurement. His criteria are stringent, so stringent that no area of the discipline meets all the tests. In fact, the judicial area stacks up very well in some respects, such as the extent to which researchers have moved beyond the national level to extend the scientific enterprise to the state and local levels. Too often our studies of institutions treat the national institutions as unique and miss the variance that exists below the national level. However, the judicial literature that Gibson cites does a better job of extending science to the state and local levels than is the case for the legislative literature cited by Dodd or the executive literature cited by Rockman, possibly because most legal cases begin at those levels. Yet Gibson's standards help remind us what we must all achieve to merit the designation of science.

The consideration of the institutional nexus concludes with Gary Miller's and Terry Moe's discussion in chapter 8 of the science of hierarchies as reflected in our understanding of organizations and public administration. This chapter reviews developments in the new economics of organization as well as social choice perspectives on hierarchy. It shows how firms and hierarchies can be examined as being composed of multiple decision makers with (possibly) conflicting values, so that the problem of control can be studied from a general theoretical perspective. The result is a theoretically exciting new framework for consideration of problems of hierarchy and bureaucracy.

The differences among the conclusions about the state of science reached in chapters 4–8 reflect the authors' different understandings of science as much as the different statuses of the subfields they review. Formal theory building is beginning in some institutional fields, but explanation is still the dominant mode. Prediction is rarely raised as a criterion, though there is beginning to be some sensitivity to the importance of understanding institutional change.

There is every reason to be excited by the new beginnings that are in evidence in the institutional areas, but caution remains necessary. There is a very real sense in which the best explanations of real political situations are still provided by less theoretical efforts. Rockman shows that one can be demanding scientifically without moving to a theoretical level. Unfortunately, the other efforts too often explain less even if they are more theoretical. Yet this may be a distinction between the short run and the long run, where formal theory building will lead to better explanations in the long run even if a more inductive approach is more useful in the short run.

THE SCIENCE OF POLITICAL BEHAVIOR

The final section of this book turns to the science of political behavior. We have come far in the development of the science of behavior, but this often just serves to highlight how much remains to be done substantively, but also methodologically. As political science has become more scientific, we have had to become more sensitive to matters of methodology. It has become clear that we must confront complex methodological issues ourselves rather than hope to leave them to other disciplines.

Methodologically, we have long been in the situation of borrowing from other disciplines sophisticated analysis procedures which are not fully appropriate for our data. As the most recent example of this continuing problem, the use of structural equation models is increasing in our data analysis, particularly through the use of such procedures as Joreskog's LISREL program for covariance structure analysis. However, political science data are often weaker than such modelling assumes. In particular, our dependent variables are frequently "limited" in the sense that they cannot assume any numeric value, but only a limited range of values as in the case of categoric variables. In chapter 9 Charles Franklin and John Jackson extend the science in our work by providing the first effort at a statistical model with the full complexity of structural equation modelling for such limited variables.

Although the mathematics of their effort can be difficult to follow, the Franklin and Jackson chapter is exciting as a first effort to solve an important statistical problem, and their solution will be useful in theory testing in political science. The chapter is theoretical rather than applied, with one potential example outlined. Hopefully, this work will soon be followed by presentation of a computer program embodying this procedure, along with a report on

Monte Carlo tests of how successfully such a program recovers structural relationships.

Another methodological problem in our research on political behavior is that our procedures too often preclude valid analysis of continuity and change over time. This methodological problem quickly becomes substantive in the sense that many of the most important substantive questions about dynamic processes cannot be studied without more appropriate data. In chapter 10, Richard Niemi considers the needs for the study of analysis of public opinion change over time. He argues the importance of more dynamic studies of public opinion, partly by pointing to some interesting cases of such work. At a very practical level he suggests methods which should be adopted to facilitate such work, though he does not provide a commentary on the comparative utility of different research designs for dynamic analysis of public opinion.

Turning directly to substantive matters, in chapter 11 Paul Allen Beck focuses on the science of electoral behavior research, an area which has often been regarded as the most scientific area in our study of politics. He considers questions of "choice, context, and consequence" in our decision as to how to approach the study of voting behavior. In particular, he discusses these questions as they have been handled in what he terms the dominant "Michigan Model" of voting behavior. His summary of the state of science in this field also includes a review of recent modifications in the Michigan Model, including the development of "realignment theory" to provide an analytical understanding of electoral change.

Another perspective on the state of science in political behavior research is given in the last chapter of this book with my analysis of model choice in political science. This essay retraces the development of the field of voting behavior during the period in which the inductive Michigan Model was formulated and shows that since then it actually has coexisted with an important deductive model of voting, the "Rochester Model," which limited its dominance. This chapter provides a case study of the history of science in one of our most scientific subfields.

If any element is common through these essays on science in the study of political behavior, it is the argument that we need more science in the field. We have made much progress, but more work is required in terms of analysis methods, design considerations, and model development. The inductive and formal approaches have both been insightful for our understanding of political behavior. If we have not yet achieved the goal of prediction, at least we better understand the importance of examining the dynamics of change. But the cure for the remaining weaknesses is seen as further development of the scientific approach.

THE SCIENCE OF POLITICAL CHANGE

One of the least developed areas of our understanding of the science of politics is dealing with political change. Yet change is an ever present feature of political life. Thus the worst nightmare for inductive science is the specter of finally achieving a perfect understanding of a political event, such as a complete explanation of the variance in the vote in the last presidential election, only to have the relevant factors change completely by the next event (or election in this instance).

Unfortunately, our models are generally more static than dynamic. Too rarely do they focus on change or permit parameters to change over time. Yet the political system is one that constantly changes. Indeed change is the politician's remedy for prediction, for perfect prediction would mean that everyone knows who the loser will be; so change must be introduced to make the system less predictable. Walter Mondale's selection of Geraldine Ferraro as his running mate in 1984 is just a single example of the use of change by politicians to increase unpredictability.

Change can be incorporated into scientific models in different ways. In inductive work, change sometimes just means the altered importance of certain variables, though the more important question is determining the factors that influence changes in causal parameters. Such models as the realignment theory that Beck describes now incorporate explicit typologies of change. Change can also be built into formal models, as by examining the effects of political candidates changing their positions on issue dimensions or changing their emphasis on different issue dimensions.

Several of the essays in this book reflect these concerns about incorporating change in our science of politics. This is most evident in Niemi's focus on the dynamics of public opinion and Dodd's selection of legislative change as a topic. Perhaps Shepsle is most sensitive to the role of change in institutions in focusing on equilibrium institutions.

Explaining change is a useful criterion for helping us to choose among the different approaches to theory and science, as inductive and deductive approaches often differ in their ability to cope with change. Thus if Rockman gains in explanation by trying to focus on science rather than theory in the study of the executive, his approach may lose the most if the governance changes radically since the vital distinction between unreliable observation and changed processes can be made only within the context of theory. The problem, as Dodd reminds us at the beginning of his chapter, is that we have too few theories of change.

In the end, change is the most challenging of the topics discussed here. Can our science of politics remain valid and robust if the political system were to change even in minor ways? How can we make our science of politics one that will remain useful in another fifty or one hundred years? The ability to cope with change is precisely what will make the difference between a study of history and a science of politics.

CONCLUSIONS

Political science has become more scientific over the years, but the reader of the essays which follow will find that scholars differ considerably in how they use that term. Some emphasize the formal modelling approach, others the empirical data analysis approach. Some emphasize the goal of prediction, others the goal of explanation. Understanding political change is more critical to some than others. If some authors are relatively sanguine about the status of science in their field, others are deeply concerned about the lack of sufficient science. All together, these several views provide a basis for reflection as to where we are going in the study of the science of politics.

CHAPTER 2

POLITICAL SCIENCE AS SCIENCE

Gerald H. Kramer

Before he sets out to convince others of his observations or opinions, a scientist must first convince himself. Let this not be too easily achieved; it is better by far to have the reputation for being querulous and unwilling to be convinced than to give reason to be thought gullible. If a scientist asks a colleague's candid criticism of his work, give him credit for meaning what he says. It is no kindness to a colleague — indeed, it might be the act of an enemy — to assure a scientist that his work is clear and convincing and that his opinions are really coherent when the experiments that profess to uphold them are slovenly in design and not well done. More generally, criticism is the most powerful weapon in any methodology of science; it is the scientist's only assurance that he need not persist in error. All experimentation is criticism. If an experiment does not hold out the possibility of causing one to revise one's views, it is hard to see why it should be done at all.

P. B. Medawar, *Advice to a Young Scientist*

It goes without saying that much of political science, as our discipline is called, is not science, which is not to say it is not valuable, or interesting. I personally think, for example, that much of the best scholarship in political science, in terms of sheer craftsmanship, seriousness of purpose, and breadth of vision, occurs in political philosophy, and clearly this field regularly attracts many of our best and brightest. But at the same time, many political scientists are in the business of trying to produce scientific knowledge about politics, of at least a rudimentary kind, and it's that part of our endeavor I want to address here.

I suppose we all know roughly what science is. Einstein (1970) described it as "the attempt to make the chaotic diversity of our sense-experience correspond to a logically uniform system of thought." The central object of scientific inquiry is to understand some part of the empirical world, by discovering the principles governing its behavior, and showing how they do. Data collection, measurement, and experimentation are important parts of the process, but only in the context of our ability to understand and account for them in a systematic way:

> At every moment of our life we perceive data. . . yet by recording them we do not get science. Science begins only when we create a system of symbols which can bring order into our experience.

> . . .the main activity of science does not consist in producing abstractions from experience. It consists in the invention of symbols and in the building of a symbolic system from which our experiences can be logically derived. This system is the work of creative imagination which acts on the basis of our experience." (Frank, 1958)

This system of symbols we might call a "theory," or set of theoretical principles. To be meaningful such principles must be precise enough to enable clearcut empirical implications to be deduced from them, and to be of much interest, the principles should be some distance from the empirical phenomena they are intended to explain, and they should also have clear and potentially falsifiable implications in other empirical areas as well, against which they can be tested and validated. Prediction and control are often useful byproducts (and the ability to generate falsifiable predictions which can be tested is of course a vital reality test), but the central object is understanding: being able to organize or "explain" a range of empirical phenomena by finding the underlying principles or laws which account for them. Principles which are simpler, fewer, more general, or more precise are more valuable in this endeavor.

There are other kinds of understanding, of course, and other "systems of thought." One of particular relevance to political science is the philosophical. Philosophical and scientific systems are sometimes related, and often borrow from each other; but they are not the same. Isaiah Berlin notes some of the differences in describing why he left philosophy (for history, in his case):

> . . .because I found I had a strong desire to know more at the end of my life than I knew at the beginning. Philosophy is not a subject that leads to an increase of knowledge about the world—to an increase of insight, of understanding, of self-knowledge, perhaps. But it is not a cumulative discipline. No scientist needs to read ancient science. Physicists do not *have* to read previous physicists. They can start in the present, at the point reached by physics. . . . In philosophy that is not so. . . . We do not say there is not need to read Plato, to read Aristotle, because they are obsolete, because we have gone far beyond them. The questions Plato asked are still being asked today. You cannot say: We know more than Plato did; as philosphers, we know more philosophy. However modern we are the relevance of the major thinkers remains. (Berlin, 1983)

Philosophical knowledge—or perhaps we should say philosophical understanding—is more timeless and enduring than scientific knowledge, and therefore less cumulative. To some degree this may simply reflect the way in which the various disciplines define themselves. When a longstanding philosophical problem is finally solved—the problem of the theory of value, for example—perhaps it simply ceases to be part of philosophy and becomes part of economics, or some other discipline. This would mean that philosophy always has to deal with the leftovers, the problems we still don't know how to attack scientifically and begin cumulating knowledge on. However that might be, it's clear that philosophical and scientific understanding are different things, with different ground rules and different aims. Indeed, the appropriate validity tests for a philosophical explanation are themselves subjects of considerable philosophical controversy; but whatever they are, in political philosophy at least they don't often seem to involve real confrontation with potentially disconfirming empirical or analytical findings. As Wittgenstein suggested, "One might give the name 'philosophy' to what is possible *before* all new discoveries and inventions" (quoted in Frank, 1958).

It is a curious and distinctive feature of political science that we use the term "theory" to encompass understanding in both the philosophical and scientific senses. An unfortunate consequence of this ambiguity is that we sometimes get confused, and imagine we're doing science when we are actually doing philosophy, or vice versa. One example is the field which has come to be called "democratic theory." Far from being a well-defined theory (or set of theories) of how democratic systems do or might operate, or should, as one might expect from the label, the subject is instead a rather curious amalgam of historical studies of the evolution of democratic institutions, some simple quantitative empiricism (as in the "prerequisites of democracy" literature), and explications and refinements of the views of influential political thinkers of the past (as in "American political theory").

While there are occasional ventures into systematic deductive analysis of one kind or another, the level of analytical rigor or depth is usually not high, and more seriously, most such attempts seem to operate in the context of an unwritten axiom to the effect that all post–1900 theoretical developments in the social sciences (notably in microeconomics and social choice theory) shall be steadfastly ignored. Many of the component parts of the field, considered alone, are both interesting and important; but the whole is rather less than the sum of its parts, for the main common thread seems to be more a conviction that democracy (or equality) is a good thing, and we should have more of it, rather than any coherent theoretical structure or conceptual framework attempting to account for some set of well-defined empirical phenomena or problems in a serious way.

The current (or perennial) pluralist-radical controversy is a topical case in point. This sometimes looks a bit like a new scientific debate, with rival conceptual frameworks for explaining various empirical aspects of contemporary society, such as the persistence of inequalities; and the pluralist view, at least, has inspired a great deal of empirical work. It's true the debate is not a particularly quantitative or rigorous one, but that seems beside the point: any naive faith that these qualities can themselves lead to scientific truth is quickly dispelled by looking at the situation in our sister discipline, economics, where after several decades of intensive and increasingly sophisticated research on macroeconomics, the situation is so chaotic and unsettled as to become the stuff of *New Yorker* cartoons, with heavy political and even ideological overtones.

But on closer examination, there is nevertheless and important sense in which the Keynesian-monetarism debate is at core a scientific one, while the pluralism-radicalism controversy is not. This concerns a very basic, and very old, aspect of the scientific method: "To Voltaire, Newton was supremely important for having demonstrated the effectiveness of a new method of . . . discovery . . . the famous method of analysis and composition" (Frank, 1958). Or as a modern biologist puts it:

> . . . the tactic of natural science is analysis: fragment a phenomenon into its component parts, analyze each part and process in isolation, and thereby derive and understanding of the subject . . . . There is an intensity of focus in [this approach] . . . . The scientific approach focuses rigorously on the problem at hand, ignoring as irrelevant the antecedents of motive and the prospectives of consequence. (Sinsheimer, 1978)

Grand conceptual schemes and broad-gauge theory are certainly not confined to philosophy; but in science, a grand whole is composed of concrete, carefully defined parts, connected in well-defined ways. A lot of time and painstaking, careful effort is devoted to studying these little parts one by one, because it is only by getting a clear understanding of them that we can hope to get to the larger picture right. Max Weber put it nicely: "whoever lacks the capacity to put on blinders, so to speak, and to come up to the idea that the fate of his soul depends upon whether or not he makes the correct conjecture of this passage of this manuscript, may as well stay away from science" (Weber, 1958).

If we ignore the sound and fury and look closely, I think the Keynesian-monetarist debate can be seen to be operating within something like these ground rules. Both sides accept the conceptual framework of the national income accounts, and recognize the distinction between actual and potential output, and agree on the main determinants of each. There is thus a wide area of serious conceptual and methodological agreement. Their differences, within this framework, are over specific parts of the whole: the interest elasticity of the velocity of money, and the extent and sources of disequilibrium within certain key markets. There is considerable agreement on what kinds of empirical evidence or theoretical insight could in principle resolve these differences. For a variety of reasons (including the inapplicability of the experimental method in macroeconomics), the available evidence falls far short of this ideal, of course, so in practice these differences are not easy to resolve, and are unlikely to be any time soon; but they do hinge on delimited, well-defined parts, so economists from both camps can "put on their blinders" and get on with the scientific task of trying to understand them in isolation, ignoring the irrelevant "antecedents of motive and prospectives of consequence."

It seems quite doubtful that the differences between the pluralists and radicals could be isolated in this manner, or in fact that either paradigm could be fully decomposed to a set of component parts susceptible to precise formulation and careful analysis. There are what seem to be key elements of each, which happen also to be subjects of intensive scientific analysis: the theory of value, the consequences of different distributions of property rights, the role of the political agenda, and the behavior of majority voting processes. By bringing this knowledge to bear, we might conceivably resolve some of the issues, or at least clarify them sufficiently to turn them into well-defined, answerable research questions. But in my experience attempts to narrow the debate down to such specifics usually don't get far. They serve mainly to alarm both sides, and to inspire them to recast their formulations in new, more complicated ways, to make them immune to such intrusions. For all their substantive differences, the two camps seem to share considerable methodological ground, or at least a preference for philosophical "theory" over the scientific kind.

Such attitudes have had unfortunate consequences for political science, since empirical work in any discipline is inevitably heavily influenced by its prevailing theoretical paradigms. A philosophical *Gestalt* inspiring empirical research is simply not the same thing as a well-defined theoretical hypothesis confronting data and risking falsification. A serious scientific hypothesis is a more fragile and vulnerable thing, much more at risk; that is why scientific hypotheses are often revolutionized or abandoned altogether, while so much of our political theory persists indefinitely.

There is another difference which is also worth noting: in science, explanatory hypotheses are not only more precise, they are typically simpler as well. This is no accident; the natural sciences have simple principles because they look for them, even insist on them. Consider the following account by a biochemist, describing what happened in biology as it became infiltrated by chemists, to create the new field of biochemistry:

> The field itself [was new] since, until the 19th century, a theoretical barrier was supposed to exist between the inorganic world and the organic, or vital, world. The chemists who breached this wall were faced with formidable technical and theoretical difficulties, and [others arising from] different languages and different ways of thought. . . . There is still another difference: chemists (and physicists) have great respect for the Reverend Occam's razor, and endeavor to limit their assumptions to the minimal number essential for an explanation, in accordance with the principle of conservation of hypotheses; whereas some biologists have no respect for the Reverend's weapon, and fearlessly bolster an ailing (and unnecessary) assumption by another similar one. As a result, the chemist, who thinks he stands on firm ground, is frequently astonished to find himself facing a whole company of unnecessary assumptions, which he expected to disprove, rather than lop off with William of Occam's weapon. . . . It is not surprising, therefore, that the history of biochemistry is a chronicle of a series of controversies. . . . These controversies exhibit a common pattern. There is a complicated hypothesis, which usually contains an element of mystery and several unnecessary assumptions. This is opposed by a more simple explanation. . . . The complicated one is always the more popular one at first, but the

simpler one, as a rule, eventually is found to be correct. The process frequently requires 10 to 20 years. The reason for this time lag was explained by Max Planck. He
remarked that scientists never change their minds, but eventually they die. (Northrup, 1965)

This preference for simplification—and precision—is a very fundamental
part of science. In this, pure science is different from applied science or engineering, whose task is to deal with the world, rather than just understand it.
Pure science is even more different from much research in the humanities, in
which texture, nuance, and evocation of the contradictions and dilemmas of
the human condition are not merely acceptable, but often constitute the essence
of the scholarly contribution. The task of science, in contrast, is to demystify
experience, and simplify it, not to extol its complexities. Robert Oppenheimer,
in relating the development of relativity theory, describes Einstein's four postulates, and then mentions "the fifth that nobody can ever translate: the theory
must be a very simple thing" (Oppenheimer, 1964). Or as a decidedly un-
theoretical experimental physicist puts it, in more personal terms:

> I think there must be very general, very simple features of everything that happens.
> The moment you read a formula that extends for lines and lines, you know it is all
> wrong. The true formulas are all simple.

> Everything that is true is very simple, once we understand it. It's only complicated
> when we don't. I look for simplification, because that's the only way I can under-
> stand. (Matthias, 1966)

It's hard to imagine a political scientist saying that he'd be afraid of appearing naive, or unsophisiticated. In political theory, but in our empirical work as
well, we tend to prefer the philosophical or humanistic norm in which texture,
context, nuance, and indirection all have their place. We tend to mistrust simple, rigid (i.e., precise) principles, and to prefer flexible ones, multimodal explanations, contextual effects, and the like. No doubt our subject matter is
more complex. But I think it is also clear that we don't have more simple
explanations because we do not look that hard for them. Our research norms
do not encourage simplicity, or value it; indeed we often seem uncomfortable
when we find it.

A partial exception to all this is the subfield which has come to be called
"positive" or "formal" theory: here, often, we do at least find a commitment
to precision and simplicity. Moreover in its initial phases, formal theory was
strongly motivated by well-defined empirical issues, and was regularly tested
against real-world political data. The extensive body of theoretical and empirical work on coalition formation, particularly that on parliamentary cabinet for-
mations and portfolio composition is perhaps the clearest example, though
some of the early work on electoral competition and candidate ambiguity was
also strongly empirically motivated. Subsequently, however, formal theory has
to some degree evolved away from these empirical roots, and at present much

of the more sophisticated and rigorous theoretical research has had little inter-action with the great body of empirical work on politics, to the probable detri-ment of both.

In part this reflects the particular historical development of formal theory in political science, associated as it was with the discovery (or rediscovery) of cyclical majorities, Arrow's Paradox, and the like. This led to a heavy emphasis on impossibility results and instability theorems for a period. In one sense, an impossibility theorem is rather like a negative experimental result. To show that a particular set of premises is inconsistent, or that a certain model does not have an equilibrium (and therefore can't make any clear-cut empirical predic-tions which could be tested against data) is to show, basically, that the model has problems: these premises can't account for much. Certainly it is a contribu-tion to show the inconsistency, particularly when the premises themselves are so appealing and empirically plausible. If nothing else, the impossibility results have vividly demonstrated the futility of "middle-level" theorizing, and of the hope that gradually building up a collection of low-level empirical generaliza-tions will necessarily lead to a coherent or even consistent body of theory. But there is a point of diminishing returns in this endeavor. Having shown the prob-lems, and that the problems are deep and pervasive, the real task is then to fix the model, or to find a new way of formulating the problem.

Formal theory is now moving beyond the impossibility results stage, and we now have positive models of political processes of various kinds. But many of these models, particularly the more rigorous and deeper ones, still cannot be seriously tested against quantitative real-world data. In part this reflects a lack of suitable data, but in part it also reflects the fact that many of these models simply don't make many of the kind of operationalizeable, restrictive, compar-ative statics predictions which permit strong empirical tests. There may be good reasons for this: since compelling, empirically plausible assumptions all too of-ten lead to instabilities or inconsistencies, and because these fundamental prob-lems are so pervasive and intractable, it may well be an optimal research strat-egy to study them in simple form at a high level of abstraction until they are better understood, before trying to construct more detailed and operational models. But in any event, the fact remains that much of formal theory, whether for good reasons or bad, is simply not very rich in testable empirical content at present. This is one reason why political science doesn't see much of the close interplay and confrontation between theory and evidence which is such a vital element in the natural sciences, and even economics.

But there are other, equally important reasons to be found on the empirical side as well. In political science we have a wealth of data, and a great many em-pirical studies. But much of this empirical evidence—and even, paradoxically, some of the most quantitative and statistically sophisticated, and therefore pre-sumably most scientific—is simply not the stuff of which theory can be tested, and is not all that useful to a theorist trying to get some sense of the empirical realities his models should be explaining. There are various reasons for this. For one thing, empirical political scientists, being interested in different questions and trained in different research traditions, don't often happen to do the critical experiments of most interest to theorists. Another, more mundane—and less excusable—reason is our somewhat casual tradition in reporting research results. But there are also deeper and more fundamental problems. Max Planck describes how in its infancy, the subjects of physics were grouped to correspond roughly to the senses—mechanics, heat, sound, and optics:

> In the course of time, however, it was seen that there was a close connection between these various subjects and that it was much easier to establish exact physical laws if the senses are ignored and attention is concentrated on the events outside the senses. . . . Once the specific physical perceptions of the senses as fundamental concepts of physics had been abandoned . . . it was a logical step to substitute suitable measuring instruments. . . . The assumption that measurement gave immediate information about the nature of a physical event—whence it followed that the events were independent of the instrument used for measuring them—now became the foundation of the theory of physics. On this assumption a distinction must always be made, whenever a physical measurement takes place, between the objective and actual event, which takes place completely independently, and the process of measuring, which is occasioned by the event and renders it perceptible. Physics deals with actual events, and its object is to discover the laws which these events obey." (Planck, 1936)

This distinction, between an actual event and our measurement of it, is an absolutely crucial one—the "basis of all natural science," Einstein called it.

The difference between the two is, of course, error. In every science I know anything about, researchers worry a lot about error, and the quality of their measurements. They spend a lot of time calibrating their instruments, discovering their characteristics, and finding out what kinds of tasks they can do and what they can't. Awareness of the fallibility of our measurements, and of the possibility—indeed, probability—of error, is a really major preoccupation. It's easy enough to generate experimental data; it's much harder to do a good experiment, which actually succeeds in establishing something definitive about the external events which exist outside our fallible measuring instruments. One has only to read accounts of some of the famous experiments in science to realize how exceedingly hard this often is. They were usually preceded by a series of false starts and unsuccessful attempts; and the successful experiment often turns out to be a very complex and roundabout one, which proceeds not by trying to measure or detect the event directly, but rather by looking for some subtle and indirect trace of it. It requires creative ingenuity to figure out what kinds of traces could give reliable indications and a great deal of painstaking, careful work to succeed in actually detecting them empirically.

In political science we're not nearly so self-conscious about error. There is, to be sure, a methodological literature on measurement error and response bias, and on errors-in-variable estimation, but this work occupies something of a methodological ghetto and has had little impact on the normal workaday empirical research article. It's still rare, in our substantive journals, to find results qualified by any serious analysis of error; indeed, it's uncommon to find much real awareness of error, or even a clear recognition that there is a fundamental difference between the preferences or perceptions a respondent is willing or able to articulate and those he actually possesses, or between the latter and the objective reality which is being perceived or recalled. We teach our students how to sample and design questionnaires, but it's not part of our prevailing research norms that the very first, elemental thing they should do with their questionnaire is to calibrate it and find out how error-prone it is, or that findings based on subjective survey data should as a matter of course be systematically cross-checked against other bodies of evidence before taking them at face value.

There are many instances. For example, we now have a variety of different measures of candidate preference: vote intention, approval ratings, thermometer scores, like/dislike counts, and so on. But how many studies begin by doing the first and most elemental task of systematically calibrating and comparing these various instruments to actual behavior, to see just what they are measuring, how accurately, and whether there is any stable relationship between them? Instead, all too often, we more or less arbitrarily select one particular measure, because it yields an interval scale, or gives "better" results, or whatever.

As another example, a currently popular explanatory variable in voting studies is family financial well-being, as reported by the respondent. Family financial well-being can be defined and, in principle, measured objectively, from household financial records and the like. But to my knowledge this has never been attempted, or even seriously contemplated, in any of the many studies of economic influences on voting; instead all simply take the respondent's subjective, self-reported evaluation at face value, and proceed blithely on as if this were reality. There is ample reason for suspecting a great deal of error and systematic distortion in the subjective measure (Sears et al., 1983), and thus that these findings are as much reflections of perceptual noise as of any real behavioral effect. *The American Voter* (Campbell et al., 1960), some 20 years ago, was at least aware of the problem, and did go some modest way in the direction of attempting to calibrate the subjective measure. But few subsequent studies have even paid lip service to the problem, and none has attempted to actually deal with it in a serious way.

The pervasiveness and importance of the error problem is quickly revealed by even a casual perusal of the methodological literature. Response errors are ubiquitous and substantial in magnitude. The error rates vary with subject area, question wording, and screens, but error nearly always contributes a sizeable portion of the total variation. Moreover, the errors are usually not random "white noise," but are typically systematically biased in complicated ways. For example, self-reported voting behavior tends to exaggerate registration and turnout and shows "bandwagon" and proincumbent biases (Katosh and Traugott, 1981; Eubank and Gow, 1983); recall data tend to exaggerate intertemporal consistency (Niemi et al. 1980); and in general there seems to be a pervasive tendency for respondents to try to present themselves in a more favorable light by "rationalizing" their perceptions to make them appear consistent (Sears and Lau, 1983), by inventing opinions to seem well-informed (Bishop et al., 1980), or by misremembering earlier events in self-serving ways (Powers et al., 1978).

It is thus well documented that the subjective survey response constitutes a very tricky and error-prone measuring instrument. And it is equally clear that such errors can be enormously consequential and can lead to seriously misleading conclusions. For example, Achen (1975) shows that the usual statistical measures of intertemporal attitude stability are highly vulnerable to even random measurement error, and that correcting for this yields quite different results, which show considerably less instability. Similarly, Bishop et al. (1978) and Sullivan et al. (1978) demonstrate that standard measures of individual consistency across different attitudes can be quite sensitive to apparently minor changes in question wording, and they suggest this as a major reason for the apparent change in attitude consistency in the 1960s reported by various researchers.

There is still a further dimension of the problem. With concepts like candidate preference or financial well-being, the meaning of error is more or less well-defined, and it's clear at least in principle how we should go about measuring it and calibrating our instruments; this is also true, at least in principle, for many perceptual variables. These are what we might call the category I concepts.

But what does it really mean when a respondent says that he "approves" of the way the President is handling things, or that the "most important problem" nowadays is inflation rather than unemployment? Is there some concrete behavioral meaning to this, or is it "most important" simply because that's what the TV commentators have been talking about lately? What are the external events against which these measures should be compared, to see if our respondent is lying, or mistaken? The question doesn't make sense: there simply is no external standard, even in principle, for these kinds of measurements. These are what we might term category II measures.

We use a lot of category II measures in political science. They do have one major advantage, of course: the question of validity doesn't really arise, so in designing such measures we can stick to secondary criteria like maximizing reliability or response rates, which are much more tractable. But in bypassing the awkward problem of error in this way we pay a heavy price. We forgo any real chance of saying something meaningful about the external world of real events, which lies beyond our measuring instruments. In effect, we elect to content ourselves with just studying the internal properties of our measuring instruments instead.

Our formal theories of politics, however tentative they may still be, are at least trying to deal with actual political events, for example, votes cast, bargains struck, coalitions formed. They're not trying to deal with measuring instruments. And whatever the shortcomings on the theoretical side, a further major reason for the gap between theory and evidence in political science is that so much of the latter is based on a tradition of measurement and conceptual framework in which events and their measurements are hopelessly intertwined and cannot be clearly distinguished even in principle. If the experience of the natural sciences is any guide, these concepts are unlikely to lead to any very deep understanding of our proper subject matter, which is the real world of politics and actual political behavior, not respondents' images or rationalizations of that world (which is not to suggest that the latter may not sometimes be useful for understanding the former).

The "behavioral revolution" broadened the scope of political inquiry beyond institutional and legal forms to encompass the real world of politics in all its aspects; but in subsequent years, "political behavior" has come all too often to mean, in practice, the study of just one kind of only tangentially political behavior, the verbal behavior exhibited by an impatient respondent when confronted with an (often ill-defined) question on current events by an interviewer. In some respects we may actually have retrogressed in the analysis and interpretation of these data, for earlier studies tended to be more conscious of some of the underlying conceptual issues and the error problem. In the decades since, as surveys have become more widespread and survey research has become a more routinized activity, its conceptual foundations have come to be taken for granted, and they have seldom been reexamined. But this policy of benign neglect has probably outlived its usefulness. This is not to suggest that we should abandon survey research. For many problems of central concern to political scientists, surveys remain the best, and in many cases the only, source of systematic data, and are indispensable. But more quality control, and more careful thought about and attention to some of the underlying measurement and conceptual issues, is surely overdue.

There are other bodies of evidence and other strategies for bypassing the problem of error that we might do well to exploit more fully. In particular, a more indirect strategy of the kind which is common in the natural science can also work in the social sciences. One good example of this is the permanent income hypothesis in economics. Permanent income is a latent variable, which cannot be measured directly. [Friedman (1957) proposed some ways of estimating it, but most have found his estimates unconvincing.] Yet at the same time most economists—even those who agree with Friedman on little else—take the permanent income hypothesis very seriously, and regard it as quite persuasive empirically. But the evidence for it is all indirect. The investigation proceeds by formulating the hypothesis in precise form, working out its empirical implications in a wide variety of areas, and then testing these implications against very different kinds and bodies of data. The resulting mosaic is quite persuasive. Friedman's *A Theory of the Consumption Function* could serve as a useful paradigm for political science: a precise, simple, but powerful explanatory hypothesis, rich in empirical implications, tested indirectly against many different bodies and kinds of evidence.

Many of our key concepts in political science also involve latent variables like permanent income, for example, subjective probabilities, expectations, and of course, perceptions. But there is one difference: expectations or perceptions are everyday concepts, and if you ask people about them, they can respond, and generally do. On the other hand it's fruitless to ask people directly about subjective probabilities, or what their permanent income is; the concepts are too unfamiliar and complicated for most people to understand. We can only find out about them indirectly. But in many ways this is really a blessing in disguise: being obliged to rely on indirect tests requires carefully formulated hypotheses, from which we can deduce far-reaching consequences; that we think through their empirical implications in many areas, not just one; and that we test them against a wide variety of data, whose different errors and shortcomings can to some degree offset each other.

In contrast, the apparent (though deceptive) ease with which we can measure perceptions by just asking people about them has permitted us to avoid all this hard work. The result is that we've been able to get by with casually formulated, often rather complicated and ad hoc hypotheses, tested against narrow bodies of evidence; and that all too much of even this knowledge rests on the treacherous sands of unknown but undoubtedly substantial measurement error.

We should surely be making more use of such indirect tests in political science. One ripe area would be on the sociotropic voting hypothesis—an interesting and important question, whose answer is by no means clear, at least to me. We could learn a great deal by carefully formulating the hypothesis and thinking through its implications for different groups in different kinds of elections, and then testing these against objective economic and voting data. I suspect we would learn much more that way than any amount of continued tinkering about with self-reported perceptions and of personal and collective interests.

There may be a more general lesson in all this. If the deeper explanatory principles of the natural sciences are typically characterized by simplicity, their empirical investigations more often display complexity, subtlety, and indirection.

In political science, on the other hand, empirical research seems much easier: all you need is a computer, a hypothesis, and some new data. But if our preference in data and measurement is for straightforwardness and simplicity, our explanatory paradigms are more often characterized by subtlety, nuance, and indirection. Thus, in important respects, we seem to have precisely reversed the roles of complexity and simplicity.

Maybe we should think about that.

REFERENCES

Achen, C. H. (1975). Mass political attitudes and the survey response. *American Political Science Review* 69: 1218–1231.

Berlin, I. (1983). In "An interview with Isaiah Berlin," by Enrique Krauze. *Partisan Review* 50: 7–28.

Bishop, G. F., Tuchfarber, A. J., and Oldendick, R. W. (1978). Change in the structure of American political attitudes: the nagging question of question wording. *American Journal of Political Science* 22: 250–269.

Bishop, G. F., Oldendick, R. W., Tuchfarber, A. J., and Bennett, S. E. (1980). Pseudo-opinions on public affairs. *Public Opinion Quarterly* 44: 198–209.

Campbell, A., Converse, P. E., Miller, W. E., and Stokes, D. E. (1960) *The American Voter* New York: Wiley.

Einstein, A. *Out of my Later Years.* Westport, Conn. Greenwood Press, 1970.

Eubank, R. B., and Gow, D. J. (1983). The pro-incumbent bias in the 1978 and 1980 National Election Studies. *American Journal of Political Science* 27: 122–139.

Frank, P. (1958). Contemporary science and the contemporary world view. *Daedalus* 87: 57–66.

Friedman, M. *A Theory of the Consumption Function.* New York: National Bureau for Economic Resarch, 1957.

Katosh, J. P., and Traugott, M. W. The consequences of validated and self-reported voting measures. *Public Opinion Quarterly* 45: 519–535.

Matthias, B. (1966). In "Interview with Bernd Matthias." *The Way of the Scientist*, by the editors of *International Science and Technology*. New York: Simon and Schuster.

Medawar, P. B. (1979). *Advice to a Young Scientist.* New York: Harper & Row.

Niemi, R. G., Katz, R. S., and Newman, D. Reconstructing past partisanship: the failure of party identification recall questions. *American Journal of Political Science* 24: 633–651.

Northrup, J. H. (1965). Biochemists, biologists and William of Occam. In *The Excitement and Fascination of Science.* Palo Alto, Calif.: Annual Reviews.

Oppenheimer, J. R. (1964). *The Flying Trapeze: Three Crises for Physicists.* London: Oxford University Press.

Planck, M. *The Philosophy of Physics.* New York: Norton and Simon.

Powers, E. A., Gaudy, W. J., and Kieth, P. M. The congruence between panel and recall data in longitudinal research. *Public Opinion Quarterly* 42: 380–389.

Sears, D. O., and Lau, R. R. (1983). Inducing apparently self-interested political preferences. *American Journal of Political Science* 27: 223–252.

Sinsheimer, R. (1978). The presumptions of science. *Daedalus* 107: 23–35.

Sullivan, J. L., Piereson, J. E., and Marcus, G. E. (1978). Ideological constraints in the mass public: a methodological critique and some new findings. *American Journal of Political Science* 22: 233–249.

Weber, M. (1958). Science as a vocation. *Daedalus* 87: 111–134.

CHAPTER 3

THE SCIENCE OF POLITICS AND ITS LIMITS

Duncan MacRae, Jr.

I am concerned in this chapter with two questions. The first is, to what extent is the scientific study of politics possible? Second, if it is possible, what have been and what will be its fruits? Sometimes it is easiest to leave these matters alone. If our discipline is accepted in the university, we can publish our findings and hope to advance knowledge without asking where it will all lead. Indeed, one of the virtues of work in a well-developed science is that the researcher is to expect the unexpected and to look for progress without a fixed image of the future.[1]

Yet there seem to be limits to what we can do. At dinner parties, friends from the natural sciences ask me to predict the result of the next presidential election, and it is not easy for me to respond. What is more, after more than three decades in the scientific study of politics, I have seen apparently promising lines of work languish; I have seen apparently solid generalizations fail to predict new events when relevant parameters changed; and I believe that the hopes for scientific progress in our field have been exaggerated. The aim of this paper is to specify limits beyond which our generalizations cannot extend, even though generalization is possible and valuable within these limits. The questions involved extend beyond political science to the social sciences generally, most of which overlap with political science.[2]

What is science? What is politics? And to what extent can there be a science of politics? These are questions that we must address at the start. The definitions of science and politics will place limits on their conjunction; only science in a certain sense, and politics in a certain sense, can be joined.

The defining feature of a science that I shall put first is successful *prediction*. It must include the prediction of things not known by laymen, or by the persons whom we study.[3] But, in addition, science must predict by means of well-defined *methods*, which can be taught openly to all comers.[4] It must rest on *generalizations*; not isolated statements, but bodies of theory that link these generalizations together consistently. These generalizations are especially esteemed if they are elegant, predicting a great deal from a simple formulation.[5] The openness of a science to all implies that anyone who has learned the necessary skills can carry out the relevant predictions, test whether they have been borne out, and criticize the logic of other scientists. These methods and predictions are thus *shared* (to a considerable degree) by a community open to newcomers. We must be able to say what will happen, say it for good and general reasons, and say it openly, preferably in print; and for the established body of knowledge in a science, a number of persons (perhaps most of the scientific community) must be able to do so.[6]

The very notion of prediction bears closer examination, however. I shall use the term in the extended sense of predicting observations not known to the predictor before, even though the events they reflect may have occurred before (postdiction). We thus include geological or paleontological observations; or the replication of a hypothesis on a random subsample set aside from a larger sample. An important question is whether we need to predict the future, and the "natural world" (Riker, 1982, p. 753). We might, for example, develop a "science of the past" that held only within an institutional or cultural framework that has ceased to exist; a "science of the artificial" (Simon, 1969); or a "science of the laboratory" that can be verified only under conditions that we control. One reason for insisting on prediction, in this general sense, is that it puts our hypotheses to a harder test and weeds out mere rationalizations that have been fitted to our prior observations. But this alone would not require prediction of the future, or of events in the natural world. If the test of science were only our delight in solving puzzles, or the esthetic satisfaction of revealing general and elegant organization in the world, we might not care what domain prediction applied to. The elegance of our solutions depends, however, on the scope of their applicability; thus when Newton showed that the same laws applied to celestial and terrestrial objects, the elegance of mechanics was greatly increased. Similarly, if a "science of the past" becomes linked to the future as well, the result is again greater generality. Beyond the question of generality and elegance, however, also lies that of practical application, which must concern the future and the world in which we act (whether it be natural or artificial).

What, then, is politics? That part of it about which we try to be scientific can be given a first or preliminary definition by the content of our discipline: electoral behavior (together with participation, opinions, and attitudes), political parties, the judiciary, the legislature, the executive, comparative politics, international relations. Many of these subjects can be studied at different levels of government or politics, from the international arena down to the organizational level, and we also study the relations among these levels. Such a list suggests the diversity of the discipline and the possibility that these subjects may not all be equally amenable to scientific study.

Yet there have been differences of opinion as to what politics is. Leo Strauss (1962, p. 320), characterizing "the new political science," asked on its part (ironically), "Can we not observe human beings as we observe rats, are decisions which rats make not much simpler than the decisons which humans frequently make, and is not the simpler always the key to the more complex? We do not doubt," he continued, "that we can observe, if we try hard enough, the overt behavior of humans as we observe the overt behavior of rats." Whether by selecting a manner of observing, or a type of things to observe, we may choose to call some things "politics" that are more easily studied scientifically but are of less practical relevance than others to which that term might be applied. Strauss suggested that sometimes the most interesting political circumstances are those that are unprecedented (1962, p. 312).

In exploring these questions, I shall first examine two "case histories" of research in areas in which I have worked. In interpreting them I shall suggest that for the social sciences generally, two problems arise. The principal problem is that the subject matter of these sciences changes over time as a result of collective symbol formation by human beings. The lesser problem is that we social scientists are not always as rigorous as we might be in defining terms, stating relationships, testing hypotheses, criticizing the empirical inferences of our colleagues, and building on previous work. As regards political science in particular, I shall later suggest that problems of conflict and strategy lead to special difficulty in prediction. Within these limits, however, I shall contend that there are scientifically fruitful and practically useful lines of research to pursue, but that this work needs supplementation by less scientific approaches.

CONDITIONS FOR PREDICTION

In order to be confident that a type of prediction can be made successfully on scientific grounds, we should like to see it made repeatedly. We need repetition to rule out the possibility that a prediction succeeded by mere chance, especially when it contains little information (such as the prediction that one of two parties will be chosen). Alternatively, for a rarely available observation we need a carefully designed procedure to rule out alternative explanations.

The need for repetition raises two other problems of social sicence: that confirming instances usually coexist with counterexamples, and that we cannot usually say clearly under what conditions our generalizations hold (MacIntyre, 1981, p. 86). If our repeated observations are a random sample of a larger population, we can generalize to other samples of that population by the procedures of statistics, but when we seek to generalize to new populations we are less certain (Cronbach, 1982a,b). These problems of repetition and sampling are less acute in natural science as practiced in the laboratory, or in the study of the artificial creations of the technology of natural science, but they still exist in complex applications such as those of agronomy or medicine. For all of these problems of generalization it seems necessary to combine statistical tests with theoretical development, seeking to extend our theories to hard cases, and at the same time limiting the complexity of the systems on which we test them.

We should also like the basis of our prediction, in nature or society, to be lasting. Eyeing natural science, we think of the assumed uniformity of nature (Natanson, 1963, p. 20). We then wish "nature" to remain constant, while the scientific community that admits and educates new members also persists. When both endure, we feel that our findings endure and are real. More generally, we should like to see a continuing scientific community with continuing opportunities to see and predict events, to improve its knowledge of them, and to take account of possible changes in the things observed. If its new theories subsume the old, this is consistent with an unchanging subject matter (Szmatka, 1983); if they do not, either the science is subject to fads or its subject matter has changed.

We might also like our theories or models of human activity (behavior) to be useful for predicting the activities of large numbers of persons, not just as sums but as systems or institutions, and at the same time to be based on a sound model of individual behavior. Economics predicts the aggregate behavior of many; this has practical value, but also reflects the reluctance of the discipline to put its postulates about the behavior of individuals to direct empirical tests (Rosenberg, 1980, p. 85). We might also, in this perspective, seek theories of the action of political parties, bureaucracies, or nations that do not rest explicitly on theories of individual behavior.[7]

To examine whether we can meet these requirements, let me take two examples from areas in which I have worked,[8] showing limits to progress in the scientific community and changes in the things studied. These concern studies of the relations between legislators and their constituencies, and the occurrence of critical elections, as well as other questions growing out of these studies. I shall suggest that up to a certain point we can shape a better science of politics by adhering more closely to the methods and reasoning of science; but that beyond that point we face a social and political world that itself changes, posing much more difficult problems.

LEGISLATORS AND CONSTITUENCIES

In 1952 I published a paper on "The Relation between Roll Call Votes and Constituencies in the Massachusetts House of Representatives" (MacRae, 1952). I was working with V. O. Key and following the work of his student, Julius Turner (1951). My paper showed that, over two decades, representatives with closer election margins tended to come from districts socially atypical of their parties; and that among representatives who came from such districts those who had had close electoral margins tended to show less loyalty to their party's position in their roll-call votes than did representatives with wide margins. These findings were consistent with a model of rational behavior aimed at reelection (Downs, 1957; MacRae, 1958, pp. 358–370). This paper was cited extensively (though not always accurately) in the years that followed, and replicated for Massachusetts by Pertti Pesonen (1963). I replicated it for the Eighty-First Congress with the aid of several cumulative scales, finding that it held for Republicans but not for Democrats (MacRae, 1958, pp. 284–289).

In the course of normal science (Kuhn, 1962), I would have hoped that this finding would constitute part of a foundation for wider theoretical generalizations. Converse (1982, p. 85) sees this building process, involving an "endless scrabbling around in the foothills," necessary if political science is to have its Newton or Einstein, to bring about "the final day's climb up Everest from the last base camp." For over twenty years, however, there was little evidence of such cumulation. For example, Fiorina stated that "Taken as a whole, the literature [on the subject was] noncumulative, noncomparable, confusing, and sometimes contradictory" (1974, p. 2). In this work (Fiorina, 1974), he conducted a careful review of the literature, proposed a new theoretical framework, and contributed to a more systematic approach that is still being used and developed.

We may ask three questions about the development of this area of research. (1) Why did it take two decades for these advances to be made? (2) What were Fiorina's contributions that helped to systematize the field? (3) What are the prospects at present for part of a "science of politics" to arise from this field?

Without detracting from Fiorina's accomplishment, I believe the slow development of this field was due partially to the fact that the rest of us—including myself and a number of well-known political scientists—may not have followed the methods of science as closely as we could have. We did engage in empirical replication, though not always with precision. This lack of precision reflected an insufficient guidance by empirically relevant theories such as Fiorina eventually proposed. Some researchers did propose principles that anticipated Fiorina's theory, but they were not selected and perpetuated in the literature. I suspect that the "invisible college" of legislative researchers was not bound together tightly enough by the mutual criticism that would sharpen our concepts and lead us to seek out the broader conditions under which particular empirical regularities held. These conditions might have been suggested by positive theory, or by broadening our perspective across political systems and over time.

Among the contributions that Fiorina and others have made to this field are a more explicit consideration of the motives of representatives; a recognition that constituencies can include conflicting groups who may be moved to opposition as well as support by a legislator's vote; and a recognition that the degree of interparty competition in a constituency can result from the diversity of groups in it, a condition that also affects other relevant variables.

But while our scientific generalizations have improved, the very subject matter under study has also changed; "the world turns, and yesterday's truth is today's fiction" (Fiorina, 1977, p. 24). Fiorina hypothesizes in this later work (1977, chap. 5) that the disappearance of many marginal congressional districts in recent decades may be attributed to a greater availability of nonconflictual goods that incumbents can give out to their constituents through pork-barrel and casework activities, fostered by an increasing federal role. Perhaps legislators still respond in their votes to the subjective probabilities of electoral defeat, but responses other than voting are increasingly available to change those probabilities. The increased independence of legislators from their parties, deriving from these new opportunities, signals important practical problems of representative government (Fiorina, 1981, p. 211), even while it makes prediction difficult.

In reviewing research on Congress, Peabody also suggested that "the Congress, like Heraclitus' river, is forever changing" (1982, p. 10). He, too, is "less sanguine about the prospects" of developing a more "general, or overarching theory of congressional behavior" (p. 1) in spite of the quantity and quality of work in the field. He suggests, too (p. 10), that "an integrated theory of the Congress would have to be almost as comprehensive as a study of American politics itself." He thus states explicitly that our findings are time-bound, and implies that they may be culture-bound as well. However satisfying it would be to achieve a theory of American politics, this might not be a theory of the politics of other countries.

In an effort to submit propositions about legislative behavior to more severe tests (Popper, 1965, p. 242), I began a study of French legislative behavior under the Fourth Republic. The existence there of a system of proportional representation, with multimember districts, allowing coalitions among party lists, seemed to make my earlier hypothesis about constituency relations irrelevant (as it did many of the American behavioral hypotheses I took across the Atlantic). Under such a system, if a legislator wished to remain in office he would first have to be sure that his party placed him high on its list, and then try to form advantageous coalitions between his own list and others. As in the United States, other motives were undoubtedly combined with the quest for reelection; but in seeking reelection the French legislator had far less opportunity than the American to further this goal by distinctive individual voting. It is possible to formulate systematic models of coalition formation in such a system (Rosenthal, 1969a,b). Conceivably such models could be synthesized across different political systems, but the task seems difficult and the likely result more a catalogue than a single elegant law of science.[9]

Scientific findings about legislative behavior in the Fourth French Republic might then have several sorts of significance. They might, at worst, be part of a "science of the past," explaining the working of a regime that no longer exists.

Even if that regime had continued, or if another like it were formed, the study of it might be an institution-bound science, possibly useful and enlightening within those bounds but not beyond them. Alternatively, as in Rosenthal's (1970) analysis, they might provide valuable and otherwise unavailable tests of a theory of coalitions, possibly extending to a number of other concrete domains, including international relations.

The difficulty of extending United States behavioral theories to France illustrates a problem characteristic of comparative studies in social science. Differences among institutional frameworks affect the form, and the validity, of particular behavioral propositions. There are indeed propositions that transcend particular frameworks, such as Duverger's law (Riker, 1982), but not all propositions do so. In comparative studies we seek to test propositions of this sort in which only a manageable number of independent variables vary, either by comparing similar systems or by examining phenomena that are not dominated by institutional structures (voters' choices for parties of the left and right, social mobility). But we may also seek problems that have practical significance. After the Fourth Republic was overthrown, not only was its electoral system changed, but the very testing of behavioral propositions on Fourth-Republic data began to seem less important than the question of why the regime had fallen. I thus moved to the study of this latter question, using some behavioral methods and findings as "building blocks whose placement in the larger structure requires judgment more than strict deduction or statistical inference" (MacRae, 1967, p. ix).

The capacity of a scientific community to predict successfully depends on the agreement among its members, and the continuity over time, in their interpretation of their observations, as well as the concordance of these interpretations with the world. This process of interpretation is characteristic of natural as well as social science (Knorr-Cetina, 1981). In social science, however, not only the scientific community but also the social system under study may change its interpretations. Not only formal institutions, but informal norms and understandings, can differ over time and among social systems. Thus we must cultivate justifiable agreement (by training observers and interviewers, by precise empirical definitions, and by immersion in the culture under study) but also be on guard for changing interpretations or motivations on the part of those whom we study.[10]

In my studies of legislative behavior, most of the basic concepts and their measurements have rested on common sense notions of their meaning, shared with the participants, as well as on certain limiting contextual conditions. In Massachusetts, I made use of our general nonscientific knowledge of legislatures, political parties, and representation to some extent. There, as well as in other legislative studies, I spent time sitting in the gallery and interviewing participants; even then, I underestimated the role of patronage and graft. The major left-right dimension that distinguished the two parties was known, and had a particularly simple character in a largely urban state. A moderate degree of party discipline was understood to exist—neither the complete indiscipline of groups in the Confederate Congress (Alexander and Beringer, 1972) nor the discipline of contemporary British parties. The legislators' presumed desire for reelection may well have mattered more than in city councils in small cities (Eulau and Prewitt, 1973, pp. 457–460). When I replicated the study for Congress, I had to build a number of cumulative scales, interpret the meaning of each, and choose a suitable socioeconomic measure of constituency characteristics to correspond to each.

Even though I did not test the same sort of constituency hypotheses for France, I did construct a number of cumulative scales. There, even more than in the United States, I had to interview knowledgeable participants in the political process (mostly ex-deputies), as well as read political commentaries and records of legislative debates in order to be sure that the scales meant what I thought. To understand numerous other features of the French political system, I also had to read extensively and question people.

These elementary requirements of social research simply illustrate the likelihood that our generalizations and predictions will depend on common sense understandings: a feature of social science that need not prevent agreement or prediction within a scientific community, but can set limits on both when these understandings change.

CRITICAL ELECTIONS

My second example comes from the study of critical elections, in which V. O. Key's work played an even more important part. This is a crucial area for testing the generality of our science; the study of voting behavior looms large among our accomplishments, but realignments are changes in the bases of the vote. They also change the relation between party and constituency that legislators face (Brady, 1978).

The behavioral voting studies of the 1950s seemed somewhat ahistorical, and Key's (1955) examination of the antecedents of the 1896 and 1928 elections revealed that the bases of voting had not always been the same, even in our own political system, but had changed markedly in periods of a few years. Key called attention to several aspects of this type of change and conjectured about its origins. He defined a critical election as one in which "the depth and intensity of electoral involvement are high, in which more or less profound readjustments occur in the relations of power within the community, and in which new and durable electoral groupings are formed" (1955, p. 4).

Following Key's lead and collaborating with the late James Meldrum, I studied a series of critical elections in Illinois, including those of 1856, 1896, and 1928 (MacRae and Meldrum, 1960, 1969). Meldrum's historical knowledge provided essential insights into the perceived political worlds of earlier years.

We chose to work with the "new and durable . . . groupings," using a factor-analytic technique that refined Key's "opening-scissors" graphs. These graphs and related techniques actually provided a more precise definition of this aspect of "realignment" than Key's verbal definition: a lasting change in the degree of association between the party vote and some background characteristic. This aspect of realigment is also stressed by Sundquist (1983, chap. 2). Further, Nexon defines a critical election as "one in which the correlates of habitual party support change" (1980, p. 54).

At the same time, another aspect of Key's definition, dealing with "relations of power," was used by Burnham (1970) to identify a set of "critical elections" that turned out to be nearly the same ones we had found using our alternative definition. Instead of factor analysis or the related autocorrelation method (Burnham, 1970, p. 8), he used the discontinuity of moving averages of the aggregate national party vote, identifying midpoint years of 1854, 1874, 1894, and 1930 (1970, pp. 13–15). The corresponding presidential years in which the new vote level began were 1856, 1876, 1896, and 1932. He characterizes the 1876 change, however, as continuing the "third, or Civil War, party system in its 'normal' or stable phase" (p. 17). We agreed with Burnham on 1856 (though we had to "explain away" an unexpected local reorientation in Illinois in 1864); did not explore 1876 with factor analysis; agreed on 1896; and found 1928 rather than 1932 to be the year in which the "new and durable groupings" were initiated.[11] Key's implicit hypothesis that these two aspects of his definition went together was largely supported, but unfortunately neither we nor Burnham gave them separate names. Their logical distinctness is still not sufficiently recognized, although Nexon (1980, pp. 56–57) states it clearly. Sundquist (1983, p. 3) has referred to the terminological problem here by referring to "the muddied concept of party realignment."

I was led, as many have been (e.g., Beck, 1982), to predict a fourth critical election—at least by 1968, if not sooner. It has not yet occurred. With an interval of at least 52 years from the last critical election (defined in terms of the social base of the vote), a serious departure from the earlier intervals of 40 and 32 years seems to have occurred.[12]

If this were to be a really scientific generalization, however, and not merely an empirical one, we should have to know *why* these three critical elections occurred, and then as "the exception proves [tests] the rule," we might find reasons why the fourth had not (yet) occurred. The topic has attracted other investigators, including historians. The apparent limitation of the prior short-term behavioral findings of the 1950s was remedied, as we always hope it will be, by larger generalizations extending to the structure of the systems within which voting takes place. Two major mechanisms have been proposed for these realignments, concerning party organization and voters' party identification. Perhaps we can verify such a mechanism, but a long time may be required to do so.[13] Indeed, the political world may have changed in a way that we were unable to predict—and it may do so again. Perhaps in historical retrospect we shall be able to go on "explaining" such major changes, but we may *never* be able to predict them very long in advance.

This example illustrates a process that we follow repeatedly in trying to put our propositions to severe tests: to test their limits of applicability and to encompass these propositions, if possible, in more general ones (Nagel, 1963, pp. 206–209). We may begin with propositions about individual behavior, for which survey techniques have provided us with large N's on which to develop and test our models.[14] The contextual features of the system or situation in which people act, such as those of historical periods or institutional systems, must be studied with smaller N's, however. Our inferences in this domain seem less certain: a pessimistic interpretation might say that we were making separate generalizations for separate periods, and that we should indicate this separateness by specifying the intervals involved. Converse (1982, p. 86) suggests that the historical aspects of the social sciences might well pattern their aspirations on those of geology, and on "messy" theories such as that of plate tectonics, rather than on Newtonian physics. I suspect, however, that the multiple precise observations underlying plate tectonics have little parallel in historical-comparative social science.

These two examples of research suggest that up to a certain point we can follow scientific methods more closely in our definitions, theories, and empirical inferences, and can encourage this tendency in the education of researchers as well as in the activities of scientific communities. Beyond this point, however, the parameters of the systems that we observe are likely to change in ways that cannot be anticipated but can be understood only in retrospect. As long as these parameters do not change, and if we have a satisfactory understanding of the system, we can predict some future political events. We must now go beyond these two examples to consider more generally the conditions under which unpredictable changes in parameters can occur.

UNDERSTANDING, COMMUNICATION, AND THE ROBUSTNESS OF MODELS OF INDIVIDUAL ACTION

The people we study can and do change their collective understandings of their situations over time. These understandings can change with changes in either formal institutions (such as electoral systems or constitutions) or informal social norms. In the case of legislators' constituency relations, a gradual change in federal policy involvement seems to have changed the possibilities of a representative role. In the case of the missing critical election, party organizations may have become more responsive, or voters' party identifications may have become more labile, or a single deep cleavage may not be ready for national expression. The very meaning of constituency relations, of party organization, or of voters' adherence to parties, may have changed.

These changes of collective understanding are of special importance, because when the world changes it sets limits beyond which the cleverest and most persistent scientific community cannot predict.[15] Some of the most conspicuous changes in the social world thus result from social movements. Such movements in earlier times gave rise to Protestantism and labor organizations and affected party configurations. Those of recent decades in the United States, for minorities and women, have changed the social meaning of the labels or roles of these groups. Generalizations about their behavior, including those as simple as the proportion of women employed, have to be changed. Such movements are easier to organize in a free society (Solow, 1982, p. 24); a controlled society might be good for social science—as long as researchers did not ask embarrassing questions—as well as for its rulers. Alternatively, social scientists might be able to control some such parameters in laboratory settings.

Such changes, which can invalidate our predictions of the future, have been numerous. The Republicans, initially the party of Lincoln, are no longer distinguished by their concern for black Americans. The fact of segregation, taken in the *Brown* case as an indicator of an impaired self-concept on the part of blacks, has a somewhat different significance when black groups organize their own separate activities. Organizations have become less hierarchical over a period of decades; the unquestioning acceptance of authority has declined. The very changes in the dimensionality of our electoral decision space, including critical elections, are hard to predict qualitatively even if we know when one is coming; a previous minority party is expected to form a coalition with an unrepresented interest; but just how will the coalition be defined and organized?[16]

Even in economics, where the maximizing model of action is expressed in ways that seem unqualified by place or time, changes have occurred. A maximizing model may well have been most realistic "in the era of nineteenth-century capitalism . . . under the pressure of mass poverty, unbridled competition, and a Puritan value system," as Lowe (1963, pp. 154–155) argues. He goes on to observe that "the consummation of the industrial revolution . . . has liberated the broad masses from the bondage of extreme scarcity; self-organization of producers and the interventions of the welfare state have mitigated the fierceness of competition; and the inherited system of values is giving way to capriciousness, typical of an 'affluent society.' " Or as Solow (1982, p. 24) notes, "Much of what happens in economic life depends on social institutions, attitudes, standards of acceptable behavior, and the like. These things change, partly for reasons quite outside of economics [for which the discipline is absolved of responsibility?], partly in response to what has happened in the recent past."

Most of social science rests on our understanding, based on our shared cultural knowledge, of the intentions of other persons, and of the meanings that they give to their situations.[17] As Schutz (1963, p. 241) expresses it, "the commonsense knowledge of everyday life is the unquestioned but always questionable background within which inquiry starts and within which alone it can be carried out." This fact has led to controversies as to whether such understanding or *Verstehen* (Abel, 1948) is a suitable basis for social science. Such understandings can be shared by a community of social scientists and the persons whom they study, facilitating prediction. Researchers can also construct new understandings, built on common sense understandings and even eventually affecting them. Alternatively, different observers may differ in their interpretation of the actions of those observed, leading to lack of consensus on predictions. Equally serious, however, is the case in which members of a scientific community agree with one another, but are all in error as to the bases of their subjects' actions; this can occur when, over a period of time, actions predicted as based on one set of understandings come to be based on another set.

We can try, as scientists, to escape from the infuence of such changing interpretations. One such approach is to characterize behavior in natural-science terms. There are limited ranges of social science in which interpretation is apparently absent or minimal (in which we study people as we would rats or ants), such as the study of the spatial distribution of persons in a room, of the length of time each of two conversation partners talks before the other responds, and the study of the auditory pitch with which each partner speaks in an interchange. Some aspects of biopolitics appear to deal only with nonsymbolic aspects of interaction, widespread among hominids, that do not require knowledge of a language and culture for their interpretation (Masters, 1983; Schubert, 1983). But for the most part, political science requires and deals with interpretation. Moreover, when we come to relate such "objective" measurements to our theories, we usually find that the latter require interpretation of these measurements in terms of meaning and intention.

A second such approach is that of economics; though as I have noted, it is not immune to these problems. In this discipline the motives of individuals are assumed to involve maximization in terms of objectively definable variables such as quantities of goods: utility, despite our difficulties in measuring it, is typically assumed to depend on objectively observable conditions and not on perceptions of them. If, however, individuals' utility functions (or tastes) change, economists can start their analyses over again, preserving the form of the equations but not their specific parameters, asking other disciplines to perform for them the task of predicting tastes. Moreover, the empirical validity of the maximization motive is protected from direct testing because questioning of respondents is usually deemed an inappropriate test (Becker, 1976, p. 7; Rosenberg, 1980, p. 85).

The practice of economics in making generalizations that do not depend on the precise values of parameters has parallels in other social sciences. We may predict an association rather than the absolute value of a variable; or the sign of an association rather than the coefficients of a regression equation. We thus abstract in certain ways from the concrete totality of the situations about which our predictions are made. Characterized in this way, our procedures resemble those of any science. If an economist cannot predict the price of a commodity, he can at least say what will make it rise or fall, *ceteris paribus*; perhaps our analogous task would be to say what makes the popularity of a president rise or fall, even when we cannot say who will win the election. Fiorina, discussing the goals of theorizing about legislator-constituent relations, contends that "generalizing about the values of the decision components [specific groups and issues], which may be quite variable and short-lived, seems far less profitable than generalizing about the way in which the components, whatever they are, affect the decision" (1974, p. 66).

Despite these efforts to circumvent the problem of interpretation and understanding, it remains. It does not preclude the existence of a science of politics or other social behavior, based on interpretation, provided only that the principles of interpretation in the scientific community and in society *remain constant* and consistent with one another. To rest our scientific knowledge on common sense knowledge (Strauss, 1962, p. 315) need not vitiate the findings of science. With a metal framework, a building can be built on foundations of stone, and these in turn rest on the surface of the earth, without our denying the special virtues of metal for construction. But if the earth should move, as in an earthquake, the metal framework of the building can become unstable. In the same way, changes in society can undermine our generalizations in social science, even while leaving intact the methods with which we can build new structures of generalizations and allowing these methods to improve over time. Insofar as society's common sense understandings of political entities and events change over time, and insofar as we cannot predict these changes, then the durability of our scientific findings (though perhaps not of our science) is limited. This does not mean that our findings are not scientific while they last, or that they lack practical utility, for they can have both these features; but they have limits, and especially for practical purposes we must seek to know these limits.

This is why we can understand the past more easily than we can predict the future. We can add parameters to our analysis if the Civil War or the labor movement has intervened, or exclude certain periods such as World War II from our economic time series. We can (if we have the insight) systematize the entire process of development of overlaid party cleavages in Europe, as Lipset and Rokkan (1967) have done, starting from the rise of representative institutions and the effects of the Reformation; these mechanisms of changing cleavages seem to have been an alternative to critical elections. We can generalize about the interrelations between religion and economy as Weber did. We can enter into the style of thought, and the symbolic environment, of earlier times through careful study. We can extrapolate some of these findings, with caution. But we cannot so easily predict a new set of such events.[18]

In this respect, the study of comparative politics resembles the study of earlier historical periods. By immersing ourselves in other languages and cultures, we can see the perceptions of politics that prevail in these other systems—until they themselves change. We can seek common elements and set aside nationally specific parameters and institutional factors. The number of variables differentiating these systems from one another may be greater than those in the history of a single system; but if we select somewhat similar sets of polities (Western Europe; the countries colonized by English settlers), we may be able to compare better.

A major problem for prediction is thus the *robustness* of our models of human action. Conceivably, some causal generalizations about behavior are more likely than others to remain valid even when regimes change, though these generalizations may be the ones studied by disciplines other than political science. Some may be relatively constant with historical change, or with respect to policy interventions. We can look for those aspects of political life in which such models of behavior are most robust; perhaps they will involve the self-interested, economic types of motives. We can also look for stable regimes, in which the institutional expression of particular motives remains relatively constant over time. As Solow puts it for economics: "If we study aspects of . . . behavior that are strong enough to be clear through the inevitable noise, persistent enough so that we can eventually collect and analyze a wide range of data, and academic enough so that they do not get too deeply involved in politics and its yen for simple answers, we do actually learn how the modern capitalist economy works" (1982, p. 27).

We may also seek persistence of motives, as well as simplificaitons of the systems under study, by doing our studies in the laboratory (Fiorina and Plott, 1978; Plott, 1982). The instructions given to the subjects, the control by the experimenter of the place where action occurs, and perhaps even the choice of cooperative subjects, can facilitate the orderliness of our studies. We are reminded now and then, however, that even in the laboratory our subjects can reinterpret the situation (Plott, 1982, p. 1490n).

The life of the laboratory is often seen by orthodox economists or political scientists as too little related to the real world; thus critics see the findings of laboratory studies as inapplicable or unimportant (Fiorina and Plott, 1978, pp. 592–593). They may of course not be so; time will tell. But this criticism suggests that the domain of a social science cannot be chosen completely arbitrarily; feelings of reality and importance enter to some degree into our judgment of the significance of findings. In another sense, however, the life of the laboratory is too much related to the real world. Think only of the difficulty in setting up a reasonable imitation of a medieval village in the laboratory: the subjects' whole external life, and their previous education, would have to be controlled.

CONFLICT AND STRATEGY

Changes in the things we study can also occur for other reasons. Not merely social movements, but even more direct efforts by participants to win the stakes of politics affect our predictions. The struggle to win elections with the aid of surveys and television may have changed the nature of campaigns and voting; and to a much greater degree, the availability of nuclear weapons has transformed international relations. The lessons of earlier military history may tell us something about possible modern wars, but they cannot tell us everything.

Wohlstetter has called attention to this problem in his essay on "theory and opposed-systems design" (1968). He notes that even in contemporary international strategy, the players change the terms so that the technology of one period will not be that of ten or twenty years later. We cannot predict inventions (Strauss, 1962, p. 313); but technological invention is stimulated by the need to prepare for war. Thus the political or strategic scientist who wishes to predict (if not to influence) the course of international conflict must be continually attuned to new technical developments, even seeking to penetrate those secrets that one nation keeps from another.[19] Not only material technology, but the political alternatives, are likely to change as one skilled player tries to defeat another. There is thus a strong interest in changing the rules of the game: "The problem about real life is that moving one's knight to QB3 may always be replied to with a lob across the net" (MacIntyre, 1981, p. 94).

The very fact that strategic opponents seek to win by changing the terms of their "games," and that they often do so by engaging the best minds available, implies that we as outsiders cannot easily tell who will win in a situation of conflict. Even in a game whose rules remain fixed, such as chess, we cannot predict in fine detail who will win, though we can do so in broad outlines from indices of players' skill. Before Vietnam, we thought we could predict the outcome when a very large nation fought a very small one, just as some predicted that Goliath would defeat David.

My inability to tell my natural-science friends how political science would predict the result of the next election thus results in part from a pervasive feature of politics. A second definition of politics is that it deals with strategic conflict.[20] Predicting who will win, in such major conflicts, is not easy. It is true that there are many easily predictable contests, such as those between parties in one-party legislative districts (which potential opposition candidates can make more predictable by not entering them). Political scientists can predict their outcomes, but so can anyone else who knows the situation. But in the spring before the presidential nominating conventions we are unlikely to know who the candidates will be or what the economic conditions will be as the election approaches. Knowing these things would help us predict. But even knowing the identities of the candidates will still not tell us the strategies they will adopt.

We are better able to make *contingent* predictions about conflicts than to predict who will win. Thus we predict the relation between voting and economic conditions, or between the votes given to a party and the seats it obtains in the legislature, or between voters' social class and their party preferences. We do not seem to have predicted the "gender gap" in support for President Reagan, but perhaps we will start to predict its recurrence.

The same sort of limitations can be seen in the prediction of certain aspects of expert chess play. Between experts, evenly matched, we cannot easily say who will win; and even in shorter intervals of the game, an important type of unpredictability can be shown. Leifer showed this by studying eighteen tournament chess games (1983, pp. 82–87). With the aid of a chess-master consultant, he defined 239 multiple-move "plans," or sequences of moves by a player that appeared to be "organized toward an outcome" or a realized goal. Within each such set of moves he studied the amount of time the player spent in thinking about each move. He wished to examine the distribution of planning activity (time between moves) over the course of each plan, and classified it as to whether this activity increased or decreased over the course of a plan. If the time spent per move decreased, he classified that sequence of moves as consistent with an "intentional" mode of action, corresponding roughly to rational planning. If it increased or remained constant, he classified the sequence as more consistent with an "interaction" model, roughly equivalent to incremental decision making, yet (as we shall see) found it to be associated with a higher level of skill and with a condition of equal power between players.

Leifer found that the most skilled players (as measured by a chess rating index) were least likely to engage in rational planning in the above sense; they often spent a long time on each of a sequence of moves. But most interesting for our purposes, highly skilled players showed more rational planning when they were ahead in the game and less when the power relation in the game (as judged by the master consultant) was balanced. Similarly, players of all skill levels showed higher numbers of moves in their plans or chains (linked sequences of plans) when ahead in the game (Leifer, 1983, pp. 88, 129).

At first glance these results suggest that we can generalize about a game such as chess if we look beyond the question of winning and losing, and that when we do, we can reveal aspects of the game and of its play that are not obvious. But more deeply, these findings are a metaphor for rational analysis and planning in situations involving conflict and strategy. In closely matched conflicts even the best players cannot plan ahead rationally. More important for a science of politics, the relation between a social-scientific observer and a skilled player devising strategies in political conflict may be similar to that between players. We, as observers, may be best able to predict strategies in uneven conflicts; and in balanced conflicts between skilled players we may fail to predict the opponent's moves. Leifer suggests that in such contests our interpretation must be *ex post*.

Leifer's view of the skilled player's interactive strategy resembles the conventional notions of incrementalism (Braybrooke and Lindblom, 1963) in that the player faces an unpredictable situation, reexamining it after each move. It differs, however, in suggesting not a simplified style of play focusing on "disjointed" goals, but rather a style of play that is calculated to be relatively insensitive ("robust") to the opponent's moves. Such a style of play can allow a move to serve multiple purposes and can deliberately introduce ambiguity as to one's intentions.

A science of "chess behavior" thus seems most attainable when the players are unevenly matched (for then their intentions are clearer), and when we as observers are more skilled in our judgment than the players.[21] Leifer, in fact, made judgments of "subtle" outcomes by comparing the master consultant's judgments with those of an amateur. If we are to understand the subtle moves of political actors, we must then meet severe standards. These standards seem distinctively characteristic of politics as conflict and add to the difficulty of establishing a science of this aspect of politics. For this reason a science of political feasibility will not come easily (MacRae and Wilde, 1979, chap. 6). Simple, unreflective behavior such as that of the average voter is within the scope of our science; complex, strategic action between skilled and evenly matched opponents is less so.

THE LIMITS OF A SCIENCE OF POLITICS

In sum, our predictive capacities seem greatest when we can test our generalizations with numerous repeated observations (as in studies of individual, nonelite behavior); when the persons we study are not collectively reinterpreting their worlds (as in the study of historically nonrevolutionary times or in laboratory experiments with controlled conditions); and when the people we study, if they are engaged in strategic conflict, are either unevenly matched or less aware of strategic possibilities than we are.[22] Or, from another viewpoint, we are likely to be most successful when the things we try to predict are *not* the outcomes of major conflicts, but relatively unchanging background features of these struggles or persistent features of stable systems.

These background features include some of the predictions of which our discipline is proudest. The cumulative Michigan voting analyses have enabled us to see and predict many aspects of elections other than their outcomes (the distribution of party identification may enable us to place *some* bets on outcomes, but only in the long run, until the distribution changes). Theories of coalitions may tell us who will join with whom, though not necessarily who will win in real-life situations.

Have we then attained a science of politics—or will we? Whether we do so may depend on whether scientific knowledge is our only goal. In the domain of science, our choice of subject matter seems arbitrary. If so, we can then choose subject matter that is amenable to scientific study (Natanson, 1963; Strauss, 1962). The apparently most insignificant phenomena acquire scientific significance when connected by theory: fruit flies and bacteria in the study of genetics and evolution; uncommon or ill-smelling substances in organic chemistry; experimental groups or groups with trivial functions in the theory of group decision making (Strauss, 1962, p. 312). Because such phenomena have been linked in the past with matters of practical importance, or with central features of our world view, we expect that still others will come to be. In this view, if we can produce a well-organized science of some aspects of politics, it may well become practically significant; and in the eyes of some, we should not even ask whether it will. If we are interested in knowledge for its own sake, ought we not to look in all domains and find where the marginal returns in knowledge, for a given amount of resources, will be greatest (Solow, 1982, p. 31)?

If knowledge is our goal, we are freer to choose our subject matter than if we are concerned with practical uses of knowledge. We can choose areas of study that are simple and well organized (Poincaré, 1952 [1914]). Becker contends that in the field of pure sociology, "A playful attitude prevails" (1982, p. 24). Strauss was less charitable when he said of "the new political science" that "it fiddles while Rome burns," but "it does not know that it fiddles, and it does not know that Rome burns" (1962, p. 327).

But if we are interested in practical action as well as knowledge for its own sake, we must not lose sight of the nonscientific aspects of knowledge, which are also part of our discipline. The intuition of an experienced observer can aid our predictions. Our concern with normative political theory keeps before us the goals we are seeking and the ways in which regimes may contribute to them, even if not known with the same precision of method as some other things. Our knowledge of statecraft supplements our scientific knowledge of international relations. Our knowledge of history expands our behavioral horizons in the assessment of contemporary politics.

The nonscientific aspects of our discipline not only alert us to goals and means, but remind us of problems that may arise from our devotion to science itself. Our use of scientific terms to refer to matters of common speech may strip away some of the valuative meanings necessary for citizens' discourse (Pitkin, 1972, pp. 280–286). And Strauss warned us that if in seeking general theories we try to compare all regimes, including democracy and tyranny, we may lose sight of major valuative distinctions (1962, pp. 318–319). Earlier,

Weber (1946 [1919], pp. 147–148) warned of "the disenchantment of the world," though without the same stress on science's direct contribution to it.

Other incidental effects of scientific analysis should also be of concern to us. An excessive confidence in science may lead us to expect more than is possible from those who claim to make use of science, and a devotion to the values of science may lead us to expect more harmony and rationality than we should from others' actions (Morgenthau, 1946). Our findings, too, may be misused as well as ignored unless we look beyond discovery and verification to their use.

Political science is an unusual science. It stands, in a way, at the opposite end of a spectrum of the sciences from mathematics and physics. Our aspirations for it may thus be somewhat different, even though it shares many features with other sciences. This difference may be summed up by recalling a toast to pure mathematics, attributed to G. H. Hardy: "May it never be of use to anyone!" Turning Hardy's toast on its head, I should like to give you "Political science: may it never be *merely* a science!"

Acknowledgments. For helpful comments I am indebted to S. Shepard Jones, William R. Keech, Michael Lienesch, Jeffrey L. Obler, James W. Prothro, George Rabinowitz, James W. White, Eric Leifer, Robert C. Kelner, and an anonymous reviewer.

NOTES

1. Converse (1982, pp. 84–89) sees evidence of progress and warns us against expecting Newtonian laws immediately. It would be interesting, however, to look back and see whether one generation's signs of progress were still acknowledged by the next as having been valid.
2. These issues were extensively debated between the behavioralists and traditionalists as the behavioral approach to politics gained in popularity in the 1950s and 1960s. Looking back at these debates, however, I see much acrimony and little effort to seek a middle ground.
3. I set aside the more difficult task of making predictions of what would occur if we acted, and acting on them successfully—especially in a democratic regime where we are only minor actors. Also set aside are predictions of well-known things, such as the tides or the customs of other cultures; but the deduction of these things from general and less obvious theories counts in favor of the theoretical structure by which a science is organized.
4. We thus seem to set aside "clinical prediction," useful as it may be for practice. Well-trained economists seem to be able to predict the course of the economy slightly better than their computer models (Ascher, 1981, pp. 249–250); if both were better than businessmen's predictions, it would seem that economics as a science should get some credit. Perhaps, too, a panel of distinguished political scientists could predict elections better than a sample of persons with doctorates in other fields; and if they made a careful study of the situation, they could do better than

by offhand guesses. But if Mayor Daley had been better able to predict Chicago elections than any political scientist, we still might have denied him the title of "scientist." As regards openness to all, Strauss proposed a stronger requirement for "the new political science": "it must supply us with a ladder by which we can ascend, in full clarity as to what we are doing, from common sense to science" (1962, p. 308).

5. Some of the most compelling bodies of theory are those that connect the properties of larger systems (gases, organisms, social institutions) with statements about properties of their component units (molecules, cells, persons). In contrast, the prediction of the result of an election from an election-eve survey rests on a relatively isolated and less surprising statement.

6. We have left unspecified the degree of success required in prediction; the nature of the socialization process into a scientific community (are the procedures of anthropological field work sufficiently explicit?); the exactness required of measurement and of formulation of statements; and the part played by systematic observation in prediction (Euclidean geometry being an extreme case where most of the reasoning is simply logical). Moreover, questions arise as to whether a scientific community can have either excessive consensus (fads) or excessive dissensus (ideological cleavage) based on "irrelevant" beliefs or allegiances held by its members. A scientific community (or "invisible college") may also be characterized sociologically by networks of citation, by journal rejection rates, and by attitudes toward the community itself or common symbols.

7. The distinction between action and behavior is significant to some critics of the idea of political science (Pitkin, 1972, pp. 242–243; Braybrooke, 1965, pp. 2–4).

8. These examples may be unrepresentative, they are limited in scope and they may not reach sufficiently to the forefront of contemporary research. I remember taking a critical view of Berns' (1962) review of voting studies because it did not reach to the most current studies of that time. A younger generation may feel that its elders did not cultivate science as effectively as they themselves can. But if there can be a science of politics, I should have expected to be able to see it easily by now, and a retrospective view over several decades has some advantage.

9. In comparing representative regimes with different electoral systems, we may still aspire to scientific conclusions with practical relevance for the choice of political institutions. Comparative behavioral studies may well contribute to such conclusions. Converse and Dupeux (1962), for example, showed similarities between French and United States voters in the relation between education and political participation. There are also a number of larger problems that can be studied if one rises above the perspective of a single regime such as the Fourth Republic and compares it with other regimes. These include problems of regime change; of the evolution of European party systems; of consociationalism and the failure to achieve it; and of the effects of electoral systems on party systems.

10. Consistency between the scientific community and the social system may also result from self-fulfilling prophecies or from our educating others to certain actions or beliefs. We should not count this consistency to the credit of science as a study of natural systems, but it may well be useful and desirable for practical purposes. The feeling that scientists and citizens are engaged together in a worthwhile enterprise

may enhance the success of our actions; educating people in the rules of probability may improve their choices. In assessment of a possible science of politics, however, we here make the simple assumption that we are dealing with nonreactive measures and theories.

11. Erbring et al. (1983) have shown, by a more detailed analysis of aggregate regressions of the vote on proportions in various ethnic groups, that there were marked shifts in association between 1928 and 1936, with greater stability in regression coefficients after 1936.

12. If 1936 is taken as the date of the most recent critical election, the intervals become 40, 40, and over 44 years; but it is not clear when the next one is due.

13. Burnham has posed a persuasive set of hypotheses linked to his "mainspring" metaphor (1970, pp. 181–183). "Developmental change in the socioeconomic system" may be contrasted with "its absence in the country's political institutions." He sees "a profound incapacity of established political leadership to adapt itself. . .to emergent political demand. . . ." This approach is consistent with an interval of a generation between realignments. It could be tested, for example, by studies of seniority and attitudes among party leaders. Thus peaks in the average age of losing congressional incumbents seem to have occurred in 1896 and 1932 (Seligman and King, 1980, p. 165).

An alternative explanation of the sources of stability and change that give rise to critical elections lies in the party identifications of the electorate (Andersen, 1976, 1979). Changes in the correlates of party identification can be related to the "attraction of new voters" as in 1928, or to the "crossing of party lines" as in 1896 (Key, 1955, pp. 16–17n). If party identification in general declines, critical elections may be replaced by "a more volatile electorate" (Nie et al., 1976, p. 290). This explanation of critical elections provides detailed support for a mechanism of change at critical elections, as well as for our failure to observe one recently, but the resulting system of propositions seems to apply only to the past.

14. Here we make probability statements, and this feature of the statements is evident to us because the large N's allow us to see the dispersion of observed values of a variable. In order for such statements to have a precise statistical meaning, they must be associated with well-specified populations.

15. I have not emphasized the problem of complexity of subject matter and the analogy to meteorology; it is important, but I wish to show what problems would arise even if it were not an obstacle. Even when our subject matter is simpler, we cannot predict "radical conceptual innovation" (MacIntyre, 1981, p. 89); this includes not only scientific innovation but also institutional and cultural innovation more generally. Poincaré characterized the complex subject matter of sociology with the observation that that field "is the science with the greatest number of methods and the least results" (1952, pp. 19–20). This problem also exists for other social sciences and may derive from changing subject matter as well as from complexity.

16. A separate question is whether the new coalition wins or loses: this is the question of predicting results of strategic conflicts, which we discuss below.

17. We can sometimes understand others' motives without making use of their conscious view of them. Unconscious motives exist, and people can be mistaken as to the effects of their actions (Pitkin, 1972, p. 254). We can also sometimes impute to others a type of motive that encompasses or channels a variety of more specific motives: economic maximization, waiting in a queue, driving a car in the prescribed

fashion; corporate actors such as nations may also sometimes be treated in this way. This concern with motives is sometimes seen as distinguishing the social sciences from the natural (Machlup, 1961, p. 176–177); but Samuelson (1971) contends that the maximum principles of economics have close parallels in physics.

18. Culture change is difficult to predict; but if it is change toward a known culture, as in the case of westernization, it may facilitate application of a preexisting set of social-scientific (e.g., economic) categories.

19. MacIntyre (1981, p. 93) suggests that in game-theoretic situations, the winners may be those who most successfully misinform other players as well as external observers; thus we are more likely to be able to understand those who were defeated, or predict the behavior of those who are going to be defeated.

20. By strategic conflict I mean situations in which actors stand to gain or lose from discrete outcomes and must calculate their own courses of action by anticipating others' actions. The action of firms in a competitive market does not fall in this category, but bargaining or bilateral monopoly more nearly does.

21. Simon notes that the theory of games has taught us "how difficult is the prediction of human behavior in situations involving conflict of interest combined with mutual uncertainty of intentions" (1982, p. 5). The possibility of our being more skilled than the players seems more remote when we realize that the other side can also hire social scientists. Knight wrote that in a free society, "Prediction and control cannot be mutual; but what each naturally wants is to predict and control the rest, and wants social science to tell him how" (1956, p. 16).

22. Our prediction is not necessarily best, however, when those whom we study are ordinary citizens rather than leaders. Aside from the fact that greater numbers of ordinary citizens may be studied, special groups such as legislators may be more predictable because their attitudes are more highly organized or because they are subject to a set of influences that they can assess clearly.

REFERENCES

Abel, Theodore (1948). The operation called *Verstehen*, *American Journal of Sociology* 54 (3): 211–218.

Alexander, Thomas B., and Beringer, Richard E. (1972). *The Anatomy of the Confederate Congress.* Nashville, Tenn.: Vanderbilt University Press.

Andersen, Kristi (1976). Generation, partisan shift, and realignment: a glance back to the New Deal. In Norman H. Nie, Sidney Verba, and John R. Petrocik, *The Changing American Voter* Cambridge, Mass: Harvard University Press.

Andersen, Kristi (1979). *The Creation of a Democratic Majority, 1928–1936.* Chicago: University of Chicago Press.

Ascher, William (1981). The forecasting potential of complex models. *Policy Sciences* 13 (3): 247–267.

Beck, Paul Allen (1982). Realignment begins? The Republican surge in Florida. *American Politics Quarterly* 10 (4): 421–438.

Becker, Gary S. (1976). *The Economic Approach to Human Behavior.* Chicago: University of Chicago Press.

Becker, H. A. (1982). Some methodological problems of measuring "progress" in sociology. Paper presented at the World Congress of the International Sociological Association, Mexico City, August 1982.

Berns, Walter (1962). Voting studies. In Herbert J. Storing (ed.), *Essays on the Scientific Study of Politics.* New York: Holt, Rinehart, and Winston.

Brady, David W. (1978). Critical elections, congressional parties and clusters of policy change. *British Journal of Political Science* 8(1): 79-99.

Braybrooke, David (1965). Introduction. In Braybrooke (ed.), *Philosophical Problems of the Social Sciences*. New York: Macmillan.

Braybrooke, David, and Charles E. Lindblom (1963). *A Strategy of Decision*. New York: Free Press.

Burnham, W. Dean (1970). *Critical Elections and the Mainsprings of American Politics*. New York: W.W. Norton.

Converse, Philip E. (1982). Response to lecture by Professor Cronbach. In William H. Kruskal (ed.), *The Social Sciences: Their Nature and Uses*. Chicago: University of Chicago Press.

Converse, Philip E., and Dupeux, Georges (1962). Politicization of the electorate in France and the United States. *Public Opinion Quarterly* 26(1): 1-23.

Cronbach, Lee J. (1982a). Prudent aspirations for social inquiry. In William H. Kruskal (ed.), *The Social Sciences: Their Nature and Uses*. Chicago: University of Chicago Press.

Cronbach, Lee J. (1982b). *Designing Evaluations of Educational and Social Programs*. San Francisco: Jossey-Bass.

Downs, Anthony (1957). *An Economic Theory of Democracy*. New York: Harper, 1957.

Erbring, Lutz, Nie, Norman H., and Hamburg, E. (1983). Realignments in the American party system. Paper presented at annual meeting of the American Political Science Association, Chicago, Sept. 2, 1983.

Eulau, Heinz, and Prewitt, Kenneth (1973). *Labyrinths of Democracy*. Indianapolis: Bobbs-Merrill.

Fiorina, Morris P. (1974). *Representatives, Roll Calls, and Constituencies*. Lexington, Mass.: D. C. Heath.

Fiorina, Morris P. (1977). *Congress: Keystone of the Washington Establishment*. New Haven: Yale University Press.

Fiorina, Morris P. (1981). *Retrospective Voting in American National Elections*. New Haven: Yale University Press.

Fiorina, Morris P., and Plott, Charles R. (1978). Committee decisions under majority rule: an experimental study. *American Political Science Review* 72(2): 575-598.

Key, V. O., Jr. (1955). A theory of critical elections. *Journal of Politics* (February), no. 1, pp. 1-18.

Knight, Frank H. (1956). Science, society, and the modes of law. In Leonard D. White (ed.), *The State of the Social Sciences*. Chicago: University of Chicago Press.

Knorr-Cetina, Karin D. (1981). Sociology and scientific method or what do we make of the distinction between the natural and the social sciences? *Philosophy of Social Science* 11: 335-359.

Kuhn, Thomas S. (1962). *The Structure of Scientific Revolutions*. Chicago: University of Chicago Press.

Leifer, Eric (1983). Robust action: generating joint outcomes in social relationships. Unpublished dissertation (Sociology), Harvard University.

Lipset, Seymour Martin, and Rokkan, Stein (1967). Cleavage structures, party systems, and voter alignments: an introduction. In S. M. Lipset and S. Rokkan (eds.), *Party Systems and Voter Alignments: Cross-National Perspectives*, pp. 1-64. New York: Free Press.

Lowe, Adolph (1963). Comment. In Maurice Natanson (ed.), *Philosophy of the Social Sciences: A Reader*, pp. 152-157. New York: Random House.

Machlup, Fritz (1961). Are the social sciences really inferior? *Southern Economic Journal* 27(3): 173-184.

MacIntyre, Alasdair (1981). *After Virtue: A Study in Moral Theory*. Notre Dame, Ind.: University of Notre Dame Press.

MacRae, Duncan, Jr. (1952). The relation between roll call votes and constituencies in the Massachusetts House of Representatives. *American Political Science Review* 46(4): 1046-1055.

MacRae, Duncan, Jr. (1958). *Dimensions of Congressional Voting. University of California Publications in Sociology and Social Institutions* 1(3): 203-390.

MacRae, Duncan, Jr., and Meldrum, James A. (1960). Critical Elections in Illinois: 1888-1958. *American Political Science Review* 54(3): 669-683.

MacRae, Duncan, Jr. (1967). *Parliament, Parties and Society in France, 1946:1958.* New York: St. Martin's Press.

MacRae, Duncan, Jr., and Meldrum, James A. (1969). Factor analysis of aggregate voting statistics. In Mattei Dogan and Stein Rokkan (eds.), *Quantitative Ecological Analysis in the Social Sciences.* Cambridge, Mass.: M.I.T. Press.

Masters, Roger D. (1983). The biological nature of the state. *World Politics* 35(2): 161-193.

Morgenthau, Hans J. (1946). *Scientific Man Versus Power Politics.* Chicago: University of Chicago Press.

Nagel, Ernest (1963). Problems of Concept and Theory Formation in the Social Sciences. In Maurice Natanson (ed.), *Philosophy of the Social Sciences: A Reader.* New York: Random House.

Natanson, Maurice (1963). Introduction. In M. Natanson (ed.), *Philosophy of the Social Sciences: A Reader.* New York: Random House.

Nexon, David H. (1980). Methodological issues in the study of realignment. In Bruce A. Campbell and Richard J. Trilling (eds.), *Realignment in American Politics,* pp. 52-65. Austin: University of Texas Press.

Nie, Norman H., Verba, Sidney, and Petrocik, John R. (1976). *The Changing American Voter.* Cambridge, Mass.: Harvard University Press.

Peabody, Robert L. (1981-82). Research on Congress: the 1970s and beyond. *Congress and the Presidency* 9, no. 1.

Pesonen, Pertti (1963). Close and safe state elections in Massachusetts. *Midwest Journal of Political Science* 7(1): 54-70.

Pitkin, Hanna (1972). *Wittgenstein and Justice.* Berkeley: University of California Press.

Plott, Charles R. (1982). Industrial organization theory and experimental economics. *Journal of Economic Literature* 20(4): 1485-1527.

Poincaré, Henri (1952). *Science and Method.* New York: Dover (English translation first published, 1914).

Popper, Karl R. (1965) *Conjectures and Refutations: The Growth of Scientific Knowledge.* New York: Harper & Row.

Riker, William H. (1982). The two-party system and Duverger's Law: an essay on the history of political science. *American Political Science Review* 76(4): 753-766.

Rosenberg, Alexander (1980). A skeptical history of microeconomic theory. *Theory and Decision* 12(1): 79-93.

Rosenthal, Howard (1969a). A study of the effect of coalitions on voting behavior, Carnegie-Mellon University, Graduate School of Industrial Administration, Research paper WP-76-69-7.

Rosenthal, Howard (1969b). The electoral politics of Gaullists in the Fourth French Republic: ideology or constituency interest? *American Political Science Review* 63(2): 476-487.

Rosenthal, Howard (1970). Size of coalition and electoral outcomes in the Fourth French Republic. In Sven Groennings, E. Woody Kelley, and Michael Leiserson (eds.), *The Study of Coalition Behavior,* pp. 43-59. New York: Holt, Rinehart, and Winston.

Samuelson, Paul A. (1971). Maximum principles in analytical economics. *Science* 173(4001): 991-997.

Schubert, Glendon (1983). Evolutionary politics. *Western Political Quarterly* 36(2): 175-193.

Schutz, Alfred (1963). Concept and theory formation in the social sciences. In Maurice Natanson (ed.), *Philosophy of the Social Sciences: A Reader.* New York: Random House (originally published 1954).

Seligman, Lester G., and King, Michael R. (1980). Political realignments and recruitment to the U.S. Congress, 1870-1970. In Bruce A. Campbell and Richard Trilling (eds.), *Realignment in American Politics.* Austin: University of Texas Press, 1980.

Simon, Herbert A. (1969). *The Sciences of the Artificial.* Cambridge, Mass.: M.I.T. Press.

Simon, Herbert A. (1982). Are social problems problems that social science can solve? In William H. Kruskal (ed.), *The Social Sciences: Their Nature and Uses.* Chicago: University of Chicago Press.

Solow, Robert M. (1982). Does economics make progress? *Bulletin of the American Academy of Arts and Sciences* 36(3): 13-31.

Strauss, Leo (1962). An Epilogue. In Herbert J. Storing (ed.), *Essays on the Scientific Study of Politics*. New York: Holt, Rinehart, and Winston.

Sundquist, James L. (1983). *Dynamics of the Party System* (rev. ed.). Washington, D.C.: Brookings.

Szmatka, Jacek (1983). Correspondence principle as a tool explaining the growth of social science. *Philosophy of the Social Sciences* 13(1): 47–53.

Turner, Julius (1951). *Party and Constituency: Pressures on Congress*. Baltimore: Johns Hopkins University Press.

Weber, Max (1946). Science as a vocation. In Hans H. Gerth and C. Wright Mills (eds.), *From Max Weber: Essays in Sociology*, pp. 129–156. New York: Oxford University Press. (Original German version published in 1919.)

Wohlstetter, Albert (1968). Theory and opposed-systems design. In Morton A. Kaplan (ed.), *New Approaches to International Relations*. New York: St. Martin's Press.

Part II
The Science of Political Institutions

CHAPTER 4

INSTITUTIONAL EQUILIBRIUM AND EQUILIBRIUM INSTITUTIONS

Kenneth A. Shepsle

Several years ago, Morris Fiorina and I, writing for a conference on the topic of political equilibrium, began our paper: "Perhaps it overstates matters to say that there is a crisis in formal political theory, but it is apparent that much mischief has been caused by a series of theorems that depict the chaotic features of majority-rule voting systems. . . .[W]hen majority rule breaks down, it breaks down completely; and it 'almost always' breaks down" (Fiorina and Shepsle, 1982). We went on to describe how that chaos—the "disequilibrium of tastes"—had been overinterpreted by political scientists, in our judgment, much as the apparent equilibrium of tastes in idealized markets had been overinterpreted by general equilibrium economists. In this paper I take a somewhat different point of view. The crisis has not yet passed, but surely it is passing as formal theorists devise and discover new ways to reason about the problems of voting instability. We have begun to accept the disequilibrium of tastes as a permanent condition. Reviewing the intellectual history of this lesson, Riker (1980) concludes: "And what we have learned is simply this: disequilibrium, or the potential that the status quo be upset, is the characteristic feature of politics." But in accepting this fact, we formal theorists, along with many others in political science and economics, have (re)discovered that tastes and their expression are neither autonomous nor necessarily decisive.

First, we have begun studying theoretically the ways in which preferences are induced or molded, on the one hand, and how, on the other hand, they are channeled, expressed, and revealed. The endogenous treatment of preferences permits us to focus on particular configurations of tastes while, at the same time, turning to environmental features and their effects.[1]

Second, the autonomy or exogeneity of tastes aside, it is becoming increasingly clear that the empirical relationship between social choice and individual values is a mediated one. Standing between the individual *qua* bundle of tastes and the alternatives comprising available social choices are institutions. A configuration of institutions—a framework of rules, procedures, and arrangements—prescribes and constrains the set of choosing agents, the manner in which their preferences may be revealed, the alternatives over which preferences may be expressed, the order in which such expressions occur, and generally the way in which business is conducted.

To observe that tastes are neither autonomous nor decisive, and that social choices are mediated by institutional arrangements, is the first step in a return to an older scholarly interest in the structures of society, polity, and economy. I do not here recommend such a return visit merely to mimic our predecessors. While their focus was (more often than not) squarely on *arrangements* and *outcomes*, their modes of scholarship—history writing, description, and normative discourse—were not principally scientific and have beeen improved upon during the intervening generations. The price we have paid for the methodological and theoretical innovations of the post-World War II era, however, is the inordinate emphasis now placed on *behavior*. Our ability to describe (and less frequently, to explain) behavior—the casting of a vote, participation in committee deliberations, campaigning, the rendering of a judicial or administrative ruling—has diminished the attention once given to institutional context and actual outcomes. On net, the behavioral revolution has probably been of positive value. But along with the many scientific benefits, we have been burdened by the cost of restricted scope in our analyses. One of the purposes of this essay is to elevate and reemphasize some of the older themes and to suggest how they might be incorporated into the domain of positive political theory.

The theme of this chapter is institutions. I bring to this theme both the more traditional interest in structures of society, polity, and economy, and the more contemporary microeconomic, rational-actor methodology with its emphasis on equilibrium outcomes. First, I briefly review the equilibrium orientation of positive political theory. Second, I consider the world of institutions and the outcomes they produce, encourage, or enforce. There I contrast *preference-induced equilibrium* (Riker calls it an "equilibrium of tastes") with *structure-induced equilibrium*. The latter focuses on organizational conditions, formal arrangements, institutional practices, and their channeling effects on the revelation and aggregation of individual preferences. Third, I stand the analysis on its head. If institutions matter, then *which* institutions are employed becomes a paramount concern. In particular, the selection, survival, adaptation, and evolution of institutional practices need to be understood. Throughout, I make reference to legislative institutions which, I claim, stand as something of an exemplar for modeling institutions more generally. From empirical familiarity with legislatures, I have come to appreciate the tension in modeling between the substantive demands for complexity, on the one hand, and the theoretical necessity of deductive interrogatability on the other. This tension constitutes a challenge to positive political theorists.

THE EQUILIBRIUM PERSPECTIVE
OF POSITIVE POLITICAL THEORY

It is useful to begin the discussion with a brief consideration of equilibrium, for surely this has been the primary concern of positive political theory dating back to Black's (1948) early work. In one sense, however, the prevailing focus on equilibrium stands in tension with some of the dominant theoretical facts of positive political theory, namely, Arrow's Theorem, the pervasive cyclicity of majority rule, the indeterminateness of logrolling, vote trading, and general exchange, and the instability of coalitions. Equilibrium theory, consequently, is a peculiar moniker for the development I have in mind, since the thrust of more than three decades of social choice theory is that voting systems in general, and majority rule in particular, *lack* equilibrium properties. This condition of disequilibrium is captured most elegantly in the theorems of Plott (1967), Cohen (1979), McKelvey (1976, 1979), Schofield (1978), Schwartz (1981), and Slutsky (1979).

Let $N = \{1,2,. . .,n\}$ be a committee or legislature consisting of n agents who must choose, by majority rule, an element of the set X (normally modeled as a multidimensional Euclidean space). Assume each agent has well-defined preferences over the points in X satisfying certain technical requirements (typically continuous and strictly convex preferences, but these technical features need not detain us). Let P_i represent agent i's preferences (xP_iy means x is preferred by i to y). For two points x and y in X, x is said to be majority preferred to y (xPy) if and only if

$$|xP_iy| \; > \; |yP_ix|$$

(where $|A|$ means the number of agents in the set having property A). For any point $y\epsilon X$, we may describe the points which majority-defeat it:

$$W(y) \; = \; \{x\epsilon X \,|\, xPy\}$$

$W(y)$ is called the *win set* of y.

The "universal instability" result may now be characterized in either of two ways.

1. For "almost every" configuration of preferences, $W(y) \neq \varnothing \quad \forall y\epsilon X$.
2. For any two arbitrary points, $x,y\epsilon X$, and "almost every" configuration of preferences, there exists a finite sequence $\{x, z_1,. . .,z_m, y\}$ such that $z_1\epsilon W(x)$, $z_i\epsilon W(z_{i-1})$ for $i=2,. . .,m$, and $y\epsilon W(z_m)$.

The first statement asserts the generic nonemptiness of win sets: no point is invulnerable to defeat in a majority-rule contest. The second statement asserts not only that win sets are nonempty, but also that their content is sufficiently rich to permit any point to be reached, via a sequence of majority-rule contests, from any other point. In short, there is no equilibrium of majority tastes.

These results are compatible with either of two different interpretations. If there is a monopoly agenda setter, i.e., someone who is uniquely and completely empowered to pick and order the alternatives on an agenda, then the results say that there is always sufficient opportunity for him to manipulate the sequence of votes to produce any final outcome he desires; the preferences of other agents are ultimately no constraint on the final outcome. On the other hand, if the agenda is built randomly or by an "open" process in which any agent may propose an alternative, then the results imply that, no matter where the process commences, there is no telling where it will end. Majority rule may "wander anywhere" since all the alternatives are part of one preference cycle. Put slightly differently, the world of the monopoly agenda setter is a well-behaved one in the sense that an equilibrium outcome is associated with it: the ideal point of the agenda setter. It is not, however, an equilibrium of majority tastes, for this does not exist. Thus, in some constructed worlds an equilibrium outcome appears. But in a world only of majority preferences, we cannot even count on this.

I emphasize these interpretations, not because I think either is terribly general or helpful, but rather because they represent two widely separated points in the "space" of institutional arrangements. The former is the extreme one in which a distinguished agent makes social choices, constrained only by majority preferences. The nonobvious insight provided by McKelvey and others is that, for all intents and purposes, this case is indistinguishable from that of the dictator, since the majority preference relation, exploited by the monopoly agenda setter, is not binding on the final choice.

The monopoly agenda setter and dictator mechanisms may appear arbitrary and highly special. Let me emphasize, however, that *so, too, is the completely open agenda process*. The "open" process of pure majority rule (PMR), like the other alternatives just discussed, is one, rather special, operationalization of a choice process governed by a cyclic *P* relation. I claim that this observation has not been fully appreciated in the literature. Just as the nonempty win sets property of majority rule implies *different* things about two of its operational forms (equilibrium with a monopoly agenda setter and pervasive disequilibrium with an "open" process), so it is more generally. There are, in fact, *many majority rules*, and the cyclic *P* relation need not imply disequilibrium for all of them.

Elsewhere I have discussed general issues pertaining to equilibrium (Fiorina and Shepsle, 1982; Shepsle and Weingast, 1984a; Shepsle, 1985), so let me here dwell on the fact of "many majority rules." The spate of instability/disequilibrium results have been overinterpreted in light of this fact. While these theorems characterize PMR, and contain truisms about the cyclicity of the P relation, they have been uncritically imported into substantive realms not characterized by PMR.[2] To see this, it is revealing to examine the structure these theorems take as fixed and exogenous.

The instability theorems of majority rule typically begin with an undifferentiated set N of decision makers. A central feature of many decision contexts, however, is differentiation. Superimposed on N are a variety of partitions: a committee system in a legislature, divisions of a firm, departments in a university, bureaus of an agency. Thus, each house of the Congress is more accurately described not by N but rather by a family of subsets of N, $C = \{C_1, \ldots, C_m\}$, where each C_j is a subset of N, and each i is an element of at least one C_j.

Similarly, the theorems of majority rule take as undifferentiated the set X of alternatives from which choices are made. The elements of X represent, in effect, comprehensive government programs in most applications. Yet, in institutional settings we rarely observe choices posed in terms of one platform of programs versus another (indeed, this orientation is a vestige of models of electoral competition; Downs, 1957). Rather, the set X, too, is partitioned into what may be called jurisdictions over which property rights are assigned to organizational subunits. Thus, the undifferentiated sets N and X of our formal theories of majority rule are, in practice, collections of subsets and bundles of "rights" differentiating the agenda and choice authority of the subsets of N over jurisdictions in X.

Both of these institutional features should raise a flag of caution. They do nothing to mitigate the results of Plott, Cohen, McKelvey, Schofield, Schwartz, and Slutsky. It is still true that the majority preference relation is ill-behaved ($W(x) \neq \phi$), and this instability underlies and affects ultimate choices. What is now no longer apparent is whether the behavioral interpretations of these theorems, derived for undifferentiated sets of agents and alternatives, apply in full force to organizationally more complex arrangements. In short, equilibrium theories to date have only just begun to depart from their institution-free, atomistic formulations.

There is a third feature that bears on this discussion. Most theories of PMR assume that any social comparison is permissible. This, too, is a vestige of models of electoral equilibrium (viz., candidates may choose any platform on which to run). In organizationally and procedurally more complex settings, however, the partitioning of the alternative space into jurisdictions combines with germaneness rules to constrain comparisons. Agenda agents (say, the Rules Committee in the House of Representatives) may impose restrictions (only certain amendments are in order) over and above those already specified in formal rules of deliberation (e.g., the status quo ante is voted on last).

Each of these caveats is not a brief for complexity. Organizational behavior theorists often get hung up on complexity, losing sight of the fact that we always want to preserve in a model the possibility for deductive interrogation. At the opposite extreme, however, lie the theories of PMR, elegant but utterly simple. In terms of structure and procedure, they constitute very special, if not extreme cases. The sensitivity of their interpretations to institutional arrangements comprises an important agenda of new research.

Such research will, I believe, revitalize equilibrium theories because it will highlight the ways in which the underlying P relation is embedded in a structure of arrangements among agents (division of and specialization of labor), rules of comparison, and mechanisms by which choices and behavior of subgroups are monitored by the entire set of agents. This structure, along with the P relation, constitutes an *institutional arrangement*. In evaluating, predicting, or explaining outcomes of an institutional arrangement, we need no longer be tongue-tied by nonempty win sets, a prospect I consider in more detail in the next section.

INSTITUTIONAL EQUILIBRIUM

Throughout the previous discussion I have taken PMR to describe a majority-rule system in which individual preferences (defined in advance) over a multidimensional space of alternatives (also given in advance) induce a cyclic P relation. Alternatives are considered (motions are made) by some random device: either individuals are recognized randomly for the purpose of moving alternatives or the alternatives themselves are sampled randomly. This arrangement has no equilibrium outcome, since $W(x) = \phi$ for no $x \epsilon X$, so that the process will never come to any resting place. For any alternative, x^0, constituting the current status quo, some new alternative will ultimately appear which majority-defeats it. If the process does produce a final outcome, it is only because of some unexplicated feature such as an arbitrary stopping rule, fatigue on the part of agents, etc. In general, however, the absence of equilibrium in PMR implies complete and pervasive instability.[3]

The instability results of the PMR model would come as something of a surprise to students of empirical commitees and legislatures. The PMR formulation, itself, is but a mere shadow of the complex procedures and structural arrangements of real decision-making bodies. Compare, for example, the preceding paragraph, where PMR is described, and the 600-plus pages of *Deschler's Procedures of the U.S. House of Representatives*. Now it is entirely possible that the minutiae of institutional life are just that, and not the stuff of theoretical significance. I simply claim that it would come as a surprise to legislative scholars, for the bulk of their attention is devoted to detailing the complex politicial process entailed by the procedures and structural arrangements of decision making. They devote considerably less space to describing the instability of results. Even in those legislative studies which emphasize the cyclicity of majority preferences (Riker, 1965; Blydenburgh, 1971; Enelow, 1982), it is clear that the cyclic *P* relation is only part of the story, a prominent fact of institutional life that takes on significance because it may be exploited by agents in various institutional niches.

There is, however, one serious ex ante objection to embedding PMR in a richer institutional structure which I shall mention here and take up in more detail in the next section. If institutional arrangements affect social choices, and if majority preferences over social choices are cyclic, then won't the induced majority preferences over institutional arrangements also be cyclic? That is, will social preferences over institutions *inherit* the cyclicity of social preferences over outcomes? These are extremely pertinent questions, first raised convincingly by Riker (1980). Their thrust reasserts the fundamental nature of cyclic majority preferences, because they suggest that cyclicity and instability cannot be finessed by "institutionalizing" PMR. The question of instability, repressed at the level of choice over outcomes, reemerges at the level of choice over institutions.

The *inheritability hypothesis* is interesting, however, only if institutions do matter. For this reason alone, it makes sense to pursue the question of institutional equilibrium first before turning to that of equilibrium institutions. Consequently, for the purposes of discussion in this section, I will take institutional arrangements as exogenous. I neither suppress such arrangements, as is done in most of the literature on multidimensional voting models, nor explain it, as I will attempt to do in the next section.

Following my earlier development of institutional arrangements (Shepsle, 1979), I now describe some building blocks of institutions: division of labor, jurisdictional specialization of labor, and monitoring. To motivate these considerations, consider the difference between global winners and more restrictive winners.

Winners

A *global winner* is an element $x^* \epsilon X$ with an empty win set: $W(x^*) = \phi$. Such a point is a *majority core point* since $W(x^*) = \{y \mid yPx^*\} = \phi$; so it is a "retentive" equilibrium. Once the process reaches x^* it can never escape (absent exogenous change). If, in addition, the voting game is strong, so that xPy or yPx for all $x,y \epsilon X$ (no ties), then x^* is a *Condorcet point*. In this case we have two distinct properties satisfied by x^*:

(i) $W(x^*) = \phi$
(ii) $x^* \epsilon W(y)$ for every $y \neq x^*$

If there are no barriers to entry onto the agenda for x^*, then it is both a "retentive"[property (i)] and an "attractive"[property (ii)] equilibrium. The problem, of course, is one of existence: "almost never" do the x's of properties (i) and (ii) exist.

A more general notion of equilibrium than that of the Condorcet/core condition may be considered. For any $A \subset X$, define

$$W_A(x) = \{y \epsilon A \mid yPx\}$$

$W_A(x)$ contains the elements of the subset A which majority-defeat x. If $A = X$, then $W_A(x) = W(x)$, so the Condorcet/core condition for equilibrium is a special case in this construction. If, however, A is a proper subset of X, and is specified by the rules governing comparisons as containing the only feasible contenders against x, then, since x can only be compared against elements of A, $W(x) = \phi$ is an inappropriate condition for equilibrium. Since $A \subset X$, it follows that $W_A(x) \subset W(x)$ and, therefore, that $W_A(x)$ *may be empty even if* $W(x)$ *is not*. The point of this development is that the emptiness of $W(x)$ is often an inappropriately extreme standard against which to assess the equilibriumlike character of an alternative.

The set A is the collection of feasible agenda elements. If $W_A(x^*) = \phi$, then x^* is said to be an *A-restricted winner* (in contrast to a global winner). The question now becomes one about the features of decision making that restrict comparisons to A. I argue that a more general treatment of the sets N and X, heretofore undifferentiated in traditional multidimensional voting models, provides the key.

Jurisdictions

The idea that a motion may be declared "out of order" suggests that institutions embody principles of proper order. Thus, even if the majority preference relation is complete, with xPy or yPx for every $x,y \epsilon X$, some social comparisons are proscribed. To give some concreteness, I develop the idea of jurisdiction. For the space of alternatives, X, a convex subset of R_n^+, let $E = \{e_1,...,e_n\}$ be an orthogonal basis, where e_i is the unit vector for the ith dimension. A *jurisdictional arrangement* is a covering of E.[4] Thus, $\beta = \{\beta_1, \ldots ,\beta_k\}$ is a jurisdictional arrangement if $\beta_i \subset E$ and $U\beta_i = E$. Each $\beta_i \epsilon \beta$ is a jurisdiction consisting of one or more dimensions of E.

Defining the status quo ante as the origin of the space, we shall say that a motion or proposal is *jurisdictionally germane* if and only if it is entirely within a single jurisdiction. Thus, $B_j = \{x \mid x = \Sigma \lambda_i e_i, e_i \epsilon \beta_j\}$ is the set of proposals germane to the jth jurisdiction. By definition, the status quo is an element of every jurisdiction.

I shall not review all of the discussion in Shepsle (1979). Let me simply note that a jurisdictional arrangement may be simple (each jurisdiction a single basis vector), complex (each jurisdiction a subspace consisting of several basis vectors), overlapping (some basis vectors common to more than one jurisdiction) or, in the extreme, global (every basis vector in a single jurisdiction). The latter, of course, is the construct of traditional multidimensional voting models.

A jurisdictional arrangement β allows an institution to split up the various dimensions of choice by permitting only jurisdictionally germane proposals. The agents of an institution may desire this sort of arrangement for any number of reasons. If, for example, an agent's preferences are separable by jurisdiction, so that his preferences over alternatives in one jurisdiction are unaffected by choices made in other jurisdictions, then jurisdictional germaneness may be regarded as an efficient and straightforward way to proceed. That is, though it need have no effect on the final vector of outcomes, it economizes on the costs of doing business by allowing agents to focus on a jurisdiction at a time. No doubt this reason stands behind numerous structural and procedural provisions of organizational decision making.

It is not, however, the whole story. What I argue about legislatures, and perhaps organizations generally, is that the specialization of decision making in jurisdictionally germane ways is partially a response to internal forces. The specialization of decision-making allows agents to differentiate their energies and attention, rationally allocating their resources to those jurisdictions that matter most to them.

Committees

Having parceled the space X into jurisdictions $\beta = \{\beta_1,...,\beta_k\}$, we may develop the idea of committees in a parallel fashion by parceling up the set of agents, N. Put simply, a *committee system* is a covering of N. Thus, $\alpha = \{\alpha_1,...,\alpha_k\}$ is a committee system if $\alpha_i \subset N$ and $U\alpha_i = N$.[5] A simple committee system is a partition of N: $U\alpha_i = \alpha_i \cap \alpha_j = \phi$ for all i, j. Each agent $i\epsilon N$ is a member of exactly one committee. A complex committee system, like that of the U.S. House of Representatives, does not possess this property, since each $i\epsilon N$ may be a member of more than one committee. Finally, in the extreme, α contains exactly one element, i.e., $\alpha = \{N\}$. This, the Committee-of-the-Whole, is the familiar structure of traditional voting models, labeled "committee," "electorate," "society," etc. It is apparent, then, that the traditional multidimensional model, consisting of a committee-of-the-whole structure with global jurisdiction, $\alpha = \{N\}$ and $\beta = \{E\}$, is easily embedded in this more general framework and, more importantly, is seen to be a rather extreme special case.

Jurisdictions as Committee Property

A jurisdictional arrangement may make some sense, even in the absence of a division of labor. In the earliest Congresses (through Jefferson's presidency and into Madison's), for example, the House divided deliberations according to a crude jurisdictional scheme, but operated almost entirely in Committee-of-the-Whole.[6] This point aside, however, the interesting and more common circumstance is that in which a jurisdictional arrangement and a committee system are interconnected. Roughly speaking, I assume that jurisdictions emerge in the form of more-or-less "naturally" separable policy domains, and subsets of agents gravitate to particular jurisdictions because they wish to have disproportionate influence there. The latter, an informal division and specialization of labor, is formalized as a committee system.

In terms of the scheme given above, there is a formal rule, F, that associates a $\beta_j \epsilon \beta$ with each $\alpha_i \epsilon \alpha$. Although perhaps a bit restrictive, it suffices for our argument to make α and β sets of equal cardinality and to assume F is a one-to-one mapping of α onto β. Thus, a committee has exactly one jurisdiction, and a jurisdiction exactly one committee.

I conceive of the association between committees and jurisdictions as a kind of property right. A committee is a monopoly provider of proposals to alter the status quo in its jurisdictional domain. Committee assent, therefore, is a necessary condition for change. Conversely, committee opposition to change is sufficient to sustain the status quo. Committees, then, are both *monopoly proposers* and *veto groups*.

At first glance this arrangement may seem a bit odd. Why would the set of all agents institutionalize an arrangement in which only a subset of them had extraordinary influence in each jurisdiction? This poses the general issue of decentralization and delegation. The rationale for decentralization resides in ex ante calculations by agents about the relative importance to them of various jurisdictions. Decentralization is the product of a circumstance in which agents are willing to trade off influence in many areas in exchange for disproportionate influence in the jurisdictions that matter most to them (Weingast, 1979). The rationale for delegation derives from the ability of the parent body to exercise some control over the committees to which it delegates disproportionate influence. In the case of both decentralization and delegation, then, there is a two-sided calculation in terms of the advantages to each $i \epsilon N$ of having disproportionate influence in some jurisdictions and the costs to that same i of allowing others disproportionate influence elsewhere. Each weighs his own advantages against the potential for opportunism by others.

Monitoring and Amendment Control

In the theory of agency (Ross, 1973; Mitnick, 1975; Jensen and Meckling, 1976; Holmstrom, 1979; Fama and Jensen, 1982), agents may be controlled by their principals in two distinct ways. First, agent compensation can be tied, if only imperfectly, to outcomes in a manner that gives agents proper incentives to pursue outcomes valued by the principal. The agent compensation or fee schedule is *output*-related. The second mechanism of agent control by principals is *input*-related. Principals may expend resources in monitoring the input contributions made by agents, bestowing rewards on agents whose input contributions are believed to contribute to achieving goals valued by the principal, and inflicting penalties on "shirking" and other counterproductive agent behavior. Organizations characterized by decentralization and delegation typically employ some mix of these two control devices, the relative proportions depending upon their relative costs to the principal.

A committee stands in an agency relationship to its parent body, and the parent body controls its agent in both input- and output-related fashions. In the U.S. House, for example, committees often contain some members who insure that party and institutional leaders are kept informed of deliberations and who serve as vehicles for transmitting leadership preferences. Thus, some monitoring by the parent body, as personified by its leaders, does take place. In many organizations this is the principal device for securing agent compliance. Yet this is resource-intensive and, in legislatures at least, monitoring is done in more indirect ways, on the one hand, and control is exercised on the output side, on the other.

Let me pursue this conjecture briefly. From my work on House committee assignments (Shepsle, 1978), I came to the conclusion that committee composition is determined essentially by self-selection. On the whole, members gravitate to the committees where they wish to exercise disproportionate influence. Party leaders play a relatively reserved role in assignment process proceedings, only occasionally making their assignment preferences known and thus influencing actual assignments. Leadership monitoring occurs more indirectly, by listening. Interested others such as lobbyists, constituents, presidents, and other legislators follow detailed committee deliberations and, when committee-qua-agent behaves opportunistically and at variance with the preferences of others, these others howl! Monitoring by party and institutional leaders takes the form of reading the decibel-meter and interpreting the howls (Shepsle and Weingast, 1984c, fn 4).

So, in legislatures some monitoring does take place. But too much monitoring would defeat the major purpose of decentralization, for it would retrieve for noncommittee members precisely the influence they were prepared to trade away in exchange for their own jurisdictional influence. It is my own view that, indirect monitoring aside, the chief form of protection against opportunistic behavior by committees occurs on the output side. Committee proposals must survive emendation by the parent body and, at the final stage, must secure a majority vote against the status quo (that is, must be an element of $W(x^0)$).

Let $x \epsilon B_j$ be a jurisdictionally germane proposal by committee α_j. The set $M(x) \subset X$ is called an *amendment control rule* if any alternative $y \epsilon M(x)$ may be offered as a substitute proposal for x by any $i \epsilon N$. Thus, committee $\alpha_j \epsilon \alpha$, in choosing to propose a modification x to x^0, opens the door to a set of possible further modification proposals, $M(x)$.[7] The parent body stands as the final arbiter in that it chooses, according to established procedures, among a committee proposal x and any proposed modifications $y \epsilon M(x)$.

On the one extreme, $M(x)$ poses a trivial constraint on α_j ($M(x) = \phi$). Here, α_j is a monopoly provider not just of proposals, but of final policy outcomes in β_j. Slightly less extreme is the *closed rule*, entailing no amendments and an "up or down" vote between x and x^0 ($M(x) = \{x^0\}$). On the other extreme, there are no constraints on the parent body's capacity to amend, i.e., $M(x) = X$, the *open rule*, so that any substitute proposal is in order. Between these extremes lie alternative amendment control rules which may be partially ordered by set inclusion. Typical of such rules is germaneness. For $x \epsilon B_j$, $M(x) = B_j$ requires *jurisdictional germaneness* for any substitute proposal. More restrictive still (in which $M(x) \subset B_j$) is *proposal germaneness*, which admits a substitute proposal y only if $y_i = x^0_i$ whenever $x_i = x^0_i$. The former germaneness rule admits any substitute alternative from the jurisdiction of which x is an element. The latter allows only those substitute alternatives from the same jurisdiction as x that change the status quo along the same dimension as the original motion does. Of course, if x proposes changes in x^0 on every dimension in β_j, then the two forms of germaneness are identical.

In my earlier work I took $M(x)$ to be given exogenously, so that if α_j did indeed move $x \epsilon \beta_j$, it did so knowing ex ante the amendment possibilities, $M(x)$. In this fashion, $M(x)$, together with the majority preference relation P of the parent body, serves as an incentive structure for each $\alpha_j \epsilon \alpha$. That is, if $M(x)$ were set in advance, well-defined (though not necessarily identical) for different classes of $x \epsilon X$, and chosen to induce agent behavior compatible with the values of the parent body (or at least not drastically destructive of them), then it would look something like the optimal fee structure of the classic principal-agent problem.

This formulation for amendment control rules provides a theoretical perspective on the arrangements of delegation and decentralization in institutions. In tying together the amount of delegation with the amount of "parental" control, though not necessarily in any straightforward way, it offers a way to model delegation structures which I hope will be pursued in further research on institutional arrangements.[8]

However, and this is an important qualification, it may not be appropriate to assume that $M(x)$ is provided exogenously. This institutional fact varies across institutions. For example, it is an acceptably accurate description of university personnel decisions. Departments are the decentralized agents of the university whose personnel proposals, in the form of particular nominees for particular positions, are governed essentially by a closed rule. A department's dean (the principal in this case) may approve or veto an agent's appointment proposal. If the latter, then the status quo prevails unless the agent makes a new proposal. What the dean ordinarily may not do is substitute his own candidate in place of the department's nominee and then transmit an offer. For committees of the U.S. House of Representatives, on the other hand, $M(x)$ is endogenous. The Rules Committee, and ultimately a majority of the entire House, determines an amendment control rule *only after* α_j proposes x.

Institutional Equilibrium

With a committee system α, a jurisdictional arrangement β, a property rights system linking monopoly proposers $\alpha_j \epsilon \alpha$ to jurisdictions $\beta_j \epsilon \beta$, and amendment control rules $M(x)$ for every x falling in some B_j, we have the building blocks of an institution. As noted, the traditional multidimensional voting model of pure majority rule (PMR), $\alpha = \{N\}$ and $\beta = \{E\}$, falls out as a special case. Because of this special case, we know in advance that the prospects for equilibrium are not independent of institutional structure. On the other hand, however, precisely because PMR is a special case, it no longer follows that the conclusion of generic disequilibrium extends to every institutional arrangement. To see this, let $B_j(x) = \{y \mid y = x + \Sigma \lambda_i e_i, e_i \epsilon \beta_j\}$. $B_j(x)$ consists of the jurisdictionally germane ways α_j may alter x. It is the opportunity or feasible set for α_j when x is the status quo. Next, let $W_j(x)$ consist of the points preferred by α_j to x, and $W(x)$ the points preferred by N to x.[9] A point x is said to be *vulnerable* if there is a $y \epsilon B_j(x)$ available to some $\alpha_j \epsilon \alpha$ (jurisdictionally germane), preferred by that committee to x, and preferred by a majority of N to X:

$$x \text{ is vulnerable if } B_j(x) \cap W_j(x) \cap W(x) \neq \phi$$

Conversely, if nothing preferred by any committee to x falls within its jurisdiction or, even if there is such a point, if it is opposed by a majority of N, then x is invulnerable. Invulnerable points are equilibria in the sense that an institution cannot depart from them. Clearly, invulnerable points may exist even if $W(x) \neq \phi \; \forall \; x \epsilon X$. A generically cyclic P relation is insufficient to render all x vulnerable.

Institutional equilibria, however, are not restricted to invulnerable points. Suppose, for committee α_j, that there were a $y \epsilon B_j(x) \cap W_j(x)$ and that yPx, i.e., x is vulnerable. However, suppose further that $M(y)$ were such that members of α_j feared that, if they proposed y, it would then be amended by some $z \epsilon M(y)$ that ultimately prevailed, i.e., $z \epsilon W(y) \cap W(x)$, but that $z \notin W_j(x)$. That is, by "opening the gates" with its proposal of y, α_j ultimately produced the outcome z, which it preferred less than the original x it sought to modify. Under such circumstances α_j will not open the gates and x will be an equilibrium even though it is vulnerable.

Letting

$$V_j(x) = B_j(x) \cap W_j(x) \cap W(x)$$

provide the criterion of vulnerability, we define institutional equilibrium in the following way. First, following Denzau and Mackay's (1983) excellent development, define a *legislative outcome function*, $L(y,x,M(y))$, to be a function whose range is the element that prevails if a committee seeks to alter x by proposal y, with $M(y)$ the existing amendment control rule. Presumably, if $y=x$, i.e., if the committee makes no proposal, keeping the gates closed instead, then x prevails:

$$L(x,x,M(x)) = x$$

With the function L we endow each committee with a modest amount of foresight (Denzau and Mackay, 1981), permitting its members to predict what will ultimately transpire if they seek to change x.[10] Now we say that an $x \epsilon X$ is a *structure-induced equilibrium* (SIE) if, for any $y \epsilon B_j$, $L(y,x,M(y)) \not\epsilon W_j(x)$.

Case 1. If $V_j(x) = \phi$ for all j, then the relevant possibilities are (i) $B_j(x) \cap W_j(x) = \phi$, (ii) $W_j(x) \cap W(x) = \phi$, or (iii) $W(x) = \phi$. Condition (i) implies that each committee prefers to veto any change in x in its jurisdiction and so will keep the gates closed. Condition (ii) finds each committee at odds with its parent body. Condition (iii) states that x is a Condorcet/core point. In each of these cases x is invulnerable so that $L(y,x,M(y))$ either results in x itself, or in some z which the committee regards as inferior to x. In neither case is $L(y,x,M(y))$ an element of $W_j(x)$. Notice that $W(x) = \phi$ is a special case of $V_j(x) = \phi$ for all j, so that the Condorcet/core condition of equilibrium common in traditional multidimensional voting models is a special case of SIE.[11]

Case 2. Suppose $y \epsilon V_j(x)$ for some j, so that x is vulnerable. If the committee forecasts a $z \epsilon M(y) \cap W(y)$ that will be offered as an amendment, with $z \not\epsilon W_j(x)$, then it anticipates either $z = L(y,x,M(y))$ or $x = L(y,x,M(y))$. The latter occurs if $z \epsilon W(y)$ but $z \not\epsilon W(x)$.[12] In either case $L(y,x,M(y)) \not\epsilon W_j(x)$.

Discussion

In Shepsle (1979) I proved existence for SIE under extremely simple structural arrangements. I regard that result as parallel to Black's equilibrium theorem for one-dimensional choice sets and single-peaked preferences (indeed, it was precisely his theorem that I exploited). Surely, it is not the last word. The SIE concept has been extended and embellished by Denzau and Mackay (1981, 1983), Koehler (1982), Enelow and Hinich (1983), and Shepsle and Weingast (1981a,b), among others. I draw this section to a close with the following comments.

1. SIE generalizes the Condorcet/core equilibrium concept (PIE) by incor-

porating structural arrangements. The nonempty win set condition for equilibrium is a special case of SIE under general structural arrangements, and is identical to the SIE when $\alpha = \{N\}$ and $\beta = \{E\}$.

2. SIE places a premium on the channeling effect of institutional arrangements. The committee system, α, creates monopoly proposers and veto groups, and the jurisdictional arrangement, β, renders certain social preferences irrelevant because it makes certain social comparisons infeasible.

3. An SIE is a "retentive" equilibrium, but it need not be "attractive," as Denzau and Mackay (1983) have illustrated. This, in turn, raises the whole issue of dynamics, the path by which the process moves off a nonequilibrium point and ultimately (?) settles on a retentive equilibrium.

4. Procedures, about which I have said little to this point, will figure prominently in characterizing dynamics: the order of voting and motion making, constraints on amendments, the form of the amendment process, etc.[13]

5. Informational and expectational conditions, behavioral assumptions (sophistication, sincerity), and preference characteristics (attitudes toward risk) need to be incorporated more fully and explicitly.

This agenda of research issues, I am pleased to report, suggests a genuine renaissance of the "institutional connection." Formal models are beginning to touch base with some of the empirical regularities long the concern of substantive students of politics. We may now begin to model real institutions, inquiring about their operating characteristics and equilibrium properties.

Two important omissions have permitted the above discussion to proceed, but it is now appropriate to raise them explicitly, if only briefly. The first, which I examine more systematically in the next section, takes institutional arrangements as exogenous. Yet agents choose such arrangements so that, while such choices normally precede actual decision making, they need to be made endogenous. Why do the agents in N do things the way they do? Why do changes in procedures and structural arrangements take on particular new forms?

The second omission is the failure to make agent preferences endogenous. In most multidimensional voting models, preferences are taken as entirely exogenous, the work of Denzau and Parks (1979) standing as something of an exception. In any case, agents are taken as the final bearers of burdens and enjoyers of benefits. In most institutional settings, however, agents are really agents, acting on behalf of and (at least nominally) in the interest of "relevant others." Agent preferences, then, are derivative, and the mechanisms by which these "derived" preferences are induced are of considerable interest.

Some work has begun in this area as it pertains to legislative agents elected from geographic constituencies. Formal models of geographic incidence (Weingast, Shepsle, and Johnsen, 1981; Shepsle and Weingast, 1984c; Fiorina, 1983; Cox, McCubbins, and Sullivan, 1983) have sought to give formal representation to the substantive context of a decade's worth of research on Congress and the "electoral connection" (Mayhew, 1974; Fiorina, 1977; Fenno, 1978). Here, too, then, the institutional setting has proved important in raising the issue of the sources of induced preferences, which was left exogenous in the traditional, structure-free, multidimensional model.

EQUILIBRIUM INSTITUTIONS

I have not, to this point, ventured to define what an institution is, nor shall I. Before proceeding, however, it will be useful to describe two competing views of institutions, each of which possesses elements that will be valuable to retain in our discussion.

Riker (1980) gives a modern treatment to the subject of institutions by referring to them as "congealed tastes." He elaborates:

> The people whose values and tastes are influential live in a world of conventions about both language and values themselves. These conventions are in turn condensed into institutions, which are simply rules about behavior, especially about making decisions. Even the [Delphic] priestess in her frenzy probably behaves according to rules and, for certain, her interpreter is constrained by specifiable conventions. So interpersonal rules, that is, institutions, must affect social outcomes just as much as personal values (p. 4).

Institutions, for Riker, are "condensed conventions" reflecting tastes and values about "interpersonal rules." In referring to these tastes about rules as "congealed," Riker transmits the sense that they possess a sort of constancy that social preferences about outcomes lack, the latter characterized by intransitivity and instability. He is quick, however, to retreat from this unqualified view. Though congealed, tastes about institutional arrangements are still tastes. Therefore, ". . . rules or institutions are just more alternatives in the policy space, and the status quo of one set of rules can be supplanted with another set of rules. Thus the only difference between values and institutions is that the revelation of institutional disequilibrium is probably a longer process than the revelation of disequilibrium of tastes. . . . If institutions are congealed tastes and if tastes lack equilibria, then also do institutions, except for short-run events" (Riker, 1980, p. 22).

Riker, then, views institutions as congealed tastes about interpersonal rules. They consist of attitudes, beliefs, expectations, and preferences about "the way things are done around here."[14] Most important for us, Riker treats institutions like ordinary policy alternatives in an important respect: they are *chosen*. Thus, institutions reflect the same sort (or at least some sort) of the instrumental calculus that rational actors bring to policy choices.

There is an older view of institutions, more sociological, macrohistorical, and almost mystical. This tradition is represented in its most developed form in studies of the origins and foundations of the law, but it is also well-developed in the study of other political institutions as well. It is a view that emphasizes glacial evolution, long periods of constancy, mutation like accident in the form of experiments with new institutional ideas, and the survival of some of these new practices via a sort of natural selection. It is an impersonal process, and neither it nor the institutions it fashions is explicable to the individuals whose behavior conforms to them. Sait (1938), for example, asserts that "private property, slavery, a stratified society—such institutions arose naturally out of altered circumstances and not through any 'intelligently controlled approach.' New social forms originate and old social forms die without any clear perception, by contemporaries, of what is happening" (p. 15). For him, "when we examine political institutions, one after the other, they seem to have been erected, almost like coral reefs, without conscious design" (p. 16).

For Sait, the microeconomic rational actor methodology would be of little utility in the study of institutions for, in his view, the latter cannot be regarded as objects of choices, as the products of an "intelligently controlled approach." The question he sought to address instead involved the puzzle of commonality: How did it come to be that widely separated communities, in space and time, possessed institutions that shared many common elements? On some occasions, as in the case of similarities between English common law and Roman law, he argues in favor of the *convergence hypothesis*, according to which a practice evolves from its environment (Sait, 1938, pp. 201–253; especially p. 202). Commonalities are accidents of parallel development, and in no manner reflect imitation by one community of the practices of another. Thus, practices in communities converge toward one another because their respective environments made such practices propitious. On other occasions, as in the case of representative institutions, Sait's argument supports the *diffusion hypothesis*, according to which conscious adaptation and imitation by one community of institutions created in another is the predominate mechanism (Sait, 1938, pp. 467–499; especially p. 469). In either case, his emphasis is on the survival of practices, not on their choice. Institutions, however they originate (and, according to Sait, historical methods, not "theoretical approaches," are the appropriate ones to answer the question of origin), survive "unless the soil proves uncongenial. All that we can foretell with assurance is this: there will be accommodation to the environment" (Sait, 1938, p. 529).

Riker emphasizes a rational calculus and the congealing of tastes around "unstable constants." Institutional choices differ from policy choices in degree, not kind. They have more durability (but not much more). Sait, on the other hand, rejects any conscious selection process for institutions. Nature "adopts"; man does not "adapt."[15]

The remainder of this essay seeks to marry these two incompatible views. In this more speculative endeavor, I embrace Riker's emphasis on choice of institutional arrangements, yet reject his view that choosing rules and choosing policies according to these rules represent differences in degree, not kind. On the other hand, while rejecting Sait's more mystical views on natural selection and his in-principle rejection of conscious choice of institutions, I embrace his emphasis on the survival of rules regimes.[16] I begin with the "Riker objection" and the "inheritability hypothesis."[17]

The Riker Objection: Inheritability

In the last section, the idea of institutional equilibrium (SIE) was formalized. An alternative x^* is an equilibrium because it cannot be dislodged. Competitors in $W(x^*)$ cannot be brought to a comparison against x^*. This may prevail because of formal rules governing comparisons (e.g., germaneness, the closed rule), because of preference differences embedded in the division of labor (e.g., $W_j(x^*) \cap W(x^*) = \phi$), because x^* is a Condorcet/core point (i.e., $W(x^*) = \phi$), or because of foresight and sophisticated calculation by agenda agents relative to monitoring arrangements via amendment control (i.e., $L(y,x^*,M(y)) \notin W_j(x^*)$ for all j and all $y \epsilon B_j(x^*)$). I shall assume here that a specific institutional arrangement possesses such an x^*, that the set SIE is nonempty.[18]

If institutional rules and arrangements produce stability in majority-rule decision making, then the manner in which the rules, themselves, are chosen must be confronted. Riker (1980) argues that preferences over outcomes, combined with well-grounded expectations about the "institutional outcome function," lead naturally to an induced set of preferences over institutional arrangements. Thus, if institutions p and q have SIEs x_p and x_q, respectively, then individual i prefers p to q if and only if he prefers x_p to x_q. From this it follows that a decisive coalition of agents prefers p to q if and only if each of its members prefers x_p to x_q. If the social preference relation defined by decisive coalitions is cyclic over outcomes, then the cyclicity will be *inherited* in social preferences over institutions.

The Riker objection asserts that instability in policy choice, suppressed by some particular institutional regime, reemerges in the selection of regimes. The latter selection process inherits the disequilibrium inherent in preferences over final outcomes. Let me first take the Riker objection as true and see where that leads. Then I will suggest why I believe the inheritability hypothesis should not be accepted at face value.

Inheritability: Suppose Q is Cyclic

If Q_i is the induced individual preference relation defined on the "space" of institutions, i.e., pQ_iq if $x_p P_i x_q$, then, as Riker suggests, while Q_i will be acyclic, Q, the social preference relation over institutions, normally will not be. But, of what significance is this condition? I have developed in the last section an argument claiming that the cyclicity of P may not be freighted with the significance given it by the universal instability theorems. The same argument applies to the cyclicity of Q. Even though a given institutional arrangement may not be a Condorcet/core point in comparison to other institutional arrangements, the procedures by which institutional arrangements themselves are selected may inhibit change.

Any consideration of changes in the practices of the U.S. Congress, for example, is restricted in some relevant ways by the Constitution. Neither the House nor Senate may alter the basis of representation (proportional to state population in the former and equality by state in the latter). All revenue bills (and by liberal generalization all appropriations bills) must originate in the House. A presidential veto requires a two-thirds vote in each chamber to override. The "chairman" of the Senate must be the Vice President of the United States. And so on. In short, against an existing regime of rules, some alternative regimes may not be compared (short of exogenous change in the form of a constitutional amendment). Constitutionality plays a restraining role on institutional comparisons much like germaneness plays on policy comparisons. Some comparisons are proscribed.[19]

Second, the relevance of the cyclicity of Q, like the counterpart fact about P, may be qualified by the manner in which choice among institutional rules is conducted. Specifically, the division and specialization of labor, monitoring arrangements, and the beliefs, expectations, and degrees of sophistication of institutional actors all are relevant here. For example, each chamber of the U.S. Congress has a Committee on Rules possessing jurisdiction over rules changes. They, in turn, have a chairman, a structure of standing subcommittees, and an occasional, specially charged select subcommittee. I shall not here repeat the story of the previous section, but it should be apparent that a parallel to the structural restrictions on the cyclic P relation exists in similar restraints on the cyclic Q relation. This is my first qualification of the Riker objection, even granting the inheritability of a cyclic Q relation.

My second response begins to drive a wedge between choice of policy and choice of institutional arrangements, suggesting the latter is not merely an instance of the former. In the policy game in a legislature like the U.S. Congress or a state legislature, to take a prominent example, there is an attitude of live and let live. Each legislative agent seeks to obtain benefits for his constituency and, even in failure, he can claim credit for having fought the good fight. Each agent behaves essentially this way and expects all others to behave similarly. Although there are some exceptions, the general rule does not impose sanctions on those who seek to place the distributive and regulatory powers of the state in the service of their constituents. That's the system.

Consider, on the other hand, an effort to change the rules. Could turn-of-the-century progressive legislator George Norris anticipate no sanctions if he tried but failed to reduce the powers of Speaker Joseph Cannon? I hardly think so. It is risky to try to change institutional arrangements in a manner adverse to the interests of those currently in control. Failure has its consequences so that anyone initiating such attempts at change must weigh the expected benefits of success against the certainty of sanctions if he fails. In short, even though some legislative majority might prefer arrangement p to the existing arrangement q (pQq), efforts to promote p will be damped by the risks of failure. These risks would seem not to play nearly so prominent a role in the politics of ordinary policy. Thus, the inherited cyclicity of Q may bear less on the instability of institutional arrangements than the cyclicity of P is alleged to bear on the instability of ordinary policy.

These contentions suggest that even if Q inherits *cyclicity* from P, institutional arrangements do not necessarily inherit *instability* from policy. At any rate, a regime of rules may persist over long periods so that it makes sense to refer to it as an equilibrium of sorts. It is a congelation that resists change unless a sufficient amount of heat is applied.

This view and its supporting arguments concede the truth of the inheritability hypothesis, but qualify its force. It is time now to develop a bolder response to the Riker objection, which casts doubt on the inheritability hypothesis itself. I shall argue that agent calculations about institutional arrangements differ from those about policy alternatives. To approach this argument, a brief digression on cooperation is necessary.

Cooperation and Institutional Bargains: A Digression

Cooperation, as it is technically treated in game theory, entails two prominent features: (i) preplay communication and correlation of strategies among agents is possible, and (ii) agents may enter into binding agreements. Thus, in pure economic exchange (Shapley and Shubik, 1967), coalitions are formed among traders which are, in effect, binding contracts enforceable through well-defined property rights, legal principles (contract law, liability law, torts), and enforcement institutions (courts, sheriffs, state attorneys, etc.). In money economies, analogously, a coalition forms between a "buyer" and a "seller." Preplay negotiation and strategy correlation—bargaining, haggling, "shopping around," and ultimately striking a deal—are clearly characteristic of such phenomena. So, too, is the idea of enforceable agreements (so long as the institutions of enforcement are treated as exogenous to the phenomena of exchange). Hence, a cooperative game formulation in which economic exchange is modeled as a coalition formation process among traders seems eminently reasonable because enforcement is left entirely exogenous.

Communications conditions, while a necessary part of what we regard as cooperation, are often the less problematic of the two features given above for cooperative formulations. Schelling (1960), for example, has persuasively argued and demonstrated that strategic correlation may be arrived at between agents *implicitly*.[20] The key, rather, is enforceability of agreements (a point also stressed by Schelling). How do agents convince one another that promises made ex ante will be honored ex post? *A* can promise to trade votes with *B* across two policy issues. But what is to prevent his reneging on that promise after he has secured *B*'s support?

Clearly, if there were an exogenous enforcement mechanism, like an umpire or a court of law whose services were costless to employ and certain to be forthcoming, then promises could be made binding. Gains from exchange would then be consumated through promises because individual agents would be assured ex ante of restraints on ex post reneging by their partners. Such is the logic (if not the practice) behind the legal enforcement of contract.

The problem, however, for cooperation among criminals, politicians, or sovereign nations is precisely the absence of exogenous enforcement (see, e.g., Laver, 1982; Taylor, 1976; Wagner, 1983). There are no (or few) exogenous mechanisms of enforcement so that cooperation among agents, absent additional features to be mentioned in a moment, will normally be truncated in frequency, scope, and duration. The ex ante prospect of ex post cheating strongly qualifies the ability of agents to exhaust gains from cooperation.

All is not lost. Some cooperation does take place even among politicians, criminals, and suspicious states, since some forms of cooperation are self-enforcing. In situations, for example, in which there is repeated play, an agent's calculations about cooperating or cheating at any one play will be affected by the impact of current behavior on future plays. Specifically, as Axelrod (1981) and Taylor (1976) have argued, an agent will contemplate cheating on an agreement if the one-time windfall from such behavior exceeds the expected net benefit of all future dealings that are jeopardized by the cheating.[21]

One such mechanism that enables cooperation to occur even in the absence of exogenous enforcement is *reputation*. A reputation for honest dealings enhances one's ability to enter into new cooperative ventures. Criminals and politicians surely understand this logic, which sustains the maxim, "Your word is your bond." Thus, in the example alluded to above, if *A* reneges on his promise to support *B*'s bill, the prospect of *B* ever doing business again with *A* declines precipitously. Indeed, if *A* develops a reputation for reneging, then even those agents who have never been personally victimized by *A* will not enter into coalitions with him. Similarly, firms develop *brand names* in order to associate virtues of quality, economy, reliability, etc., with their products.

Unfortunately, self-enforcement via reputation and brand names may not provide a sufficiently firm foundation for cooperation.[22] First, cooperation may be sustained by reputational forces on a bilateral basis between two agents engaged in frequent dealings; but it may be insufficient for multilateral cooperation or intermittent dealings. Thus, a reputation for honest dealings between a retailer and his wholesaler or customer, or between two career legislators on matters in which each is decisive ("favor-doing"), may be sufficient to allow cooperation to transpire. But what of two legislators whose cooperation extends across an election which neither can be certain of surviving? Would *A* do *B* a favor, at some personal cost or risk, or would the frequency of such exchanges be very high, if he could not count on *B*'s ability to reciprocate (either because *B* was subsequently defeated for reelection or *A* was)? Legislative scholars like to talk about a system of "generalized IOUs" in contrast to specific quid pro quo cooperation in the Congress. The problem with the former, and hence the truncated form in which cooperation based on it develops, is the events which may intervene to short-circuit exchanges.

Multilateral cooperation based on reputation has equally troublesome problems. The identification of cheaters, free-riding behavior, and problems with imposing sanctions (who will do the punishing?) all reduce the efficacy of reputation as a form of self-enforcement (Laver, 1981).

A final point about individualistic forms of self-enforcement of agreements follows from the difficulty of specifying contingencies. Cheating is not dichotomous (cheat, not cheat) and there are many forms of opportunistic behavior. Legislator *A*, for example, pledges loyalty to his party, except on matters of conscience or constituency. But who is to determine when the exceptional circumstance has arisen? Or, to give another example, legislator *A* may agree to support *B*'s bill but subsequently claim that his support was only for a weak form of that bill, or for a form that did not contain a particular title, or only for a form that included a specific amendment. In short, it is often costly to negotiate an agreement that pins down the parties to precise terms which reputation can then enforce.

Weingast (1983) likens individualistic forms of agreement and enforcement to a "spot market." If economic agents were unable to write long-term contracts governed by exogenous enforcement, they, too, would be limited to spot-market transactions. Such transactions are more costly, more limited in scope and durability, and generally less satisfactory than alternative ways of doing business (the long-term contract being one such way). Williamson (1975), too, develops an argument which contrasts the problems of spot-market transactions, with all the possibilities for cheating, reneging, and opportunism, with other forms of agreements (e.g., long-term contracts, franchising, organizational integration).[23]

The point here is that, absent exogenous enforcement, the reputational basis for enforcement of agreements, is fraught with problems. And because various forms of opportunistic behavior are still possible, cooperation based on enforcement by reputation does not exhaust otherwise mutually advantageous exchanges. Some exchanges, that is, which are regarded as beneficial to the cooperating parties, will not take place because of (self)enforcement problems.

Institutional Solutions to Problems of Cooperation

I conjecture that the development of political institutions and specific ways of doing things is partly a response to cooperation problems.[24] Political agents come to a situation and wish to extract as much advantage as they can. But not knowing how conflicts will shape up, now or in the future, they develop mechanisms which enable positive collective action, on the one hand, but which possess aspects of insurance against reneging, opportunism, and other adverse circumstances, on the other hand.

One telling example is the practice, in every legislature with which I am familiar, of voting the status quo, x^0, last. Any bill or motion must survive a "vote on final passage," a "motion to table," a "motion to recommit to committee," a "proposal to strike the enacting clause," etc. In terms of my argument in the previous section, any bill or motion, however perfected by amendment, must be an element of $W(x^0)$ if it is to survive as the final outcome. Consequently, no amount of strategic behavior, opportunism, cheating, or reneging on promises can ever produce a final outcome which makes any decisive coalition worse off than they were under the status quo ante.[25] Because of this institutional practice, some forms of self-enforcement are possible which do not require the force of reputation.

This feature of legislatures permits other insitutional practices to evolve, prosper, and survive. Legislators, for example, have differential concerns. Some care principally about one bundle of policy dimensions while others are mostly concerned about some different bundle. These differences in salience suggest the possibility of gains from trade, each group trading off influence in one area in exchange for disproportionate influence in the other. One possible solution, for example, is the *omnibus*. Let each set of legislators have disproportionate influence in molding a proposal in their respective areas of concern. But instead of voting each proposal separately, tie them together into a single bill composed of distinct sections. Such a solution is, in fact, the predominate practice in the U.S. Congress in those policy areas that recur with some regularity, e.g., the biennial omnibus rivers and harbors bill (see Ferejohn, 1974).

However, all the problems of spot markets emerge if these exchanges must take place de novo at each occasion. Deals struck risk coming unstuck. In short, it would seem that, except for those circumstances that recur frequently, the omnibus solution is costly to transact and enforce. A more efficient solution, still entailing protection against opportunism, is complete decentralization via a committee system with the proviso of voting x^0 last. This is Weingast's (1983) persuasive argument for the emergence of a division-of-labor arrangement in the U.S. Congress. Each committee may be composed of "interesteds," or Niskanen's (1971) "high demanders," and bills may emerge from committees without the requirement that they be linked in an omnibus (thereby economizing on transactions costs). But the proviso of voting x^0 last is sufficient to protect every decisive coalition from exploitation by committees. If, on the other hand, committees were not merely monopoly *proposers* of policy in a given jurisdiction, but monopoly *providers* of final outcomes, in which case they need not observe $W(x^0)$ as a constraint, then no such protection is afforded, and it is unlikely that the strong committee system we observe today would ever have developed.

Decentralization to committee, in turn, permits a kind of cooperation that is far more unlikely at the level of atomistic legislators. At the level of *committees*, reciprocity agreements are self-enforcing in a way that they are not at the level of individual legislators. Individual legislators come and go; committees persist. The identity of the legislative agent from any specific district may change; the identity of the decisive coalition on a committee changes much more slowly. Thus, the committee system permits reciprocity and other forms of cooperation *between committees* because self-enforcement is more easily facilitated.

Institutions as Ex Ante Agreements

The argument developed only briefly here is that cooperation that is chancy and costly to transact at the level of individual agents is facilitated at the level of institutions. Practices, arrangements, and structures at the institutional level economize on transaction costs, reduce opportunism and other forms of agency "slippage," and thereby enhance the prospects of gains through cooperation, in a manner generally less available at the individual level. Institutions, then, look like ex ante agreements about a structure of cooperation.

What is beginning to emerge in this argument is a wedge between choosing outcomes and choosing cooperation structures. The latter, chosen in advance of policy choice, must be assessed over many policy choices and evaluated over the duration it is expected to survive. When legislators in the very first Congress, for example, agreed to let the Speaker appoint all select and standing committees, the likely composition of no one committee dominated this decision. Rather it was the "on average" assessment and was compared to another "on average" assessment of the contending alternative (electing each committee). Both uncertainty and indifference made appointment by the Speaker appear desirable in comparison to a time-intensive alternative.[26]

Institutional Survival

When Riker (1980) describes institutions as "congealed tastes" and "unstable constants," he conjoins opposites: "congealed" and "constants" versus "tastes" (known to be cyclic) and "unstable." Institutions, then, are something of a paradox for him. They seem to maintain themselves over short horizons, but ultimately succumb to the instability they repress. For Sait (1938), too, institutions are paradoxical. Strongly conditioned by their environment, which changes only slowly, institutions look constant; but occasional abrupt environmental changes, coupled with imitation and diffusion, invest institutions with a longer term dynamic undetectable to individuals in the shorter term of, say, a human lifetime.

What is to be made of this paradox? Let me suggest a paradox of my own. Suppose institution p leads to a determinate SIE, x_p. Then, subject to the caveats I have developed in this section about the mechanisms by which institutions are chosen, p inherits the vulnerability it represses in x_p. Since $W(x_p) \neq \phi$, a decisive coalition may prefer some other structural arrangement, q, for which $x_q \in W(x_p)$. Suppose, on the other hand, that p does not lead to a determinate SIE.[27] For example, as I have shown elsewhere (Shepsle, 1979), and Denzau and Mackay (1983) have developed further, even when SIEs exist, they rarely are unique. Thus, for any institution p, the set SIE(p) is normally not a singleton. Ex ante, then, individuals may be uncertain about what the adoption of p implies in policy terms. Their priors will not be as flat as those they would attach to pure majority rule, since probabilistic support is concentrated on SIE(p). But, since SIE(p) is a (possibly dense) set, their priors will not be spiked either.

The paradox I propose is the following. A modest amount of uncertainty, e.g., about individual preferences, about which element of SIE(p) will emerge ex post, etc., may be sufficient to congeal tastes about institutions. One such argument that proposes this logic is Weingast's rational choice model of the norm of universalism (Weingast, 1979). In distributing some fixed pie by pure majority rule, the unstable world of hard ball politics and minimum winning coalitions (MWC) applies. Uncertainty, ex ante, over which MWC will ultimately prevail, induces a preference by individuals for a specific, for-certain, sharing rule (in the perfectly symmetric case, this is the "rule of $1/n$"; see Weingast et al., 1981). This sharing rule is a maximal element relative to the set of all sharing rules and relative to MWC politics.

At the level of institutional choice, the uncertainty is twofold. Ex ante, p may prevail over q because SIE(p) is preferred to SIE(q), where the SIE($\cdot$) are now set over which individuals have prior beliefs. Although I have done no analysis, it would be worth inquiring whether the conjecture that Q has maximal elements is plausible under various conditions, i.e., whether inheritability is short-circuited by uncertainty.[28]

There is, however, a second form of uncertainty. A given institutional arrangement, p, however uncertain its outcome implications ex ante, becomes relatively better known ex post. While always subject to the vicissitudes of exogenous change—new elections bring a different configuration of preferences to a legislature, for example—it may even get stuck on a specific $x_p \in$ SIE(p). Now the uncertainty equation gets turned around. Will every effective set of agents prefer x_p to what they would expect (given uncertainty) from some alternative institution, q? If so, then p possesses a stability, even though x_p is not P-maximal.

CONCLUSIONS

It is difficult to bring this essay to a close on so conjectural a note, especially since it, in turn, is based on a more fundamental conjecture. Even though I sought to drive a wedge between policy choice and institutional choice, and thereby qualify the hypothesis of inheritability, I have accepted the common premise of both Riker and Sait that institutions persist in ways that ordinary policies do not. The sources of my belief in this premise are the role institutions play in facilitating cooperation and solving agency problems, and the restricted mechanisms by which institutional change may transpire. I think, however, that this premise requires further scrutiny, both empirically and theoretically.

Are institutional arrangements as stable (relative to policy outcomes) as Riker, Sait and I presume? Any brief history of the House of Representatives points to particular high-water marks of institutional change: the establishment and general use of standing committees, the accrual of powers by the Speaker, the establishment of a separate appropriations process, various "legislative re-organizations," etc. But between these high-water-mark events (and frankly, even they occur with some frequency) are many "smaller" changes and many more failed efforts at change. I suppose we really have not yet found a precise scientific language in which to characterize institutions and assess magnitudes of change.

And this is where I leave the discussion. Institutions, I have claimed, by their very structure induce an element of stability in policy outcomes that does not emerge in the more atomistic world of pure majority rule. I have further pro-posed that choices over institutional arrangements, based on ex ante beliefs and calculations about cooperation problems, need not inherit the instability of preferences over outcomes. Yet I have left vague exactly what it is that consti-tutes an institutional practice or arrangement. I have begun the task of charac-terizing the "institution space" in my discussion of a division of labor, jurisdic-tions, specialization of labor, and rules of comparison and monitoring. These, in turn, imply particular practices in the formation of agendas and lay bare the strategic character of institutional choice (Shepsle and Weingast, 1981b, 1984a). But these hardly constitute a beginning.

Acknowledgments. The author acknowledges the research support of the National Science Foundation (SES-8112016) and the John Simon Guggenheim Memorial Foun-dation. He is also most appreciative of the many useful conversations over the years with Professor Barry Weingast of Washington University. His comments on this paper, as well as those of the author's research assistant, Brian Humes, were especially helpful.

NOTES

1. I refer here not to the work on socialization, which is not at all formal, but rather to the work on incentive structures and the preferences they induce. See the citations in note 24 below on agency theory, as well as the now voluminous literature on incentive compatibility and demand-revealing mechanisms.

2. This discussion is based on Shepsle and Weingast (1981a).

3. I should mention at this point, as Fiorina and I (1982) emphasized, that there are different levels of analysis and hence different degrees of equilibrium. Thus, even in the absence of equilibrium of PMR at the level of outcomes, there are other equilibrium concepts that exist. Ferejohn, McKelvey, and Packel (1981), for example, show that the open agenda process of PMR may be modeled as a Markov process with a stationary limiting probability distribution. Under various conditions they establish the existence of an *equilibrium distribution*. In short, PMR, lacking a core point in the space of outcomes, possesses a stochastic equilibrium in the space of probability distributions over outcomes.

4. For any set, S, a *covering* of S is a finite collection of subsets $\Sigma = \{\sigma_1,...,\sigma_k\}$ such that $U\sigma_i = S$. If $\sigma_i \cap \sigma_j = \phi$ for every $\sigma_i, \sigma_j \epsilon \Sigma$, then Σ is a *partition* of S.

5. For simplicity of exposition, I have written α and β as sets with the same number of elements so that, shortly, we can conveniently match the elements of α and β. While not necessary, it does permit us to avoid notational nightmares.

6. Committees existed, but the important decisions were *first* made in the Committee-of-the-Whole only after which a bill or resolution was sent to a committee to be drafted formally. Moreover, the committees were required to report back, thus eliminating any veto power. See Shepsle (1978, chap. 1), Harlow (1917), and Cooper (1970).

7. For a game-theoretic treatment of a special version of this—in the form of a two-person game between a legislative committee (which picks a motion) and a rules committee (which picks a single amendment)—see Shepsle and Weingast (1981b).

8. As I write, these precise issues are being debated on the front pages of the nation's newspapers. On June 24, 1983, the Supreme Court decided the case of Immigration and Naturalization Service v. Chadha, in which it invalidated the "legislative veto." A crucial issue emerging now is how much Congress would have delegated (will delegate) to executive agencies or the President if it did not have (no longer has) an opportunity for a "second look" and an opportunity to negative those exercises of delegated authority of which it disapproves.

9. $W(x)$ is the majority win set defined earlier by the majority P relation. I remain silent on $W_j(x)$ inasmuch as the ideas below apply to any arrangement by which the $\alpha_j \epsilon \alpha$ arrange their decision-making rules.

10. A more general expectational model is developed in Denzau and Mackay (1983). Also see Enelow and Hinich (1983) for a related development in which expectations are probabilistic rather than deterministic.

11. In Shepsle (1979), I called any $x \epsilon X$ for which $W(x) = \phi$ a *preference-induced equilibrium* (PIE) and proved that the set PIE of such equilibria is contained in SIE, the set of structure-induced equilibria.

12. If each $i \epsilon N$ is sophisticated, he would not vote to amend y by z, even though $z \epsilon W(y)$. See Shepsle and Weingast (1984a) and Ferejohn, Fiorina, and McKelvey (1981). If, on the other hand, the $i \epsilon N$ are not (or are constrained from being) sophisticated, then the possibility in the text exists.

13. In the House, for example, bills are perfected a title at a time whereas, in the Senate, an amendment to any title is in order at any time.

14. For explicitly formal treatments of conventions, norms, and institutions, see Lewis (1969), Ullman-Margalit (1978), and Schotter (1981), respectively. Schotter, in particular, takes a game-theoretic perspective in which institutions are regularities in social behavior that (i) are agreed to by the members of a community, (ii) specify behavior in recurrent situations, and (iii) are either self-policed or exogenously enforced.

15. For a more thoroughly modern development of this latter argument, see Alchian (1950).

16. This latter emphasis is experiencing something of a theoretical revival in economics. See Nelson and Winter (1982) and Hirshleifer (1982).

17. To keep matters somewhat concrete in what follows, let me be clear in restricting my discussion to formal political and organizational practices, i.e., structural arrangements and procedural methods. I shall have little to say about some of the things Sait took as institutions, e.g., "private property, slavery, a stratified society." For a treatment similar in spirit to mine of these more macro practices, however, see Demsetz (1967).

18. This is clearly false in general, since we know the "traditional" arrangement with $\alpha = \{N\}$ and $\beta = \{E\}$ possesses no equilibrium. That is, the existence of SIEs is not general and must be established institution by institution. Except for some relatively simple settings (Shepsle, 1979; Shepsle and Weingast, 1981a; Denzau and Mackay, 1983), there are no general existence results to report. The assumption in the text, however, permits me to address matters of equilibrium institutions in a deterministic fashion without having to resort to stochastic arguments that would be necessitated by nondeterministic outcomes. Shortly, I relax this stricture by assuming that SIEs exist but are not necessarily unique.

19. In response it might quite correctly be argued that just as an institutional arrangement may suppress policy cycles, so too a *constitutional* arrangement may suppress institutional cycles. But then, it might further be argued, would not the cyclicity of P, inherited by (but suppressed in) Q, in turn be inherited by the social relation T over constitutional regimes? That is, haven't I just pushed the problem back still another step? The answer, I suppose, is yes. But for this to be important one must continue to maintain that, because preferences are induced from the narrow level to the next broader level, choices at each level are essentially the same, deriving from the same calculus. Riker has argued that choosing over institutions is essentially the same as choosing over policies (since the P_i's induce Q_i's): "In [this] sense, rules or institutions are just more alternatives in the policy space. . ." (Riker, 1980, p. 22). Now the same must be argued about constitutions. I find this implausible on its face, but will develop the argument further below.

20. I should add, however, that communications conditions constitute an important aspect of an institutional arrangement—as in rules governing debate and discussion. Such rules may enhance or inhibit cooperation by affecting the transactions costs of coalition formation. This point is developed at some length in Shepsle and Weingast (1984b) in our commentary on an experimental study of cooperation by McKelvey and Ordeshook (1984).

21. The strongest form of sanction against a cheater is that of no future cooperation. This requires that agents be able to identify the cheating and the cheater. In informationally poorer circumstances, cheating may secure a one-time windfall at the risk of some *probability* of no future cooperation with the cheater. Laver (1981) has pointed out some of the problems associated with punishing cheaters.

22. This point is developed in more detail in Shepsle and Weingast (1984b). Recently

my colleague, Barry Weingast, completed an early draft of "The Industrial Organization of Congress," in which he applies principles of the theory of agency and the theory of industrial organization to legislatures. This is an outstanding intellectual effort from which I have borrowed heavily.

23. Also see Klein, Crawford, and Alchian (1978).

24. These are called agency problems in the industrial organization literature. See Holmstrom (1979), Jensen and Meckling (1976), Fama and Jensen (1982), and Ross (1973), among others.

25. This provides probabilistic insurance to each individual. In a simple majority rule legislature, for example, the odds are better than even, on average, that any individual is part of a decisive coalition whose wishes serve to constrain final outcomes.

26. As the slavery issue overwhelmed all others from the 1830s on, so that Speakership appointments (especially to the Committee on Territories) took on global significance, Speakership elections became protracted and bitter, and efforts to strip the Speaker of committee assignment authority grew more frequent (see Shepsle, 1978, chap. 1).

27. See note 18 on the nonuniqueness of SIEs.

28. This orientation equates an institution with a lottery over outcomes, and institutional choice with choice among lotteries. This is precisely the view taken by Fiorina (1982) in modeling the legislative choice of alternative modes of regulation. Some technical results about choice over lotteries is found in Fishburn (1972), Shepsle (1972), McKelvey (1980), and McKelvey and Richelson (1974).

REFERENCES

Alchian, Armen A. (1950). Evolution, uncertainty, and economic theory. *Journal of Political Economy* 58: 211–221.

Axelrod, Robert (1981). The emergence of cooperation among egoists. *American Political Science Review* 75: 306–318.

Black, Duncan (1948). On the rationale of group decision making. *Journal of Political Economy* 56: 23–44.

Blydenburgh, John C. (1971). The closed rule and the paradox of voting. *Journal of Politics* 33: 57–71

Cohen, Linda (1979). Cyclic sets in multidimensional voting models. *Journal of Economic Theory* 20: 1–12.

Cooper, Joseph (1970). *The Origins of the Standing Committees and the Development of the Modern House.* Houston: Rice University.

Cox, Gary W., McCubbins, Matthew, D., and Sullivan, Terry (1983). Policy and constituency: reelection incentives and the choice of policy intervention. Mimeo. University of Texas, Austin.

Demsetz, Harold (1967). Toward a theory of property rights. *American Economic Review* 57: 347–360.

Denzau, Arthur T., and Parks, Robert P. (1979). Deriving public sector preferences. *Journal of Public Economics* 11: 335–352.

Denzau, Arthur T., and Mackay, Robert J. (1981). Structure induced equilibrium and perfect foresight expectations. *American Journal of Political Science* 25: 762–779.

Denzau, Arthur T., Mackay, Robert J. (1983). The gate keeping and monopoly power of committees: an analysis of sincere and sophisticated behavior. *American Journal of Political Science* 27: 740–761.

Downs, Anthony (1957). *An Economic Theory of Democracy.* New York: Harper & Row.

Enelow, James M. (1982). Saving amendments, killer amendments, and a new theory of congressional voting. Mimeo. SUNY, Stony Brook.

Enelow, James M., and Hinich, Melvin J. (1983). Voting one issue at a time: the question of voter forecasts. *American Political Science Review* 77: 435–446.

Fama, Eugene F., and Jensen, Michael, C. (1982). Agency problems and the survival of organizations. Unpublished paper. University of Rochester.

Fenno, Richard F. (1978). *Home Style.* Boston: Little-Brown.

Ferejohn, John A. (1974). *Pork Barrel Politics.* Stanford: Stanford University Press.

Ferejohn, John A., McKelvey, Richard D., and Packel, Edward (1981). Limiting distribution for continuous state Markov voting models. Mimeo. Caltech.

Ferejohn, John A., Fiorina, Morris P., and McKelvey, Richard D. (1981). A theory of legislative behavior on divisible policy. Mimeo. Caltech.

Fiorina, Morris P. (1977). *Congress: Keystone of the Washington Establishment.* New Haven: Yale University Press.

Fiorina, Morris P. (1982). Legislative choice of regulatory forms: legal process or administrative process? *Public Choice* 39: 33–66.

Fiorina, Morris P. (1983). Some observations on policy relevant models of legislative decision making. Delivered at Annual Meeting of Midwest Political Science Association. Chicago.

Fiorina, Morris P., and Shepsle, Kenneth A. (1982). Equilibrium, disequilibrium, and the general possibility of a science of politics. In Peter C. Ordeshook and Kenneth A. Shepsle (eds.), *Political Equilibrium*, pp. 49–65. Boston: Kluwer-Nijhoff.

Fishburn, Peter C. (1972). Lotteries and social choices. *Journal of Economic Theory* 5: 189–207.

Harlow, Ralph V. (1917). *The History of Legislative Methods in the Period Before 1825.* New Haven: Yale University Press.

Hirshleifer, Jack (1982). Evolutionary models in economics and law. *Research in Law and Economics* 4: 1–60.

Holmstrom, Bengt (1979). Moral hazard and observability. *Bell Journal of Economics* 10: 74–91.

Jensen, Michael C., and Meckling, William H. (1976). Theory of the firm: managerial behavior, agency costs, and ownership structure. *Journal of Financial Economics* 3: 305–360.

Klein, Benjamin, Crawford, Robert, and Alchian, Armen (1978). Vertical integration, appropriable rents, and the competitive contracting process. *Journal of Law and Economics* 21: 297–326.

Koehler, David (1982). Structure induced equilibrium in the legislative process. Paper presented at the Annual Meeting of the American Political Science Association, Denver.

Laver, Michael (1981). *The Politics of Private Desires.* Harmondsworth, U.K.: Penguin Books.

Laver, Michael (1982). The politics of crime and vice versa. Paper presented at the Public Choice Workshop, Washington University, St. Louis.

Lewis, David K. (1969). *Convention.* Cambridge, Mass.: Harvard University Press.

Mayhew, David (1974). *Congress: The Electoral Connection.* New Haven: Yale University Press.

McKelvey, Richard D. (1976). Intransitivities in multidimensional voting models and some implications for agenda control. *Journal of Economic Theory* 2: 472–482.

McKelvey, Richard D. (1979). General conditions for global intransitivities in formal voting models. *Econometrica* 47: 1085–1111.

McKelvey, Richard D. (1980). Ambiguity in spatial models of policy formation. *Public Choice* 35: 385–402.

McKelvey, Richard D., and Richelson, Jeff (1974). Cycles of risk. *Public Choice* 18: 41–66.

McKelvey, Richard D., and Ordeshook, Peter C. (1984). An experimental study of the effects of procedural rules on committee behavior. *Journal of Politics* 46: 182–205.

Mitnick, Barry (1975). The theory of agency: the policing 'paradox' and regulatory behavior. *Public Choice* 24: 27–43.

Nelson, Richard R., and Winter, Sidney, G. (1982). *An Evolutionary Theory of Economic Change.* Cambridge, Mass.: Harvard University Press.

Niskanen, William (1971). *Bureaucracy and Representative Government.* Chicago: Aldine.

Plott, Charles R. (1967). A notion of equilibrium and its possibility under majority rule. *American Economic Review* 67: 787–806.

Riker, William H. (1965). Arrow's theorem and some examples of the paradox of voting. In John M. Claunch (ed.), *Mathematical Applications in Political Science.* Dallas: Southern Methodist University Press.

Riker, William H. (1980). Implications from the disequilibrium of majority rule for the study of institutions. *American Political Science Review* 74: 432–447. Reprinted in Peter C. Ordeshook and Kenneth A. Shepsle (eds.), *Political Equilibrium*. Boston: Kluwer-Nijhoff. [Citations to latter source.]

Ross, Stephen A. (1973). The economic theory of agency: the principal's problem. *American Economic Review* 63: 134–139.

Sait, Edward M. (1938). *Political Institutions—A Preface*. Boston: Appleton-Century-Crofts.

Schelling, Thomas C. (1960). *The Strategy of Conflict*. Cambridge, Mass.: Harvard University Press.

Schofield, Norman (1978). Instability of simple dynamic games. *Review of Economic Studies* 45: 575–594.

Schotter, Andrew (1981). *The Economic Theory of Social Institutions*. Cambridge: Cambridge University Press.

Schwartz, Thomas (1981). The universal instability theorem. *Public Choice* 37: 487–502.

Shapley, Lloyd S., and Shubik, Martin (1967). Concepts and theories of pure competition. In Martin Shubik (ed.), *Essays in Mathematical Economics in Honor of Oskar Morgenstern*, pp. 63–82. Princeton: Princeton University Press.

Shepsle, Kenneth, A. (1972). The strategy of ambiguity: uncertainty and electoral competition. *American Political Science Review* 66: 555–568.

Shepsle, Kenneth, A. (1978). *The Giant Jigsaw Puzzle: Democratic Committee Assignments in the Modern House*. Chicago: University of Chicago Press.

Shepsle, Kenneth, A. (1979). Institutional arrangements and equilibrium in multidimensional voting models. *American Journal of Political Science* 23: 27–60.

Shepsle, Kenneth A. (1985). The future prospects of formal models of legislatures. *Legislative Studies Quarterly* 10: 5–20.

Shepsle, Kenneth A., and Weingast, Barry R. (1981a). Structure-induced equilibrium and legislative choice. *Public Choice* 37: 503–519.

Shepsle, Kenneth A., and Weingast, Barry R. (1981b). Structure and strategy: the two faces of agenda power. Paper presented at the Annual Meeting of American Political Science Association, New York.

Shepsle, Kenneth A., and Weingast, Barry R. (1984a). Uncovered sets and sophisticated voting outcomes with implications for agenda institutions. *American Journal of Political Science* 28: 49–74.

Shepsle, Kenneth A., and Weingast, Barry R. (1984b). When do rules of procedure matter? *Journal of Politics* 46: 206–221.

Shepsle, Kenneth A., and Weingast, Barry R. (1984c). Political 'solutions' to market problems. *American Political Science Review* 77: 417–434.

Slutsky, Steven (1979). Equilibrium under α-majority rule. *Econometrica* 47: 1113–1125.

Taylor, Michael (1976). *Anarchy and Cooperation*. New York: Wiley.

Ullman-Margalit, Edna (1977). *The Emergence of Norms*. Oxford: Oxford University Press.

Wagner, R. Harrison (1983). The theory of games and the problem of international cooperation. *American Political Science Review* 77: 330–347.

Weingast, Barry R. (1979). A rational choice perspective on congressional norms. *American Journal of Political Science* 23: 245–263.

Weingast, Barry R. (1983). The industrial organization of Congress. Mimeo. Washington University, St. Louis.

Weingast, Barry R., Shepsle, Kenneth A., and Johnsen, Christopher (1981). The political economy of benefits and costs: a neoclassical approach to distributive politics. *Journal of Political Economy* 89: 642–664.

Williamson, Oliver (1975). *Markets and Hierarchies*. New York: Free Press.

CHAPTER 5

THE CYCLES OF LEGISLATIVE CHANGE: BUILDING A DYNAMIC THEORY

Lawrence C. Dodd

The subject of legislative change first captured my attention in the summer of 1975. I was teaching a course on Congress; I had started the semester with the theoretical arguments of David Mayhew (1974) and was ending with a review of the recent budgetary reforms. As the course drew to a close an exasperated student raised two questions: "Mayhew presents a static Congress; why is Congress changing? Mayhew describes a fragmented Congress; why is Congress centralizing?"

I had no answer for the student, nor could I find one in the legislative literature. Scholars from Wilson (1885) to Huntington (1965) to Polsby (1968) had described congressional change and noted its critical implications. Parliamentary analysts such as Bryce (1924) and Bracher (1971) had treated change—the decline of legislatures—as one of the great themes of twentieth century politics. And Blondel (1973), surveying all contemporary legislatures, had found cyclical change to be legislatures' most widely shared characteristic. Yet none of these writers provided a coherent explanation of change.

The questions posed by the undergraduate student had uncovered a major flaw in the study of legislatures. The problem did not lie with inadequate methods. Legislative scholars had pioneered the use of mathematical models (Ferejohn, 1974; Fiorina, 1974; Shepsle, 1978), sophisticated statistics (MacRae, 1970), and participant observation (Fenno, 1966, 1973, 1978; Huitt and Peabody, 1969; Jones, 1961; Oppenheimer, 1974; and Peabody, 1976). The problem did not lie in a paucity of data; scholars had abundant access to roll call votes, election statistics, and first-hand interviews. Nor was the problem an absence of historical research. A solid body of literature existed by the mid 1970s that traced the outlines of congressional history in some detail (Bolling, 1965; Brady, 1973; Cooper, 1971; Ripley, 1969a,b; Rothman, 1969; and Young, 1966).

The problem lay in the absence of theory. The student's questions—why change? why centralization?—demanded explanation, demanded theory. With theory the student could understand the movement of Congress from one organizational structure to another, and then hypothesize perhaps the emergence of a third. With theory legislative scholars could visualize and research the critical patterns of change that static analysts might overlook or misunderstand. But no theory of change existed to guide students or scholars.

A decade has now passed since the congressional reforms led my undergraduate student and others across the country to challenge the static nature of legislative theory. And today, just as in the 1970s, the creation of a theory of change remains an unfulfilled task (Rieselbach, 1984). A growing body of scholars focus on the historical research necessary for developing and testing theory (Aydelotte, 1977; Cooper and Brady, 1981). But legislative theory itself remains preoccupied with static models that bear little relationship to the turbulent change of modern legislatures.

Against this backdrop the purpose of this essay is to encourage scholars to build theories of change. Given the relative absence of theory perhaps the best way to provoke such work is to construct a theory. To this end let us first examine some major studies on which we can build.

THE INTELLECTUAL FOUNDATION

The theoretical work of Anthony Downs (1957), presented in *An Economic Theory of Democracy*, provides us a useful starting point. Downs is important not so much for what he says about legislatures as for the insights he provides into building theories of change. He focuses on the behavior of parties and elections in a world that closely resembles a British parliamentary system. Parties are goal-oriented teams of members seeking to gain power by winning elections. To win the support of the electorate, parties reflect dominant ideological positions of voters. As large groups of voters shift their ideological stands, the parties alter their policy positions. Such jockeying among parties can alter the number and size of parties in the party system.

Downs' theory demonstrates that the goals of political actors can shape and explain changes in their political behavior. Moreover, micro level motivations, such as actors' desires for power, can shape macro phenomena such as the changing structure of the party system. These conclusions suggest that legislative scholars, who after all are studying the same politicians as Downs, should examine the impact that legislators' goals have, not simply on elections and parties, but on the politics of the institution. Just as a focus on politicians' goals can generate a deductive theory of electoral and partisan change, it may also produce a coherent understanding of legislative change.

Downs' influence on general legislative theory is seen most clearly in the work of David Mayhew (1974). In *Congress: the Electoral Connection*, Mayhew provides us the first full-fledged attempt to build an economic theory of legislative politics. He draws his inspiration from Downs' emphasis on the goal-oriented nature of politicians. Mayhew argues that the goals of legislators, specifically, their desire for reelection, shapes the structure and functioning of a legislature. The effort by members to gain reelection leads to common patterns of behavior such as credit-claiming and to the creation of a decentralized Congress designed to serve members' reelection needs.

Mayhew's work is a major step toward a general legislative theory. Unfortunately, his theoretical strategy suffers from two shortcomings (Dodd, 1978). First, the book contains a logical flaw. In order for Mayhew to explain the existence of mechanisms such as the Rules Committee that keep Congress functioning, he argues that legislators receive side payments of power for service on these committees; these side payments induce members to serve on such committees even though service may limit their opportunity to pursue their reelection interests. The reelection motive by itself cannot account for the existence of these committees and thus fails to explain fully the organization of the legislature. A second problem, as noted above, is the static nature of Mayhew's Congress. He develops no argument to explain how or why the legislature may change.

These theoretical shortcomings should not mask the great contribution of Mayhew's work. Early efforts such as this to build a theory are bound to have conceptual and logical flaws; but the effort itself is a vital part of a process of theory building that will span several generations of scholars and explore many dead-end paths. The important point is that Mayhew directs us to a potentially fruitful strategy for studying legislatures: linking members' goals to institutional politics and structure. He also identifies an argument, the emphasis on reelection, that undoubtedly has widespread applicability in the legislative world.

Mayhew's work was published almost simultaneously with Richard Fenno's pathbreaking study of congressional committees (Fenno, 1973). Fenno's empirical work directly addressed the central problems of Mayhew's theory. Whereas Mayhew focused on one narrow goal, Fenno introduced three goals: reelection, policy, and influence. Members pursue these by serving on committees that facilitate one or another of the goals. These findings suggest that legislators may in fact create different committees to serve these different career goals. An explanation of the structure of the committee system and thus of Congress must incorporate all three goals.

Fenno's analysis also suggests that a certain hierarchy of goals may exist among members. While Fenno does not develop the topic himself, the move from reelection to policy to influencing committees parallels an increase in the average seniority of committees' members and in the power and prestige of committees (Rieselbach, 1973; Smith and Deering, 1984). These patterns suggest that legislators may share some very general goal such as power that they pursue through orderly stages of career advancement, moving from a reelection to a policy to an influence stage (Dodd, 1977). The pursuit of power then would be the underlying factor determining the type and relative status of committees in the legislature.

Fenno's second contribution was to link legislators' goals with organizational change. This development comes in his exploration of the House Post Office Committee. In the postwar years, Fenno argues, the members of that committee pursued a reelection goals so avidly—by raising civil service pay while keeping postal revenues low—that they undermined the fiscal integrity of the postal service. Their continued pursuit of the reelection goal eventually produced a fiscal crisis; in response, Congress stripped the committee of its jurisdiction and created a postal service commission. The uninhibited pursuit of members' short-term goals had crippled the committee's capacity to perform responsibly and had forced Congress to change the committee's role.

The tension evident in Fenno's micro-level analysis of the Post Office Committee is writ large in the ambitious work of a fourth scholar, Joseph Cooper (1975, 1976). Cooper argues that a key way to see legislatures and legislative change is from an organizational perspective (see also, Davidson and Oleszek, 1976). Whereas Fenno sees tension between the individual and a committee, Cooper sees tensions involving the individual, the overall legislative structure, and the legislature's external environment. These tensions shape and constrain the individual's career development and thus the sort of structure and process he supports for the legislature.

Of the scholars discussed here, Cooper is the one for whom legislative change is really a major issue. Cooper is particularly concerned with macro change. Just as Downs is interested in changes in macro level phenomena (shifts from a two party to a multiparty system, for example), Cooper is interested in knowing why a legislature may change from a party dominated to a committee based structure. Cooper reminds us that our real explanatory task is to explain the institution itself: its broad patterns of organization, behavior, and change. We will possess an incomplete and unreliable understanding of legislative behavior until we can explain how the general structure and processes of the legislature shape the behavior of its members.

A similar concern with macrolevel analysis is reflected in the growing research into congressional realignments (Brady, 1978; Carmines and Stimson, 1985; Sinclair, 1982; and Sundquist, 1973). Key (1955) and Burnham (1970) saw realignments as the critical engines of electoral change; the students of congressional realignments see them as critically connected with policy decisions in the legislature. Such scholars demonstrate, for example, that the coming of realignments may be preceded by sustained shifts in the legislature's policy outputs. They also show that a realignment itself may produce policy changes in the legislature.

These studies invite us to look closely at the interconnection between electoral and institutional change. They suggest, first, that we explore the institutional consequences of realignment. When a realignment brings new members and a new policy agenda into the legislature, for example, it may generate pressures for the legislature to reorganize so that it can better meet members' career goals and process their new policy proposals.

Similarly, consider the observation that policy shifts in the legislature foreshadow the coming of realignment. These patterns suggest that the legislature itself may play a role in the genesis of realignments, with the policy actions or inactions of the legislature fostering electoral upheaval. The research conducted by students of congressional realignment, though still at an early stage, could have important implications: realignments may arise from a legislature's internal politics and then spark change in the legislature itself.

This emerging concern with realignment reflects an increased attention to historical research on legislatures. The pathbreaking analyses of Bolling (1965), Huntington (1965), Polsby (1968), Ripley (1969a,b), and Young (1965) have brought to our attention the existence of different historical eras with very different patterns of organizational behavior. A second body of scholars (Bullock, 1972; Fiorina, Rohde, and Wissel, 1975; Kernell, 1977; King, 1981; Loomis, 1982; Price, 1975; and Rohde, 1979) stress the critical impact of careerism on legislative behavior. A third theme, seen in the work of Blondel (1973) and Sundquist (1981), is the cyclical nature of change. Legislatures tend to experience long periods of decline followed by short periods of resurgence and organizational reform.

Together these empirical and theoretical studies are moving toward a general theory of legislative change. They exhibit a common focus on the career goals of legislators (Downs, Fenno, and Mayhew). The goals shape the organizational structure and behavior of the legislature (Cooper and Mayhew). Yet legislators' pursuit of personal goals also may be in conflict with the maintenance of a viable decision-making process (Cooper and Fenno).

The consequent inability of the legislature to make responsible policy decisions can foster societal crisis (Bolling, Huntington, and Sundquist), provoke party realignment, and thereby alter the legislature's policy agenda and organizational structure (Brady and Sundquist). Tension between members' personal goals and their broader environment thus can reshape the fundamental operation of the legislature (Cooper). The resulting change tends to be cyclical in nature (Blondel and Sundquist).

BUILDING A CYCLICAL THEORY

The foregoing studies fit together in a suggestive way, pointing toward a theory of change. The key missing element is a proposition that can pull the discussion together into a structure of reasoned and logical argument. Such a proposition can be found, I suggest, by treating legislators as power seekers whose preoccupation with career advancement undermines the policy-making integrity of the institution.

In what follows, I develop this proposition into a theory of change. The theory begins with a micro-level discussion of legislators' goals and career cycles. It then details the impact of this micro-level behavior on the legislature at a macro level, focusing on the progressive emergence of fragmentation, realignment, and reform. The conclusion to the essay considers the empirical applications of the theory.

Legislative Goals and the Career Cycle

Let us assume that a politician enters a professional legislature to gain policy-making power. He enters a legislature in which all formal decision making is collective and based on formal equality among members. The legislature's rules establish the procedures and work groups through which policy is created and approved. These rules give special resources to a limited number of members who are to lead and coordinate the activities of the legislature. These resources are highly valued because they allow such members to have special power in policy making.

Career advancement is the process whereby legislators gain mastery over the resources that are necessary for this exercise of power (Muir, 1982). To become a successful power wielder, a legislator must exercise mastery of four types of resources: those associated with reelection, policy development, institutional influence, and organizational control. The quest for policy-making power is thus an extended pursuit of legislative mastery.

Legislative Goals and the Stages of Mastery

The development and exercise of mastery follows a certain natural order. A member first must ensure his reelection; the realization of all other goals depends on this goal. As a result, the newly elected legislator must focus extensive attention on reelection politics, gaining the resources and learning the skills that best nurture his security in his district (Fenno, 1978; Jacobson, 1983).

As the legislator gains mastery of reelection politics, his concern necessarily turns to policy making: advocating and presenting specific policy proposals. Policy making is an immediate concern in part because it is so closely linked to constituent concerns—to fulfilling specific promises (Clausen, 1973; Kingdon, 1973). It is also important, however, because it provides the legislator with the knowledge and experience he needs before he can address broader societal problems and before he can gain legitimacy in the eyes of the legislators whom he seeks to influence and lead (Matthews, 1960).

With reelection and policy-making mastery, the legislator can turn his concentration to influence over the members and control of the organization. Influence, the ability to persuade and bargain effectively with legislators, is generally required before a legislator has the support to win a position of organizational control. Influence will come as a member gains leverage over resources—campaign funds, information, constituency appropriations—that other members want. Control of the organization means authority to appoint members to the legislature's work groups, to schedule debates and votes on bills, to rule on parliamentary conflicts, and to regulate policy debates. Such control allows a legislator to shape the policy agenda and policy decisions of the legislature (Sinclair, 1983).

Legislators gain these four types of mastery primarily through membership and service in political parties. The resources of the legislature, such as staff, office space, and committee positions, are allotted to the parties according to their majority or minority status, with the majority party receiving a greater than proportional share. Each party distributes its resources in accordance with a well-established body of rules and norms. These rules and norms regulate the availability of the different types of resources.

Since the goal of each party is to govern, each seeks to use its resources to build a large group of supportive legislators who can help it gain and exercise institutional power. As a result each party spreads its reelection and policy resources widely, hoping to ensure members' electoral security and their satisfaction with the party. Yet precisely because a party seeks to govern, it must ensure that party leaders can coordinate the party's members and pursue the party's general interests. Thus party rules and norms create a small number of influence and control resources that generally go to long-term members who are knowledgeable, loyal, and electorally secure.

The rules and norms of legislative parties thus create a hierarchy of resources which parallels the goal hierarchy of members. Each party's quest for power leads it to distribute reelection resources widely among its members, followed in progressively smaller amounts by policy, influence, and control resources. Party rules thus create a set of resource stages that are similar to and reinforce the four stages of mastery. A complete legislative career will begin by focusing on reelection mastery, both because of the legislators' personal desire to solidify reelection and because the rules and norms of the legislature guide new members toward reelection activities. The legislators' goals and the legislature's resource structure then focus him progressively on policy making, organizational influence, and organizational control.

Movement from one career stage to the next generally requires a congruence between goals and resources: legislators must both want to achieve new goals and have access to the necessary resources before a new stage of mastery can be pursued effectively. The development of organizational mastery thus may involve tensions and frustrations, particularly when legislators pursue organizational goals but are denied access to appropriate resources. Such tensions are inherent in legislative life.

Organizational Resources and the Career Cycle

In a highly professional legislature, where a large proportion of the members seek long-term careers, the rules and norms restrict the availability of organizational resources and thus hinder rapid career advancement. While numerous re-election and policy-making resources are normally available so that most legislators can realize their early career aspirations, influence and control resources are limited in number and restricted primarily to more seasoned legislators. Because a large number of careerist legislators compete for a relatively small number of highly desirable resources, the career path, or career cycle, that legislators desire falls far short of the career cycle that they actually experience.

The legislators' desired career cycle is shaped by their aspirations to gain legislative mastery as early in their careers as possible. Otherwise the vagaries of electoral politics or the organizational success of other legislators may deny any one member his opportunity for power. The amibitious legislative profesional thus seeks the desired career cycle illustrated in Figure 1. He wants to move rapidly through the stages of career development, spending a short and concentrated amount of time gaining skills and resources necessary to master each stage. The bulk of his career can then be spent in the exercise of policy-making power.

In actual practice, the professional legislator spends the bulk of his career not in the exercise of mastery but in its pursuit. The rules and norms of the legislature control resources and severely limit the availability of influence. Such re-

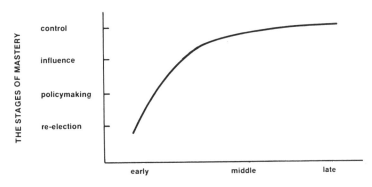

FIG. 1. The desired career cycle.

sources generally are possessed by senior legislators whose electoral and organizational mastery ensures their long-term reelection to the legislature and to its positions of power. Young and midcareer legislators thus face a long struggle in their pursuit of valued resources.

Figure 2 illustrates the actual career path a professional legislator will experience. While the legislator may move rapidly through the reelection stage and into the policy stage, owing to widespread availability of resources, legislators then are caught in a midcareer stall that diverts them from influence and control; rather than a career focused on broad policies they spend the bulk of their time concerned with narrow and middle range issues, always under the influence and control of the more advanced careerists.

The basic message of Figure 2 is that the core of a professional legislator's career will be spent in frustration. Experiencing such frustration, younger and midcareer legislators will necessarily seek ways out of their predicament—ways to speed up their career advancement. The most obvious and direct way is to change the rules of the legislature and make the desired resources more avail-

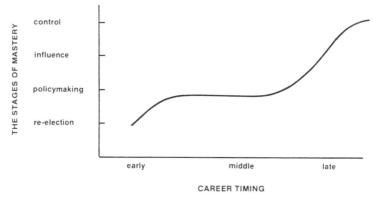

FIG. 2. The actual career cycle.

able to the less senior members. The consequences of such efforts are clearest if we examine legislators' behavior beginning with the creation or reorganization of a legislature.

Career Goals and Organizational Fragmentation

Let us assume that a legislator enters a professional legislature with a large group of new professionals at a time when the legislature is reforming. A significant aim of this organizational reform is to strengthen the governing capacity of the legislature while securing the broad career interests of its members. The reforms create numerous reelection and policy resources to serve the large junior contingent. They establish a relatively limited number of influence and control resources to meet the career needs of the senior legislators and the coordination and leadership needs of the insitution.

A new legislator will have few initial quarrels with this distribution of resources: it readily fulfills his reelection and policy-making interests. But as the new legislator, his cohorts, and succeeding classes seek access to the stages of influence and control they face a more difficult circumstance. The career advancement of the new generation is hindered by the limited number of available resources and by the dominance of senior legislators. To end their shared frustration and gain desired resources, these junior and midcareer legislators use their collective voting power and pass reforms designed to spread resources more widely among all members.

Over time, the legislature will experience the organizational fragmentation pictured in Figure 3. The period immediately following the creation or reorganization of the legislature will witness very little fragmentation. The new organizational structure and the career interests of legislators mesh fairly well. But with the aging of the new generation, the legislature will witness a steady rise in fragmentation, with the junior and midcareer legislators using their growing numbers to pass the necessary reforms. The fragmentation process, however, will not occur in identical ways through all segments of the legislature.

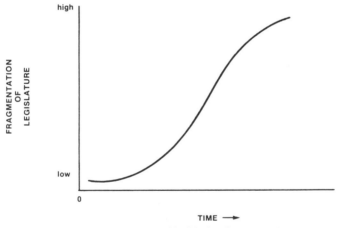

FIG. 3. The pattern of legislative fragmentation.

Countercyclical Fragmentation Among Work Groups

The general pattern of fragmentation in Figure 3 is a composite of the specific patterns that characterize the diverse work groups of a legislature. When we characterize groups such as legislative committees according to the primary career goal they serve, we see the more complex fragmentation patterns of Figure 4. As this figure indicates, the pattern of legislative fragmentation will differ dramatically among different groups.

The move toward fragmentation occurs primarily in those work groups where new and midcareer legislators exist in large numbers, work groups which are most concerned with reelection and policy making. It is in these groups where a sufficient number of frustrated legislators exist to force the creation and redistribution of resources. Unable to move out of these work groups, legislators will attempt to use these groups and their resources as surrogates for the influence and control resources they lack.

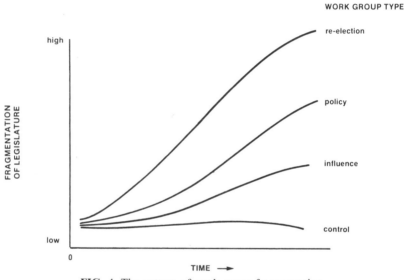

FIG. 4. The pattern of work group fragmentation.

The continued presence of legislators preoccupied with influence and control means that reelection and policy-making work groups will increasingly disintegrate over time. Their membership will be concerned with an incompatible mix of goals that undermines the work groups' capacity to establish coherent decision rules and perform their allotted tasks. The breakdown of such work groups, and the spread of their resources among uncoordinated individuals, makes it difficult for the majority party to maintain control of the electoral and policy making resources of the legislature.

The process of organizational change is quite different among the influence and control groups. Few early and midcareer legislators serve on such groups; thus it is difficult to reform the groups from within. Attempts to reform such groups from the outside are equally difficult because the senior members can use their parliamentary power to stop the passage of reforms through the legislature. In the fight against outside interference the members of these work groups may actually develop greater group cohesion.

Fragmentation and Crisis

Over time, then, work groups within a professional legislature experience a countercyclical pattern of change. Those groups most open to new and midcareer legislators, the reelection and policy groups, should fragment extensively. The groups most dominated by the advanced careerists, the influence and control groups, will fragment least and possibly centralize somewhat in their effort to offset the reformist assaults. The bulk of the legislative organization, the reelection and policy-making groups, thus disintegrates over time while the governing groups may actually experience increased integration.

The various groups direct their attention not toward working with each other but toward working against each other. The result is a breakdown in the mechanisms for coordination and leadership of the legislature. As the decision-making capacity of the legislature declines, the legislature increasingly loses its ability to make policy and govern. Severely immobilized, the government will have difficulty performing its most basic and seemingly routinized functions. Such extensive immobilism will generate or exacerbate serious national crises and set in motion a period of electoral upheaval.

The Institutional Genesis of Party Realignment

The foregoing patterns of fragmentation and policy immobilism are generated by the organizational ambitions of legislators. Members' success in their power quest rests on the ability of their party to provide them scarce legislative resources. The party's ability to provide such resources is tied to its effectiveness in gaining and maintaining control of the legislature.

In a two party (or two factional) setting, which we will assume here, the party that gains the attachment of the largest number of voters becomes the long-term governing party. The minority party continually challenges the governing party and is prepared to take power if the public loses faith in the government's performance. The performance of the governing party rests in part on how well organized the legislature is to make policy decisions. The fragmentation of a legislature, thus, can have substantial consequences for the electoral fortunes of the majority and minority parties.

The Majority Party

The most obvious impact of legislative fragmentation is on the majority party, particularly the party's perceived performance. Because fragmentation immobilizes policy making, it limits the party's ability to fulfill its promises to the public. And because immobilism ultimately fosters societal crisis, it undermines public confidence in the party's ability to govern. Legislative fragmentation thus cripples the majority party's performance and erodes public support for the party.

Ironically, legislative fragmentation has a somewhat opposite effect on the immediate fate of majority party incumbents. As fragmentation undermines the capacity of the majority party to coordinate legislative resources, it increases the autonomous control that junior and midcareer party members have over resources, particularly those connected with reelection and policy making (Sundquist, 1973, 1981). This individual control of resources increases the capacity of majority party incumbents to engage in constituent services and strengthen their reelection chances (Fiorina, 1977). Fragmentation thus aids the reelection of majority party incumbents and may actually increase their margins of victory.

In a fragmented legislature the apparent electoral strength of the majority party incumbents hides the party's increasing vulnerability and weakness. Because the party lacks coordinated control of its own resources, it can neither create a record that will elect its candidates nor provide campaign assistance to the candidates who could use it most effectively. The party's legislative majority depends on incumbents who are attractive for their constituent service rather than their policy views. Yet such legislators are particularly vulnerable when periods of extreme national crisis allow strong minority challengers to stress the overriding importance of the nation's policy problems.

The Minority Party

The experience of the minority party is quite different. The minority party lacks control of the legislature. Before minority legislators can gain extensive legislative resources, their party must win a legislative majority. To do so minority party members must focus their attention primarily on nurturing the electoral and policy success of the party (Jones, 1970). Minority party members thus will protect the cohesion of the party and oppose moves to fragment the organizational resources that it does control. Only after the party gains secure majority party status will party members focus their primary attention on personal competition for resources.

The cohesion of the minority party gives it an increasing electoral advantage as the legislature fragments. It can coordinate the electoral resources that it does possess within the legislature, utilizing those resources in the manner best designed to expand the party's delegation in the assembly. It can coordinate policy-making resources to create a coherent and visible party program that presents an image of party unity, policy competence, and governing capacity. Such a policy image, publicized by a well-coordinated and well-financed body of candidates, generates public support for the party and its legislative team. Minority party incumbents thus can win in increasing numbers (Cook, 1980; Light, 1980).

The General Pattern

During the period of fragmentation, then, the two parties follow very different paths. The majority party experiences an apparent increase in the security of its incumbents accompanied by a largely unseen *decline* in the public support for the party itself. The minority party members experience an increase in the electoral performance of its members accompanied by a *growth* in the party's public support. As incumbent security increases, and as the parties converge in the degree of public support they enjoy, the growth in legislative fragmentation leads the legislature deeper into policy immobilism and crisis.

The coming of severe national crisis provides the minority party a golden opportunity. The crisis highlights the inability of the majority party to govern effectively and encourages the public to voice its hidden discontent with the party. It also encourages normally inactive citizens to participate in politics and oppose the governing party. Such political upheaval casts a shadow over the electoral future of the majority party and encourages ambitious junior politicians to join the minority party. These attractive candidates then can mount effective campaigns on a nationwide basis by attacking the policy failure of the majority party and by dismissing the value of incumbent's constituent services in the face of national crisis.

The nationwide challenge by the minority party uncovers the underlying vulnerability of the majority party and produces its massive electoral defeat. The great fall of the majority party is not the result of sudden displeasure on the part of voters. The public had long ceased to identify with the majority party. The great fall occurs because the electoral strength of the party or dominant faction was more apparent than real, resting on incumbents who also were open to defeat when seriously challenged (Mann, 1978). The national crisis activates serious challenges, leading the public to throw the old rascals out, and gives the governing mandate to a new party.

We can talk, then, of the institutional genesis of electoral realignments. The fragmentation of the legislature leads to the rise of policy immobilism, a decrease in majority party support among voters, and the eventual national crisis that activates electoral upheaval. The electoral upheaval brings to the legislature a new majority party dedicated to new policy solutions. It also brings into majority status new legislators concerned with career advancement.

Organizing to Govern

Upon gaining majority status, the victorious party confronts the central dilemma that undercut the former majority party: it must organize the legislature so that it can govern effectively. In approaching this task, the party inherits the fragmented legislature created by the outgoing party. This organization can cripple the new majority party just as it undermined the governing capacity of the old party. Yet the severity of the national crisis demands immediate policy changes and allows little time for elaborate organizational reforms.

During the early days in power, the new majority party offsets legislative fragmentation by drawing on two distinct advantages. It possesses a relatively cohesive party organization within the legislature because it avoided extensive fragmentation when in the minority. In addition, the new party majority contains a large number of new legislators preoccupied with reelection and policy advocacy and not yet concerned with using resources to exercise influence and control. The party thus can govern effectively despite a fragmented legislature. It can move rapidly to end the crisis of immobilism.

Soon the honeymoon ends, however, and the new majority party faces the dilemmas of governing. The legislators elected during the realignment upheaval gain mastery of reelection and policy-making resources. They increasingly pursue the numerous resources available in the fragmented legislature and use these resources to gain influence and control. The capacity of the party to lead and coordinate its members declines, and within two to three elections the legislature experiences renewed immobilism (Patterson, 1977).

Policy immobilism after realignment is even more difficult for the legislature to resolve than before. The new majority party is hesitant to deny its members the legislative rewards for which they worked so hard while in the minority. The party members, concerned with their personal career success, fail to connect the policy failures of the party with their pursuit of personal power. The new party thus embraces the politics of fragmentation and watches its governing mandate flounder. Seeing the legislature stifled even with a fresh infusion of new members and new ideas, public disenchantment with legislative decision making grows.

Legislative immobilism and the public disillusionment invite the executive to usurp the policy-making power of the legislature in order to break policy immobilism and end the national crisis. The executive initially succeeds because the legislature is too fragmented and disorganized to oppose it effectively and because many members of the legislature and the public see executive intervention as necessary to save the republic. As the executive attempts to consolidate power, however, legislators come to realize that the institution is on the verge of permanently losing its governing power. Such a loss would make members' resources and status in the legislature worthless. The legislators support for the strong executive thus turns to fear and opposition.

Executive intervention demonstrates to legislators that they must strengthen the legislature if they are to save their personal power. They respond by reducing fragmentation and creating a more coherent decision-making structure. With the reformed structure in place, the new majority party is now prepared to govern until career frustrations lead its members to fragment the legislature once again (Dodd, 1977).

The Organizational Cycle: An Overview

The thrust of the foregoing argument can be summarized in one phrase: professional legislatures are characterized by an organizational cycle. The struggle of legislators for career advancement leads them to press for a fragmentation of legislative resources. This fragmentation eventually cripples the governing capacity of the institution and requires members to reorganize it along more coherent lines. During such cycles the legislature passes through six stages (Figure 5):

Stage one: organizational stability
Stage two: fragmentation
Stage three: immobilism and crisis
Stage four: electoral upheaval and realignment
Stage five: interventionism
Stage six: reorganization

This organizational cycle and the six component stages results from the internal politics of the legislature and the effect that such politics has on elections and the broader governing process. This cyclical perspective provides scholars with a theoretical framework they can use to explore legislative change in a more systematic manner.

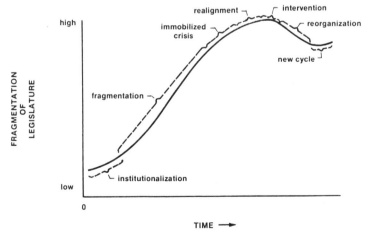

FIG. 5. The organizational cycle.

CONCLUSIONS

The value of this theoretical framework depends primarily on its ability to help us explain changes in legislative behavior. A test case is the legislative reforms of the mid-1970s. The prospect that the Congress would centralize itself seemed farfetched to legislative scholars during the postwar years. Legislators preoccupied with reelection would necessarily create a decentralized structure in order to maximize their ability to play constituent politics. They would never create a centralized policy process that could confront them with unpopular policy decisions.

The decisions in the 1970s to strengthen party leadership and create a new budget process proved otherwise. The budget procedures, in particular, built difficult policy choices into the annual roll call votes in Congress. These reforms thus confronted legislative theorists with a challenging task, to explain why a professional legislature of reelection-oriented careerists would enact reforms that could complicate their reelection. The theory of cycles provides such an explanation.

Careerist politicians are drawn to legislative service, the theory argues, not primarily for job security. They are attracted by a desire for policy-making power. Reelection is an essential component of the quest for power. But long-term reelection is in itself rather valueless without power. Members thus must maintain the fundamental policy-making integrity of the institution if their career advancement is to provide them with personal power to make policy.

Throughout the postwar years, the members of Congress pursued their needs for reelection and personal power by fragmenting the committee system and eroding the integrity of the policy process (Dodd and Schott, 1979). They failed to understand that the value of personal power depends on the capacity of the institution to govern. The resulting policy immobilism on issues of civil rights and social welfare provoked the 1964 realignment that produced the Great Society (Burnham, 1970; Sundquist, 1973; Carmines and Stimson, 1985). Yet the coordination and funding of the new policy agenda soon ran afoul of a highly fragmented Congress. The national government, attempting to pursue social and military spending that Congress could not coordinate, faced a growing fiscal crisis (Ellwood and Thurber, 1977; Schick, 1980).

The fiscal crisis provided the executive with a ready-made justification for usurpation of congressional power: the argument that Congress could not coordinate spending in a responsible manner. Richard Nixon embraced this argument to justify unconstitutional impoundments of domestic appropriations (Fisher, 1975). His intervention demonstrated to legislators the institutional and personal price of single-minded careerism. Legislators had crippled the processes of leadership and coordination in Congress much as Fenno's Post Office Committee members had destroyed the policy-making integrity of their committee. Post Office Committee members lost their prized jurisdiction; under Nixon, members of Congress reformed the policy process just in time to defuse presidential cooptation of the budget.

The centralizing reforms of the seventies thus illustrate the explanatory value of the theory. But the theory should fit this case, if no other, since it was created in response to these reforms. The more interesting question is whether the theory can actually be generalized beyond the Congress of the seventies. Can it explain congressional change in earlier decades? Can it explain the widespread pattern of cyclical change among other professional legislatures?

The U.S. House of Representatives, as the world's best-researched legislature, offers us an opportunity to address these questions. In the House the serious growth of legislative professionalism began with the ending of the Civil War. By 1885 Woodrow Wilson could argue that the struggle for power and resources within the House was a central influence on legislative politics. He emphasized the acquisition of resources, particularly committee resources, as a major concern of the members. He also recognized the inherent tension between a central party leadership and fragmented committee politics; he saw this tension as shaping the ongoing life of the institution.

From Wilson's day to the present time this struggle for power has fostered fragmentation, crisis, and reform (Bolling, 1965; Huntington, 1965). Fragmentation in the late nineteenth century centered on the committee system, which grew by approximately 50% in size from the 1860s until the reforms of 1920. From 1920 to 1946 congressional fragmentation centered on the proliferation of a variety of special committees and subcommittees, a process reversed by the 1946 Legislative Reorganization Act. And from the early 1950s to the early 1970s, the committee system experienced a growth in the number and autonomy of standing subcommittees and subcommittee chairs. In each of these periods we witness roughly similar sequences of change in which fragmentation is followed by realignment (1890s, 1930s, 1960s) and then reorganization (1910-1920, 1946, 1970-1975).

Our faith in the theory is reinforced by the patterns of countercyclical change that we see in the postwar House. The theory argues that reelection and policy work groups should fragment to a much greater extent than influence and control groups; this is precisely the pattern that emerges when we examine the reelection (constituency), policy, and prestige committees identified by Smith and Deering (1984). From the mid-1950s to the early 1970s, for example, reelection and policy committees increased by approximately 50% the average number of members holding committee or subcommittee chairs. By contrast, the more prestigious influence and control committees, such as Appropriations and Rules, experienced no increase in members holding chair positions; the powerful Ways and Means Committee fragmented only with the party reforms of 1974 (Rudder, 1977). These patterns conform to the expectations of the theory.

Micro-level patterns in the House likewise correspond to the general expectations of theory. Career cycles in the House are seen in such empirical patterns as the tendency of junior and senior legislators to concentrate on different electoral strategies (Fenno, 1978; Parker, 1984) and on different types of committee and subcommittee assignments (Smith and Deering, 1984). The linkage between career aspirations and organizational structure is shown by the long-term tendency of the House to fragment as the proportion of careerist members grows (Huntington, 1965; Polsby, 1968). And the linkage between career frustration and fragmentation is shown by the organized efforts of disadvantaged groups such as House liberals in the 1950s to gain personal power and policy influence by pursuing decentralized reforms (Stevens, Miller, and Mann, 1974).

The history of the House thus suggests that the theory has broader relevance than the reforms of the 1970s. In the long term, I hope that the theory also will prove applicable to other legislatures besides Congress. While congressional politics provided the theory's stimulus, its analytic arguments are not necessarily restricted to Congress. Just as Downs could build a general electoral theory by starting with assumptions that resemble British politics, so legislative scholars may find clues in the study of Congress that unlock a general legislative theory. The trick is to discover in Congress phenomena that professional legislatures have in common and to build on this discovery a general theory that is applicable to them all.

The common phenomena I identify is the existence of ambitious career legislators with deep frustrations over the maldistribution of institutional resources (Loewenberg and Patterson, 1979; Schwarz and Shaw, 1976). To the extent that such legislators are present, the concepts and hypotheses of this theory should apply to any legislature. The fragmentation of the British House of Commons over the last 15 years, for example, would seem a possible consequence of the frustrations that a growing number of career members have with the limited resources available to them (King, 1981). Likewise the historic immobilism and cyclical restructuring of the French parliament can be analyzed from the perspective of career ambitions and frustrations of parliamentarians.

The theory thus identifies an extensive research agenda for scholars of professional legislatures, pointing them to such little explored phenomena as goal hierarchies, career cycles, career frustration, cyclical and countercyclical fragmentation, policy immobilism, and organizational reform. It also introduces hypotheses that address some of the most important unanswered questions of electoral and institutional analysis, not only the impact of careerism on institutional change, but the impact of institutional structure on policy immobilism, incumbent security, and electoral realignment.

The answers offered by the theory are necessarily tentative: there are too many gaps in empirical knowledge and theoretical logic for me to argue the theory's general validity. But the theory does provide a foundation, one strengthened by support from the work of Downs, Mayhew, Fenno, Cooper, and others, on which scholars can build.

Empirical efforts to build from this theory will require scholars to modify and interpret the theory before they apply it to a particular legislature. Parliamentarians may be more likely to seek positions in cabinet ministries and party committees, for example, than in standing committees. Parliamentary fragmentation thus may be more adequately measured by examining the cabinet ministries and party committees than the standing committees. Similarly, policy immobilism in a multiparty parliament may not generate an American-type realignment because the electorate may find it difficult both to determine the parties responsible for policy failures and to identify the viable governing alternatives. The realignment that occurs may come in the parliament itself as members fundamentally restructure the parliament's governing coalition.

Efforts at empirical application also require additional developments in the theory itself, one of which I will mention in closing. The cyclical theory treats the legislature's external environment as constant unless the internal decisions of the legislature alter it. In real life, of course, the external environment does change quite independently of a legislature's decision. New technologies can arise, a war can erupt, an international depression can occur, all unprovoked by the legislature.

Such external change can alter the policy problems of a society and confront the legislators with demands to create a new legislative structure designed to address the new policy problems. The legislators themselves, however, have their careers deeply enmeshed in the old structure and may be unwilling to alter it substantially (Davidson and Oleszek, 1976). Reforms pressed by external groups, after all, are primarily designed to help the groups pass their desired policies rather than promote the resources and power of legislators.

This tension between external and internal forces is absent from the cyclical theory and could pose great problems for it. External groups, for example, could force legislators to reform at the "wrong" time in terms of the predictions of the theory. Likewise, legislators could refuse to reform and challengers with "new ideas" could defeat them, thereby causing electoral upheaval and reform that come out of sequence with the theory.

These and other scenarios indicate that theorists must consider closely the interaction of external and internal factors (Strom and Rundquist, 1978). For myself, I believe that the two dimensions can be integrated into an even richer cyclical theory in which the organizational cycle remains the core pattern of legislative change and external factors determine how extensive the process of change will be. Such a theory would explain why some cycles experience greater fragmentation that others, why some realignments are more policy oriented, and why some reforms actually transform legislatures into new policy-making bodies (Dodd, 1985).

Acknowledgments. I have benefited greatly from the comments of numerous colleagues who read earlier versions of this essay. My special thanks to the panelists who critiqued the original convention paper, Joseph Cooper, Gary Jacobson, Charles O. Jones, and Kenneth Shepsle; and to those who provided me feedback as this final essay was completed, particularly Michael Berkman, Edward Carmines, Richard Champagne, Carolyn Cooke, Jon Hale, Russell Hanson, Calvin Jillson, Glenn Parker, David Prindle, Leroy Rieselbach, Barbara Sinclair, and Herbert Weisberg.

REFERENCES

Aydelotte, William O. (1977). *The History of Parliamentary Behavior.* Princeton, N.J.: Princeton University Press.

Barry, Brian M. (1970). *Sociologists, Economists and Democracy.* London: Macmillan.

Blondel, Jean (1973). *Comparaitve Legislatures.* Englewood Cliffs, N.J.: Prentice Hall.

Bolling, Richard (1965). *Power in the House.* New York: E. P. Dutton.

Bracher, Karl Dietrich (1971). Problems of parliamentary democracy in Europe. In Herbert Hirsch and M. Donald Hancock (eds.), *Comparative Legislative Systems.* New York: Free Press.

Brady, David (1978). Critical elections, congressional parties, and clusters of policy change. *British Journal of Political Science* 8: 79–99.

Brady, David W. (1973). *Congressional Voting in a Partisan Era.* Lawrence, Kan.: University of Kansas Press.

Bryce, James (1924). The decline of legislatures. *Modern Democracies*, Vol. II. New York: Macmillan.

Bullock, Charles S. (1972). House careerists: changing patterns of longevity and attrition. *American Political Science Review* 66: 1295–1300.

Burnham, Walter Dean (1970). *Critical Elections and the Mainsprings of American Politics.* New York: W. W. Norton.

Carmines, Edward, and Stimson, James (1985). The politics and policy of race in Congress. In Wright et al., eds., *Congress and Policy Change.*

Clausen, Aage R. (1973). *How Congressmen Decide.* New York: St. Martin's Press.

Cook, Rhodes (1980). National committee given major role in fall campaign. *Congressional Quarterly Weekly Report*, July 19, 1980, p. 2011.

Cooper, Joseph, and Brady, David W. (1981). Toward a Diachronic Analysis of Change. *American Political Science Review* 75: 988–1006.

Cooper, Joseph (1971). *The Origins of the Standing Committees and the Development of the Modern House.* Houston, Tex.: William Marsh Rice University.

Cooper, Joseph (1975). Strengthening the Congress: an organizational analysis. *Harvard Journal on Legislation* 12: 307–368.

Cooper, Joseph (1977). Congress in organizational perspective. In Dodd and Oppenheimer, eds., *Congress Reconsidered.*

Davidson, Roger H., and Oleszek, Walter J. (1977). *Congress Against Itself.* Bloomington, Ind.: Indiana University Press.

Davidson, Roger H., and Oleszek, Walter J. (1976). Adaptation and consolidation: structural innovation in the U.S. House of Representatives. *Legislative Studies Quarterly* 1: 37–65.

Dodd, Lawrence C. (1985). A theory of congressional cycles. In Wright et al., eds., *Congress and Policy Change.*

Dodd, Lawrence C. (1978). Review of David R. Mayhew. Congress: the Electoral Connection. *American Political Science Review* 72: 693–694.

Dodd, Lawrence C. (1977). Congress and the quest for power. In Dodd and Oppenheimer, eds., *Congress Reconsidered.*

Dodd, Lawrence C., and Schott, Richard L. (1979). *Congress and The Administrative State.* New York: Wiley.

Dodd, Lawrence C., and Oppenheimer, Bruce I., eds. (1977). *Congress Reconsidered.* New York: Praeger.

Downs, Anthony (1957). *An Economic Theory of Democracy.* New York: Harper & Row.

Ellwood, John W., and Thurber, James A. (1977). The new congressional budget process. In Dodd and Oppenheimer, eds., *Congress Reconsidered.*

Fenno, Richard F., Jr. (1966). *The Power of the Purse.* Boston: Little, Brown.

Fenno, Richard F., Jr. (1973). *Congressmen in Committees.* Boston: Little, Brown.

Fenno, Richard F., Jr. (1978). *Home Style.* Boston: Little, Brown.

Ferejohn, John A. (1974). *Pork Barrel Politics.* Stanford, Calif.: Stanford University Press.

Fiorina, Morris P. (1977). *Congress: Keystone of the Washington Establishment.* New Haven, Conn.: Yale University Press.

Fiorina, Morris P. (1974). *Representatives, Roll Calls and Constituencies.* Lexington, Mass.: Lexington Books.

Fiorina, Morris P., Rohde, David W., and Wissel, Peter (1975). Historical Change in House Turnover. In Ornstein, Norman J. (ed.), *Congress in Change.* New York: Preager.

Fisher, Louis (1975). *Presidential Spending Power.* Princeton, N.J.: Princeton University Press.

Huitt, Ralph K., and Peabody, Robert L. (1969). *Congress: Two Decades of Anaysis.* New York: Harper & Row.

Huntington, Samuel P. (1965). Congressional Responses to the Twentieth Century. In David B. Truman (ed.), *Congress and America's Future.* Englewood Cliffs, N.J.: Prentice Hall.

Jacobson, Gary C. (1983). *The Politics of Congressional Elections.* Boston: Little, Brown.

Jones, Charles O. (1970). *The Minority Party in Congress.* Boston: Little, Brown.

Jones, Charles O. (1961). Representation in Congress: the case of the House Agricultural Committee. *American Political Science Review* 55: 358-367.

Kernell, Samuel (1977). Toward understanding 19th century careers, ambition, competition and rotation. *American Journal of Political Science* 21: 669-693.

Key, V. O. (1955). A theory of critical elections. *Journal of Politics* 17: 3-18.

King, Anthony S. (1981). The rise of the career politician in Britain—and its consequences. *British Journal of Political Science* 11: 249-285.

Kingdon, John W. (1973). *Candidates for Office.* New York: Random House.

Light, Larry (1980). Republican groups dominate in party campaign spending. *Congressional Quarterly Weekly Report,* November 1, 1980, pp. 3235-3239.

Loewenberg, Gerhard, and Patterson, Samuel C. (1979). *Comparing Legislatures.* Boston: Little, Brown.

Loomis, Burdette (1982). Congressional careers, legislative behavior and policy outcomes. Paper prepared for the 1982 Midwest Political Science Convention.

MacRae, Duncan, Jr. (1970). *Issues and Parties in Legislative Voting.* New York: Harper & Row.

Mann, Thomas E. (1978). *Unsafe At Any Margin.* Washington, D.C.: American Enterprise Institute.

Matthews, Donald R. (1960). *U.S. Senators and Their World.* New York: Vintage Books.

Mayhew, David P. (1974). *Congress: The Electoral Connection.* New Haven, Conn.: Yale University Press.

Muir, William K., Jr. (1982). *Legislature: California School for Politics.* Chicago: The University of Chicago Press.

Oppenheimer, Bruce I. (1974). *Oil and the Congressional Process: The Limits of Symbolic Politics.* Lexington, Mass.: Lexington Books.

Parker, Glenn R. (1984). Stylistic changes in the constituency orientations of U.S. Senators: 1959-1980. Paper prepared for presentation at the 1984 Midwest Political Science Convention.

Patterson, James T. (1977). *Congressional Conservation and the New Deal.* Lexington, Ky.: University of Kentucky Press.

Peabody, Robert L. (1976). *Leadership in Congress.* Boston: Little, Brown.

Polsby, Nelson W. (1968). Institutionalization of the House of Representatives. *American Political Science Review* 62: 144-168.

Price, Douglas (1975). Congress and the evolution of legislative professionalism. In Norman J. Ornstein (ed.), *Congress in Change.* New York: Praeger.

Rieselbach, Leroy N. (1973). *Congressional Politics*. New York: McGraw-Hill.

Rieselbach, Leroy N. (1984). The forest for the trees: blazing trails for congressional research. In Ada W. Finifter (ed.), *Political Science: The State of the Discipline*. Washington, D.C.: American Political Science Association.

Ripley, Randall B. (1969a). *Majority Party Leadership in Congress*. Boston: Little, Brown.

Ripley, Randall B. (1969b). *Power in the Senate*. New York: St. Martin's Press.

Rohde, David W. (1979). Risk bearing and progressive ambition. *American Journal of Political Science* 23(Feb.): 1–26..

Rothman, David T. (1969). *Politics and Power*. New York: Atheneum.

Rudder, Catherine (1977). Committee reform and the revenue process. In Dodd and Oppenheimer, (eds.), *Congress Reconsidered*.

Schick, Allen (1980). *Congress and Money*. Washington, D.C.: The Urban Institution.

Schwarz, John E., and Shaw, L. Earl (1976). *The United States in Comparative Perspective*. Hinsdale, Ill.: Dryden Press.

Shepsle, Kenneth A. (1978). *The Giant Jigsaw Puzzle*. Chicago: University of Chicago Press.

Sinclair, Barbara (1983). *Majority Leadership in the U.S. House*. Baltimore: Johns Hopkins Press.

Sinclair, Barbara (1982). *Congressional Realignment, 1925-1978*. Austin, Tex.: University of Texas Press.

Smith, Steven S., and Deering, Christopher J. (1984). *Committees in Congress*. Washington, D.C.: Congressional Quarterly, Inc.

Stevens, Arthur G., Miller, Arthur H., and Mann, Thomas E. (1974). Mobilization of liberal strength in the House, 1955-1970: the Democratic Study Group. *American Political Science Review* 68: 667-681.

Strom, Gerald, and Rundquist, Barry S. (1978). On explaining legislative organization. Paper presented at the Annual Meeting of the American Political Science Association, New York.

Sundquist, James (1973). *Dynamics of the Party System: Alignment and Realignment of Political Parties in the United States*. Washington, D.C.: Brookings Institution.

Sundquist, James (1981). *The Decline and Resurgence of Congress*. Washington, D.C.: The Brookings Institution.

Wilson, Woodrow (1885). *Congressional Government*. Glouster, Mass.: Peter Smith (reissued, 1973).

Wright, Gerald, Rieselbach, Leroy, and Dodd, Lawrence C. eds. *Congress and Policy Change*. New York: Agathon Press (forthcoming).

Young, James S. (1966). *The Washington Community, 1800-1828*. New York: Columbia University Press.

CHAPTER 6

PRESIDENTIAL AND EXECUTIVE STUDIES: THE ONE, THE FEW, AND THE MANY

Bert A. Rockman

In a lengthy review article, lamenting the state of scholarly progress in the field of presidential and executive studies, Anthony King offered the view that the existing literature was scant, mainly descriptive and atheoretical, composed mostly of rehashed essays rather than original research, and evocative only of political rather than scholarly controversy (King, 1975, p. 173). A more recent and exceptionally well-done review of the subfield by Joseph Pika (1981) notes that while we have made some improvement on the empirical side, we are lacking commensurate progress from a theoretical standpoint. This is so because, according to this contention, conceptualization of the field of study has been inadequate and insufficiently systemic.

We have been preoccupied, so Pika argues, with a relatively narrow range of problems "focusing on the presidential person and his political fortunes" (p. 32). All "nonpresidential" variables have been poured through a "presidential filter." To see the president as the exclusive object of study, it is argued, is inevitably limiting, and leads neither to interesting theoretical questions, nor to careful explication of methodological and normative assumptions.

Reviewing a subfield inevitably raises the obvious question, What are we doing? There are, however, two additional questions that any review of a subfield should address. One is, How well are we doing? The second is, Why are we doing it? The first suggests some kind of standard or yardstick by which to calibrate "progress," though such imagery can be more ruinous than revealing. I will return to this issue a bit later and more or less persistently. The second question, however, is foremost. What is it we want to know about government and politics that a focus on executives can help us to answer or to puzzle anew, and why should we want to know it? This last question is both breath-taking and heart-sinking.

My primitive assumption about why we study the executive is that it helps us to grapple with issues of governability, just as study of the legislature helps us to grapple with issues of representation. Further, my assumption is that we study the chief executive because we expect this to be a central source of political leadership, especially so in the case of the U.S. presidency.

My focus here is on the presidency, though by implication also, other chief executives and accordingly other executive officials. As a review, it is a selective one, omitting regrettably many works of stature and of value. In rough order, I first discuss briefly why we cannot, and should not, avoid linking the study of the chief executive to normative questions about political leadership. Second, I also briefly set forth my understanding of the terms "science" and "theory" and relate these to the state of the subfield. With these preliminaries in hand, I want to focus, thirdly, on the theoretical assumptions and scientific possibilities of three types of presidential studies—those focusing on the officeholder himself (the one), those focusing on interdependencies with other elites (the few), and those focusing on broader societal or mass interdependencies (the many). Finally, I offer some comments regarding the role of, and paths to, the study of the chief executive.

Political controversy engulfs the study of the presidency. Presidential studies, after all, are at the vortex of issues dealing with the shape and functioning of the political system—of both the possibilities and limits of political leadership. So it could hardly be otherwise. Controversy is inevitable because we lack a consensual notion of how the presidency ought to function. Despite the dim prospect of attaining such a consensus, we do urgently need to clarify the premises we hold as to how the presidential role should be fulfilled, for how we think the role should be fulfilled also illuminates the model of governance we hold. Studies of the presidency, therefore, must be driven in part by concerns that are fundamentally political-philosophical.

NORMATIVE ROLES FOR THE CHIEF EXECUTIVE

What kind of role should the president play? How should power be exercised, and for what purposes? These qustions, it is fair to say, have been debated for two centennia. Their answers, a skeptical observer might claim, are dependent upon the officeholder himself and the extent to which his "plans" are coincident with the observer's. A less cynical but equally contingent interpretation, advanced by Erwin Hargrove, suggests that our interpretations of the leadership role of the president are greatly conditioned by the times, and in this, "we necessarily study ourselves and our own beliefs about power and purpose" (Hargrove, 1973, pp. 819-821).

Some writers have advanced bold, if not always precise, ideas as to what the leadership role of the president should be. James MacGregor Burns, almost two decades ago, proclaimed the need for "exuberant leadership" deriving from a responsible party alignment and strong "party leadership" in the White House (1963, pp. 323-340). Neustadt (1980),[1] seeing little likelihood that such a party alignment would develop in the foreseeable future, instead emphasized the skill factor in the presidency. What sort of person with what kinds of instincts ought to inhabit a role that is both constrained in power and yet the expected source of effective leadership? Such a person would have to be possessed of a keen nose for power and willingness to seek opportunities for exercising it. Leadership, in brief, would have to come from a president with instincts for power. For these instincts would have to serve in lieu of more potent tools of governance. Yet in seeking power in this way, it has been argued that the ends to be served are essentially more self-aggrandizing than promoting of the public good (Burns, 1978, pp. 385-397; Cronin, 1980, pp. 119-142).

A different view of the office, however, places less stress on the leadership function, and more on the legitimating function. The main (or at least a principal) task of the president is to ensure the legitimacy of the political system, its institutions, and his office. Leadership is bargaining, but bargaining that is duly respectful of other power centers in the system. Necessarily, this view diminishes emphasis on "the great man" as president. (Wildavsky, 1975; Ceasar, 1978, 1979; Polsby, 1977; Greenstein, 1982). In a system of shared power but separate institutions, this view celebrates the president who can instill trust in the system and its institutions through the moderation and intermediation of conflict. Such a president would seek accommodations and not avail himself of all opportunities to heighten his profile or maximize his advantage. He would be inclined to take small steps rather than leapfrog over points of opposition. Inevitably, though, an important question raised by such a model of the presidency is whether he, or his governance (two linked yet separable matters), would be effective, and if not effective, could trust be produced?

Yet another perspective treats the chief executive as neither engineer or conscious accommodator, but mostly as a frequently harried decision maker sporadically attentive to matters that cry for a response (March and Olsen, 1976, 1983). To borrow a felicitous phrase, governing, in this view, is more like gardening than engineering (March and Olsen, 1983, p. 292). Putting this a bit differently, since government does numerous things, no overall rational plan to give coherence to the numerous things is apt to be attainable (Rose, 1976; Peters, 1981; March and Olsen, 1983). "Attention is a scarce resource," and "the core reality [in governing] is the organization of attention" (March and Olsen, 1983, p. 292). Such a focus contrasts quite spectacularly with the larger visions of coherence, design, and attention to be found in macro-level theories of political leadership and governance. From this perspective, the idea of meaningful action is, in a word, meaningless. Only in the long run can a change in symbols affect the short run problematics of attention, in which case these implications take us beyond government to broader social forces and technologies.

A further perspective on the relationship between leader and leadership is offered by Valerie Bunce (1981a,b). Bunce combines intention and environmental forces. Changes in the chief executive, Bunce demonstrates (1981b), rather universally bring forth substantial changes in the direction of public expenditures, suggesting that political change is substantial as well as rhetorical. Her analysis restores our faith that intentions have effects. The logic of this relatively uniform pattern is to extend our search for the causes of this initial burst of nonincremental policy change beyond variability in the leaders themselves. The process of leadership change rather than the leaders themselves is her focus, and the dynamics of that process her explanation.

To presidency scholars, the first group of works, which emphasize, however differently, the leadership and accommodative roles of the president, is familiar territory, employing familiar language, focusing on the system at the macro level, and operating with familiar assumptions about the role of the officeholder and the beliefs and values that influence his behavior. The second group, which emphasize limited attentiveness, organizational complexity, and relatively uniform recurrences, is less familiar and more alien to traditional ways of thinking about presidents as autonomous and purposeful actors.

Puppet or puppeteer? Refractor or director? These are vintage questions in the study of political leadership (Searing, 1969). What should the role of the president be? This is, I believe, another way of asking what should the role of governing be: to reflect and refract or to lead and direct? Such questions are wrestled with by scholars belonging to the first group. But what the role of the president can be turns also not just on what we want government to be, but what governing can be. These questions are focused on by scholars in the second group. Taken seriously, these are all hard questions to answer. Yet, how we answer them is linked closely to core assumptions in studying the presidency. Clearly, we need to be conscious of what our first order assumptions about political leadership and governing are, and where they lead us in terms of conceptualizing the role of the president in the American system.

Empirically valid theories are, however, a necessary abrasive by which to test the consistency of these assumptions. Yet there is a widespread consensus that few such theories exist of much relevance to the presidency, or to executives more generally; that we have at best cosmological speculation, journalistic tidbits, and theoretically unconnected description. To be certain, there are difficulties attendant to data generation in presidential studies, but far more in gaining a basis for scientific analysis and even more attached to theory building, a term that I use here to mean a linked network of empirically derived and valid generalizations. Such problems are obviously central to the status of science and theory in presidential-executive studies.

SCIENCE, THEORY, AND PRESIDENTIAL-EXECUTIVE STUDIES

One way of measuring scientific progress in a field of inquiry is to judge the amount of uncertainty reduced by theoretically developed generalizations arising from explanations of regularly recurring events or behaviors. Despite our stress on this ideal, it is questionable that science achieves such linear progress. Indeed, if "progress" is measured in this manner, our path will no doubt be a tortuous one.

Not all knowledge is scientific, at least as I am about to define that word here. Much of what we know about the presidency as an institution and about particular presidents is the result of research (and some simply the result of ideas) that cannot meet the strict tests of scientific method. In my view, this fact alone grants it no higher or lower status. I dwell on the scientific mode here only because of the Rodney Dangerfield syndrome that presumably afflicts the study of the presidency—the belief that "there is a lack of respect for research on the presidency" (Edwards, 1981, p. 146).

Science, simply put, is a method of reality testing requring knowledge to be public, therefore explicit, therefore precise in order for it, and the conditions under which it has been obtained, to be evaluated. By this definition, certain ancillary characteristics follow. The first of these is *precision* in meaning; the second is *operationalization*; the third is *quantitative*, more properly statistical, procedures of analysis; the fourth is *experimental or quasiexperimental* (the latter meaning properly specified multivariate) techniques of analysis so as to remove confounding influences from real ones, to assess the relative magnitude and form of potential influences, and to set forth a structure of explanation. Overall, like the rest of political science, more quantitative work on the presidency is being done, particularly in the "joints" between the president and legislative elites, and especially between the president and public opinion.

Note, however, that my strict definition of science does not include theory; the latter being drawn from, and consistent with, scientific evidence, but not necessarily produced by it. It is (or has been) a commonplace assumption that the more science we have, the more likely this is to lead to unifying theoretical development (Shull, 1979, p. ix). A key assumption here seems to be that we have the essential structure of the puzzle and need only to fit the pieces together.

I do not want to linger too long over this point. I want only to argue that better science does not equal better theory despite the usual assumptions linking the two.[2] Science is frequently messy and conditional because it is essentially controlled description. Pretheory, whether axiomatic or casually stated, is cleaner but untested. Any theory drawn from a limited range of empirical observations is often overgeneralized or incautiously specified, which is the state of most of what we call "theory" in political science.

Both King and Pika urge us to do more comparison, to extend both our temporal and spatial horizons. And I agree we should, indeed, must. But it does not follow from this that we will have more unifying propositions. Indeed, it is quite conceivable that our initial simple ideas will become more impure as we expose them to further observations.

This is not to say, of course, that we should cease trying to find appropriate points of spatial and temporal comparison, to find what is stable and what is volatile. Nor is it to say that we should cease efforts to theorize. It is, however, to say that we are apt to have slivers of explanatory theory focused on explaining a relatively narrow range of patterns that are themselves often unstable. The implication of this point is that better science should enable us to test elements of our theories more readily than to help us constitute new ones. The tests themselves, of course, are conditional, a feature we sometimes forget. In this respect, the subfield is little different from the rest of the discipline, which is to say relatively kaleidoscopic. Just when we think we have found the conceptual apparatus to apprehend newly discovered "facts," we often find the power of the apparatus diminishing. In this view, "science" and "theory" are not so much congenial allies, the one naturally produced from the other, as they are in a continuous state of tension. As in other maturing fields of inquiry, we are led to wonder, are we knowing more and comprehending it less? And beyond this, how does what we know link to normative perspectives on governance and the role of the chief executive in it?

The selective review that follows reflects a relatively traditional way of thinking about the chief executive. Thus we analyze the person (the one), interdependencies with other elites (the few), and interdependencies with broader publics (the many). Indeed, this scheme of organization, however, commonsensical it now seems, owes much to Richard Neustadt's *Presidential Power* (1980). For Neustadt's analysis remains, whatever its flaws, the closest thing we have in the literature on the U.S. presidency to a general theory.

THE ONE: ANALYSES OF THE PRESIDENT

At the core of studies of individual presidents is the simple idea that people do make a difference in how the office is conducted, and that obviously there is variability in the people who have held the office. In some ways, the data base for studying individual presidents is growing as presidential archives are enriched. Yet in other ways, it is also subject to the criticism of "softness" regarding capacities to operationalize data. Evidence usually is based on biographical materials, narratives of events, and cases of decision making. Moreover, analyses of a single individual are sometimes idiosyncratic and theoretically casual, while analyses that do compare individuals are prone to dress up preferential judgements in sleek analytic garb. Biographical and archival work on individuals, lacking a formal scheme for codifying and selecting material, inevitably is subject to much scholarly interpretation on the selection of relevant evidence and rules for drawing inferences therefrom.

Analyses of the role of the individual in the presidency focus on three points: (1) the style of leadership employed; (2) the psychological disposition of the individual; and (3) the process of selection. These are connecting links and, for the most part, in studies focusing on variation among individual presidents, all of these focal points are threaded together. This we see in Figure 1, where the

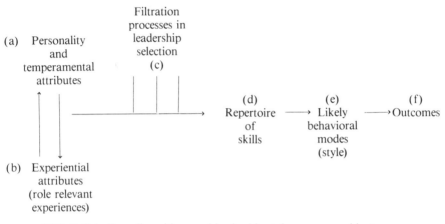

FIG. 1. Selection, disposition, and leadership style among presidents.

links are drawn more fully. Studies focused on leadership *style* typically emphasize points *e* and *d* in the figure, often arguing back from point *f* as evidence of the worthiness or limits of these styles. Usually, they will proclaim the importance of points *a*, *b*, and *c* to the emergence of "effective" leadership styles. But points *e* and *d* are the real focus. Analyses of the leader's *psychology*, however, look mainly at point *a*, using points *d* and *e* as evidence to buttress how it is that *a* becomes behaviorally relevant. Finally, studies of the *selection process* focus on point *c*, typically claiming that *c* influences the probability that persons with only certain experiential attributes *b* and personality-tempermental characteristics *a* will be selected, and this, in turn, will increase the probability that individuals with a given repertoire of skills (*d*) will come to office and behave in a given range of ways (*e*).

Leadership Style

If the importance of a book is judged by the extent to which other scholars pay it continued attention over the years, Neustadt's *Presidential Power* is undoubtedly still the magnet that holds together so much of the research literature on the presidency. The main components and emphases of the book are well known, and still a source of both reference and controversy whenever one speaks of how the presidential role should be fulfilled. The book, however, spins off, if implicitly, numerous hypotheses (disguised as assertions) such that it has created whole research enterprises within the larger body of presidential studies (Wegge, 1981). Neustadt's impressionistic discussion regarding the link between political prestige and presidential influence in Washington has spawned a spectacular increase in studies (if not clear conclusions) on the subject. Although a number of Neustadt's impressionistic assertions do not hold up well under documented evidence, for example, those regarding the time in the term during which the president is apt to be most influential (Light, 1981, 1982) or the extent to which the presidential staff by its proximity is a controllable presidential resource (Heclo, 1981), the book has been a gold mine in producing ideas to be more systematically evaluated.

However, when *Presidential Power* was first published in 1960, the features most seized upon were the apparent prescriptions for presidential behavior. While there is no avoiding the prescriptive nature of Neustadt's analysis—the astute political entrepreneur required for an active and effective presidency—the parts of the book that are best and require virtually no revision are those setting forth the Madisonian logic of the institutional framework. Not the separation of powers, Neustadt says, but separate institutions sharing power.

This theme, the individual versus the system, is, in fact, the distinguishing feature of Neustadt's analysis. How does a president bring his influence to bear so as to advance his goals in a system resistant to the straightforward advance of any singular set of goals?

The theme of the interrelationship between leadership style and the political system is developed in other case and biographical analyses, most notably J. M. Burns' study of Franklin Roosevelt (1956) and Fred Greenstein's work on Eisenhower (1982). Whereas Neustadt sees a president, of necessity, having to live by his wits alone in a system not readily conducive to his aspirations, Burns sees the leadership role as a careful balance between adherence to role imperatives and the transformation of role structures so as to alter the parallelogram of forces in society. On balance, Burns actually demands far more of the leadership role than Neustadt. For where Neustadt sees entrepreneurial manipulation within a given set of role parameters as all that can be maximally expected, Burns (1978) contends that such an expectation is too limiting, that the ultimate test is a transformation of environmental forces.

Burns and Neustadt each hold a view, however, that is in accordance with an active presidential role at the "head" of a government busily engaged in directing social change. Neither seems to question much the limitations of this "director" model of presidential governance. Each is interested in overcoming the natural proclivities of the American system, these being resistant to central direction.

Greenstein's sketch of Eisenhower as president, however, produces a very different model of presidential conduct, but also a more contingent one. Here,

Greenstein focuses on the idea of leadership as legitimation, and the president as selective activist and purposeful delegator rather than continually interventionist and programmatic leader. The arts of organizational politics in which Eisenhower presumably was steeped engender the style of indirection and the appearance of delegating responsibility. Although Greenstein was not the first to take note of these political abilities in Eisenhower (Wills, 1970), he amplifies them fully into a theory of political leadership not so much at odds with, as merely distinct from, the more aggressive and directing forms identified with Neustadt and Burns.

In this regard, Greenstein notes that no single model of leadership is appropriate; that any model is a function of the objectives a president wishes to achieve. The special virtue of the Greenstein analysis, whether one agrees with all of its particulars or not, is to rescue the model of presidential leadership from an exclusive focus on the mythologized presidency of Franklin Roosevelt (with John F. Kennedy thrown in from time to time as a prospective FDR cut short). There being no *one* model of presidential leadership but rather alternative models contingent upon objectives, these objectives may be devoted to important, if unglamorous, purposes, ones that often minimize a president's activist profile. Thus, one recent study of the McKinley presidency extensively cites Greenstein's analysis of Eisenhower as a model for rescuing the reputations of less glamorous presidents (Latcham, 1982). Finally, Greenstein shows us that concern for relatively formal organizational procedures and staffing, matters which suffer from malign neglect in Neustadt's analysis, can be relevant to effective decision making.

No one, of course, can conclude from inquiries into leadership style that the person in the office is the most important feature of a president's successes or failures, words that brim with subjectivity. But that the person holding the office is the most interesting and controversial element in the assemblage of factors that account for successes and failures is reasonably certain. The subject matter is soft, though, and rarely can be quantified in ways that are sensible. Formal content analytic schemes can bring forth some rigor in terms of standards of evidence, but by themselves (problems of validity aside) do not resolve the problem of selectivity in the use of evidence, which boils down essentially to a sampling problem. Moreover, formal coding schemes are often very abstract and unlikely to be useful in detailing the nuances of leadership style, i.e., the problem of validity. In the absence of clear, operational criteria for judgment, however, words used in praise of one president well thought of by the writer of them are sometimes perceived as applying equally well to presidents perhaps not so well thought of by the writer. Traits Neustadt used to describe Kennedy's willingness to absorb facts and resist ex parte advocacy, for instance, could equally well have been applied, using less laudatory language, to Carter (Rockman, 1980).

Two problems are of even greater centrality, however, in being able to predict leadership style. One is the problem of defining criteria in selecting those likely to produce desirable leadership characteristics. The second is the problem of connecting stylistic factors to policy making in a more theoretically developed way.

As to the first problem, Neustadt postulates (at least in the initial edition before these issues became further obscured) that presidents would have to be recruited from a tiny pool of professional politicians of extraordinary temperament. Although "professional politician" in the United States is not an unambiguous tag, it is clearer than "extraordinary temperament." Such temperaments, arguably, have been lacking in those recruited to the presidency, whether professional politicans or not, since Franklin Roosevelt. The possible exceptions granted in Neustadt's terms were Kennedy (whom he liked, whatever his actual level of accomplishment) and Johnson, whose temperament was indeed devastatingly extraordinary.

If professional politicans, by their trade, cannot assure us of having "the right stuff," we also have a similar problem with generals, just in case we might think Eisenhower's craft to have been well suited as a training ground for the style of political leadership he produced. Between Washington and Eisenhower only one general, Andrew Jackson (with a leadership style much unlike Eisenhower's), could be considered a success in the presidency. And Jackson was at least a hybrid—military officer and professional politician. In short, we are pretty well mystified in coming up with criteria more systematic than the corns on our feet for selecting someone with "the right stuff."

As for the second problem, to be sure, Neustadt, Burns, and Greenstein all give us some clues as to how the presidents they examine act as policy makers. But at this point, they are just that—clues. Although there is no denying that very complicated operational problems arise when we try to systematize presidential policy making styles, Lloyd Etheredge (1978) tries to link temperamental characteristics of several presidents, secretaries of state, and other foreign policy elites to predictions about their orientations to the international political system. Cottam and Rockman (1984) attempt to link features of a president's psychological style (his policy attentiveness and policy thinking) with features of his organizational style to predict the extent to which specific criteria in policy making (in this case, foreign policy making) are apt to be met. Very major analytic and empirical problems lie in the path of such attempts, but if presidents are worth studying as leaders, they are surely worth studying as policy makers.

Psychological Disposition

Another body of work that is focused on the president as individual emphasizes psychological makeup and early socialization. There is, to be sure, inevitable overlap with studies primarily focused on the president's leadership style, for this body of work also tries to explain (or starts from) particular presidential behavior traits. The focus here, however, is more on the president's personality than his political psyche.

The study of personality is clearly a tricky business, even more so, in my estimation, than style. In focusing on it, we are seeking consistent patterns of behavior (indeed, maybe seeking them out) and an essentially prepolitical explanation for them. On the whole, this genre of analysis tends to look at presidents as disasters on their way to happen, or if they have happened already, why they could be traced back to earlier personality deformations. The intractable character of Woodrow Wilson's stances reflect, in the Georges' account (1956), a need to demonstrate his commitment in the face of concerns about his own worthiness; a need to prove himself, to constantly test himself while craving for, and anxious about, self-respect. The result was inflexibility, ultimately producing great policy and personal disaster.

Now, let us listen to what Betty Glad (1980) has to say about Jimmy Carter: "Strong reactions to criticism and potential failure suggest that underneath Carter's self-confidence he suffers . . . from fear of not being worthwhile" (p. 502). Later, "His negative reactions to opposition and criticism sugest that he may have trouble learning from his mistakes" (p. 504). And, "his anxiety is based on the assumption that being less than perfect is terrible indeed" (p. 502). At one level, the problem is that for all of the apparent similarities in the psychological makeup of Wilson and Carter, their behavior in office by all accounts was often opposite. Whereas Wilson refused to bend, Carter was thought to be infirm and protean.

The train of linkages from generalized personality formation to presidential behavior is an exceedingly long one. If similar personality types can behave differently, then the obverse probably is also true; that is, different personality types can behave similarly. Another, less generous, way of putting this is to ask, do we begin with behaviors we find faulty (or praiseworthy) and then work our way back to a reconstructed logic of personality development that is consistent with (though not necessarily causative of) them?

Alexander George's critique (1974) of James David Barber's much celebrated work on presidential character (1972) makes two points that reflect my own unease with the genre. First, to what extent do the deeper psychological patterns cohere to fit *exclusively* with a particular type of surface or phenomenological behavior? Second, to what extent, given the inevitable richness of evidence that one might look for, is it likely that we quite naturally would be inclined to emphasize dominant features of the case that accord with the presidential behavior being examined?

Although presidents and candidates for the presidency can exhibit persistent traits of behavior that are worth paying attention to, causal attribution based on the construction of inner psychological needs and dynamics may be excess baggage. If similar inner psychological needs can produce different symptoms of behavior, then of what worth is it to devise explanations based on inner psychological drives? I suspect only at the outer margins are we apt to see patterns so clear that we could predict a behavioral outcome from them given the proper behavioral opportunities. Such behavioral patterns, the Georges' thought, were there in the case of Wilson (George and George, 1956); Barber, I believe, thought that to be so in the case of Nixon.

In his critique of Barber, George (1974) distinguishes between "scientific" and "policy" uses of characterological analysis, fearing that we may move from the unfinished product of the former to the dogmatic application of the latter. George seems to be suggesting that a specific syndrome of behavior, apparent in other roles as well, must be specified before links can be drawn. I am more inclined to think that we might see a pattern of behavior more evidently than be able to explain it in either a non-ad hoc or nonreductionist way. To the extent, it seems, that we have borrowed from psychoanalytic and clinical theories, we also have borrowed their frailties.

The problem of sorting out meaningful patterns in a person's life is a difficult, though not impossible, task. Explaining, and predicting from, these patterns is even more uncertain. This is one instance in which I think we are apt to be better off focusing our attention on those patterns relevant to the conduct of the office. The ways in which presidents and aspiring presidents organize themselves for dealing with politics and policy are more focused and politically relevant, though perhaps less interesting than their inner turbulence or serenity, their sibling and familial relations, and their drives to achieve perfectability or fulfill their mother's aspirations for them. If we are to borrow psychological tools to understand presidential behavior, I suspect, but cannot definitively conclude, that more benefits will be derived from those of cognitive, organizational, and social psychology than from psychiataric premises.

A somewhat different twist can be found in Bruce Buchanan's book, *The Presidential Experience* (1978). Buchanan asks not how does one shape the office, but how does the office shape its holder? In some ways, his analysis accords with (but of course is not responsible for) the numerous cliches that abound regarding the burdens imposed by the office on the visibly deteriorating countenance of the president. Briefly, Buchanan sees an overload of expectations and too little sharing of responsibilities; a view that, without the psychological overtones, is shared by Aaron Wildavsky (1976). Rather than emphasizing the right person, Buchanan entertains options for how the presidency (as well as the political system and the society) may be reformed so as to reduce some of the worst impact it has on its incumbents. In the end, however, lacking faith in the likelihood of his "solutions" being adopted, he concludes that we probably will have to search for those who seem well balanced to begin with. Whether one finds his conclusion satisfactory or not, the virtue of Buchanan's analysis is that it suggests that emphasizing "industrial psychology" is apt to be as useful for looking at persistent patterns (problems?) of presidential behavior as emphasizing the person is for looking at how those patterns might vary.

The Selection Process

How can we select presidents who are both temperate and competent? How can we, simply put, select presidents who are apt to be successful by whatever reasonable criterion we employ? The answer, despite a good bit of inveighing to the contrary, is pretty simple. No one knows.

Much particularly has been made of nomination processes, their change over time, the lesser role that professional politicians have played in the process and the effects on a president's ability to navigate effectively. A few things are certain, of course. Since the days when nominees were selected by the congressional caucus, most everything about politics, its organization and channels of participation, have changed. Particularly over the last decade (with some modest reversal now within the Democratic party), the process of nomination has reached outward via the expansion of presidential primaries and party caucuses, putatively lessening the role of traditional power brokers at the party conventions while expanding the role of mass elements and ideological activists. The result, it is thought, are nominees who owe nothing to their party, are frequently unfamiliar with party stalwarts and with Washington in general. Above all, therefore, such presidents (or nominees) are apt to be unconcerned with their party except as a tool of convenience. They are apt to be immoderate, isolated, and/or ineffective.

The basis for this perspective can be found in a number of works (Polsby and Wildavsky, 1980, pp. 210–286; Wilson, 1962; Kirkpatrick, 1976; Ranney, 1975), but it has been eloquently distilled and argued by James Ceasar (1978; 1979; 1982). The evidence on behalf of this accumulation of assertions, however, is remarkably scant. Presidents of varying quality, in fact, have been chosen by a variety of schemes. In some instances, party stalwarts have been willing to dump their peers overboard to find someone more attractive. The Democrats' effort to entice Eisenhower, who hardly could have had many ties with political leaders, and dump Truman in 1948 is a classic case. On the other hand, without "public" voice in the nomination process (however smaller then than now), it is highly likely that the Republican nominee in 1952 would have been the stalwarts' favorite, Taft, rather than Eisenhower. The point is not that one system is overwhelmingly superior to another but, instead, that from the standpoint of producing "good" presidents—whatever the term may mean—the null hypothesis is fundamentally correct.

If anything, there is a modicum of evidence to suggest that the standard litany of characteristics, cited above in the critique of recent developments in the selection process, are negatively related to quality in presidential performance. This would not surprise Lord Bryce, of course, who argued that for the party it was better to have a good candidate than a good president (1881, p. 108). Using Barber's typology, Michael Nelson claims that presidents in the postreform era seem to be psychologically better fit than those selected in the prereform era (1982, p. 103), whatever the validity one may attach to that observation. Ironically, as well, though it was the McGovern nomination that brought about a reaction to the reforms, it was the candidate of the (at that time) nonreformed convention (Nixon) who brought disaster to the presidency. Certainly, to the extent that stalwarts under the old system were to select candidates experienced and wise in the ways of political life, one would think that experience in government should be positively related to reputational success. Alas, no such relationship exists except to the extent that a congressional career is inversely related to success in the presidency (Rockman, 1984).

Any search for the candidate (and president) with the right ingredients is shrouded in mist because what we think the right ingredients are, as well as who it is we think embodies them, is a highly subjective matter. Yet, it is important. For what we are looking for in a president and in a selection process should bring to the surface our first order assumptions about the personal elements of leadership and the model of the presidency we hold.[3] As important as the person and the selection process are, analysis of each remains at a fairly soft level, while judgments often are rendered with a certainty bred more from conviction than from rigorous, conceptually precise, and logically consistent inquiry.

THE FEW: ELITE INTERDEPENDENCIES

A system of shared powers is also a system of interdependencies. No system is without them, of course, because nowhere does power flow freely. Structurally, the American system conduces to an immobilized president. But it need not happen that way. Much depends on the nature of political alignments. Even more important is the attitude of the elite toward governance.

James Young's extraordinary account (1966) of the political life of the capital touches on all of these elements. From separated institutions and unstructured political alignments, a president's cabinet members easily could become his rivals, often more closely linked to Congress than to the president. A politics based on unclear alignments ultimately would later reflect the importance of state and locality despite the later growth in the importance of party. Elements of the Neustadtian emphasis on the skills of political leadership enter into the analysis, Jefferson being a more mobilizing and resourceful president than Madison, for example. But mainly Young attributes the immobilization of political leadership to the confluence of complexity in political structure, fluidity in political alignment, and an elite culture disdainful of governance. Critiques of the "unstructuredness" of early political alignments subsequently have surfaced (Hoadley, 1980), and party later would become an engine of revived national political forces (Kleppner, 1979).

Early politics was not determining of every subsequent later feature of the American polity. Indeed, ultimately, power would have to be driven outward through mass political parties and democratization in order for it to be reestablished at the center in the presidency. How much power would be reestablished at the center and how much the antigovernance attitudes of the elite linger are matters of continued controversy. In contrast to European systems, the American system still seems less munificently endowed in the capacity for governance (Rose, 1980c). And there is little doubt that the complexity of the governing structure, in the absence of forces to overcome it, would produce an extraordinarily complex network of interdependencies. If presidents ultimately would escape from being under the dominion of Congress, they, in turn, could not dominate Congress or shut off the relationship between agencies of the executive and the committees of the Congress.

One writer, consequently, has argued that the traditional three branches of government in the U. S. have evolved into five, with three alone being part of the executive: the president with his political and policy advisory team, the politically appointed officials in the departments and agencies of the executive branch, and the legion of career officialdom in the executive (Merry, 1980). So defined, there now may be a lot more branches than five if one looks at the staffing and support agency growth in Congress. At the very least, each branch has supported numerous twigs.

In the various parts of this section, I will be examining work dealing with presidential interdependencies with the executive, with the Congress, and with the nongovernmental elites of the Washington based media. In doing so, I realize that several other interdependencies will not be separately addressed here. For example, I do not address party elites, because I think that much that is relevant on this score is best expressed through the president's relations with his party in Congress. That which is relevant to selection processes, I have whisked over in the prior section. The judiciary is an important point of interdependency also, and has been a growing one for some time. As the courts have become more involved in administrative decision making, such intervention may come at the expense of both the president's ability to control the executive (Shapiro, 1981) and now, if *Chadha* v. *Immigration and Naturalization Service* is an indication, perhaps also the ability of Congress to do similarly. I shall merely note this last linkage of the presidency and the judiciary, while anticipating that in the future more attention will be paid to this link.

Presidential-Executive Interdependencies
The Presidential Office: Theories and Evidence

No government, not even West Germany or Canada with their ample central agencies and numerous central officials, possesses the amount of high level staffing around the chief executive as the United States does. Whatever the particular reasons for this, the hired help has grown in quantity, but especially in importance, ever since the Brownlow report asserted the need for it. Sporadic scholarly attention was aimed at the White House staff and EOP agencies (Neustadt, 1954, for instance), but the impetus for scholarly attention has been especially prominent over the course of the last decade. Perhaps some of this was a result of the belief that operations in the Nixon administration reached a zenith in their centralization, and that traditional departmental functions were being usurped (or at least duplicated) by a more extensive White House apparatus than previously had been known.

This growth in the president's "organization" has stimulated a fair amount of research, commentary, and conceptual development where once little attention, for understandable reasons, had been paid. In fact, we now have two major studies that have emphasized comparative analysis of the office of the chief executive, one cross-nationally (Campbell, 1983), and the other temporally (Kessel, 1975, 1983a,b). Following upon his study with George J. Szablowski of Canadian central agencies (1979), Colin Campbell extends the compass of inquiry to the United Kingdom and the United States. Analyzing both systemic differences and leadership style differences, Campbell develops a theoretical framework for the latter based upon the chief executive's goals and priorities, the extent to which authority is centralized within the chief executive's office or delegated to line departments, and the extent to which competitive versus discrete jurisdictions are encouraged. Through the use of intensive and extensive interviews with leading officials in the three countries, Campbell's analysis helps to illustrate how stylistic factors interact with, indeed are conditioned by, structural differences. Ironically, the American executive system appears to be overcentralized and understaffed relative especially to its British counterpart, and even its Canadian one. Relative to the Canadian and British systems, American executive operations are infused with personalism, which is evidence in important ways of underinstitutionalization, a matter which I will touch on again.

While Campbell compares systems, John Kessel compares American presidential administrations over time in order to identify constant and variable features regarding the White House staff. Kessel's odyssey begins with the Nixon administration, from which the major base line work is published (1975), and then takes in both the Carter administration and now also the Reagan administration (1983a,b). Kessel's analysis focuses on the structures of White House organization; in particular, his efforts are aimed at identifying issue structures in the White House staff, communications networks, influence structures, and organizational characteristics. Kessel's supposition is that the growth and importance of the White House staff (and agencies therein) means that it likely will be internally differentiated. Even though the White House does not carry the earmarks of a highly complex organization, characteristic of the more classically organized line departments, it is complex enough to warrant examination of its diversity and of how the parts integrate, if they do. Kessel's approach is essentially survey analysis with a strong emphasis on the sophisticated use of quantitative description. Where Campbell's analysis is physiology, Kessel's is anatomy.

A White House staff and its operations could well be changeable depending upon at what point in a term one encounters it, or what events it is responding to or being traumatized by. Alas, this is not easily controllable. Taking these limits into account, Kessel's findings indicate, not very surprisingly, that the personnel based structures show more cross-administration variability than the organizational ones, even though organization, to some extent, evolves around both personalities and differing priorities across administrations. Issue structures, therefore, are most variable. Whereas the Reagan White House is remarkably cohesive in outlook, the Carter White House was equally remarkably incohesive. The Nixon White House, Kessel's evidence shows, was somewhere between the two. As interesting as the differences are, there also are fascinating similarities. Here, especially, the deployment of quantitative technique shows that impressionistic discussion can be misleading. For all of the scuttlebut that the NSC staff had been relegated to a peripheral role in the Reagan administration, Kessel's data show quite the contrary (1983b, p. 31).

Following Kessel's line of analysis, other work seems to suggest the relative importance of various staff agencies. A staff agency's mark of importance in the U. S. may be the reduction of its continuity and an increase in the likelihood of its politicization. Heclo's discussion of the layering in phenomenon at OMB (1975) by which a whole new stratum of politically appointed officials (program assistant directors) was created to monitor the work of the careerists below fits nicely with the relative organizational importance of OMB, especially in Republican administrations. Covington's analysis of staff turnover rates (1981) in EOP agencies implies a growing shift in personal over institutional forces, and also demarcates which agencies are apt to be given prime presidential attention.

Growing attention to executive dynamics at the top also has been fruitful for demonstrating certain uniformities in the presence of systems as diverse as those of the U. S. and the U. K. For example, Thomas Cronin's observation (1980, pp. 274–290) that the cabinet can be divided between insiders and outsiders, that is, incumbents of posts whose functioning requires frequent presidential consultation and those whose functioning lies on the periphery of presidential attention, is also verified by Richard Rose's discovery (1980a, pp. 32–43) that much the same can be said of Britain, although, of course, the cabinets themselves in the two countries play different roles. But the evidence that Rose presents is that the matters in the U.S. which are peripheral to the attention of the president are likewise so in the U.K. Though neither cites one another on this point, the Cronin-Rose hypothesis seems to be a vintage case of an empirical regularity that should tell us, among other things, that ministerial influence is not autonomy, and ministerial autonomy is similarly not influence. It should suggest to us as well that the power of clientele groups and bureaucratic routine are most evident when the boss is paying (because the boss has) only limited attention. In turn, the primacy factor should help explain to us why recent American presidents generally have been concerned with a compatible NSC but less concerned with changing faces in an EOP agency such as the Council on Environmental Quality (CEQ), at least until a president with a strong interest in altering policy lines came into office.

While focusing on features that are relevant only to the U.S., some studies have pointed, nonetheless, to interesting evolutionary tendencies that require a revision of prevailing maxims. Heclo (1981), for instance, emphasizes how increasingly White House public liaison has come to represent external political constituencies to the president. As interest networks have grown more complex, so has their representation. Heclo's interesting analysis hints that White House staff personnel, to the extent that they become spokespersons for this or that constituency, also gain some measure of autonomy, even indispensability. Neustadt's belief in his earliest edition of *Presidential Power* that proximity made for controllability is apparently amended by the thrust of Heclo's analysis. Still, Heclo's interpretation may be based heavily, perhaps even exclusively, on a Democratic presidency (the Democrats are a party seemingly of more constituencies than principles) and on a president with peculiar outreach needs to those constituencies. Heclo's very interesting analysis cries out for some continuous attention, without which the findings of the day (in this case yesterday!) may become engraved into stone as the latest in a quickened series of durable truths.

Advisory Systems: Models and Prescriptions

Providing advice on how to render advice also has become a growth industry in applied social science. Elements of organization theory and the psychology of small group behavior have been brought to the task. Strictly speaking, such advice rendering predates the advent of the Harvard Kennedy School, although then much of the advice came in the form of commission reports—Brownlow and Hoover I and II, for example. The art of advice giving on how to organize a presidency, however, received a strong push from the omnipresent Richard Neustadt in his equally omnipresent *Presidential Power.* Keep a lot of pots boiling and keep them stirring was his message.

The process of scholarly analysis of advisory processes, however, received a special impetus from the Johnson and Nixon presidencies: in Johnson's case because the decisions that led to engagement and involvement in Vietnam and the tactics that followed were believed to be disastrous for Johnson's own political prospects and for the country. In the case of Nixon, foreign policy especially had been extracted from its institutional roots and not subject to effective staffing, however effective or ineffective the policies actually may have been. In various other respects, the subsequent presidencies of Ford, Carter, and Reagan have illustrated the importance of good advisory processes, if, perversely, by their frequent absence.

Foreign policy especially is an area of intense interest in promoting effective advisory systems. The main problem is how to make use of institutional competence yet remain open to new ideas (Rockman, 1981). No easy matter. Decision making during the Cuban missile crisis serves frequently as a case in which alternatives did get aired in a fairly undistorted manner (although one could question the effective range of the options). The problem would be how to transmit this free flow of options and to take advantage of the diversity that naturally is generated from the varied elements of the foreign-national security policy apparatus while, at the same time, providing for orderly management of it. Even more to the point: How can this be done outside of the context of a crisis situation?

Three relatively early responses to the problem could be characterized roughly as (1) providing neutral traffic management (George, 1972); (2) grafting responsiveness on to competence (Destler, 1972); and (3) diversifying the institutional socialization experiences of foreign-national security policy officers (Allison and Szanton, 1976). The first and second appraisals particularly come into conflict because the first tries to define a role for the national security assistant while the second tries to eliminate the role. Roger Porter's study (1980) of the Economic Policy Board (EPB) under President Ford suggests particular advantages of the multiple advocacy approach, initially promoted by George, and plays off characteristics of the multiple advocacy system with those of two other "systems" of advice: "ad hocracy" and centralized management. In large part, however, the EPB worked as a multiple advocacy system because its coordinator, William Seidman, played the honest broker and coordinator roles that George envisioned for the NSC staff director. Among other factors cited in the ability of the EPB to bring options to the surface was the style of Seidman himself, who was a person willing to subordinate his own views to a process of sifting views in an unjaundiced way for the president. Few persons of this sort are now to be found in Washington, especially in foreign policy. Above all, Porter duly notes, organizational factors are themselves contingent upon a president's operating style and tolerances.

Porter's analysis and George's own development of advisory schemes (1980) are clearly efforts at applied social science. They also are thoughtfully conceptualized in terms of delineating the conditionals under which various organizational schemes might be applicable to particular goals. George (1980) particularly makes the case for policy relevant theory, distinguishing it from pure social science theory. The latter presumably seeks broad generalizations spanning time and space, whereas the former emphasizes conditional generalizations relevant to particular policy phenomena. Generally speaking, this also is about where we stand in applied organization theory—more conditionals than broad-scale generalizations.

Central-Departmental Relations

From the "inner sanctum" of the executive to broader relationships with the line bureaucracies, there is impressive evidence of persistent White House efforts to seek thoroughgoing political control. An initial survey of the federal executive (Aberbach and Rockman, 1976) and its political attitudes apparently served to reinforce the suspicions of Republican presidents, while it helped to renew scholarly attention to the question of presidential relations with the line bureaucracy. Randall (1979) and Nathan (1983) make it clear that when presidents are persistent and clear in their willingness to gain control over the apparatus, and when that control can be measured in contracting rather than expanding or coordinating activities, it can be achieved (see also, Mowery et al., 1980). It is a question of attention and goals.

This remains an area, however, in which we are very limited in our generalizability. Some phenomena do appear to be secular. For example, the layering-in phenomenon discussed by Heclo (1977) and the diminution in stature of senior civil servants speculated on by Polsby (1981). All of these are symptoms of an unrelenting drive across recent presidential administrations toward the politicization of the bureaucracy.

Yet, other areas show change. A later attitudinal reexamination of the senior federal executive reveals attitudes more in line with those of the presidential administration under which it was serving (Cole and Caputo, 1979), evidence perhaps of personnel change. More important, we have as yet not differentiated the concept of presidential "control" that has been so casually tossed around. Precisely what does control mean? Do administrations differ, especially as between Republicans and Democrats, in their definitions of, and approaches to, presidential control? Further, if motivations for control differ, is it not probable (especially now in view of the Supreme Court ruling on the legislative veto) that the relative ease with which control can be imposed is a function of the type of control it is? Contracting is less daunting than coordinating or integrating, for example. What we need here, it seems, is one of those good conditional theories that George has spoken of. But first we need to specify the dependent variable(s).

Research: Problems and Opportunities

Whatever other conclusions one may reach regarding the state or quality of research on the executive connections to the presidency, this is an area of research no longer suffering from neglect. At the same time, the dynamic aspects of chief-executive/executive relationships seem terribly foreboding for cross-national inquiry, however critical the latter will be to expanding our thinking, conceptualizing, and theorizing. How do dissimilar structures function around similar problems? And how do similar appearing structures function differently?

While inquiry into the dynamics of executive behavior probably will initially derive from single country studies or from comparative studies without very explicit frameworks, eventually any real test of our theories will have to develop theoretical frameworks sufficiently comparable, yet sufficiently precise, that they can serve as effective guides to the analysis of diverse policy-making systems and the role of the chief executive in them. Moreover, they will have to be mindful of all the intrasystem variability that one would have to be conscious of in a single country study. For example, to what extent does the party in power affect the constellation of policy forces? To what extent are issues so diverse in the policy constellations that develop around them that we are inhibited from making broad-scale generalizations about any country's policy process (Pempel, 1977, pp. 308–323; Spitzer, 1982; Lowi, 1972)? And to what extent can political influence from the center be exerted on autonomous or semiautonomous organs of the state—the Federal Reserve Board in the U.S., for example (Beck, 1982)?

Presidential-Legislative Relations

I divide this topic into two sections. The first focuses on efforts of the president, or his staff, to influence Congress through lobbying operations. The second body of work is focused more on presidential successes with Congress in the aggregate, and the conditions for success.

Lobbying and Congress

How much influence can a president exert with Congress above and beyond the fixed parameters of the distribution of seats and the propensities for incohesion in the majority and minority parties? Good will and other charms produced by effective liaison and lobbying activities are not context free. It is easier to generate good will in the presence of ample majorities (Manley, 1978); it is easier to do so, one suspects, earlier in a term than later (Light, 1981, 1982); and it may be easier to do so when programs are expanding rather than being contracted.

No one, I doubt, would contest Stephen Wayne's point that "Despite the institutionalized aspects of congressional-presidential interaction, there is no escaping the fact that the character of the relationship is very much affected by the president himself" (1978, p. 173). It is not easy though, to show precisely what that effect is.

In important respects, it appears that lobbying overall is a defensive measure. While it is hard to convert good relations into legislative success, it is easier to transform sour relations into legislative defeats. And defeats beget further vulnerability (Davis, 1979a). By examining the "lobbying" question within this fairly limited context, both Manley (1978) and Davis (1979a) are able to illustrate that lobbying is an activity taking place within a given set of political parameters that are themselves likely to be a lot more important that the lobbying activity itself.

Thus, scholars have tended to focus more on congressional characteristics than on presidential manipulations as key influences in the relationship. Several studies have emphasized the atomization of congressional power structure as an increasingly important deterrent to presidential legislative ambitions (Manley, 1978; Davis, 1979b; Oppenheimer, 1980). The net effect of changes in congressional structure has made it harder to compose stable majorities. Additionally, these changes have exposed members of Congress to greater pressures from the outside. It is unlikely, though, that the changes affect all presidential agendas equally. The greater the complexity of the agenda or proposal, the more adversely it is affected. Yet some changes, especially in the House of Representatives, have veered toward greater centralization, permitting passage of the ambitious budgetary designs of the Reagan administration's first year.

Presidential Success with Congress

Obviously what influences presidential programmatic success with Congress involves a complex of factors; least of which, George Edwards (1980b) appears to show us, is a president's personal skills, and most of which, Jeffrey Cohen (1982) points out, historically involves the partisan distribution of seats and party cohesion. By comparing the support proferred in Congress by party and region, Edwards (1980b) demonstrates that differences across presidents in the structure of their support are not as strong as is commonly supposed. He infers, therefore, that numbers are the main source of presidential success or failure, and that changes in agendas, the structure and culture of Congress, and in the atmosphere of the country more generally are far more powerful determinants than presumptions of legislative legerdemain.

Agendas, and their timing, are also crucial to the prospects of legislative success. A particularly impressive analysis by Fishel (1980) demonstrates the importance of agenda change in the latter stages of the Carter administration to the prospects for success. Agenda change, of course, is substantially imposed by circumstances, and the circumstances bringing about change in the Carter agenda were ones apt to make it difficult to follow traditional Democratic party programs. The Carter case, it turns out, was not at all unique at least in terms of the general pattern of agenda displacement over the course of the presidential term. Such displacement affected all presidents except for Kennedy, whose

term was tragically cut short. The remedies sought by Carter for a hyperinfla-
tionary economy, however, were not easily swallowed by his party (Fishel, pp.
40-62).

Since events impose themselves over time on presidents rather than vice versa, Paul Light contends that presidents who fail to move rapidly on their
domestic agenda are likely to face a declining stock of resources with which to
work their will. Presidents differ in the extent to which they press that agenda
immediately, but the more compelling point is, as Fishel emphasizes, the extent
to which external forces come to disturb and erode initial plans.

Clearly, studies of presidential success with Congress benefit empirically
from the fact that they are as much studies of Congress as they are of the presidency. This means a greater opportunity to do relational analysis in quantitative
form. Although measures of success have their flaws as do the measures of
many of the independent variables, analyses here have demystified some of the
legends surrounding our presidents as legislative geniuses (or incompetents).
Systemic forces appear as much larger determinants of outcomes than personal
manipulations, despite the amount of journalistic ink spilled on the latter relative to the former.

Yet it is unlikely that personal efforts are of no consequence. Not only does
that seem implausible, it undoubtedly is. What we are confronted with, however, is a classic problem of levels of analysis. The effects of presidential manipulations are nested within these larger forces that tend to cut across administrations or which have similar cyclical impacts within administrations
(Rockman, 1984). In the broad scope of things, there is no doubt which has the
more powerful effects. What we need to know, however, is how personal exer-
tion interacts with the broader determinants, and that is difficult to do at the
same level of analysis and inference. The problem is controlling environmental
circumstances for presidential strategies.

Charles O. Jones (1983) takes a stab at conceptually intertwining these
forces: the givens of the political situation and the style of legislative leadership
exerted by the president. However, it would be reasonable to say that we are a
far way from theoretically and empirically blending the behavioral and systemic elements. Indeed, this may not be a soluble analytic problem.

The Washington Media

Another elite of great importance to presidents, if only because presidents
think it is, is the community of reporters based in Washington—those directly
and indirectly covering the White House and the president. Two recent studies
(Hess, 1981; Grossman and Kumar, 1981) have focused on the characteristics
and behavior of the Washington community of reporters, on the coverage of
the media, and on strategies of the White House for developing favorable or at
least nonharmful relations. Together, the studies suggest that, paradoxically,

while the Washington reporters are afforded greater independence by their distance from, and the bureaucratic organization of, their newspapers, they often behave and report in similar ways. Part of the latter symptom is what has come to be referred to as "pack journalism." The overt political bias of an earlier era when the publishers themselves took a big hand in the content of the news has dramatically receded, thus awarding the Washington correspondents more independence. On the other hand, the bureaucratic characteristics of the organizations they now work for tend to diminish the possibilities of deviating from received interpretations or consensus definitions of "hot" stories (Hess, pp. 133–137).

Reporters, Hess finds from his investigation, are "talking" people, not "reading" people. Information is what someone in authority says or slips to a reporter. Few do much documentary work that would shed complexity or, above all, situational background on the stories they are covering. It is not unnatural, therefore, for personal aspects of governing to come to the fore and to downplay situational complexities. There is good news and bad news in that for presidents, of course. The good news is that favorable soft features are obviously positive for image management; the bad news is that, in the event presidents have any inclinations toward emphasizing complex analyses of problems, the general coverage of the media is not naturally predisposed toward doing that.

A particularly vexing problem in analyzing the impact of the Washington news community is whether the distrust of government that has markedly arisen over the course of the last two decades is a result of the press's scepticism toward the governors in Washington or whether the reporters merely mirror these more pervasive sentiments (Grossman and Kumar, p. 315). Do the reporters merely report on the atmosphere or help create it? An effective answer to that question really requires a consumer survey (public opinion) even more than one of reporters. Media effects seem to have more short run than long run effects in this regard, one study reports (Miller et al., 1979). Judgments of the authorities rather than the institutions of authority seem to be affected most.

The media, of course, translate reality while the authorities try to manage the translation. Realities are inevitably more complex than their capsulization can be. The strategies, tendencies, and incentives of the contestants, governors and media, bear continued watching, as does the impact they have on various publics.

THE MANY: SOCIETAL INTERDEPENDENCIES

As we move beyond elite interactions and into mass political phenomena, data have the appearance of seeming "harder" since we often are drawing inferences from survey data collections. This is more illusion than not, however.

We have more data, of course, but often less conclusiveness, a common malady of "empirical" political science.

My first focus is on the issue of the meaning and shape of public approval for the president. The second is on the impact of the media in shaping public judgments (looked at from the consumer rather than the producer side). A third issue, that of electoral coalitions, is given a very brief discussion. A last and most important, but also most difficult, issue is the relationship of the president (but effectively any chief executive) to society, and what, therefore, are the boundaries of social change imposed by the role and the path taken to get there? My discussion here can be composed of nothing more than selected highlights. Not all relevant literature can be pursued, but I hope the key relevant points can be made.

The Meaning and Shape of Public Approval for the President

Political prestige, Richard Neustadt (1980) contends, is an element in a president's ability to successfully exert power because other elites are attentive to the president's standing in the country. Assuming, however, that the relationship between public approval of the president and his legislative success is not perfect (it isn't; the correlation coefficient between approval and success from Eisenhower to Reagan is .43), the question is, through what mechanisms does approval translate into political support? While approval may influence elites outside of Congress, too, the focus of research attention, nonetheless, has been on its translation into legislative success within Congress as measured through roll call voting.

The translation process, it is clear, does not work in an undifferentiated way. In general, for the period 1955-70, Edwards found that in the House, voting support for the president's positions was consistently better correlated with his level of public support in foreign than in domestic policy and among first term members than others (Edwards, 1976). Broken down further, however, Edwards' analysis suggests that presidential popularity is mediated by congressmen via the president's standing among their own electoral supporters (Edwards, 1976, 1980a,b). Whether these findings are temporally generalizable beyond the period studied is as yet uncertain.

A different sort of dilemma, however, is that of causality; that is, in which direction does the relationship between approval and legislative support run? We tend to assume that it runs from mass approval to elite suport, in part, because Neustadt implied that and, in part, because our models of representation assume it. But those studying presidential liaison and lobbying efforts with Congress tend to concede the importance of perceptions—defeats tend to beget larger vulnerabilities. One might assume that such a process can work in the mass public as well. The more politically vulnerable a president looks in Washington, the less public prestige he may have. The disentangling of causal influences here is a quite complicated matter, but it is clear that a static correlation model cannot decide this question for us.

Beyond the issue of the relation between popularity and legislative performance, there is the question of what explains the shape of the approval curve itself. Stimson (1976) noted, for instance, that presidents through Nixon have experienced declines in approval as a function of time (with a slight upward turn at the very end). Following Nixon, the general thesis continues to hold true, though even the small end of tenure turn for the better is no longer found. Stimson wonders whether anything but time matters in accounting for the attrition of presidential support. Implicitly, Stimson's work takes off from an earlier article by Mueller (1970), which hypothesized that the diminution in presidential approval over time is a function of the dissolution of presidential coalitions: doing things makes enemies of your former friends; ignoring promises or not meeting expectations similarly turns friends into foes. Stimson hypothesizes that the downward tendency in approval can be explained best by an expectations/disillusionment theory (1976), which argues that disillusionment is a function of the extent of expectation. Put in pugilistic terms, the bigger they are the harder they fall.

There is, to be sure, a good bit of controversy about the inevitableness of this fall-off in presidential popularity (Kernell, 1978; Brody and Page, 1975; Presser and Converse, 1976; among others). Events produce political judgments, and these judgments are a function of the cumulative effect of the valence of the events. At the same time, judgments are not uniform across the population in that a president's natural political enemies, in the interpretation of Presser and Converse, register their disapproval earliest and most sharply. In another interpretation, however, presidential approval is deeply influenced by events bearing on presidential performance, but the approval shifts reflect occupational strata (class) differences more than political party ones (Hibbs, 1982).

The mysteries of mass support for political leadership and the explanations of it have received increasing attention in political science (Sigelman, 1979). Confronted with swirls of interpretive controversies, alternative variables given emphasis, and numerous theoretic-analytic models promising "better fits" streaming across the pages of our journals, we are now faced with a situation of more ingestion than digestion. For those apt to think that more and more precise data analyses will lead to more unifying theories, I recommend a steady diet of articles on the questions of who supports whom and why?

Although these controversies continue in slightly more muffled tones in other countries, the question of presidential support (or at least part of it) probably ought to be (and is, in fact, beginning to be) cast explicitly in a more cross-national mold. Obviously, given the absence of party discipline norms in the United States, the original Neustadtian hypothesis bearing on the relationship between mass support and political influence in governing is unique to the U. S.

"Success" scores in the legislature obviously are not a point of comparison. Elsewhere, approval might influence other political maneuvers, especially in multiparty governing coalitions, but this is too complicated a matter to enter into here. Rather, a simple first step is descriptive, namely, to compare magnitudes of approval (where systems are sufficiently alike) for the president/government and the magnitude of shifts in approval.

This will reveal that the unpopularity of recent American presidents is a phenomenon not specific either to American political leadership or to the American mass public. In a roughly comparable time period of about the past 30 years, for instance, the same number of British prime ministers as American presidents have been approved of at the end by more than half the public. Moreover, Lewis-Beck (1980) shows that French presidents typically have been subject to more modulated swings of disapproval than have American presidents apparently because the prime minister absorbs much of the criticism without deflecting it onto the president. The sharp downward swing in current approval of Mitterand, however, suggests obvious limits to this deflection hypothesis.

Media Influences

No short statement can adequately summarize the research in this area which, in any event, appears resistant to tidy summaries. However, one body of research in particular forms the basis of my comments here, namely, the extent to which what we perceive becomes equally or more politically relevant to us than that which we directly experience. There is evidence that this may be so. And if so, this obviously raises important questions as to how the news is covered or, even more, what news is created. In other words, we probably not only need to know more about the behavior patterns of the reporters, but also those whose job it is to manage the time and space allocated to various stories.

Two researchers (Kinder and Kiewiet, 1981) have shown that news regarding economic performance is a great deal more important in terms of political behavior than personal economic expectations. Similarly, Edwards finds that evaluations of a president's economic performance are a far more important ingredient of his popularity than either the prevailing state of economic conditions or the person's own economic situation (1983).

Two recent studies designed to evaluate the effects of media reporting on particular news stories (Iyengar et al., 1982; Kinder et al., 1983) emphasize the impact of what stories are being paid attention to (television being the medium in this case), and in what light they tend to show the president. Viewers experimentally exposed to slightly manipulated "real" newscasts were primed by the stories being covered to move in directions implied by the flow of the slightly contrived events. Subjects with less information were especially vulnerable to this effect. The logic of this analysis seems to accord well with the findings of

Brody and Page (1975) that presidential approval is largely a function of the cumulation of good news over bad or vice versa.

Electoral Coalitions

Although the topic of electoral coalitions is a broad one, I want to pay attention here to the specific question of linkage between presidential and congressional electoral fates. That is, is there a nationalization of political forces or homogenizing tendency that is apt to link congressional with presidential fates? And if not, what are the likely consequences?

Evidence published in the 1960s (Stokes, 1967; Cummings, 1966) indicated a growing nationalization of political forces in the United States, apparently a function of both the New Deal alignment and nationalizing communciations technologies. The tendencies noted by researchers two decades ago may be reversing, not because there is a return to the rigid regionalism that preceded the New Deal realignment, but because party has become a less relevant factor in voting for members of Congress. Members are evaluated, according to Morris Fiorina, increasingly on service rather than policy grounds, whereas presidents are evaluated on the basis of policy performance (1981, especially, pp. 201–211). Consequently, one is unhinged from the other, and the cord of responsibility is severed. If this is so, then president and Congress have become separated institutions in more than the strictly constitutional sense. Indeed, one might conclude that Neustadt's analysis begins where Fiorina's ends.

President, Society, and Social Change

We return now from the scientific back to the speculative. What can we expect of the president as an agent of social change? By himself, probably not much, chime in several scholars (Miroff, 1976, 1980, 1981; Cronin, 1980; Burns, 1978). In one view, the presidency could be the fulcrum of broad social change only in the presence of a galvanizing party system (Burns, 1978; Burnham, 1969), though some notable, if indirect, dissent would be forthcoming here from those in Britain, a land much fancied by American scholars for its galvanized party system (Rose, 1980b; Kavanagh, 1980; King, 1969).

A different perspective suggests that those who rise to the pinnacle of formal authority are not apt to be greatly inspired by the desire to produce significant change. Cronin (1980) hypothesizes, for example, that innovative leadership most likely will be practiced by spokespersons outside of official positions—Martin Luther King, Ralph Nader, or even Jerry Fallwell being cases in point. Miroff (1976) contends that presidents are fully accepting of the norms of the system, having been socialized extensively in its tenets, and having made extensive symbolic commitments to prevailing arrangements and mores in order to get to the top. Therefore, they are unlikely to want to bring about great change. Certainly there is evidence that elites tend to be pretty satisfied with the system that brought them their status, whether in the United States or elsewhere (Anton, 1980).

The route taken to the top, of course, is apt to influence one's calculations. The more filters one passes through, the more cautious one is about taking risks. In general, the European parties scrutinize their potential leaders from the standpoint especially of party constituencies and ideals, while American leaders play two successive games: one to appeal to their party's contituencies, and the other, to some extent, to symbolically relevant, broader constituencies. The wider game the Americans play means that they are less subject to organizational filtration processes. In this regard, the American process may be less resistant to springing antisystem surprises in a swell of populist enthusiasm than the more predictable European processes. Be that as it may, both Mr. Reagan and Mrs. Thatcher, whatever the differences in how they came to be where they are, are less known for their caution than the changes they have helped stir, though, true enough, neither would be known to harbor anticapitalist sentiments.

In fact, it seems that the route taken to the top is probably less important from the standpoint of Miroff's concerns than the proposition that all systems are biased against change in prevailing policy norms or in existing distributions of power and advantage, whether they be capitalist or Marxist-Leninist. Reagan and Thatcher can impose changes more easily than can Mitterand, despite the excellent formal position of the latter, because the needs of advanced capitalist economies are more amenable to their programs (Lindblom, 1977). On the other hand, Khruschchev was stymied by the implicit "power-brokers" in his system too (the party apparat) from generating substantial reform, and assuredly he was followed by someone safe (Bunce, 1984).

How much change is real change also seems endlessly arguable in the absence of specified standards. Nonetheless, however vague some of Miroff's language is, it is a price to be paid for thinking about fundamental questions. In this case, that is to ask: What can be the role of the leaders of governments in envisioning and generating major changes in society? Very limited is Miroff's answer. But the question posed forces one to come to grips with where, if at all, change can be produced, We appear then to have come full circle (and perhaps a generational one as well) from the belief that important changes could be generated from within Washington (Neustadt) with skillful political leadership to the more skeptical view that important changes (if they are to come at all) almost necessarily would have to be stimulated from beyond the Washington community (Miroff, 1980; Cronin, 1980).

FINALE

In his 1975 essay, Anthony King implores scholars in the field of presidential and executive studies to seek answers to soluble questions. The thrust of my review of research and ideas in what loosely may be called the subfield is that more and more answers to soluble questions are being given, especially where analysis is susceptible to multivariate quantitative inquiry. But the answers are often controversial and also often nondurable. This should not be surprising because, after all, this is what science involves: quibbles over the particulars of measurement, over the time periods used as data bases, and over the control of confounding influences. And frequently, as well, the search for empirical regularities does not lead to equally regular or consistent explanation.

We do need answers to soluble questions. For these answers to make any sense beyond aesthetically interesting compartmentalizations, however, we need to pose insoluble questions as well. We need to entertain such questions if the particulars are to be relevant to any broader ideas regarding the role of public leadership.

In this context, the study of the presidency (and I think more generally, the chief executive in any setting) is motivated by what we believe the role of the president can be, and that, in turn, is related to what we believe governing can and ought to be. Normatively, it is impossible for us to escape these questions, and the more aware of them we are, the more likely it is that our "science" will begin to make more integrative sense to us than it has as yet.

In thinking about the role of the chief executive as leader, I think it is increasingly incumbent on us to do so comparatively, especially if we are to shed stereotypes. While we are most adept at discussing formal capabilities (Thomas, 1980; Rose and Suleiman, 1980), we should also draw on comparative behavior in dissimilar as well as similar systems (Bunce, 1981b, 1984). Further, we will need to look at how governments actually function without being limited to the idea that political leadership is necessarily the source of their direction (Heclo, 1974; Ashford, 1982; Steinbruner, 1974; Allison, 1971). Nor should we automatically accept the implicit premise of a comprehensively rational agenda at work, when it may be that underlying uniformities of temporal rhythms and limited attention spans disturb, and disturbingly, inhibit that premise. Above all, it seems to me, the chief executive is, as a former president put it, a "vantage point" for focusing on governance *and* on politics and, especially, the interconnection of the two. The subfield of presidential/executive studies, I am convinced, will reach scholarly fruition when it is no longer a distinctive subfield at all, but merely a point from which to integrate our considerable store of knowledge about politics with our less considerable store of knowledge about governance.

In the meantime, the subfield will abound with a mixture of prescriptive concerns, particularistic insights, inductive (and to a much lesser extent, deductive) searches for elusive generalizations, and illuminating (if often nonoperational) pretheoretical schemes of analysis. Some of what we do will be "science" as I have quite narrowly defined that term; very little of what we will produce from that science will be "theory" as I have equally narrowly defined that term. Most of our "theories" will, in fact, simply be interesting ideas, and most of our "inductive findings" are apt to be eroded when we extend their temporal and conditional horizons, a condition noted also by a prominent economist within his own field (Leontief, 1971, p. 3). Because of the normative interest surrounding the presidency and the larger issues of governance which it gives rise to, and because of the methodological hurdles that often exist, much work will continue to be, in the language of Almond and Genco (1977, p. 520), "descriptive or historical accounts of case studies making limited use of theoretical frameworks and generalizations, and [contributing] to the aims of understanding, interpreting, and exploring political reality and policy. . . ." This will not be science as I have described it, but it will be knowledge, the Rodney Dangerfield syndrome notwithstanding.

Is everything, then, equally good or bad? Equally useful or useless? As for a standard of progress, obviously it should be to reduce uncertainty, which ideally is the theoretical achievement of scientifically tested inquiry. But science generates uncertainty. (Note the state of the absolutist Delaney amendment regarding carcinogens in the marketing of food products.) Theories do create unity—at least conditional unities—but most of our "theories" have limited empirical validity. They are really pretheories, whether arrived at formally or verbally. At the cost of sounding extravagantly tolerant, I suspect that we shall label as "progress" research and ideas that help us to answer or illuminate the questions that we as individual scholars are quite individually interested in. I suspect also that we will deal with soluble questions with more and more precision while also ultimately producing less and less clarity. That we need to continually reconceptualize the insoluble questions, I take (perhaps mistakenly) for granted. That we need the gravitational pull of those "insoluble" questions to keep us from drifting off into ever narrower and more conceptually isolated ones, I also take for granted.

Being less confident, though, that I can (or ought) to point future inquiry in this subfield to some definitive destiny through some equally definitive route, I close with the words of a formerly revered top political leader (but alas not a chief executive): "Let a hundred flowers bloom." But will they become a garden?

Acknowledgments. I wish to thank George C. Edwards, Alexander George, John Kessel, Anthony King, Richard Rose, James S. Young, and two anonymous referees for their comments on an earlier version of this chapter.

NOTES

1. I shall cite the most recent edition of *Presidential Power*, but it incorporates material from all earlier editions. At particular places in this paper where it is important to make a time related point, I shall cite the reference to the first edition (1960) or

compare the first and most recent (1980) editions. However it is cited in the text, though, all references are to the 1980 edition.

2. For an argument suggesting that crisper science can lead to stronger theoretical reformulations, see Riker (1982). Obviously, how one evaluates this argument depends on the integrating scope of theory that one presupposes. Singular propositions, of course, can be tested on their own terms when those terms are precisely specified.

3. Ceasar does exactly this in contrasting the Van Buren and Wilsonian models of the presidency.

REFERENCES

Aberbach, Joel D., and Rockman, Bert A. (1976). Clashing beliefs within the executive branch: The Nixon administration bureaucracy. *American Political Science Review* 70(June): 456–468.

Allison, Graham T. (1971). *Essence of Decision: Explaining the Cuban Missile Crisis.* Boston: Little, Brown.

Allison, Graham T., and Szanton, Peter (1976). *Remaking Foreign Policy.* New York: Basic Books.

Almond, Gabriel A., and Genco, Stephen J. (1977). Clouds, clocks, and the study of politics. *World Politics* 29(July): 489–522.

Anton, Thomas J. (1980). *Administered Politics: Elite Political Culture in Sweden.* Boston: Martinus Nijhoff.

Ashford, Douglas E. (1982). *British Dogmatism and French Pragmatism: Central-Local Policymaking in The Welfare State.* London: Allen & Unwin.

Barber, James David (1972). *The Presidential Character: Predicting Performance in the White House.* Englewood-Cliffs, N.J.: Prentice-Hall.

Beck, Nathaniel (1982). Presidential influence on the Federal Reserve in the 1970's. *American Journal of Political Science* 26(August): 415–445.

Brody, Richard A., and Page, Benjamin I. (1975). The impact of events on presidential popularity: the Johnson and Nixon administrations. In Wildavsky, ed., *Perspectives On The Presidency,* pp. 136–148.

Bryce, James (1881). *The American Commonwealth.* New York: Macmillan.

Buchanan, Bruce (1978). *The Presidential Experience: What The Office Does To the Man.* Englewood Cliffs, N.J.: Prentice-Hall.

Bunce, Valerie (1981a) The cycles of the presidency. Paper presented at the annual meeting of the Midwest Political Science Association, Cincinnati, Ohio.

Bunce, Valerie (1981b). *Do New Leaders Make A Difference? Executive Succession and Public Policy Under Capitalism and Socialism.* Princeton, N.J.: Princeton University Press.

Bunce, Valerie (1984). Of power, policy and paradigms: the logic of elite studies. In Ronald H. Linden and Bert A. Rockman (eds.), *Elite Studies and Communist Politics: Essays in Memory of Carl Beck.* Pittsburgh, PA: UCIS and University of Pittsburgh Press.

Burnham, Walter Dean (1970). *Critical Elections and the Mainsprings of American Politics.* New York: W. W. Norton.

Burns, James MacGregor (1963). *The Deadlock of Democracy: Four Party Politics in America.* Englewood Cliffs, N.J.: Prentice-Hall.

Burns, James MacGregor (1978). *Leadership.* New York: Harper & Row.

Burns, James MacGregor (1956). *Roosevelt: The Lion and the Fox.* New York: Harcourt, Brace.

Campbell, Colin (1983). *Governments Under Stress: Political Executives and Key Bureaucrats in Washington, London, and Ottawa.* Toronto: University of Toronto Press.

Campbell, Colin, and Szablowski, George J. (1979). *The Super-Bureaucrats: Structure and Behavior in Central Agencies.* Toronto: Macmillan.

Ceasar, James W. (1978). Political parties and presidential ambition. *Journal of Politics* 40(August): 708–741.

Ceasar, James W. (1979). *Presidential Selection: Theory and Development.* Princeton, N.J.: Princeton University Press.

Ceasar, James W. (1982). *Reforming the Reforms: A Critical Analysis of the Presidential Selection Process.* Cambridge, Mass.: Ballinger.

Cohen, Jeffrey E. (1982). The impact of the modern presidency on presidential success in the U.S. Congress. *Legislative Studies Quarterly* 7(November): 515–532.

Cole, Richard L., and Caputo, David A. (1979). Presidential control of the senior civil service: Assessing the strategies of the Nixon years. *American Political Science Review* 73(June): 399–413.

Cottam, Richard W., and Rockman, Bert A. (1984). In the shadow of substance: presidents as foreign policy makers. In David P. Forsythe (ed.), *American Foreign Policy In An Uncertain World.* Lincoln, Neb.: University of Nebraska Press.

Covington, Cary R. (1981). Organizational memory development in three presidential agencies. Paper presented at the annual meeting of the Midwest Political Science Association, Cincinnati, Ohio.

Cronin, Thomas E. (1980). *The State of the Presidency* (2nd ed.). Boston: Little, Brown.

Cummings, Milton, C. (1966). *Congressmen and the Electorate: Elections for the U.S. House and the President, 1920–1964.* New York: Free Press.

Davis, Eric L. (1979a). Legislative liaison in the Carter administration. *Political Science Quarterly* 94(Summer): 287–301.

Davis, Eric L. (1979b). Legislative reform and the decline of presidential influence on Capitol Hill. *British Journal of Political Science* 9(October): 465–479.

Destler, I. M. (1972). *Presidents, Bureaucrats, and Foreign Policy: The Politics of Organizational Reform.* Princeton, N.J.: Princeton University Press.

Edwards, George C. III (1976). Presidential influence in the House: presidential prestige as a source of presidential power. *American Political Science Review* 70(March): 101–113.

Edwards, George C. III (1980a). *Presidential Influence in Congress.* San Francisco: W. H. Freeman.

Edwards, George C. III (1980b). Presidential legislative skills as a source of influence in Congress. *Presidential Studies Quarterly* 10(Spring): 211–223.

Edwards, George C. III (1981). The quantitative study of the presidency. *Presidential Studies Quarterly* 11(Spring): 146–150.

Edwards, George C. III (1983). *The Public Presidency: The Pursuit of Popular Support.* New York: St. Martin's.

Etheredge, Lloyd S. (1978). Personality effects on American foreign policy, 1898–1968: a test of interpersonal generalization theory. *American Political Science Review* 72(June): 434–451.

Fiorina, Morris P. (1981). *Retrospective Voting in American National Elections.* New Haven: Yale University Press.

Fishel, Jeff (1980). Presidential elections and presidential agendas: the Carter administration in contemporary historical perspective. Working Paper #001, Center for Congressional and Presidential Studies, The American University, Washington, D.C.

George, Alexander L. (1972). The case for multiple advocacy in making foreign policy. *American Political Science Review* 66(September): 751–785.

George, Alexander L. (1974). Assessing presidential character. *World Politics* 26(January): 234–282.

George, Alexander L. (1980). *Presidential Decision Making in Foreign Policy: The Effective Use of Information and Advice.* Boulder, Colo.: Westview.

George, Alexander L., and George, Juliette L. (1956). *Woodrow Wilson and Colonel House: A Personality Study.* New York: John Day.

Glad, Betty (1980). *Jimmy Carter: In Search of the Great White House.* New York: W. W. Norton.

Greenstein, Fred I. (1982). *The Hidden-Hand Presidency: Eisenhower As Leader.* New York: Basic Books.

Grossman, Michael Baruch, and Kumar, Martha Joynt (1981). *Portraying the President: The White House and the News Media.* Baltimore: Johns Hopkins University Press.

Hargrove, Erwin C. (1973). Presidential personality and revisionist views of the presidency. *American Journal of Political Science* 17(November): 819–836.

Heclo, Hugh (1974). *Modern Social Politics in Britain and Sweden: From Relief to Income Maintenance*. New Haven: Yale University Press.

Heclo, Hugh (1975). OMB and the presidency: the problem of neutral competence. *The Public Interest* 38(Winter): 80–98.

Heclo, Hugh (1977). *A Government of Strangers: Executive Politics in Washington*. Washington: The Brookings Institution.

Heclo, Hugh (1981). The changing presidential office. In Meltsner, ed., *Politics and The Oval Office*, pp. 161–184. San Francisco: Institute for Contemporary Studies.

Hess, Stephen (1981). *The Washington Reporters*. Washington, D.C.: The Brookings Institution.

Hibbs, Douglas A., Jr., with the assistance of R. Douglas Rivers and Nicholas Vasilatos (1982). The dynamics of political support for American presidents among occupational and partisan groups. *American Journal of Political Science* 26(May): 312–332.

Hoadley, John F. (1980). The emergence of political parties in Congress, 1789–1803. *American Political Science Review* 74(September): 757–779.

Iyengar, Shanto, Peters, Mark D., and Kinder, Donald R. (1982). Experimental demonstrations of the 'not-so-minimal' consequences of television news programs. *American Political Science Review* 76(December): 848–858.

Jones, Charles O. (1983). Presidential negotiation with Congress. In Anthony King (ed.), *Both Ends of The Avenue*. Washington: American Enterprise Institute.

Kavanagh, Dennis (1980). From gentleman to players: changes in political leadership. In William L. Gwyn and Richard Rose (eds.), *Britain: Progress and Decline*, Tulane Studies in Political Science, Vol. 17, pp. 73–93. New Orleans: Tulane University.

Kernell, Samuel (1978). Explaining presidential popularity. *American Political Science Review* 72 (June): 506–522.

Kessel, John H. (1975). *The Domestic Presidency: Decision-Making in the White House*. North Scituate, Mass.: Duxbury.

Kessel, John H. (1983a). The structures of the Carter White House. *American Journal of Political Science*, 27(August): 431–463.

Kessel, John H. (1983b). The structures of the Reagan White House. Paper presented at the annual meeting of the American Political Science Association, Chicago.

Kinder, Donald R., and Kiewiet, D. Roderick (1981). Sociotropic politics: the American case. *British Journal of Political Science* 11(January): 129–161.

Kinder, Donald R., Iyengar, Shanto, Kroswick, Jon A., and Peters, Mark D. (1983). More than meets the eye: the impact of television news on evaluations of presidential performance. Paper presented at the annual meeting of the Midwest Political Science Association, Chicago.

King, Anthony (1975). Executives. In Fred I. Greenstein and Nelson Polsby (eds.), *Handbook of Political Science: Governmental Institutions and Processes*, Vol. 5, pp. 173–255. Reading, Mass.: Addison-Wesley.

King, Anthony (1969). Political parties in western democracies: some sceptical reflections. *Polity* 2(Fall): 111–141.

Kirkpatrick, Jeane (1976). *The New Presidential Elite*. New York: Twentieth Century Fund, Russell Sage.

Kleppner, Paul (1979). *The Third Electoral System*, 1853–1892. Chapel Hill, N.C.: University of North Carolina Press.

Latcham, John S. (1982). President McKinley's active-positive character: a comparative revision with Barber's typology. *Presidential Studies Quarterly* 12(Fall): 491–521.

Leontief, Wassily (1971). Theoretical assumptions and nonobserved facts. *American Economic Review* 61(March): 1–7.

Lewis-Beck, Michael S. (1980). Economic conditions and executive popularity: the French experience. *American Journal of Political Science* 24(May): 306–323.

Light, Paul C. (1981). The president's agenda: notes on the timing of domestic choice. *Presidential Studies Quarterly*, 11(Winter): 67–82.

Light, Paul C. (1982). *The President's Agenda: Domestic Policy Choice From Kennedy to Carter*. Baltimore: Johns Hopkins University Press.

Lindblom, Charles E. (1977). *Politics and Markets*. New York: Basic Books.

Lowi, Theodore J. (1972). Four systems of policy, politics, and choice. *Public Administration Review* 32(July/August): 298–310.

Manley, John F. (1978). Presidential power and White House lobbying. *Political Science Quarterly* 93(Summer): 255–275.

March, James G., and Olsen, Johan P. (1976). *Ambiguity and Choice in Organizations*. Bergen: Universitetsforlaget.

March, James G., and Olsen, Johan P. (1983). What administrative reorganization tells us about governing. *American Political Science Review* 77(June): 281–296.

Meltsner, Arnold J., ed. (1981). *Politics and The Oval Office: Toward Presidential Governance*. San Francisco: Institute for Contemporary Studies.

Merry, Henry J. (1980). *Five-Branch Government: The Full Measure of Constitutional Checks and Balances*. Urbana, Ill.: University of Illinois Press.

Miller, Arthur H., Goldenberg, Edie N., and Erbring, Lutz (1979). Typeset politics: impact of newspapers on public confidence. *American Political Science Review* 73(March): 67–84.

Miroff, Bruce (1976). *Pragmatic Illusions: The Presidential Politics of John F. Kennedy*. New York: David McKay.

Miroff, Bruce (1980). Beyond Washington. *Society* 17(July/August): 66–72.

Miroff, Bruce (1981). Presidential leverage over social movements: the Johnson White House and civil rights. *Journal of Politics* 43(February): 2–23.

Mowery, David C., Kamlet, Mark S., and Crecine, John P. (1980). Presidential management of budgetary and fiscal policymaking. *Political Science Quarterly* 95(fall): 395–423.

Mueller, John (1970). Presidential popularity from Truman to Johnson. *American Political Science Review* 64(March): 18–34.

Nakamura, Robert T., and Sullivan, Denis G. (1982). Neo-conservatism and presidential nomination reforms: a critique. *Congress and the Presidency* 9(autumn): 79–98.

Nathan, Richard P. (1983). *The Administrative Presidency*. New York: Wiley.

Nelson, Michael (1982). Sentimental science: recent essays on the politics of presidential selection. *Congress and the Presidency* 9(autumn): 99–106.

Neustadt, Richard E. (1954). Presidency and legislation: the growth of central clearance. *American Political Science Review* 48(September): 641–671.

Neustadt, Richard E. (1980). *Presidential Power: The Politics of Leadership From FDR to Carter*. New York: Wiley.

Oppenheimer, Bruce I. (1980). Policy effects of U.S. House reform: decentralization and the capacity to resolve energy issues. *Legislative Studies Quarterly* 5(February): 5–30.

Pempel, T. J. (1977). *Policymaking in Contemporary Japan*. Ithaca, N.Y.: Cornell University Press.

Peters, B. Guy (1981). The problem of bureaucratic government. *Journal of Politics* 43(February): 56–82.

Pika, Joseph A. (1981). Moving beyond the Oval Office: problems in studying the presidency. *Congress and the Presidency* 9(Winter, 1981-82): 17–36.

Polsby, Nelson W. (1977). Against presidential greatness. *Commentary* 13(January): 61–63.

Polsby, Nelson W. (1981). The Washington community, 1960–1980. In *The New Congress*, eds. Thomas E. Mann and Norman J. Ornstein. Washington: American Enterprise Institute, pp. 7-31.

Polsby, Nelson W., and Wildavsky, Aaron (1980). *Presidential Elections: Strategies of American Electoral Politics* (5th ed.). New York: Scribner's.

Porter, Roger B. (1980). *Presidential Decision Making: The Economic Policy Board*. Cambridge: Cambridge University Press.

Presser, Stanley, and Converse, Jean M. (1976). On Stimson's interpretation of declines in presidential popularity. *Public Opinion Quarterly*, 40(Winter, 1976-77): 538–541.

Randall, Ronald (1979). Presidential power versus bureaucratic intransigence: the influence of the Nixon administration on welfare policy. *American Political Science Review* 73(September): 795–810.

Ranney, Austin (1975). *Curing the Mischiefs of Faction: Party Reform in America*. Berkeley: University of California Press.

Riker, William H. (1982). The two-party system and Duverger's Law: an essay on the history of political science. *American Political Science Review* 76(December): 753–766.

Rockman, Bert A. (1980). Carter's troubles. *Society* 17(July/August): 34–40.

Rockman, Bert A. (1981). America's Departments of State: irregular and regular syndromes of policy making. *American Political Science Review* 75(December): 911–927.

Rockman, Bert A. (1984). *The Leadership Question: The Presidency and the American System.* New York: Praeger.

Rose, Richard (1976). *Managing Presidential Objectives.* New York: The Free Press.

Rose, Richard, and Suleiman, Ezra, eds. (1980). *Presidents and Prime Ministers.* Washington, D.C.: American Enterprise Institute.

Rose, Richard (1980a). British government: the job at the top. In Rose and Suleiman, eds., *Presidents and Prime Ministers*, pp. 1–49.

Rose, Richard (1980b). *Do Parties Make a Difference?* Chatham, N.J.: Chatham House.

Rose, Richard (1980c). Government against sub-governments: a European perspective on Washington. In Rose and Suleiman, eds., *Presidents and Prime Ministers*, pp. 284–347.

Searing, Donald D. (1969). Models and images of man and society in leadership theory. *Journal of Politics* 31(February): 3–31.

Shapiro, Martin (1981). The president and the federal courts. In Meltsner, ed., *Politics and the Oval Office*, pp. 141–150.

Shull, Steven A. (1979). *Presidential Policy Making: An Analysis.* Brunswick, Ohio: King's Court.

Sigelman, Lee (1979). The dynamics of presidential support: an overview of research findings. *Presidential Studies Quarterly* 9(spring): 206–215.

Spitzer, Robert J. (1982). *The Presidency and Public Policy: The Four Arenas of Presidential Power.* Tuscaloosa: University of Alabama Press.

Steinbruner, John D. (1974). *The Cybernetic Theory of Decision: New Dimensions of Political Analysis.* Princeton, N.J.: Princeton University Press.

Stimson, James A. (1976). Public support for American presidents: a cyclical model. *Public Opinion Quarterly* 40(Spring): 1–21.

Stokes, Donald E. (1967). Parties and the nationalization of electoral forces. In William Nisbet Chambers and Walter Dean Burnham (eds.), *The American Party Systems: Stages of Political Development*, pp. 182–202. New York: Oxford University Press.

Thomas, Norman C. (1980). An inquiry into presidential and parliamentary government. In Harold D. Clarke, Colin Campbell, F. Q. Quo, and Arthur Goddard (eds.), *Parliament, Policy and Representation*, pp. 276–306. Toronto: Methuen.

Wayne, Stephen J. (1978). *The Legislative Presidency.* New York: Harper & Row.

Wegge, David G. (1981). Neustadt's Presidential Power: The test of time and empirical research on the presidency. *Presidential Studies Quarterly*, 11(summer): 342–347.

Wildavsky, Aaron, ed. (1975). *Perspectives on the Presidency.* Boston: Little, Brown.

Wildavsky, Aaron (1975). System is to politics as morality is to man: a sermon on the presidency. In Wildavsky, ed., *Perspectives on the Presidency*, pp. 526–539.

Wildavsky, Aaron (1976). The past and future presidency. In Nathan Glazer and Irving Kristol (eds.), *The American Commonwealth—1976*, pp. 56–76. New York: Basic Books.

Wills, Garry (1970). *Nixon Agonistes: The Crisis of the Self-Made Man.* Boston, Houghton Mifflin.

Wilson, James Q. (1962). *The Amateur Democrat: Club Politics in Three Cities.* Chicago: University of Chicago Press.

Young, James Sterling (1966). *The Washington Community, 1800–1828.* New York: Columbia University Press.

CHAPTER 7

THE SOCIAL SCIENCE OF JUDICIAL POLITICS

James L. Gibson

Advances in the scientific study of politics have not accrued evenly or monotonically over the past three decades. For example, as early as 1961, it was asserted that the behavioral movement in political science had overtaken virtually the entire discipline. In proclaiming the success of behavioralism, Robert Dahl asserted that what had begun as a radical protest against unscientific (and largely nonrigorous) political inquiry had become so widely accepted as to constitute mainstream political science (Dahl, 1961). Twenty years later, and after political science had flirted with "postbehavioralism" (see Easton, 1969), John Wahlke was not nearly so sanguine. In his assessment of the discipline, Wahlke described political science not as "behavioral," but rather as "prebehavioral" (Wahlke, 1979).[1] In both its failure to imbed political behavior research in macro-level theories of politics, and in its reliance on flawed, mentalistic conceptions of human nature, political science could hardly be deemed to be behavioral, Wahlke argued. Most recently, the scientific status of the discipline was questioned further. Charles Lindblom has considered the claim that significant portions of the discipline are very nearly "unscientific" due to implicit ideological commitments (Lindblom, 1982). He provided several prominent illustrations of deviance from the supposed value neutrality of scientific political research. A comparison of the perspectives of Wahlke, Dahl, and Lindblom could support the thesis that the discipline may have made little progress toward becoming more behavioral and scientific.

There is little evidence that the study of judicial politics, by which I mean the study of the authoritative allocation of values by those working within legal institutions, has been successful at countering the trend that characterizes the discipline as a whole. Despite a quick start in the 1950s on the track toward behavioral and scientific inquiry, progress has been uneven. Substantial support for nonscientific frameworks for analyzing judicial politics has become evident of late; exploratory research is still more common than confirmatory research; and there has been a notable lack of progress in the level of methodological sophistication typifying the subfield. Indeed, quite in contrast to the unification of the discipline perceived by Warren Miller (1981), there is great diversity in the epistemological, theoretical, and methodological positions of judicial scholars. Although eclectic approaches to judicial politics may be desirable, there is ample room for consternation among those who favor scientific inquiry as a superior means of knowing about things judicial.

In this chapter, I review and evaluate the current state of judicial politics scholarship. At the outset, several limitations to this review ought to be acknowledged and made explicit. First, I consider the field from the perspective of the development of a *science* of judicial politics. Thus, research that contributes little to scientific inquiry, even though it may contribute to knowledge acceptable within other epistemological frameworks, is given only passing and scant attention. This also means that much of the important policy-oriented research receives little consideration here. Second, evaluations and exhortations are derived from a fairly idealized (but explicit, see below) conception of the scientific enterprise. Of course, no area of inquiry—not even natural science—approximates the ideal, but it is nonetheless useful to have some idea of what the field will look like if it ever "arrives." High standards are employed, not in an effort to paint the field black, but rather out of concern to articulate goals and to identify specific strategies for future work.

Finally, my review is to a considerable degree retrospective. It assesses the degree to which the procedures, assumptions and promises of judicial politics research in the early 1960s have been fulfilled. It might be argued by others that new directions have rendered the old roadmaps obsolete and of little interest. That is a question for full, complete, and spirited debate (see, for example, Stumpf et al., 1983), but it is beyond the mandate of this chapter.

Several continua are employed in assessing the field, including

1. The degree to which judicial politics research is generalizable, reproducible, and intersubjectively transmissable;
2. The degree to which extant theory is logically structured and capable of producing empirically testable hypotheses;
3. The degree to which measures of key concepts are reliable and valid, and the degree to which statistical models are isomorphic with the structure of the reality they purport to represent.

ESPISTEMOLOGICAL FOUNDATIONS OF JUDICIAL POLITICS

Perhaps the single most endearing attribute of scientific research is that it is intersubjectively transmissable; that is, through reproduction, knowledge generated by the scientific method can be known independently by all. Unlike nonscientific epistemologies, an attempt is made to minimize the influence of the investigator on the information produced, and thus each researcher can independently confirm the observations made by other researchers. Disagreements over the nature of reality are fairly easy, in principle at least, to resolve. Most importantly, because there are commonly accepted procedures of proof, the *falsifiability* of propositions is possible. The hallmark of scientific inquiry is its reproducibility.[2]

For political science qua science the operational definition of "science" is behavioralism. Easton provides the following list of the widely accepted premises and objectives of behavioralism:

1. *Regularities*—the assumption that "there are discoverable uniformities in political behavior."
2. *Verification*—the assumption that "validity of such generalizations about those regularities must be testable, in principle, by a reference to relevant behavior."
3. *Techniques*—the assumption that "means for acquiring and interpreting data are problematic and need to be examined self-consciously."
4. *Quantification*—the assumption that measurement and quantification, where possible, relevant, and meaningful, are essential to interpreting data and verifying generalizations.
5. *Values*—the assumption that "ethical evaluation and empirical analysis should be kept analytically distinct."
6. *Systematization*—the assumption that "theory and research are to be seen as closely intertwined parts of a coherent and orderly body of knowledge."
7. *Pure science*—the assumption that "understanding and explanation of political behavior logically precede and provide the basis for efforts to utilize political knowledge in the solution of urgent practical problems of society."
8. *[Interdisciplinary] integration*—the assumption that "political research can ignore the findings of other disciplines only at the peril of weakening the validity and undermining the generality of its own results." (Easton, 1962, pp. 6–7)

It is this conception, which of course is not the only one available or legitimate, of scientific political science that guides my evaluation of the field of judicial politics.

All social science suffers from a certain amount of nonreproducibility, and the field of judicial politics is no exception. The earliest scaling research (e.g., Pritchett, 1948; Schubert, 1965, 1974; Ulmer, 1969), in which the hypothesis that judges' values determine their decisions was tested, relied in its initial operational step on a fairly subjective classification of court cases. Other stages in the analytical process have been alleged to be arbitrary (see Tanenhaus, 1966). Identifying blocs or clusters of judges on the United States Supreme Court (e.g., Ulmer, 1965) is similarly subject to a certain amount of arbitrariness, if not subjectivity (but see Spaeth, 1968). So too are criteria for factor rotation in psychometric analyses (at least until recently; see Gow, 1979). But as the field has developed, fairly arbitrary decisions have become widely accepted as conventions, thus contributing to reproducibility. And more generally, early research on the behavior of appellate court judges was typically self-conscious about its epistemological underpinnings and their methodological implications.

Largely as a function of the expansion of judicial politics research to the study of trial courts, a significant amount of work today is characterized by much weakened ties to scientific epistemology, especially insofar as the key issue of reproducibility is concerned. For instance, instead of attempting to minimize the interaction of the observer with the observed, those favoring participant observation as a means of learning about judicial politics advocate many fewer constraints on the observer. Perhaps one of the most self-conscious, and reasonable, statements of this research perspective can be found in Ryan et al. (1980, Appendix A). Describing their research design as one of passive participant observation, they are quite candid about the relationships they developed with their subjects:

> to establish rapport [with the judges], we tried to adopt a mental set that conveyed both empathy and informed understanding of the judicial work environment. . . . Most judges came to view the observer as one who empathized[3] with him and the work environment. Usually this interpretation was quite accurate. . . . We were frequently seen by the judge as a temporary judicial colleague or ally. For our research purposes, this impression was crucial, and in many instances we did become temporary colleagues, but "emotionally detached" ones. Thus, in many but not all situations the observer tended to be accepted as an ally, someone in whom the judge could confide and to whom he could frequently complain. (Ryan et al., 1980, pp. 253–55)

Unlike many who assume such an epistemological and methodological stance, Ryan and his colleagues are concerned with the concomitant problems of reactivity, reliability, and validity, although ultimately they are unable to assess rigorously the degree of measurement error or to ameliorate the effects of such sources of error. Consequently, it might fairly be asked whether different researchers would reach the same conclusions about the court systems Ryan and his colleagues studied. Indeed, the authors themselves are even uncertain that the four members of their research team perceive reality in similar or even compatible ways. For instance, "each of the authors possesses a somewhat different intellectual and disciplinary training; no amount of effort or practice can entirely eliminate these differences in 'perspective' " (Ryan et al., 1980, p. 257). Without at least minimal standardization of the methodology, it is impossible to know that their observations can be reproduced by other judicial scholars. Absent the ability to reproduce, falsifiability is made difficult. In short, the knowledge they generated is of suspicious intersubjective transmissability.

Though such research may be valuable in and of itself, its contribution to the development of a science of the judicial process is limited.

The problem of reproducible findings is ever so much more difficult when combined with concepts that are ill-defined in the first place. Although the concept "political or legal culture" will be considered more fully below, it should be noted here that ethnography, especially, is susceptible to the problem of reproducibility. "Ethnography examines how people think about what they do and how they organize and interpret the actions of others. This is what is meant by the task of describing a culture; the task is not simply to describe the customary behaviors, but is also to describe the cultural meaning of those behaviors" (Mather, 1979, p. 3). Two important attributes of ethnography are "to describe the rules of culturally appropriate behavior rather than to predict actual behavior," and " 'to discover, not prescribe, the significant stimuli in the subject's world' " (Mather, 1979, p. 4, citing Frake, 1969: p. 124). Though social scientists can easily agree with the proscription against prescription, and, substantively, her argument that the nature of plea bargaining requires "data on the social perceptions and interactions of participants" (p. 5) is completely tenable, "culture," especially as conceptualized in this fashion, is never given the rigorous operational meaning necessary for reproducibility. Indeed, the whole research problem can be (and has been) more systematically attacked through much more scientific research designs (e.g., Howard, 1981; Asher, 1973; Kirkpatrick and McLemore, 1977). Scientists and other scholars alike perceive the importance of norms on the operation of legal institutions, but the scientific approach to the problem serves far better the generation of intersubjectively transmissable knowledge.

A myriad of implications flow from the reliance on epistemologies supporting methodologies within which reproducibility is difficult. Without adherence to a common method, it is hard to determine whether hypotheses have been supported by empirical findings. For instance, how can the ethnographer and the social scientist agree on the nature of the evidence necessary to support the hypothesis that culture influences the actions of the courts? Indeed, many of the propositions drawn from participant observation research are in some considerable sense nonfalsifiable. More generally, the cumulativeness of research, so critical to the development of a science of judicial politics, is severely constrained. Because these nonscientific methods rely so heavily on the idiographic assumption that each court is unique (see below), it is difficult to draw generalizations across different systems and across different research projects. There is also an inordinate emphasis given to description, in contrast to more analytical research. As we all recognize, to see the world as the participants see it is not necessarily the analytical *coup de grace*; rather, if useful at all, it is the point from which abstraction and analysis *begin*. Certainly, what the participants say they do is an important datum; but, as we all know, what people say they do, even when they are completely sincere and honest, is not necessarily the same as what they do in fact. And while sometimes seeming to be committed to holism,[4] participant observation research frequently is more concerned with describing in minute detail the attributes of the trees, even to the point of allowing such descriptions to obscure the outlines of the forest. It is also somewhat nonplussing to consider that lower courts are judged to be too complex to study with traditional social scientific methods, while appellate courts, as well as a host of nonjudicial institutions, are not so considered.

Ethnographic and other participant observation research strategies can make some contribution to the understanding of judicial politics, and I would not gainsay that at exploratory stages of inquiry there is some utility in such approaches (for a superb example from another field see Fenno, 1977). But, as argued below, exploration and induction must ultimately give way to deduction and confirmatory research requiring scientific methodology. From the perspective of a science of judicial politics, ethnographic research is not an end in itself; rather its utility is as a transitional epistemological position.

SUBSTANTIVE THEORY

In the past three decades, palpable progress has been made in the development of theories of judicial politics. There is today a greater awareness of the need for and the value of theoretical research, and prominent examples of highly developed theoretical areas can be found, as, for example, in research on judicial decision making. The accumulation of theory in the last thirty years has been a slow process, but there have certainly been discernible advances.

For instance, recent research on lower court decision-making processes has made tremendous theoretical strides through the application of organizational theory (e.g., Flemming, 1982; Nardulli, 1978). Rather than some ill-formed notions of interactions of the various actors in the criminal justice process, relatively well-developed conceptual schemes for analyzing the peculiar form of collegial decision making of the work group are advanced. Such schemes are capable of being generalized to the formally collegial processes of appellate court decision making, thereby contributing to theoretical parsimony. Especially as such efforts integrate micro-level and macro-level decision making determinants, as in the pioneering work of Eisenstein, Nardulli, and Flemming (1982), the theoretical gains are truly impressive.

Nonetheless, there are several limitations of extant research that must be overcome in future research. These limitations include an excessive reliance on description, to the detriment of hypothesis testing; an overreliance on induction as a means of developing theory; an aversion to theoretical complexity; a commitment to idiographic theory; and a lack of cross-level (macro-micro) theories. This is not to say that these problems are peculiar to the subfield of judicial politics; they exist to a lesser or greater degree in all areas of political science. But without solutions to these problems, it will be difficult indeed for any area of the discipline to develop much further. Thus, it is fruitful to consider each of these points in greater detail.

The Pervasiveness of Description

A considerable proportion of all research on judicial politics, and especially of research on the lower courts, is descriptive. Even some work appearing to be analytical in focus is actually little more than descriptions of multivariate frequency distributions. We occasionally think of description as involving statements about univariate frequency distributions, but, absent theory, statements about multivariate frequency distributions are also simply descriptions of data. Perhaps the most obvious example of this is the early research on judicial decision making that was concerned with scaling judges' votes. Little theory was proposed; instead, patterns, albeit complex ones, in the voting behavior of judges were described in some detail.

It should not be assumed, however, that descriptive research is of no value: instead, description is a necessary precursor to the development and testing of theory. For instance, the pathbreaking research of C. Herman Pritchett (e.g., 1941, 1948) did not really advance a rigorous theory of judicial decision making. Instead, it presented systematic descriptions of behavioral patterns. But without the precision of Pritchett's description, as well as his penetrating insights, the later theoretical work on the problem (e.g., psychometric theories, largely associated with the work of Schubert, Spaeth, Tanenhaus, Ulmer, and others) might have been long delayed. Moreover, description is itself occasionally an implicit test of a hypothesis (for instance, descriptions of court caseloads over time; see, for instance, Heumann, 1978). Thus descriptive research certainly plays an important function in scientific inquiry.

Yet, ultimately, as is widely recognized, it is essential to move beyond description. At the level of the trial courts, for instance, it is unclear that additional exploratory work is necessary. Decision making in such courts reflects a mixture of influences from individual-level propensities and from institutional-level constraints (formal and informal). Rather than being concerned to describe the endless variety of minute variations in local practices, much greater effort should be devoted to formalization of theories of individual and organizational determinants of processes. The mapping and analysis of these social networks is of foremost importance, not the cataloging of interesting but theoretically barren nuances in local practices.

There is perhaps no better illustration of the value, and limitations, of descriptive research than Heumann's study (1978) of the processes through which actors in the criminal trial courts are socialized to organizational norms and values. Heumann's research provides a number of significant insights into this process; as, for instance, in his emphasis on the initiative of the newcomer in

learning relevant norms rather than on the desire of the organization to inculcate particular values. His theoretical framework, however, would profit from
formalization so that more rigorous hypotheses can be deduced and tested empirically. A great deal of the research on lower courts is of this nature.

The Paucity of Deductive Theory

Perhaps the most significant general problem of theory in the study of judicial and other politics stems from placing greater emphasis on induction than
on deduction. Not surprisingly, given the descriptive orientation of much of
our research, theory tends to be inductively derived. Induction is certainly valuable — indeed, the theory building/testing process can be thought of successive
iterations of deduction and induction — but excessive emphasis on induction
creates a number of problems. First, inductive research contributes to the ad
hoc character of most judicial politics theory. A plethora of propositions may
be derived from empirical analysis, but all too rare is the imposition of logical
structure on the these propositions. Perhaps this is not a natural limitation of
the inductive approach, but work that collects the miscellaneous empirical propositions that emerge, that formalizes them, and that embeds them in a logical
structure is extremely ⊬aluable, though all too uncommon. And of course without the formalization of theory, it is impossible to proceed to the deduction of
nontrivial hypotheses that can be empirically tested.

And because the research design typically *precedes* theory, induction does
not generate rigorous or comprehensive theory. It is rarely possible to discount
alternative explanations, because they have not been anticipated and the proper
data have not been collected. Especially when inductive research is combined
with a nonscientific epistemology and methodology, the utility of the theory
generated is limited.

Finally, the existence of enormous quantities of measurement error (see
below) makes induction a difficult process. It is hard enough to identify patterns in data uncontaminated by random and systematic error. The presence of
such error makes induction perilous and arduous.

It is not difficult to provide illustrations of the limitations of induction. For
instance, almost all research on the social backgrounds of judges is subject to
this problem, Typically, such research proceeds with little advance theory, instead collecting data on every variable available. After correlations of everything with everything are calculated, post hoc efforts at theory building take
place and a host of essentially bivariate propositions is derived. The final step in
the process, the linking of these propositions together within a logical framework, rarely takes place, however. Thus, social background studies have generated precious little formal socialization theory capable of generating testable
hypotheses. All too frequently this is the fate of inductive research.

Unfortunately, there is a substantial amount of affection for inductive approaches to the study of judicial politics, especially at the lower court level. As Malcolm Feeley, one of the leaders in the area, asserts:

> Comparative analysis implies a deductive research strategy, elaborating on a typology, testing hypotheses, or applying a theory. At a minimum, it requires *advance* knowledge of relevant factors, for it must impose requirements on the data collection so that the data will be truly comparable and the variables operationalized in equivalent fashion. I am not convinced that current knowledge of criminal court processes is well developed, and unless or until there is a substantial body of carefully drawn descriptive and inductive research on which typologies can be drawn and until classifications are made, the benefits of an analysis of a single setting may be as great, if not greater than, those of comparative studies. (Feeley, 1979, pp. xvi–xvii, emphasis in original)

And:

> Most students of the criminal court process agree that the operations of the criminal courts are shaped by little-understood factors, and that decisions are made as a consequence of an uncharted, complex, and interdependent set of relationships. Both of these factors militate against a comparative approach which by definition must *impose* at the outset a developed framework on the research. While there have been a number of studies comparing outcomes in several court settings, by and large these have been superficial reports which did not convince even their authors that they adequately controlled for major relevant factors. (Feeley, 1979, pp. xvi, emphasis in original)

> To the extent that [the analysis provides a general explanation, one that maintains an interest in and focus on the generic rather than on the particular] . . . the researcher undertaking a study of a single setting or a single institution has no need to apologize for not adopting the hallmark of social science, comparative analysis, and in fact may be able to make the claim that, unfettered by the constraints of predetermined data collection requirements, he [or she] is freer to pursue general theory. (Feeley, 1979, p. xvii)

Thus, if "theory" requires logically interrelated sets of propositions from which nontrivial hypotheses can be deduced, then there is a paucity of theory about judicial politics. The components of many judicial politics theories are frequently inductively derived, logically unconnected propositions. Formalization of such propositions is quite difficult, but quite useful. Perhaps, however, as descriptive/inductive research accumulates at a rapid pace (e.g., Eisenstein and Jacob, 1977; Heumann, 1978; Utz, 1978; Mather, 1979; Feeley, 1979; and Flemming, 1982), it will be possible to devote greater research attention to more deductively oriented research.

The Comprehensiveness of Theory

There are some notable undertakings aimed at expanding the comprehensiveness of extant theories of judicial politics. At the level of the appellate courts, Ulmer's (1972, 1978) modeling of certiorari and merit decisions by judges of the U.S. Supreme Court represents an effort to bring together several different theoretical strains. Similarly, Baum's (1977) research on the California Supreme Court develops a quite sophisticated, multistage decision making model. Other examples could easily be noted (e.g., Eisenstein et al., 1982). Generally, though, comprehensive modeling is the exception.

Elsewhere I have argued that it is possible to construct a fairly comprehensive model of decision making from the variety of seemingly competitive decision making theories (Gibson, 1983). Basically, "judges' decisions are a function of what they prefer to do, tempered by what they think they ought to do, but constrained by what they perceive is feasible to do" (Gibson, 1983, p. 9). This simple proposition is capable of integrating attitude theory, including theories linking attitudes to case stimuli, or "cues," role theory, and theories of institutional, or "organizational," constraints on decision making. And the resulting integration clearly is a cross-level theory, considering as it does case stimuli, individual-level propensities, and institutional or contextual attributes.

Once this model of decision making is fully articulated, it becomes a fairly simple matter to link it to a host of interesting political problems. For instance, the political opportunity structure, as well as the formal and informal incentives provided by selection and recruitment systems, are terribly important in terms of selecting candidates with particular role orientations and/or socializing newcomers to particular value positions. There is a feedback loop involved as well. To the extent that the role orientations of judicial actors, for instance, encourage representative behavior on the part of these actors, citizen perceptions of and support for judicial institutions may be affected. After all, the *"IMPEACH EARL WARREN!"* road signs of the 1960s and 1970s were ample evidence of this feedback loop. Although there are many details of a comprehensive model that must be worked out, and a variety of hypotheses that need testing, the rough contours of such a model are at least discernible.

The problem of models that are not fully specified is not just an esthetic problem; instead, it leads to the extremely serious statistical problem of specification error. Statistical (and theoretical, for that matter) analyses that do not incorporate all relevant influences on the dependent variable are subject to bias in the estimates of the effects of the independent variables on the dependent variables. Because it is so unusual to understand or anticipate all or even most of the major determinants of key dependent variables, specification error is no doubt rife in empirical research on judicial politics, as it is in all other areas of political science.

Spuriousness is also a problem, as apparent in research on the effects of race on outcomes in criminal cases (e.g., Hagan, 1974). As a further example, it has been reported that prior prosecutorial experience is associated with more conservative decisions by judges (e.g., Tate, 1981). Does this mean that something about being a prosecutor influences the values of lawyers, making them more conservative? Perhaps not. It is possible that more conservative lawyers are attracted to prosecutorial positions, so that attitudes determine *both* the career experience and the decisions of judges. Thus, the relationship between prosecutorial experience and decisions would be spurious in the classical sense, with the direction of causality being misspecified in the original formulation. Finally, it must also be noted that theoretical completeness implies that the possibility of complex, nonlinear relationships has been considered. I will discuss this issue in greater detail below.

Thus, extant theories rarely purport to be comprehensive, making tests of critical hypotheses impossible, and resulting in large amounts of specification error. Although there has been considerable improvement over the simplistic, largely bivariate empirical models used in the past, complex, multivariate relationships ought to be more frequently modeled.

Nomothetic Theory

The generalizability of theory, as distinctive from the generalizability of empirical findings, is an issue that is rarely confronted by scholars of judicial politics. The generalizability of theory goes to the problem of the uniqueness of judicial phenomena; that is, whether it is necessary to develop theory that recognizes peculiarities of different court systems, the lower and appellate courts, and judicial and nonjudicial institutions. This question of uniqueness is directly associated with the role of comparison in scientific inquiry.

Scientific inquiry may incorporate in its objectives and methods one of two conflicting assumptions about the "knowability" of empirical phenomena.[5] This conflict centers on the question of the likelihood of developing general lawlike propositions about political processes. The first, the idiographic approach, asserts that

> social science statements cannot be universally true because the interaction of various characteristics within each [institution] creates unique, or at least varying, patterns of determination relative to each [institution]. Therefore, the identification of the [institution] in which a given phenomenon occurs is part of its explanation. In this extreme version of this position no general statements applicable across [institutions] are possible, and all social science statements must be confined to particular [institutions] (Przeworski and Teune, 1970, p. 7).

In the other view, the nomothetic, a fundamental similarity is assumed: *"if all relevant factors were known*, then the same multivariate statement would yield a deterministic explanation regardless of time and space" (Ibid., p. 7). Little is thought to be unique, although it is acknowledged that a deterministic model would be very, very complex. Thus, the two approaches differ in their assumptions about the fundamental similarities and dissimilarities of political phenomena.

Although this debate cannot yet be resolved by reference to empirical data, the nomothetic approach has two distinct advantages. First, if successful, propositions generated under this assumption would have greater explanatory power, but not at the expense of parsimony. Further, the nomothetic approach does not foreclose, a priori, efforts to identify all relevant variables that might account for cross-institutional differences. The idiographic assumption of uniqueness does not encourage theoretical completeness; a significant amount of unexplained variance is predicted by the model. Thus, the nomothetic approach is more compatible with the goals of scientific research.

In terms of cross-institutional research, this approach also requires acceptance of the "postulate of substitutability": *"lawlike statements are possible in the social sciences if and only if spatio-temporal parameters are treated as residua of variables potentially contributing to the explanation"* (Przeworski and Teune, 1970, p. 25). That is

> the characteristics of particular [institutions] can be expressed as general variables . . . and as such would be applicable across all [institutions]. In fact, whenever there is an [institution] specific factor that seems to be necessary for explanation, the conclusion should not be that [institutions] are unique but rather that it is necessary to identify some general factors so far not considered. This is indeed the primary function of comparative inquiry. (Ibid., p. 13)

In short, institutional names should be replaced with theoretical constructs to account for cross-institutional similarities and dissimilarities.

Institution-bound theories contribute little to the development of lawlike propositions about political processes. This should not be taken as a statement that all institutions are necessarily similar. To the extent that they are dissimilar, however, it is essential that theoretical dimensions be identified, and that institutional contexts be located on the dimensions, thus allowing the explanation of interinstitutional differences. The identification of appropriate continua offers the potential for truly general propositions explaining political phenomena.

A nice example of concern for nomothetic theory can be found in macro-level research on litigation rates. For instance, Sarat and Grossman (1975) are much concerned to develop a conceptual scheme that allows for the comparison of judicial and other dispute processing institutions. Such work thus treats courts as comparable to other political and nonpolitical institutions.

Many of those who study the lower courts adopt a fairly idiographic position, however. Illustrative of this group is the civil trial court research at the University of Wisconsin-Madison. In one of their papers that sought to link usage of the civil trial courts with political culture, the authors asserted:

> It is distinctly possible that courts, and the propensity to use them, are not nearly so well integrated into the political culture as we have assumed. A political culture explanation assumes that courts are an integral part of political society, that variance

consequently would be expected along political lines and could be explained as a function of political variables. But the data we have collected may be pointing in a different and unexpected direction. It may be that "courts are courts," and that what they (or at least the civil courts) share in common as participants in the American legal culture is more important than characteristics of the political environment in which they operate. Courts are not autonomous; they are part of a seamless web. Nevertheless, it may be that more weight should be given to "court" factors or even to random variations in the "local legal culture" or in the behavior of key individual actors (Grossman et al., 1982, p. 133)

There can be no more explicit example of an idiographic approach to theory building than is contained in the assertion that "courts are courts." Aside from a lack of parsimony, such a perspective is largely incompatible with the aspiration toward "covering law" that is common to science. The idiographic perspective is not uncommon among judicial politics scholars.

There have been a few limited attempts to generalize theory beyond judicial institutions. One of the first, and still one of the most innovative, is Danelski's effort (1970) to account for the behavior of Harold Burton as both a U.S. Senator and a U.S. Supreme Court justice. More recently, Canon and Baum (1981) exhibit concern for developing nomothetic theory in their effort to account for differences in the diffusion of innovations across judicial and legislative institutions. However, such research is rare and there still remains a need for large-scale projects aimed at developing cross-institutional explanations of political processes.

Thus, as in so many areas of political science, much of existing theory is of suspicious generalizability. This is not simply a limitation on extant empirical findings (although the proliferation of case studies makes this a serious problem as well), but instead reflects rather weak commitments to the development of nomothetic theory. Judicial institutions and processes (especially at the lower court level) are too often perceived as in some unspecified sense unique, with differences among different court systems, the lower and appellate courts, and judicial and nonjudicial institutions being so great as to render them virtually noncomparable.

The Cross-Level Problem

Little theory in the study of judicial politics is cross-level in nature. That is, adequate micro-level theories exist, as do adequate macro-level theories. But theory that crosses levels is rare.

The lack of cross-level theory is sometimes perceived as a more serious problem for micro-level research than for macro-level research. Wahlke, for instance, has been quite critical of micro-level work for its failure to identify relevant macro-level consequences. In essence, this is close to the allegation that micro-level research is not "political" enough. Thus:

It is sometimes said that political behavior research is "micro-level" study whereas political systems or governments viewed institutionally call for "macro-level" study. But, as Eulau has explained, "Commitment . . . to the individual person as the *empirical* unit of analysis . . . does not mean that research is restricted to the individual person as the *theoretical* focus of investigation (1963, pp. 13, 14, emphasis added). . . . This . . . suggests . . . another point about levels of political analysis which is almost universally neglected in political behavior research: political inquiry is rooted toward the "*macro*" end of the continuum, since it is there that the common subject matter uniting all political scientists is defined. . . . A *political* researcher can tell what aspects or elements of individual behavior are worth examining only by their ultimate bearing on such matters at higher levels of analysis (Wahlke, 1979, pp. 13, 15)

In short, the political relevance of micro-level research is suspect without cross-level linkages to macro-level theory.

For example, some might disparage micro-level research on decison making as having too much psychological content and too little political content. That may be a sophist argument, however. Those investigating the interrelationships of attitudes and behaviors do so out of the presumption that attitudes cause individual-level behaviors, behaviors that are in turn aggregated within institutional structures to create public policies. Moreover, the origin of attitudes is itself an important question, thus justifying the study of political socialization. At the aggregated level, the distribution of attitudes reflects, in part at least, the nature of the selection system and the incentives and disincentives to potential participants. At the individual level, political socialization—childhood, general adulthood, and socialization to specific institutions—shapes attitudes. The fact that participation in legislative institutions constitutes one important and well-used pathway to the bench has significant implications for the nature of the linkages between judges and their constituents, for public policy, and, ultimately, for levels of institutional support. Thus, though it is rare to find a fully specified presentation of the model, it is not entirely fair to criticize any particular piece of work for failure to make the cross-level linkages. Nonetheless, such linkages must at some point be explicitly made.

Macro-level research may also be criticized for failing to state explicitly its necessary assumptions about micro-level processes. More specifically, disembodied macro-level theory has severe limitations. For instance,

our macro-level theories need to be given behavioral underpinnings, even in instances where micro-level data may not be available. In order to pass back and forth between the micro and macro levels on a systematic basis it is necessary to state one's assumptions explicitly, and this, of course, implies that we need micro-level theories to justify our macro-level assumptions, and perhaps vice versa. (Blalock and Wilken, 1979, p. 2)

Much too little attention, for instance, has been given to the *processes* that underlie correlation coefficients. Research on the policy outputs of the United

States Supreme Court has shown a relationship between national opinion and the policy outputs of the Court (see Dahl, 1957; Adamany, 1973; Casper, 1976; Funston, 1975; Canon and Ulmer, 1976). But what micro-level processes might reasonably account for this correlation? Are Supreme Court justices acting as instructed delegates, basing their decisions on their perceptions of majority opinion? If so, how do they learn about public opinion? How do they define their constituency. And, perhaps most perplexingly, why do they act that way given the freedoms from both electoral sanctions and ambition? Surely Supreme Court justices do not act as delegates; the process must be more complex. Perhaps the justices are influenced by other national elites or other departments of the government. But whatever the processes (and some important clues are provided by Cook, 1977), the credibility of the macro-level correlation between opinion and policy is quite weak unless and until the micro-level contours of the process are detailed.

It is also common to see macro-level research that fails to specify fully the micro-level processes involved. For instance, Canon and Baum (1981) examined innovations in legal policies by the supreme courts of the American states. A mixture of macro-level and micro-level variables is used to predict court innovativeness (using the court as the unit of analysis), and generally they find that the dependence of courts on others to initiate litigation makes judicial innovation processes distinctive. However, only cursory mention is made of the micro-level processes involved. They assert, for example, that "many modern judges have adopted the view that the law should be flexible and responsive to social needs, and in doing so they have developed a more favorable attitude toward doctrinal innovation" (Canon and Baum, 1981, p. 985). This is essentially a statement about the role orientations of the judges, although the authors do not explicitly recognize it as such, and it is far from being fully developed theoretically. Canon and Baum present nearly all of the pieces of a cross-level, cross-institutional theory of innovation, but in the end they fail to actually integrate the pieces into a comprehensive theory.

It is less difficult to develop and test cross-level theories if one begins at the micro level and then moves to higher level influences. As I have argued:

Individuals make decisions, but they do so within the context of group, institutional, and environmental constraints. . . . The key to comprehensive modeling is the individual: that is, comprehensive modeling must begin with the individual decision maker as the unit of analysis. At the same time, the analysis must move beyond the individual to incorporate contextual effects. But these effects must be modeled through the sensory and behavioral modalities of individuals. Perceptions may be influenced by reality, but it is perceptions, not realities, that shape the behaviors of actors in judicial institutions. Although it may be interesting for some purposes to consider the causes of perceptual accuracy and inaccuracy . . . concepts such as *norms* must be given theoretical and operational meaning at the level of the individual in order to bridge the micro-macro gap. Only in this fashion can cross-level theories be developed. (Gibson, 1983, pp. 32–33)

Levin (1977) does just this in his examination of the trial court systems in Minneapolis and Pittsburgh. He is concerned about the micro-level linkage between the attitudes and behaviors of judges, about the linkage between behavior and policy outputs, and between policy outputs and system support. At the other end of the model, he analyzes the manner in which the selection system is biased toward those with particular attitudes and values, and ultimately, the manner in which the selection system is imbedded in the larger political cultures of the two cities. Thus, with great attention to detail, Levin proposes a theory that takes us from the system level, to the institution level, to the individual level, and back up to the institution and system levels. Though the number of cases for much of his analysis is limited (i.e., it is two), Levin's research is an excellent prototype for further work on the courts.

Thus, cross-level theories of judicial politics are rare, for two distinctive reasons. First, those doing macro-level research rarely are concerned to specify the micro-level processes accounting for macro-level correlations. Second, much micro-level research fails to make obvious its macro-level (some might say "political") consequences. The failure to develop cross-level approaches to judicial politics has significantly fragmented theory in the field.

Summary

By way of summary, it is useful to identify a piece of research that approximates the ideal. There is perhaps no better exemplar than Howard's 1981 study of the U.S. Courts of Appeals. Informed by role theory, a portion of this research is focused on the individual judge and very self-consciously tests hypotheses about the relationships between propensities and behavior. In addition to the micro-level analysis, however, the Courts of Appeals are also analyzed at the institutional level, considering the court as the unit of analysis, and inter-court relations are examined as well. Thus, there are three levels of analysis: the individual judge, the court, and the court system. Moreover, the very explicit attention to theory building and testing, as well as careful grounding in extant descriptive and theoretical work, is quite laudable. Howard's research reveals a great deal about how decisions are made within these institutions, how the institutions maintain themselves in the face of rather severe disintegrative incentives, and, more generally, how values are authoritatively allocated by the federal circuit courts. Thus, this research moves well beyond description: it tests hypotheses—at both the micro and macro levels—derived from fairly formalized theory, with relatively sophisticated multivariate analysis; while treating courts as distinctive, but far from unique, political institutions. One might hope that future theoretical research on judicial politics emulates this standard.

METHODOLOGICAL FOUNDATIONS

Many of the limitations of the field of judicial politics stem from, or are closely associated with, methodological problems. There are virtually no problems of methods (by which I mean research design, measurement, and statistical analysis) that do not have serious implications for the study of judicial politics. Some of the issues arise from peculiarities of the subject matter of the field (e.g., the nine-member United States Supreme Court generates a variety of small *N* problems), but most are common to the discipline as a whole. In this section I will consider issues of statistical complexity and multivariate analysis, research designs, and measurement error.

Statistical and Theoretical Complexity

Generally, statistical models of judicial behavior rarely are isomorphic with the reality they attempt to explain; instead the models depict processes that are unreasonably simplified. At a more abstract level, Blalock and Wilken have asserted:

> Our general theories, which are intended to apply to a wide variety of situations, must be highly complex, at least in the sense that they *allow for* possible complications that do not necessarily arise in each specific application. That is, when we consider special cases of the general theory we may be willing to assume that certain variables are effectively held constant or that they appear with zero coefficients. Therefore they may be ignored in these instances, even though in other situations they may turn out to be highly important as explanatory factors. . . . [But] a theory that is too complex and that introduces too many such unknowns will yield a hopeless situation in which none of the coefficients in the equations can be estimated by *any* means. . . . This means that the theorist has to straddle the fence between two desirable characteristics of a theory: realism and testability. The theory can be made increasingly realistic by adding to its complexity. But at some point it becomes too complex to be tested, not just in the sense of becoming unwieldy in a practical way but in the more fundamental sense of containing too many unknowns. . . . The only resolution to this very real practical problem that we can visualize is through a theory-construction process that allows for many more complexities than possibly can be handled in any single piece of research. In effect this implies that our theories must 'lead' our data-collection capabilities by a reasonable amount and must be sufficiently flexible to allow for additional complications introduced whenever measurement is crude or highly indirect. . . . Given the more complete and more general theory, a critic of any particular piece may then see more easily just where the shortcomings lie and how the necessarily incomplete knowledge based on one study may be fitted together with that derived from other similarly incomplete studies. This, of course, makes the job of the critic much easier, but it also facilitates the process of linking the results of diverse pieces of research, each of which may have its own unique combination of shortcomings. . . . The major point, then, is that from the standpoint of the cumulation of knowledge based on individually incomplete empirical studies, it is essential to state our theories in such a way that we allow for many more complexities than will ever be handled in any single piece of research. (1979, pp. 3–5)

Perhaps because judicial politics theories so rarely address complex processes, the typical statistical analysis involves little more than the assessment/of bivariate and multivariate linear relationships.

The origin of modern research on judicial politics was focused on essentially a bivariate model of decision making. The widely accepted psychometric model of decision making postulates a simple and direct relationship between attitudes and behaviors. Only as researchers have changed their focus away from appellate courts, where judges are less accessible and appropriate data much more difficult to acquire, has it been possible to develop theories of how attitudes interact with other factors to predict behavior. The simple proposition that judges do what they want to do is no longer tenable given the results of multivariate research.

Other examples of essentially bivariate models can be found. For years, scholars investigated the relationship between defendants' race and the severity of sanctions they receive in the criminal justice process without consideration of the possibility of spurious relationships, relationships discernible only through multivariate analysis (Hagan, 1974). Even social background analyses, typically involving several variables, are essentially "uniconceptual" (if not actually univariate) in nature.

Sophisticated statistical analysis is a necessary (albeit not sufficient) condition to the development of scientific theories of judicial politics. This is not to say that nonquantitative work is useless—it is frequently of heuristic value. Nor is it to say that complex (e.g., multiplicative) relationships should be indiscriminantly asserted without the guidance of theory. *But the complexity of social and political reality cannot be understood without the simplicity brought about by complex quantification.* One of the most significant shortcomings of extant research on judicial politics is that it fails to consider relationships that are statistically complex.

There are of course dissenters from this position. For instance, Feeley is quite opposed to quantitative analysis of trial court processes. In his "Reflections on a Quantitative Approach" (Feeley, 1979, pp. 147–153), quantitative analysis is charged with a host of crimes of omission and commission. Basically, though, his points are two. First, quantitative analysis is said to focus only rarely on *processes*, instead contenting itself to examine *products*. Second, that which is easily quantifiable is said to be relatively unimportant to understanding the criminal courts, while that which is not quantifiable is quite important. In support of the first position he asserts that "the criminal process is a complex and interrelated series of sanctions, and the severity of punishment at any state may be determined in part by what preceded and what may follow it. To look at each stage as a wholly separate and distinct decision in isolation from the others may fragment the process beyond recognition and in turn account for the failure of quantitative studies to explain outcomes at any one stage" (Feeley,

1979, pp. 148–149). As an illustration of the sort of influence not typically considered in quantitative analyses, he asserts "in many jurisdictions prosecutors develop a 'feeling' about the reliability of individual police officers, and this affects how they respond to their arrest reports" (Ibid, p. 149). Thus, Feeley is not at all sanguine that there is profit in the pathway for future research that I advocate.

Feeley's position deserves several comments. First, *processes* can be—and Feeley is certainly correct that they ought to be—modeled statistically, using techniques ranging from path analysis to Markov chains. The *product* of one stage of a process no doubt becomes an input in later stages. This is far from being an intractable statistical problem, although complex statistical models are required. Second, discounting for a moment issues of feasibility, a host of relatively "soft" concepts can be, and have been, measured through rigorous, reproducible instruments. Eisenstein et al. (1982) have used a rather complicated Q-sort procedure in order to derive assessments, or "feelings," along several continua, of nearly all of the participants in the criminal justice processes (in nine different jurisdictions, it might be added). Perhaps the "feelings" to which Feeley refers could be indicated by a dynamometer, or even physiological measures (in the future, at least, perhaps even an unobtrusive physiological instrument). Third, if taken as a call for the reduction of specification error, Feeley's remarks have my complete support. Model misspecification is a quite serious and quite widespread problem. Finally, it should be noted that the apparent stimulus for Feeley's comments was his despair over the "general lack of predictive power" of the independent variables considered in his study. My emotion is similarly one of despair, but my response, as apparent throughout this chapter, is to call for greater rigor, greater emphasis on scientific method, quantification, and theory building as a paliative to the malady we both perceive.

Thus, a great deal of research still relies on bivariate or relatively simplistic and linear multivariate analyses. Specification error, especially that associated with the failure to incorporate nonlinear terms into equations, is particularly worrisome. Models that are capable of accommodating the complexity of reality will benefit greatly our understanding of judicial politics.

Research Design

Many of the inadequacies of statistical analysis are actually inadequacies of research design. Certainly the failure to control for key variables, and more generally, specification error, are just a few of the serious statistical problems associated with weak research designs. This problem is greatly exacerbated when researchers are forced to rely on secondary data, including data compiled by court officials, for analysis. Indeed, although the problem is not so worrisome among judicial politics scholars, Warren Miller has recently (1981) warned of the possibility of atrophy of research design skills as a result of the widespread reliance on secondary data.

A host of traditional problems of design plague our field, and Tate (1983) provides a comprehensive catalog of them. However, few—except Miller (1981)—have shown much concern for the logistics of large-scale projects, and only a handful more have voiced reservations about the role of federal funding in setting the research agendas of judicial politics scholars. With regard to the former, a host of problems, ranging from project administration to personality conflicts to mortality and, perhaps most importantly, university structures that offer disincentives to such projects, dissuade many from mounting efforts to test more comprehensive theories. And to invest a great deal of effort in a single large-scale project is a quite risky venture, especially for junior faculty. Much more must be done to remove disincentives to large-scale projects.

The monthly notices from the National Institute of Justice of the Institute's current topic of interest are hardly conducive to the development of a coherent, theoretically inspired research program. Though NIJ has funded large-scale mulitvariate applied research, its interest in theoretical work is much more limited. It is disconcerting to note that the budgets of the Political Science and Law and Social Sciences sections of the National Science Foundation were roughly 3.5 to 4.5 million dollars per year from 1980 to 1984, while the budget of NIJ was roughly five times larger each year (Special Feature: Federal Funding for Social Science Research, 1983). The comparability of these budget figures is no doubt limited, but the conclusion that basic theoretical research is supported at a far lower level is certainly accurate. The result is that the efforts of no small number of creative scholars have been siphoned off to more practical research. Perhaps this is one explanation (in a multivariate theory) of the low development of theory in the study of judicial politics.

Research designs are too frequently unable to generate data yielding definitive assessments of hypotheses. Proper research designs will minimize specification error, as well as contribute to the solution of many miscellaneous problems, such as overdetermination and the selection of the most effective unit(s) and level(s) of analysis.

Measurement

The final methodological issue I will address concerns the quality of measurement that characterizes the study of judicial politics. Three points are developed. First, there is very little attention given in published work to issues of measurement, with few identifying even the contours of a measurement theory. Second, single-item indicators are common, and many instances of simply stipulating that an indicator measures a concept can be found. Finally, much too little attention is given to index construction. Before considering these points, a few general comments on measurement error are in order.

Of the two types of measurement error, systematic and random error, it is sometimes thought that the latter is of little consequence. It is true, for example, that the primary consequence of random error is to attenuate correlation coefficients. If the total variance in Y is decomposed into explained and unexplained variance, then random measurement error is a component of the unexplained portion of the variance. So long as it is recognized that the presence of measurement error reduces the ability of theoretical variables to account for variance, it is sometimes argued, standards can be lowered with little threat of misinterpretation of findings. Thus, variables that account for at least 10% of the variance in Y are treated as substantively significant, not because 10% is such a great amount of variance, but rather because 10% of the total variance may be equivalent to as much as 50% of the variance not attributable to measurement error.

In statistical terms the above argument is impeccable. However, an important caveat must be raised. When a field is as heavily reliant upon induction as judicial politics is, and when measurement error constitutes such a large percentage of the total variance in the variables of interest, the impact of attenuated coefficients is especially severe. Induction involves drawing inferences from patterns in the data analysis and as such can be especially sensitive to minor and/or trivial perturbations. Like factor analysis, the analyst may fail to recognize patterns in the coefficients, or be overly sensitive to insignificant covariance. Furthermore, differences between studies in their findings may reflect more differences in levels of measurement error than differences in substantive processes. Trying to induce patterns from analyses that differ largely on random grounds is trying, to say the least. Were deductive research the norm, the impact would be less severe. Thus, even though random error may not have extreme methodological implications for all empirical analyses, it can significantly affect the development of theory.

Systematic measurement error is quite a different problem. With systematic measurement error, the error term e is composed of random variance and systematic variance. If the error is in the dependent variable, the systematic component is related to Y (by definition), and the equation predicting Y is misspecified. If the error is in the independent variable, then a correlation between the error term and the independent variable is necessarily introduced, resulting in biased estimates of the coefficients. Under some circumstances (e.g., survey data), systematic error may exist in both X and Y, *and* may be from the same source, thus making the relationship between X and Y partially spurious. Systematic measurement error is thus a problem of some considerable moment.

The concepts of random and systematic errors are closely related to the concepts validity and reliability. "The amount of random error is inversely related to the degree of reliability of the measuring instrument" (Carmines and Zeller, 1979, p. 13). Similarly, "invalidity arises because of the presence of nonrandom error, for such error prevents indicators from representing what they are intended to: the theoretical concept" (Ibid., p. 15). Thus, great amounts of measurement error directly threaten the validity and reliability of the measures of key concepts.

Despite this, it is not at all common to see explicit attention to measurement issues in research on judicial politics. In spite of fine examples to the contrary (e.g., Hogarth, 1971; Nardulli, 1978), measurement receives barely a mention, and conclusions are rarely qualified on the basis of measurement error. Perhaps this is due to limitations of journal space, but I suspect that many view measurement as an issue of less compelling import. It may not be essential that every piece of research estimate epistemic correlations (e.g., through LISREL), but it is necessary that at least the rudiments of a theory of measurement (e.g., the common factor model) be reported.

Perhaps inattention to measurement stems from the generally low quality of the indicators we are typically obliged to employ. For instance, it is quite common to find single-item indicators of complex concepts. Canon and Baum (1981, p. 981) use voting patterns as an indicator of the political ideologies of the American states, for example. Ideology, all would agree, is a complex and slippery concept, one surely worthy of multiple indicators. Perhaps more significantly, though the measure is employed at the aggregate (i.e., state) level, there is ample evidence that at the individual level ideology (such as it exists in the mass public) is only very weakly related to vote choices (even in the 1936, 1948, and 1964 presidential elections). More valid measures, of course, may be prohibitively expensive to collect, but Canon and Baum offer no discussion of the impact of measurement error on their findings. Indeed, from their analysis one should *not* conclude that ideology is unrelated to judicial innovation, but rather should conclude that innovation and *vote patterns* are unrelated. The practice of taking a conventional variable and tacking a new conceptual name on it is all too prevalent.

Mention of the problem of index construction must also be made. Without multiple indicators, indices cannot be constructed, so current practices are unassailable. But all too often strategies of constructing indices from multiple indicators are unsound. For instance, it is not uncommon to attach equal weights to the components of an index without an explicit justification for doing so. The implicit weighting associated with items with unequal means and standard deviations is occasionally unnoticed and uncorrected. More rigorous means of determining validity coefficients, such as factor analysis, are not common, although they are certainly becoming more widely accepted. Generally, the typical techniques of index construction lag behind the state of the art in social science.

Finally, special note should be taken of the tendency to employ unmeasured and perhaps unmeasurable concepts in popular theories of judicial politics. No more prominent examples can be identified than that provided by the concepts *political or legal culture* and *organizational norm.* Both of these are concepts that those working on trial courts find quite attractive. Yet rigorous operationalizations of these concepts are practically nonexistent, and, as a consequence, such theories border on nonfalsifiability. Institutional norms can be rigorously measured (e.g., Asher, 1973; Kirkpatrick and McLemore, 1977), but to date the norms of judicial institutions have not been properly indicated (but see Howard, 1981).

Explicit concern over the causes and consequences of measurement error is all too infrequent, with the result that research findings are often contaminated by the effects of error variance. Greater attention to the construction of valid, reliable indicators is essential.

Summary

Methodological problems abound in the study of politics. Simple statistics, and a certain antipathy toward quantitative analysis in general, are not uncommon. Perhaps the Achilles heel of the field, however, is its inattention to the validity and reliability of its measures. Advances in the development of theory—both inductive and deductive—will be severely impeded until the level of methodological awareness increases. Method does not create theory, but method and theory are so intimately interrelated as to contribute equally to the scientific study of judicial politics.

CONCLUDING REMARKS

Several conclusions or recommendations for future research can be derived from this analysis. First, there ought to be much greater attention to the reproducibility of findings. Science provides a methodology that is easily reproducible but, if non-scientific approaches are to be considered, they must be standardized to at least some degree, thus allowing falsifiability. Second, the issue of reproducibility extends into measurement as well. Careful attention must be given to developing reliable indicators of concepts. But reliability, a well-developed statistical concept, should not be allowed to detract from the less statistically well developed concept "validity." Validity is the sine qua non of empirical social science research. Beyond a much greater general self-consciousness about measurement, multiple indicators, formal measurement theories, and appropriate statistical tests will contribute to minimizing error variance in our measures. With better measures, inductive theorizing becomes a more attractive enterprise, although ultimately the goal of all research ought to be the development of logically interconnected propositions allowing the deduction of empirically testable hypotheses.

There has been considerable progress over the last thirty years in the development of a science of judicial politics. Perhaps with a greater consciousness of the epistemological, theoretical, and methodological requirements of social scientific research, the next thirty years will move the field even further and at a more rapid pace toward the goal of a science of judicial politics.

Acknowledgments. This chapter is a revision of a paper delivered at the 1983 Annual Meeting of The American Political Science Association, September 1–4, 1983. Most helpful comments on that paper were received from Burton M. Atkins, Robert A. Carp, Beverly B. Cook, David J. Danelski, Roy B. Flemming, Sheldon Goldman, Joel Grossman, Doris Marie Provine, and Karen O'Connor.

NOTES

1. Wahlke reports that only a small fraction of political science research can be considered to be behavioral. Of the over 4000 works considered in the book review section of the *American Political Science Review* between 1968 and 1977, on average no more than 4% per year were behavioral works (another 4%, on average, were quantitative in orientation, but were not behavioral). In terms of articles published in the *Review*, only about one-third per year were behavioral. It might also be noted that only 5 of the 180 behavioral articles published in this period were in the judicial politics area. On behavioralism generally, see Eulau (1963).
2. Care must be taken not to confuse the issue of reproducibility with replication. Replication has obvious value for scientific inquiry, but, of course, the incentive structure of the discipline is stacked against such research. I am not advocating here the replication of existing research; instead, I am arguing that research processes must be systematic so as to be reproducible, in order to contribute to the ability to falsify hypotheses and to the cumulativeness of research.
3. By empathy the authors mean "the ability to recognize and understand another's point of view without losing one's own point of view" (Ryan et al., p. 254).
4. For instance, "we entered the field with working assumptions based upon previous research, our own courtroom and legal experiences, and consultation with judges, but we believed that the validity of our observations would correspond to how *wholly* we responded to the events of the judicial work day" (Ryan et al., 1980, p. 250, emphasis in original).
5. This problem of uniqueness is directly associated with the logic of comparison. Because cross-national research has been most explicitly self-conscious about its methodological and epistemological foundations, this argument parallels very closely the thinking in that area, and in particular, the work of Przeworski and Teune (1970). In order to demonstrate the ease with which the cross-social system argument can be adapted to cross-institutional research, all of the quotations from Przeworski and Teune substitute the word "institution" for the word "social system" used in the original.

REFERENCES

Adamany, David W. (1973). Legitimacy, realigning elections, and the Supreme Court. *Wisconson Law Review* 1973: 790–846.
Asher, Herbert B. (1973). The learning of legislative norms. *American Political Science Review* 67: 499–513.

Baum, Lawrence (1977). Policy goals in judicial gatekeeping: a proximity model of discretionary jurisdiction. *American Journal of Political Science* 21: 13-35.

Blalock, Hubert M., Jr., and Wilken, Paul H. (1979). *Intergroup Processes: A Micro-Macro Perspective.* New York: The Free Press.

Canon, Bradley C., and Ulmer, S. Sidney (1976). The Supreme Court and critical elections: a dissent. *American Political Science Review* 70: 1215-1218.

Canon, Bradley C., and Baum, Lawrence (1981). Patterns of adoption of tort law innovations: an application of diffusion theory to judicial doctrines. *American Political Science Review* 75: 975-987.

Carmines, Edward G., and Zeller, Richard A. (1979). *Reliability and Validity Assessment.* Beverly Hills, Calif.: Sage Publications.

Casper, Jonathan D. (1976). The Supreme Court and national policy making. *American Political Science Review* 70: 50-63.

Cook, Beverly B. (1977). Public opinion and federal judicial policy. *American Journal of Political Science* 21: 567-600.

Dahl, Robert A. (1957). Decision-making in a democracy: the Supreme Court as a national policy maker. *Journal of Public Law* 6: 279-295.

Dahl, Robert A. (1961). The behavioral approach in political science: epitaph for a monument to a successful protest. *American Political Science Review* 56: 763-772.

Danelski, David J. (1970). Legislative and judicial decision-making: the case of Harold H. Burton. In S. Sidney Ulmer (ed.), *Political Decison-Making.* New York: Van Nostrand Reinhold Company, pp. 121-146.

Easton, David (1962). The current meaning of 'behavioralism.' In James C. Charlesworth (ed.), *The Limits of Behavioralism in Political Science,* pp. 26-48. Philadelphia: American Academy of Political and Social Science.

Easton, David (1969). The new revolution in political science. *American Political Science Review* 63: 1051-1061.

Eisenstein, James, and Jacob, Herbert (1977). *Felony Justice: An Organizational Analysis of Criminal Courts.* Boston: Little Brown.

Eisenstein, James, Nardulli, Peter F., and Flemming, Roy B. (1982). Comparison of macro and micro models of court decision making: a preliminary analysis. Paper delivered at the 1982 Annual Meeting of the American Political Science Association, Denver, Colorado.

Eulau, Heinz (1963). *The Behavioral Persuasion in Politics.* New York: Random House.

Feeley, Malcom M. (1979). *The Process is the Punishment: Handling Cases in a Lower Criminal Court.* New York: Russell Sage Foundation.

Fenno, Richard F. (1977). U.S. House members in their constituencies: an exploration. *American Political Science Review* 71: 883-917.

Flemming, Roy B. (1982). *Punishment Before Trial: An Organizational Perspective on Felony Bail Processes.* New York: Longman.

Frake, Charles O. (1969). Notes on queries in ethnography. In Stephen A. Tyler (ed.), *Cognitive Anthropology.* New York: Holt, Rinehart, and Winston.

Funston, Richard (1975). The Supreme Court and critical elections. *American Political Science Review* 69: 795-811.

Gibson, James L. (1983). From simplicity to complexity: the development of theory in the study of judicial behavior. *Political Behavior* 5: 7-49.

Gow, David John (1979). Scale fitting in the psychometric model of judicial decision making. *American Political Science Review* 73: 430-441.

Grossman, Joel B., Kritzer, Herbert M., Bumiller, Kristin, Sarat, Austin, McDougal, Stephen, and Miller, Richard (1982). Dimensions of institutional participation: who uses the courts, and how? *Journal of Politics* 44: 86-114.

Hagan, John (1974). Extra-legal attributes and criminal sentencing: an assessment of a sociological viewpoint. *Law and Society Review* 8: 357-384.

Heumann, Milton (1978). *Plea Bargaining.* Chicago: University of Chicago Press.

Hogarth, John (1971). *Sentencing as a Human Process.* Toronto: University of Toronto Press.

Howard, J. Woodford, Jr. (1981). *Courts of Appeals in the Federal Judicial System: A Study of the Second, Fifth, and District of Columbia Circuits.* Princeton: Princeton University Press.

Kirkpatrick, Samuel A., and McLemore, Lelan (1977). Perceptual and affective components of legislative norms: a social-psychological analysis of congruity. *Journal of Politics* 39: 685-711.

Levin, Martin A. (1977). *Urban Politics and the Criminal Courts*. Chicago: University of Chicago Press.

Lindblom, Charles E. (1982). Another state of mind. *American Political Science Review* 76: 9–21.

Mather, Lynn M. (1979). *Plea Bargaining or Trial? The Process of Criminal Court Disposition*. Lexington, Mass.: Lexington Books.

Miller, Warren (1981). The role of research in the unification of a discipline. *American Political Science Review* 75: 9–16.

Nardulli, Peter F. (1978). *The Courtroom Elite: An Organizational Perspective on Criminal Justice*. Cambridge, Mass.: Ballinger.

Pritchett, C. Herman (1948). *The Roosevelt Court: A Study in Judicial Politics and Values 1937-1947*. New York: Macmillan.

Pritchett, C. Herman (1941). Division of opinion among justices of the U.S. Supreme Court, 1939-1941. *American Political Science Review* 35: 890–898.

Przeworski, Adam, and Teune, Henry (1970). *The Logic of Comparative Social Inquiry*. New York: Wiley-Interscience.

Ryan, John Paul, Ashman, Allan, Sales, Bruce D., and Shane-DuBow, Sandra (1980). *American Trial Judges: Their Work Styles and Performance*. New York: The Free Press.

Sarat, Austin, and Grossman, Joel B. (1975). Courts and conflict resolution: problems in the mobilization of adjudication. *American Political Science Review* 69:1200–1207.

Schubert, Glendon (1965). *The Judicial Mind: The Attitudes and Ideologies of Supreme Court Justices, 1946-1963*. Evanston, Ill.: Northwestern University Press.

Schubert, Glendon (1974). *The Judicial Mind Revisited: Psychometric Analysis of Supreme Court Ideology*. New York: Oxford University Press.

"Special Feature: Federal Funding for Social Science Research." *PS* 16: 205–216.

Stumpf, Harry P., Shapiro, Martin, Danelski, David J., Sarat, Austin, and O'Brien, David M. (1983). Whither political jurisprudence: a symposium. *Western Political Quarterly* 36: 533–569.

Tanenhaus, Joseph (1966). The cumulative scaling of judicial decisions. *Harvard Law Review* 79: 1583–1594.

Tate, C. Neal (1981). Personal attribute models of the voting behavior of U.S. Supreme Court justices: liberalism in civil liberties and economic decisions, 1946–1978. *American Political Science Review* 75: 355–367.

Tate, C. Neal (1983). The methodology of judicial behavior research: a review and critique. *Political Behavior* 5: 51–82.

Ulmer, S. Sidney (1965). Toward a theory of sub-group formation in the United States Supreme Court. *Journal of Politics* 27: 133–152.

Ulmer, S. Sidney (1969). The dimensionality of judicial voting behavior. *Midwest Journal of Political Science* 13: 471–483.

Ulmer, S. Sidney (1972). The decision to grant certiorari as an indicator to decision 'on the merits'. *Polity* 4: 429–447.

Ulmer, S. Sidney (1978). Selecting cases for Supreme Court review: an underdog model. *American Political Science Review* 72: 902–910.

Utz, Pamela J. (1978). *Settling the Facts: Discretion and Negotiation in Criminal Court*. Lexington, Mass.: Lexington Books.

Wahlke, John C. (1979). Pre-behavioralism in political science. *American Political Science Review* 73: 9–31.

CHAPTER 8

THE POSITIVE THEORY OF HIERARCHIES

Gary J. Miller and Terry M. Moe

So far, positive political theory has not contributed much to our understanding of public bureaucracy. In part, this is due to the unsympathetic treatment that rational modelling has received from students of public administration. Compared to other areas of political science, public administration is known for its emphasis on normative and practical concerns, its traditional modes of analysis—and its lack of theoretical progress. The other side of the coin, however, is that positive theorists have not really made much of an effort to develop theories of bureaucracy. Their concerns have generally centered around two basic mechanisms of social choice, voting and markets. They have devoted little systematic attention to a third mechanism that is clearly of pervasive importance for an understanding of how societies and other aggregates make collective decisions. This third, relatively unexplored mechanism is hierarchy. Movement toward a positive theory of hierarchies would fill a serious gap in the social choice literature, while at the same time making a theoretical contribution that strikes to the essence of public bureaucracy, indeed of all organizations.

In fact, significant steps toward a positive theory of hierarchies have very recently been taken, but by economists, not political scientists. In small numbers, of course, economists began to make contributions to the study of bureaucracy some time ago, notably with the pioneering works of Downs (1966), Tullock (1965), and Niskanen (1971). But the new wave of theoretical work is different. Grounded in recent attempts to move beyond the neoclassical theory of the firm toward a theory of economic organizations, it is already a large, complex body of literature that is the focus of innovation and excitement among a growing number of economists, and it reflects an unusual degree of theoretical coherence and cumulative effort.

Our central purpose in this chapter is to provide political scientists with an overview of the new economics of organization, stressing its most basic concepts and theoretical arguments. First, we focus on the heart of this new tradition, work that is oriented by a distinctive approach to the study of organizations: a contractual perspective on organizational relationships, a theoretical focus on hierarchical control, and formal analysis via principal-agent models. Second, we explore a far less developed component of the new economics of organization, axiomatic social choice theory, highlighting areas of overlap and suggesting its promise for organizational analysis.

THE NEW ECONOMICS OF ORGANIZATION

The neoclassical theory of the firm is not in any meaningful sense a theory of economic organization. It centers around the entrepreneur, a hypothetical individual who, by assumption, makes all decisions for the firm and is endowed with a range of idealized properties defining his knowledge, goals, computational skills, and transaction costs. Virtually all aspects of business enterprise that organization theorists find interesting and consequential, from formal structure to social context and worker psychology to bounded rationality, adaptive search, and goal conflict, are thereby assumed away. The model firm is simply a black box that produces optimal choices automatically as a function of any given environment.

Similarly, the more general theory of perfect competition is not in any meaningful sense a theory of competition. Industries are assumed populated by large numbers of firms that take prices as given and make choices without any reference to the behavior of others. The interactive, highly strategic process we ordinarily associate with competition is entirely missing, as are the organizational forms and market-structuring devices such as vertical integration, tie-in sales, and resale price maintenance that firms often adopt in responding to the uncertainties, externalities, and transaction costs inherent in actual competitive environments. As Demsetz (1982) has suggested, it is less a theory of perfect competition than a theory of perfect decentralization—that is, a theory of how atomized decisional units, without any mechanism of central coordination other than the free-market system of prices, can produce outcomes that are optimal for the collective. The lessons learned are lessons about prices and markets, not about competition.

These models are easily criticized. But this is not new or even very disturbing for mainstream supporters of neoclassical theory, since the theory was never intended to be realistic in its assumptions nor to be descriptively accurate in its micro-level implications for individuals and organizations. Its development and use by economists over the years have generally been grounded in its value in generating formal implications for market prices and outputs, resource allocation, equilibria, and other aggregate properties of economic systems. These reflect, in some sense, the underlying purpose of neoclassical theory, and assumptions about the firm and perfect competition are vehicles by means of which this end is pursued. The explanation of organizational behavior is simply a different purpose calling for a different approach—perhaps a modification and extension of neoclassicism, perhaps a rejection of it.

An Early Departure from the Neoclassical View of the Firm

Much of the economic theory of organizations has emerged in the last ten years or so, and a good part of this new work is the product of writers whose methods and theoretical orientations are largely consistent with neoclassical tradition. Nevertheless, the origins and basic themes of the new economics of organization have been shaped most fundamentally by the pioneering views of an early dissenter from the neoclassical theory of the firm: Ronald Coase. Coase was among a diverse group of economists who contended that an understanding of economic activity required systematic inquiry into the institutional context in which such an activity takes place. While others emphasized legal institutions (Commons, 1934), Coase focused on the firm itself. In his classic article, "The Nature of the Firm" (1937), Coase raised a fundamental question: why do these organizations exist? Specifically, why do economic agents in real economic contexts tend to arrange themselves hierarchically and coordinate their decisions via central authority rather than relying upon voluntary exchange and the automatic coordination provided by the market?

His answer—that hierarchy is often more efficient—is unsurprising, but far less important than the way he goes about constructing it. He notes that real-world production processes of any complexity generally involve numerous transactions among owners of capital, labor, land, specialized knowledge, and other inputs, and that these transactions are costly. In a hypothetical world in which all production is carried out purely by means of market relationships, transaction costs of two types are particularly important. First, an agent interested in arranging for the production of a good must somehow learn the myriad prices of relevance to the transactions he enters into, thus suffering the costs of information gathering and evaluation. Second, he experiences costs—due to informational problems, haggling, strategic noncooperation, delays, etc.—preparing for, negotiating, and concluding separate contractual agreements for each transaction. Rational economic agents will naturally seek to minimize these transaction costs. The thrust of Coase's argument is that many such costs can often be eliminated or substantially reduced by shifting to an alternative, nonmarket arrangement that internalizes various of the agent's transactions with factor owners and alters his contractual arrangements with them:

> For this series of contracts is substituted one . . . whereby the factor, for a certain remuneration (which may be fixed or fluctuating) agrees to obey the directions of an entrepreneur within certain limits. The essence of the contract is that it should only state the limits to the powers of the entrepreneur. Within these limits, he can therefore direct the other factors of production. (Coase, 1937, p.391).

Thus emerges a rudimentary economic organization, the firm, centrally characterized by the authority relation and the hierarchical direction of production. The driving force behind its emergence is efficiency. Economic agents arrange production within firms—that is, they substitute authority relations for market relations—in order to reduce transaction costs and thereby produce more efficiently. Firms only emerge when this condition is met, and they will only expand up to the point where the cost of an additional transaction within the firm begins to exceed the cost of the same transaction in the market. In equilibrium, some transactions will therefore be internalized within firms of various kinds and sizes, and some will be left to the market.

Coase's article was, in his own words, "much cited and little used" (Coase, 1972) for more than thirty years after its publication. With the new wave of studies in the 1970s, however, it was effectively resurrected as a major source of theoretical ideas that, perhaps more than any other, has shaped the conceptual foundations and research directions of this emerging body of works on organizations. Several of his notions have proved especially influential: (1) Economic organizations are best understood by comparing their efficiency to that of the market. (2) In the real world, which is clearly not characterized by perfect competition, perfect information, or frictionless exchange, economic activities and alternative organizational arrangements are best understood in terms of the transaction costs inherent in any system of exchange relationships among rational individuals. (3) These relationships are essentially contractual in nature, and the firm is best understood as founded upon a distinct kind of contractual arrangement, the authority relation. Thus, in their earliest coherent statement, we have three central components of the new economics of organization: markets versus hierarchy, transaction costs, and the contractual nature of organizations.

The Emerging Paradigm

Modern work in this tradition was stimulated by Alchian and Demsetz's seminal article, "Production, Information Costs, and Economic Organization" (Alchian and Demsetz, 1972).[1] They argue, as Coase did, that the particular organizational (contractual) arrangement we identify with the capitalist firm is a more efficient productive mechanism than alternative contractual arrangements occurring purely within the market, and that the existence of firms can be derived logically from an analysis of the rational behavior of economic actors. But while their argument could be couched in the general terms of transaction costs, their theoretical focus is more narrowly defined—and, many would say, more interesting and consequential because of it. Specifically, their focus is on the "shirking-information" problem, and their claim is that the firm exists because it provides a better solution to this problem than markets do. A brief review of their argument offers us an opportunity to introduce a number of ideas.

Alchian and Demsetz note that for complex production processes there is typically a gain from cooperation. Teams of input owners (including those who only own labor) can produce more in cooperation with one another than separately, and this gives rational agents an incentive to coordinate their actions. Yet team production also suffers from a peculiar problem. Precisely because of the complex interdependence of tasks and their frequent remoteness from organizational output, the marginal products of individuals are difficult and perhaps impossible to determine; thus, in the absence of mechanisms for monitoring each individual's behavior, they cannot reward one another according to individual impacts on output. Division of the team's surplus among its members, then, must proceed according to some other rule—equal sharing, for example—that does not depend upon knowing each person's productive impact. It happens, however, that this induces a distinctive kind of reactive behavior among the members themselves: shirking.

Each individual knows that his effort has some impact on the team's reward, but that this reward is split among all members; thus, while he bears the full cost of his effort, he receives only part of what his effort produces. On the other hand, when he shirks by reducing his effort expenditures, the savings in effort accrue only to him and the resulting losses in team reward are borne largely by others. A fundamental asymmetry therefore characterizes the structure of incentives, and each member will tend to find it in his own best interests to engage in some degree of shirking. Team production and rewards fall as a result, and each member may actually be worse off than if no one had shirked from the outset.

While they may realize that their collective fate is suboptimal, that will not in itself allow them to solve the problem: they are trapped in what is essentially a prisoner's dilemma. Their cooperative effort is plagued by a public goods problem (where the public good is team reward) that promotes free-rider behavior (shirking) among members. The problem is a reflection of underlying externalities: for each individual, the fact that others benefit from his productive effort is external to his decision calculus, and he therefore chooses more leisure than is socially (for the team) desirable.

In view of this, how can member shirking be reduced? Alchian and Demsetz argue that the usual market mechanisms—e.g., allowing outsiders to bid for shirkers' places on the team—will not work, since bidders cannot know who the shirkers are and, worse, bidders would also have incentives to shirk once they join the team. On the other hand, if information could somehow be gained on the marginal products of individual members, they could agree to be rewarded on this basis. Externalities would thereby be reduced, and everyone would be made better off as a result. Thus, the way to mitigate the shirking problem is to monitor the productive efforts of team members. If monitoring were perfect, each individual's marginal product could be known with certainty, and shirking could be completely eliminated. This outcome is impossible in practice, however, because monitoring is costly. The best the team can do is to invest in monitoring up to the point where its marginal costs begin to outweigh the marginal benefits from reduced shirking. Some degree of residual shirking is thus both rational and to be expected.

How can monitoring be carried out most efficiently? To avoid hierarchy, members could rotate the job of monitor among themselves; but they would then lose the substantial efficiencies of specialization. A better alternative is to hire an outsider or to appoint a team member to be a full-time monitor. This allows for specialization, but points to still another question: who will monitor the monitor? Because his marginal product will be unknown, he will also have an incentive to shirk and thus to monitor less efficiently than he otherwise might—which implies, in turn, that member marginal products will be measured improperly, and member resources will be misallocated. Given that the monitor's role is uniquely critical to the efficiency of all other members, the key to team efficiency is to ensure that the monitor has rational incentives to do his job efficiently. The best way to do this, Alchian and Demsetz argue, is to give him marketable title to the team's rewards and to establish him as central contracting agent with all its members. He would then pay members their estimated marginal products, based on bilateral contracts between him and each member, and keep the remaining amount as personal income. This new status clearly enhances his incentives to monitor efficiently. It also gives him both the incentive and the authority to adjust payments in accordance with observed productivity and to make changes in team membership in the interests of higher team rewards. Moreover, this is an arrangement that all rational team members will tend to favor—for it promises to make them all better off by mitigating the shirking problem. The hierarchical relationship that results is not one of fiat or dominance, but a contractual quid pro quo into which they all voluntarily enter, in pursuit of greater gain.

Alchian and Demsetz thus go well beyond Coase in demonstrating why factors overlooked by the neoclassical model in fact operate to provide a rational foundation for economic organization. In the process, they put the contractual framework to use in developing innovative ideas—notably, the centrality of the shirking-information problem—that point the way toward new lines of organizational inquiry. In particular, their perspective has obvious promise in application to issues of organizational management and control, and indeed to a vast range of theoretical questions surrounding the superior-subordinate relation characteristic of all hierarchies. For their logic implies that hierarchy, monitoring, incentives to shirk, and member productivity are integrally bound up with one another. Thus, while their analysis is explicitly about firms, it rests on theoretical foundations that capture something inherent in organizational and hierarchical behavior generally. It would appear that this broad analytical scope, combined with their implicit acceptance of the optimization model, largely explains the interest and enthusiasm their article has generated. For the first time, economists had a theoretical perspective that rivalled Simon's behavioral paradigm in organizational relevance without straying too far from neoclassical foundations.

Subsequent work further generalized the Alchian-Demsetz perspective by emphasizing that contractual relationships are fundamentally shaped by incomplete information, especially when asymmetrically distributed across the contracting parties, and conflict of interest. Together, these core components offer a broader explanation of the shirking-information problem that is not tied to teams or production inseparabilities. More importantly, they also provide a more powerful framework for the analysis of hierarchical control, one with clear links to information economics, game theory, and other areas of the discipline.

We can briefly illustrate the nature and utility of this general framework by considering two concepts that have become central to the literature: adverse selection and moral hazard. Both emerged from early applied work on insurance and were incorporated into the modern work on information and organization in recognition of their much broader theoretical significance. Adverse selection derives from unobservability of the information, beliefs, and values on which the decisions of others are based.

Consider an example from the employment relation, in which an employer seeks applicants for a marketing research position requiring independent, creative work. While he would like to attract highly qualified and motivated individuals, he cannot know any given applicant's true intelligence, aptitude, or work habits. What he can do is to proceed on the basis of rough indicators, like education or job background, thus declaring his willingness to pay a certain price for individuals who are nominally qualified according to these indicators; the price is in effect a statistical average, reflecting both the estimated implications of the indicators for productivity and the estimated varition in productivity across all individuals who qualify. The individual evaluating this price, on the other hand, does know his own qualifications and work habits. If he is in fact highly intelligent, creative, and motivated, he will tend to find that the employer's proxy-based price understates his true economic value. If he is in fact quite lacking in all these desirable traits but still meets the formal proxy requirements, he will tend to find that the price overstates his true economic value. The latter type of individual is thus likely to view the job as an opportunity, while the former is likely to look elsewhere, especially for "better" jobs whose proxy categories are either more finely measured or simply pitched at a higher level. In addition to all of this, individuals who happen to place high value on leisure are likely to find this job particularly appealing, because supervision is minimal and productivity is difficult to measure; high productivity individuals, in contrast, will find the measurement problem a negative factor, since they want their true productivity to be observed and rewarded.

Because the employer cannot in general know each applicant's true "type," whereas the applicants themselves clearly do, his recruitment effort will tend to suffer from adverse selection: he will attract a disproportionate number of low-quality applicants. Moreover, even though he and the best of these applicants share a common interest—he wants to hire the best, and the best wants to be hired—this may not ease his problem, for the asymmetry remains. He cannot know for sure which applicant is truly the best, and the best applicant cannot credibly offer the truthful self-assessment that he is in fact superbly qualified, because all individuals have incentives to make the same sorts of claims in order to get the job.

Moral hazard arises from the unobservability of actual behavior in the ex post contracting situation—here, after an applicant has been hired. The employer cannot know for sure to what extent the individual is productive and instead must ordinarily rely upon proxies; e.g., quality of reports, timeliness, diligence, and responsiveness. The individual then has an incentive to redirect his efforts towad the proxy measures (a phenomenon called "goal displacement" in the sociology of organizations), rather than pursuit of the abstract goals implicit in the employment contract; and he also has an incentive to substitute leisure for productive effort, since the unobservability of his inputs allows him to achieve the benefits of additional leisure at low cost (the expected cost of being detected). Shirking behavior, therefore, is an aspect of moral hazard, with the incentive to shirk deriving from underlying information asymmetries.

Moral hazard and adverse selection are general problems whose potential is inherent in all contracting and hierarchical relationships. As theoretical concepts, they are particularly valuable for understanding situations in which one party seeks to achieve certain outcomes (such as profits) by relying on and controlling the behavior of another. These, of course, are the essence of organizational analysis, whether the substance has to do with decentralization, division of labor, formal rules, structure, communication, or ownership versus control—and all, because of information asymmetries, are shaped by moral hazard and adverse selection.

Consider what happens, for instance, when organizations decentralize. Tasks and authority are delegated to lower-level units in the expectation that they will use their specialized knowledge and productive capabilities to contribute toward organizational ends; but the inevitable information asymmetries create incentive problems. An upper-level unit soliciting policy inputs from lower-level units will pay the price of adverse selection, since only the lower-level units know what information their inputs are based upon, and they can use that to their own advantage. Similarly, a superior unit trying to increase a subordinate unit's productive efficiency will have to grapple with the problem of moral hazard, since the observability of productive behavior is asymmetrically distributed in the latter's favor. To take another example, consider the relationship between stockholders and managers. This is a variation on the same theme: stockholders want to control managers in the interests of profits, but managers tend to possess far better information both about actual organizational behavior (including their own) and about the technical and cognitive grounds on which proposals are formulated and adopted, which leads, once again, to adverse selection and moral hazard problems for stockholder control efforts.

Across these and other organizational areas, therefore, the economic analysis of organizations tends to center on certain common questions having to do with the incidence and content of information asymmetry, why the asymmetry exists, what it implies for contractual outcomes, and how the asymmetry or its consequences can be mitigated. Theoretical inquiry into these questions takes diverse forms, but one analytical framework is so eminently well suited to the task that it has emerged over the years as the dominant model within the new economics of organization: the principal-agent model. Initially developed to investigate more general questions of incomplete information and risk-sharing (Ross, 1973; Spence and Zeckhauser, 1971), its relevance for explicitly organizational analysis was quickly recognized, and applications to the central issues of organization theory are growing (Jensen, 1983).

The principal-agent model is an analytical expression of the agency relationship, in which one party, the principal, enters into a contractual agreement with another, the agent, in the expectation that the agent will subsequently choose actions that produce outcomes desired by the principal. Examples of agency relationships are legion: lawyer-client, doctor-patient, broker-investor, politician-citizen, and most generally, employer-employee. As these examples tend to suggest, a principal may seek out an agent for various reason. Often he may lack specialized knowledge or legal certification that the agent possesses, and sometimes the size or complexity of the task simply requires coordinated action by persons other than himself. But given some motivation for relying on the actions of an agent, the principal's decision problem is far more involved than simply locating a qualified agent—for there is no guarantee that the agent, once hired, will in fact choose to pursue the principal's best interests or to do so efficiently. The agent has his own interests at heart, and is induced to pursue the principal's objectives only to the extent that the incentive structure imposed in their contract renders such behavior advantageous.

The essence of the principal's problem is the design of just such an incentive structure. The difficulty, of course, is that information about the agent's actions and the inputs on which they are based is not only imperfect but skewed in favor of the agent, yielding adverse selection and moral hazard problems that must somehow be mitigated. The design of an efficient incentive structure is thus bound up with the development of monitoring systems as well as mechanisms for inducing the agent to reveal as much of his privately held information as possible. The principal must weave these interrelated components into a contractual framework that, in mitigating the informational asymmetries and structuring rewards, prompts the agent to behave as the principal himself would under whatever conditions might prevail.

The logic of the principal-agent model, therefore, immediately leads us to the theoretical issues at the heart of the contractual paradigm: issues of hierarchical control in the context of information asymmetry and conflict of interest. It is a natural framework for the economic analysis of organizations of all kinds, and adherents are enthusiastic about its promise. Thus:

> The problem of inducing an "agent" to behave as if he were maximizing the "principal's" welfare is quite general. It exists in all organizations and in all cooperative efforts. . . . The development of theories to explain the form which agency costs take . . . and how and why they are born will lead to a rich theory of organizations which is now lacking in economics and the social sciences generally. (Jensen and Meckling, 1976, p. 309)

The advantage of a simple analytical framework is that organizational issues can be cast in a clear, rigorous manner that allows for the application of conventional economic methods. A corresponding disadvantage, however, is that such a framework sometimes encourages highly complex mathematical treatment of increasingly trivial problems; form may triumph over substance, with analytical concerns taking on lives of their own that have little to do with the explanation of empirical phenomena.

The principal-agent literature reflects both these positive and negative forces. On the negative side, much of the current literature does indeed focus on matters of little substantive interest; "authors are led to assume the problem away or to define sterile 'toy' problems that are mathematically tractable" (Jensen, 1983, p. 333). The inherent substantive complexity is magnified rather than simplified by many of these efforts, and it is often unclear that theoretical progress has much to do here with arriving at better explanations of truly interesting types of organizational behavior. The real danger, critics would argue, is that the economics of organization will ultimately go the way of mainstream neoclassicism, with analytics and methods clearly dominating substance. This would be the ultimate irony—for this new area began, after all, as an effort to put realism and substantive relevance back into microeconomic theory.

Yet the principal-agent literature has clearly enhanced our understanding of hierarchical relationships and represents a major advance beyond the usual sociological methods of organizational analysis. In part, this is due to important theoretical conclusions—regarding incentive mechanisms for revealing an agent's "type" (Myerson, 1979), the role of signalling and screening devices (Spence, 1974), and conditions for the optimality of alternative reward systems (Shavell, 1979; Holmstrom, 1979) and monitoring and accounting systems

(Baiman, 1982), among others. But it is also due to its demonstrated value in clarifying what the relevant aspects of hierarchical relationships are. It cuts through the inherent complexity of organizational relationships by identifying distinct aspects of individuals and their environments that are most worthy of investigation, and it integrates these elements into a logically coherent whole.

In all likelihood, the contractual paradigm will maintain its central role in structuring economic approaches to organization, owing to its linkages to neoclassicism. But it will also continue to subsume a great diversity of approaches, some of them far more concerned than others with the empirical richness of organization. The principal-agent model, ideally suited to the analysis of issues striking at the essence of hierarchical relationships, is understandably the major means of formal modelling at present, and should become well established as an important tool of organizational analysis. Given the countervailing influences for substantive relevance, however, and given the broader tasks of organization theory, the current fervor surrounding the principal-agent model will likely give way in the long run to a more eclectic methodology within which that model plays a less pronounced but integral role.

HIERARCHY AS SOCIAL CHOICE

While neoclassical theory views the firm as an extension of a single decision maker (the entrepreneur), the new economics of organization recognizes that firms and other hierarchies are composed of multiple decision makers with plural value systems. In other words, it recognizes that hierarchy is a social choice mechanism. In this section, we will use social choice theory to examine the implications of this transformation from hierarchy as dictatorship of the entrepreneur to hierarchy as social choice mechanism. An advantage of this approach is that it will embed the theory of hierarchy in a general social choice theory which has already been used to integrate and transform the study of markets and voting processes. At this writing, very little work has been done along these lines (but see Hess, 1983; Hammond and Miller, 1985), and it remains an unfortunately minor component of the new economics of organization. We hope this introductory analysis will help to illustrate its potential.

The Advantages of Dictatorship

The neoclassical view of the firm as an extension of a single decision maker carries with it the assumption that the firm is a dictatorship. As Alchian and Demsetz noted (p. 777), "It is common to see the firm characterized by the power to settle issues by fiat, by authority, or by disciplinary action superior to that available to the conventional market." In public administration, the same perspective can be traced back to Woodrow Wilson's classic article calling for the importation of the science of administration from European despots. Wilson's argument was that once policy was made, whether by democratic or autocratic means, it could and should be implemented autocratically. Democratic politics, in other words, should stop with the formation of legislation, and accountability required that the implementation of the legislation be carried out in a rigorous authoritarian mode, just as the entrepreneur's decision for a firm. With this view of hierarchy as dictatorship, it is possible to assume a set of mutually consistent desirable traits for the organization. These are as follows.

1. *Nonrestriction of individual preferences.* For every possible combination of preferences of the individuals in an organization, the organization is capable of making some decision. That is, the organization is not stalemated or prohibited from making a decision because of any zany combination of individual preferences you can think of. This trait is clearly desirable because we would not like to think that hiring some employee whose personal views are off-beat or eccentric would bring the organization to a halt. It is also reasonable, because employees are thought to be acting as agents whose actions are constrained by the reward system of their superiors; thus organizational behavior should achieve a degree of independence from the preferences of individual actors. A dictatorship satisfies this condition because a dictator is assumed to be able to make a choice for the organization no matter what the preferences of his subordinates.

2. *Unanimity, or Pareto optimality.* This is the weakest possible "efficiency" condition for an organization, where efficiency has to do here with the satisfaction of member preferences, not with productivity. It requires only that if everyone in the organization prefers x to y, then the organization will not select y. This condition is met trivially in a dictatorship because, if he prefers x to y, then the organization will not select y. (Note: this does not mean that the organization must be unanimous to act, which would be a very strong condition indeed.)

3. *Independence of irrelevant alternatives.* Some voting mechanisms work in such a way that by introducing an alternative that is sure to lose, the winning alternative may be changed. Plurality elections are an example. A dictatorship is not manipulable in this way. When a subordinate points out to a dictator that pea soup is available for lunch, it does not change the dictator's preference for hamburgers over hot dogs.

4. *Transitivity.* This condition has to do with whether the organization makes stable, meaningful choices. Majority rule is one choice mechanism that can be unstable, since a majority can prefer x to y, y to z, and z to x, even with stable individual preferences. A legislature or committee can cycle from one alternative to another in an unstable way. This problem does not occur with a dictatorship: the dictator's transitive preferences fix the preferences for the hierarchy as a whole.

These four conditions seem to be so obviously desirable as to be boring.

There is not one condition that Woodrow Wilson or Frederick Taylor (1947) would have had to think twice about, if asked about its desirability for an administrative organization. Indeed, these conditions would seem to be descriptive of that combination of energy and rationality which Wilson felt he saw in the idealized Continental bureaucracies and coveted for American bureaucracy. A violation of any of the four conditions in an administrative organization would have seemed to Wilson absurd, bizarre, and probably rather malevolent. In this case, Wilson's intuition was correct in pressing for a "science of administration" that imitated Continental dictatorships, because we now know that *a dictatorship is the only method of social choice that is consistent with the four desirable conditions just listed.*

If Not a Dictatorship, Then What?

The problem, of course, is that no one seriously believes any more that an organization is a complete dictatorship; in fact, the new economics of hierarchy is grounded in that fact. This was anticipated by empirical studies of hierarchies by social scientists from the Hawthorne studies onward. The Hawthorne researchers "became interested in those groups whose norms and codes of behavior are at variance with the technical and economic objectives of the company as a whole" (Roethlisberger and Dickson, 1939). If multiple, conflicting value systems determine the actual performance of a simple task like assembling switchboards, then the view of hierarchy as a monocratic dictatorship seemed insupportable. By World War II, political scientists were dismissing the Wilsonian premise of a politics/administration dichotomy that supported his desired state of authoritarian administration within a democratic polity; they began to conceive of administration as a complex bargaining process among actors, each of whom had some degree of autonomous decision authority. Cyert and March discussed the firm as a "coalition" of subgroups, each of which had its own goals. Alchian and Demsetz dismissed the dictatorship view of the firm as "delusion. The firm does not own all its inputs. It has no power of fiat, no authority, no disciplinary action any different in the slightest degree from ordinary market contracting between any two people" (p. 777). Hierarchy as dictatorship was dismissed as a technical impossibility and increasingly as undesirable as well.

But if hierarchy is not a dictatorship, then the Arrow Paradox is applicable to hierarchies. Arrow demonstrated that every nondictatorship must violate at least one of the four conditions listed above. But which condition is violated in a nondictatorial hierarchy? What does it mean for an organization to violate Pareto optimality, or transitivity, or nonrestriction of individual preferences? How can we characterize the social choice properties of nondictatorial hierarchies?

While no one thinks of hierarchies as dictatorships any more, hierarchies are not exactly voting bodies, either. Although some organization theorists seem to view hierarchies as having a centralized weighted voting system, it seems much more accurate to view the organization as being nondictatorial because it is necessarily decentralized. That is, not all decisions in a hierarchy are made at the top. The subunits of the organization have greater or lesser degrees of freedom in implementing organizational goals and policies, and their decisions over the range of delegated matters contribute to the final organizational decision.

It is reasonable to think of an organization as "minimally decentralized" if, out of perhaps hundreds of thousands of alternatives facing the organization, there are at least two subunits of the organization with the power or authority to veto at least one alternative each. If organizations are minimally decentralized in this sense, then another social choice theorem provides us with further ammunition for understanding the nature of hierarchical social choice. This is the Sen paradox (Sen, 1970). The Sen paradox states that any organization that is minimally decentralized cannot simultaneously have three of the conditions listed above: nonrestriction of individual preferences, Pareto optimality, and transitivity. In other words, any organization that delegates any decision making to subunits must be subject to violations of Pareto optimality or transitivity, or it must restrict individual preferences. To put it yet another way, a decentralized organization that is prepared to make a decision for any combination of individual preferences must be susceptible to inefficiency or instability.

For example, imagine an organization in the business of producing and marketing a new product. Let's say that there are two production technologies and three sales strategies available. This means that there are six possible alternatives for the organization to choose from, as in Figure 1. The problem is for the organization to come up with the best alternative out of the six.

If it were a complete dictatorship, then the organization's rank-ordering over the six alternatives would be the same as the president's, and the organization's first choice would be the president's first choice. However, the president realizes that she cannot be a complete expert on all aspects of the organization's behavior, so she has delegated to the marketing vice-president the responsibility for rank-ordering two alternatives, x and y. She does this because that vice-president is known to be an expert in the area of marketing products made by technology II. Furthermore, the production vice-president has the responsibility for evaluating w and z. This vice-president has just been hired away from a company that had used marketing strategy III and had made the transition from technology I to technology II during his tenure. The president herself is decisive for all other pairs of alternatives.

By the assumption of nonrestriction of individual preferences, we can ask what would happen with any possible sets of preferences. That is, it is perfectly feasible for the president and the two vice-presidents to have the preferences

Marketing Strategies

		I	II	III
Production Strategies	I	u	v	w
	II	x	y	z

PREFERENCES

President	Sales Vice-President	Production Vice-President
z	u	x
v	y	w
x	z	u
w	v	y
u	x	z
y	w	v

FIG. 1. The Sen paradox in a hierarchical organization.

given in Figure 1. What must be the decision of the organization in this case?

The production vice-president claims that with marketing strategy III, production strategy I is better than II. That is, he ranks w over z. But the president (and everyone else) ranks x over w. The sales vice-president claims that y is better than x. But the president (and everyone else) ranks u better than y. The president thinks v is better than u. This gives us a ranking of v over u over y over x over w over z. But the president and everyone else thinks that z is better than v. This means that there is a cycle of preferences, violating transitivity. Someone with the authority to enforce the decision prefers something else to anything you can suggest. There is no stable, undominated outcome. The point of the Sen paradox is that, with any system of delegation, even very minimal ones of the sort used in this example, there will be some set of preferences that creates instability.

You can of course resolve this instability, but only by violating one of the other desirable characteristics. For instance, as president, you could accept the decision of your subordinates, which would lead you to some alternative like v. But this would be a violation of the unanimity principle since everyone in the organization prefers z to v. Or you could impose the alternative z, which is after all the first choice of the president. But this contradicts the supposed delegation of authority to subordinates and reveals the hierarchy as in fact a dictatorship instead of a minimally decentralized organization. A president who tries to overrule every subordinate who has delegated authority will become an overworked bottleneck; the literature mentioned above has ruled this possibility out as technically impossible and undesirable as well. In short, it is logically impossible to combine Pareto efficiency, transitivity, and minimal decentralization in an organization which is programmed to make a decision for every possible combination of individual preferences.

This example assumes very minimal accounts of delegation of decision-making authority. With more extensive delegation of entire dimensions of policy to different specialized units, the likelihood that the problem will develop is much greater. It is, in fact a particular case of a general problem associated with Kenneth Shepsle's theory of structure-induced equilibria. Shepsle (1979) considers to what extent institutional structure in the form of division of labor and jurisdiction produce equilibrium when there is in fact no majority rule equilibrium. As Shepsle notes, this amounts to an interest in the

> mechanisms of decentralization that are employed to expedite complex decision-making. Examples abound: a committee system in a legislature; a collection of schools, colleges, and departments in a university; a system of divisions in a firm; an arrangement of bureaus in an agency . . . What distinguishes these mechanisms of decentralization is that they are division of labor instruments. The different committees of a legislature or departments of a university have different (though not necessarily disjoint) domains of responsibility of jurisdictions. (p. 31)

What Shepsle does not specifically say is that each of these different domains of responsibility amounts to delegation of veto power over some elements of the organization's alternative set in favor of others. Thus, the Sen paradox applies, and organizations with the structural properties Shepsle describes will necessarily be subject to the Sen paradox.

Shepsle claims that structures can in fact guarantee stable equilibria, and indeed they can, if you make the assumption that an organization will not overrule inefficiencies that decentralization generates. Figure 2 provides an example in the context of a generalized division-of-labor organization, in which division I has responsibility for policy dimension I, and division II has responsibility for policy dimension II. Each of the five members has circular indifference curves around the given ideal point. The members of division I are players 1 and 3, the members of division II are players 4 and 5. The system of delegation of decision-making authority results in division I proposing $X(1)$ and division II proposing $Y(1)$, which results in outcome A. The outcome, however, is very clearly one which violates the unanimity principle; everyone in the organization could agree that outcome B, for instance, is better than A. But B is not a stable outcome. Division I, which after all has the authority, would always be wanting to cut back on dimension I, and division II would always be wanting to cut back on the second dimension. Moreover, outcome B is not unique, for there are

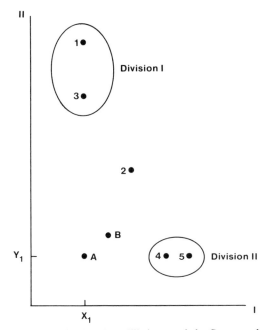

FIG. 2. Institutional equilibrium and the Sen paradox.

other outcomes that are also unanimously preferred to A. But there is a strong conflict of opinion among subgroups among the set of Pareto optimal choices. How is the organization to choose among the set of outcomes which are unanimously better than the structure-induced equilibrium? If they were to vote, in fact, there would be no problem in this case: with this system of preferences, majority rule would give a unique stable equilibrium at player 2's most preferred outcome. But that would definitely make the organization something other than a decentralized hierarchy. The dilemma is clear: if the organization is in fact using the jurisdictional division of labor that Shepsle is studying, then there is a stable inefficient outcome. If the organization is able to achieve an efficent outcome, then it is unstable. Shepsle's "structure-induced equilibrium" is an equilibrium only if the rules are capable of enforcing an outcome that no one likes. The Sen paradox states that any nondictatorial hierarchy will be faced with this dilemma for some possible configurations of preferences.

Restricting Individual Preferences: Teams and the Problem of Shirking

The simplest way out of this dilemma has been much used in the study of markets and electoral bodies. We hope to show that this solution, although much tried in hierarchies, is by no means well understood and is not generally successful.

Markets are decentralized social choice mechanisms; yet welfare economists have been able to prove that markets will result in stable, efficient outcomes. How, in the light of the Sen paradox, can this result hold? It can hold only by assuming restrictions on individual preferences. Individuals are assumed to have preferences only for their own personal consumption levels, and are indifferent to the consumption of others. If consumption externalities do exist, then markets generally fail; that is, they produce equilibria that violate Pareto efficiency.

Similarly, the easiest way to solve the Arrow paradox for voting bodies is to assume that all individuals have preferences that can be mapped as single-peaked preferences in one dimension. In this case, the median voter's most preferred outcome is stable, and, since it is someone's most preferred outcome, it cannot be Pareto dominated. If the voting space is multidimensional, however, then this nice result disappears and the paradox recurs with a vengeance.

In markets and electoral bodies, assuming such restrictions on individual preferences is simply inadequate if the assumption turns out to be false. If a consumer happens to object to another consumer's cigarette smoke or a voter happens to have multipeaked preferences, there is nothing to be done but give up on the certainty of efficient, stable equilibria. Neither a market nor a legislature can require its members to have restricted preferences.

In a hierarchy, however, restrictions on individual preferences might well be a reality of organizational design rather than an assumption. That is, hierarchies may take it upon themselves to select members who have compatible preferences, socialize members to mold their preferences, and sanction individuals who are revealed to have incompatible preferences. The evidence that organizations do concern themselves with individual preferences is overwhelming. And from the standpoint of the Sen paradox, this is virtually an organizational imperative. *Restricting individual preferences is the only way to have an organization that delegates authority without introducing simultaneously the potential for inefficiency and/or instability.*

This technique might well be successful in part. The Forest Service may benefit by recruiting and indoctrinating its foresters as carefully as it does. But how well understood is the technology for restricting individual preferences? Take the organization in Figure 2, for example. How would one go about recruiting employees for Division I and/or Division II so that the organizational division of labor would always result in a stable, Pareto-efficient equilibrium? And who would have the job of doing the recruiting? Player 2, as organizational president, would like to recruit people for Division I whose preferences on this dimension are compatible with his own, and similarly with Division II. On the other hand, if (as is more typical) Division I and Division II got to recruit their own members, there would be a self-perpetuating tendency to reproduce their own problematic preferences.

Furthermore, the restriction of individual preferences as an organizational tactic runs into the problem of moral hazard. Indeed, moral hazard can be viewed as a manifestation of the Sen paradox at the most basic organizational level.

For example, consider an undifferentiated organization that has succeeded in recruiting members who are dedicated to a single, clear measure of organizational profit. The organizational task is rope pulling. Ten individuals have been told that organizational profit is completely determined by the force exerted on the rope. Each of the ten individuals will split organizational profit equally. Let us make this a very primitive organization, one without hierarchy or specialization. The ten members simply have to grab hold of the rope and pull; the aggregate force on the rope will be measured, organizational profit calculated, and individuals paid off accordingly.

This is as simple an organization, and as simple an organizational task, as can be imagined. Furthermore, there are no policy differences among the individuals as regards profit or the means to it: more is always better. This is a severe restriction on individual preferences that should eliminate all working at cross-purposes and organizational foul-ups. Furthermore, there is only minimal delegation: the only delegated decision is simply the individual's decision about how hard to pull on the rope.

In fact, social psychologists tell us that there is a clear and reproducible problem in this simple kind of organization, known as social loafing. When confronted with a simple group task like pulling on a rope, cheering, or clapping to produce noise levels, individual effort declines with the number of coworkers. "We have found that when the individual thinks his or her own contribution to the group cannot be measured, his or her output tends to slacken." (Latane et al., 1979, p. 104) This was found to be true in both German and American cultures, and for a large number of tasks. Nor can faulty coordination of effort explain the decline in group effort. When blindfolded and convinced that others were pulling with them, "people pulled at 90 per cent of their individual rate when they believed one other person was pulling, and at only 85 per cent when they believed two to six others were pulling. It appears that virtually all of the decline in performance could be accounted for in terms of reduced effort or social loafing" (Ibid., p. 106).

The delegated aspect of organizational performance is the ineluctable minimum: "How much will I as an individual pull on this rope?" This decision is not subject to veto by anyone, nor is it even monitored. The point is that even in this organization in which delegation of authority is minimal, and in which preferences have been severely restricted in order to achieve maximum agreement on organizational goals, the Sen paradox still appears with a vengeance.

The Nash equilibrium of this game is very stable, but totally inefficient: everyone loafs, yet they all realize they would be better off if no one loafed. All members might agree to work harder; they might even hire a cheerleader to spur themselves to maximal effort. But this is clearly not a stable outcome, even if it is temporarily achieved. While working maximally, each will wonder if the others are, and the temptation will inevitably be to slacken. The best the organization can hope for is some kind of cycle in which the organization periodically agrees within itself to cooperate for greater success in organizational goals, but in which the cooperative effect is short-lived.

This situation is obviously analogous to the problem of "team" production investigated by Alchian and Demsetz. As Alchian and Demsetz point out, social loafing or "shirking" is even more of a problem in "team" production, in which the cross partial derivative of individual efforts is not zero; that is, the marginal effect of one individual's effort is itself a function of the other individual's effort. In these cases, it is not possible to solve the problem by measuring each individual's effort and rewarding individual marginal productivity. For teams, "measuring marginal productivity and making payments in accord therewith is more expensive by an order of magnitude than for separable production functions" (Alchian and Demsetz, 1972, p. 779).

How does the Alchian-Demsetz approach square with the social choice approach? Alchian and Demsetz recognize that while individuals share a common interest in the team reward, the preferences of different individuals may still be widely varied. In particular, they will have residual differences in preferences due to the fact that their own individual utility functions are based in part on their own leisure. Because both "leisure and higher income enter a person's utility function," each individual "will adjust his rate of work to bring his demand prices of leisure and output to equality with their true costs" (Alchian and Demsetz, p. 780). Alchian and Demsetz arrive at this conclusion through an analysis of member incentives to contribute toward the production of collective goods. But application of the Sen paradox leads to a general conclusion consistent with theirs: given even minimal delegation, a stable organizational outcome (universal shirking) must be inefficient, that is, there are other outcomes (including universal nonshirking) that everyone prefers.

Alchian and Demsetz make it very clear that the only kind of restriction of individual preferences that is sufficient to eliminate the trade-off of stability versus efficiency (i.e., the Sen paradox) is one in which individuals are not assumed to have leisure as a part of their utility function. Lacking this restriction, shirking is inevitable; and with shirking comes Pareto suboptimal equilibria, for as Alchian and Demsetz note, "Every team member would prefer a team in which no one, not even himself shirked." But such an outcome is not attainable without finding people who do not value leisure, or creating the absolute dictatorship by depriving employees of the freedom to work at anything less than maximal effort. As long as individuals have any degree of freedom in choosing their own leisure (minimal decentralization), and as long as individuals value leisure (nonrestriction of individual preferences), then the Sen paradox will appear.

Hierarchy as Specialized Monitoring of Shirking

To summarize the argument thus far, decentralized organizations must be vulnerable to configurations of preferences that result in either inefficiency or instability. Theoretically, this problem can be solved by eliminating the troublesome preference configurations, but Alchian and Demsetz make a convincing argument that these preference configurations will arise as long as leisure enters individual utility functions. Alchian and Demsetz claim, in fact, that the only efficient way to solve the problem is by moving away from decentralization to nondictatorial hierarchy. The purpose of this section is to see whether hierarchy can indeed solve the Sen paradox, given that restrictions of individual preferences cannot. Can hierarchies produce stable efficient outcomes where teams cannot?

Alchian and Demsetz cite several attributes or rights of the hierarchical superior in a firm. The superior has the right "to observe input behavior," that is, to monitor the behavior of individuals providing labor or services. The superior has the right to be "the central party common to all contracts with inputs." In addition, the superior has the right to terminate the contract unilaterally with any provider of labor or a service. Finally, the superior has the right to be the "residual claimant" to the surplus generated by the firm, and is authorized to sell these rights to other individuals. "The coalescing of these rights has arisen, our analysis asserts, because it resolves the shirking-information problem of team production better than does the noncentralized contractual agreement" (Alchian and Demsetz, p. 783).

The team of rope pullers must now be reorganized hierarchically. This changes the nature of the team member's problem. The question is no longer, "How hard shall I pull on this rope?" The question is now, "Shall I comply with the organization's hierarchically regulated and mandated behavior, or take a chance on being discovered as a shirker?" The existence of hierarchy and rules creates a principal-agent relationship between the monitor and subordinate. The subordinate is working for the superior, with his choices constrained by the incentive system created by the superior. They are no longer members of a team.

What does the principal/agent literature have to say about simple hierarchies like this? The classic statement of principal-agent theory by Ross (1973) argues that it is possible for the principal to create an incentive system that will lead to a stable Nash equilibrium which is Pareto efficient for the two players. This apparently flies in the face of the Sen paradox, so its assumptions clearly bear looking into.

As Ross has structured the problem, a given act by the agent may lead to a variety of possible payoffs for the principal, due to uncertainty in the environment. The Pareto efficient incentive system is one in which the agent's fee is linear with the principal's earnings. As Ross points out, this guarantees that "the agent and the principal have identical attitudes toward risky payoffs and, consequently, the agent will always choose the act that the principal most desires" (p. 136).

This sounds like an overly simple solution to the problem of hierarchy. All the superior has to do is provide every subordinate with a contract that guarantees the subordinate a percentage of the value generated by the subordinate's activities, and the subordinate will always act in the superior's best interests. The organization is decentralized (the superior has autonomy over choice of the incentive system, the subordinate has autonomy over how he performs the task), and yet it is efficient and stable.

But logically, since the Ross solution guarantees decentralization, efficiency, and stability, then some of the assumptions he uses *must* by the Sen paradox restrict individual preferences. How much of a restriction is he forced to make in order to get this idea result? As it turns out, Ross assumes that each agent has a utility function in which only the fee and risk appear. The agent, in other words, does not value leisure time, contrary to the Alchian-Demsetz argument, nor does he have preferences over the state of the world or the payoffs to the principal. If we assume that bureaucrats value leisure or policy outcomes, then the Ross result no longer applies. In particular, it is possible to construct a counterexample of a superior-subordinate relationship, in which the superior promises the subordinate a linear fee based on the superior's valuation of the subordinate's performance, and still have the dilemma of inefficient stable equilibria (or efficient nonequilibria).

As a simple example of this, consider the following statement of a minimal superior/subordinate relationship. There is one subordinate who can expend effort providing the service that is valued by the superior. Let E indicate the amount of effort spent by the subordinate, and let us assume for simplicity that the superior gets V units of value for each unit of effort spent by the subordinate. The only control that the superior has over the subordinate is the reward function, whereby the superior pays the subordinate k dollars for every unit of effort. The linear production of V in E and the linear fee for k in E guarantee that the subordinate's fee is linear in V. The superior's net payoff equals $(V-k)E$. The subordinate, however, dislikes expending effort, and in fact the marginal cost of expending effort increases with effort: $MC = c + 2dE$, where c and d are positive (Figure 3).

With these assumptions, the subordinate will only work until $c + 2dE = k$. Knowing that for every possible k, the subordinate will set $E = (k-c)/2d$, the superior can substitute that value for E into his net payoff function. Taking the

Parameters

V = superior's (constant) marginal valuation of effort   (e.g., $v = 5$)
E = subordinate's effort (subordinate's decision variable)
k = subordinate's pay per unit of effort (superior's decision variable)
$cE + dE^2$ = subordinate's psychic cost of effort   (e.g., $c = 3$, $d = 1$)

Individual Goals

superior maximizes $vE - kE$
subordinate maximizes $kE - cE - dE^2$

Superior's Strategies

	$k = 4.4$	$k = 4.0$
$E = 1$	superior earns .6 subordinate earns .4	superior earns 1.0 subordinate earns 0.0
$E = .5$	superior earns .3 subordinate earns .45	superior earns .5 subordinate earns .25

Subordinate's strategies

FIG. 3. Hierarchical compliance as a prisoners' dilemma.

derivative of this with respect to his decision variable k, we discover that the superior is best off setting $k = (V+c)/2$. This produces a level of effort by the subordinate at $E = (V-c)/4d$.

However, this will not be the efficient level of effort; with this constrained example, it will be exactly half the efficient level of effort. Both the superior and the subordinate could be better off at $E = (V-c)/2d$. But this could be achieved only by deviating from their individually rational behavior, so that the efficient outcome will be unstable.

It is obvious that if the superior knows the subordinate's cost function, it is not efficient to pay the subordinate some fixed fee for every unit of effort. It is much more efficient for the superior simply to say, "I will pay you X if you work at the efficient level $E = (V-c)/2d$, and nothing if you work any less hard." As long as X is slightly greater than his psychic cost of working at that level, then the superior could conceivably get the subordinate to work at that level, while obtaining virtually all of the surplus generated by that level of effort for herself.

However, there are two problems with this solution, ideal though it may be from the bureaucratic superior's standpoint. The first is that the superior may not know the subordinate's cost functions, and thus may not be able to find and dictate the ideal level of effort. It is, after all, internal to the employee's psyche, and the employee has no incentive to reveal that information to the superior. By a trial-and-error process, the superior and subordinate can converge to the (inefficient) intersection of their reaction functions without detailed knowledge of the other's cost or benefit parameters; but the existence of an equilibrium does not imply any specific parameters and therefore does not allow the superior to deduce the subordinate's psychic aversion to work. But without this information, the superior cannot confidently mandate a specific optimal level of effort on the part of the subordinate. The mandated level of effort, after all, is an effort on the part of the superior to require the subordinate to work harder than he would otherwise work for the level of remuneration. But this means that, with a mistake, the superior could dictate a level of work that leaves the subordinate indifferent or hostile toward working at all. The line at which the subordinate is just indifferent to quitting altogether is shown in Figure 4; any combination of effort and payoff mandated below that line would result in a negative net payoff for the employee and force him out. In other words, the superior can use the bureaucratic structure of hierarchy and rules to mandate a fixed level of effort at the optimum, but only with precise information. The bureaucratic superior is using the agenda control provided by

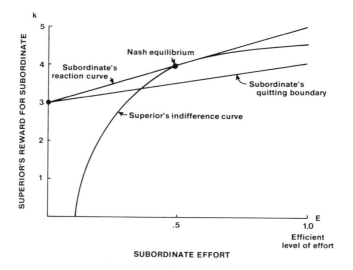

FIG. 4. Hierarchical compliance as game with inefficient institutional equilibrium.

her bureaucratic position to make a take-it-or-leave-it offer to the subordinate, but the line below which the subordinate would leave it must be known by the superior.

Another problem is that by using the bureaucratic structure to force the subordinate to deviate from his reaction function, the superior is requiring another level of enforcement. The suboptimal Nash equilibrium is self-enforcing in that the subordinate picks his rational degree of effort given the reward structure. But when a bureaucracy mandates through hierarchy and rules a fixed level of effort that is not the subordinate's best choice given the reward structure, then the superior suddenly has to create the machinery to enforce that mandate. As Gouldner noted, the use of impersonal rules in a bureaucracy, motivated by the superior's need to control subordinate behavior, has the effect of providing information to the subordinate about minimal acceptable levels of work (Gouldner, 1954). Given that subordinates tend to resent the authoritarian model of supervision and control that is implied by the rule- and hierarchy-enforced level of effort, they are certainly unlikely to go beyond this bare minimum. This leads to increasing attempts to require extra effort through more levels of hierarchy, which in turn leads to more resentment on the part of subordinates, a drop in morale and motivation, and an increase in interpersonal tension that might in fact lead to a change in the subordinate's psychic costs of effort. This leads to a vicious cycle known in organizational behavior circles as the rigidity cycle, and must result in a rightward shift in the subordinate's "quitting boundary," meaning more turnover and decreased efficiency.

Furthermore, even if the superior does know the subordinate's cost function, then the superior's ability to impose her ideal solution by means of a set of rules requiring minimal performance is still dependent on the subordinate's lack of bargaining ability. If the subordinate possesses some other ready sources of employment, then it would be just as possible for the subordinate to impose his ideal solution: "I will work at the level you mentioned [$E = (v - c)/2d$] because this is the level of effort that maximizes our organization's overall consumer surplus; however, I will work at that level of effort only for a total wage slightly less than your evaluation of it." Of course, either side's ability to impose either ideal solution is dependent on relative bargaining ability determined by numerous factors, including relative balance of information asymmetries, the number of other potential employees competing for the employee's job, the number of other employers competing for the employee's time, etc. In general, there is no reason to believe that the superior will be able to impose her ideal solution any more than the subordinate will be able to impose the other. Virtually all one can say about the simple hierarchy is constrained by the Sen paradox: the equilibrium outcome is unstable, and the efficient outcomes can be reached only by potentially unstable bargaining between the superior and the subordinate. The hierarchic relationship proposed by Alchian and Demsetz is no more

immune to the Sen paradox than the team production problem which motivated the solution.

Specialized Hierarchies

The preceding section discussed what the Sen paradox might imply about
simple hierarchies consisting of one superior, one subordinate, and a rule specifying some exchange relationship between them. It was argued that even under
conditions that are more favorable than reality (a superior who is able to monitor subordinate behavior with no error, and with total control over the subordinate's payoffs), the existence of hierarchy and rules does not imply the existence of a Pareto optimal stable outcome. The subordinate's control over his
own degree of cooperation is sufficient "liberalism," in Sen's sense, to introduce the paradox. Either a suboptimal equilibrium will occur with some degree
of control loss, or instability will be likely.

But in fact, the problems in actual bureaucracies are normally much worse
than that. The normal bureaucratic superior has more than one subordinate to
supervise. The advantage of bureaucracy, it is commonly argued, is due in large
part to division of labor and specialization. The normal superior, therefore, has
multiple specialized subordinates who are assigned the responsibility of carrying out specialized aspects of the organization's task. This compounds the
problem, because even if each subordinate is perfectly compliant and sincerely
attempting to pursue his portion of the task, the aggregation of a lot of specialized tasks done well is not necessarily optimal over all. This is once again an immediate implication of the Sen paradox.

McCubbins and Schwartz[2] have proved this with regard to the theory of
principals and agents. They assume a principal who has at her disposal a series
of agents, each of whom is responsible for a few specialized dimensions of
tasks. They further assume that each agent is a perfect agent, that is, one that
will act within his own task dimensions in the principal's interest. In Figure 5,
the convex indifference curves are those of the principal. Let us assume that the
X agent has picked $x(1)$, and the Y agent has picked $y(1)$. Each of these behaviors is best for the principal, given the other agent's choice. Neither agent can
unilaterally change his behavior without either harming the principal or exceed-
ing the budget constraint. Both agents can justify their behavior as being that
of a loyal and selfless agent. The problem is that the budget constraint has introduced nonseparability into the problem. Each agent's best choice is dependent on the other agent's choice. The point determined by $x(1)$ and $y(1)$ is an
inefficient equilibrium, resulting from the decentralized delegation of authority
to perfect specialized agents.

The obvious response to Figure 5 is that the problem is simply one of coordination. But this obvious response, while correct, begs the question. Is it possible to introduce enough centralized coordination to guarantee stable efficient

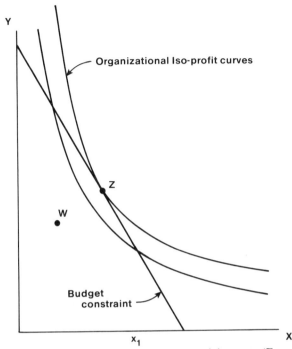

FIG. 5. Inefficient, stable equilibrium with perfect, special agents. (From McCubbins and Schwartz; see note 2.)

outcomes without introducing dictatorship? The Sen paradox says that this is the trade-off, without offering the hope of an optimal outcome on any trade-off possibility frontier. If the principal has enough information, for instance, she could perhaps require the exactly efficient choices of agents X and Y, given the budget constraint. However, if the principal has enough information to do this, then one wonders why she needs agents in the first place.

The same argument is true for hierarchies. If it were possible for one person to know all about the effects of the X and Y dimensions on organizational profit, then the superior could make all the decisions regarding those two dimensions herself, without the aid of specialist subordinates. The problem is, of course, that most superiors cannot know everything, and therefore can neither dismiss the specialists nor be guaranteed of coordinating their behavior efficiently as long as they are in the organization. The information asymmetry, so important to the new economics of organization discussed in the first section of this paper, is central to understanding the social choice analysis of power relationships as well.

Organizations have specialized subordinates because they presumably provide specialized expertise. It is this expertise that gives a special "bite" to the problems that have been discussed so far in this section. The Alchian-Demsetz solution to the problem of team shirking was to create a hierarchical superior who has an incentive to monitor subordinate behavior. But the problems of shirking, monitoring, adverse selection, and moral hazard all become especially problematic when the subordinate is hired for a supposed expertise that the superior lacks.

If one wants to hire the best theoretical physicist or plant pathologist available for a given amount of money, the problems of adverse selection and moral hazard are obviously more intense if you yourself are not a physicist or plant pathologist. Once you have hired an individual with the credentials which you hope support your choice, then how do you go about monitoring his effort or performance? When the subordinate says that technical problems made greater success in his research and development division impossible this year, how do you know whether that is the truth or an excellent cover for shirking? Even if you are convinced that your subordinate-expert is sincerely trying to work in the organization's best interests, how do you know whether his expertise has not in fact blinded him to the superior option which is simply regarded as unacceptable given the professional training he received? If two of your subordinate-experts are sincerely trying to coordinate behavior for the organization's well-being, isn't it possible that there is a superior combination of specialist decisions that they do not see? And if you, as the superior, do believe that there is a superior option available that the specialists do not see because of their "trained incompetence," as the sociologists see it, can you enforce that unorthodox option on your supposed subordinates, or does their expertise give them the power to enforce their incorrect choices on the decentralized organization?

The tension between the authority of expertise and the authority of hierarchy has been one of the most noted empirical generalizations about modern organizations. Talcott Parsons, in his introduction to Weber (1947), specifically contrasted the two systems of authority and instigated thereby a great deal of research on the inefficiencies and conflict generated by the unresolved conflict between the two. A single example serves to illustrate the problem. During the Cuban missile crisis, Chief of Naval Operations Admiral George Anderson claimed the authority to command the blockade forces based on naval expertise. Secretary of Defense McNamara used the hierarchical authority of the presidency to demand that the blockade be managed in a different way to decrease the possibility of a nuclear confrontation. Upon insistent questioning by McNamara,

> Anderson replied that he had outlined the procedures in the National Security Council meeting and that there was no need to discuss it further. Angered but still calm, McNamara began to lecture the admiral. . . . At one point McNamara asked An-

derson what he would do if a Soviet ship's captain refused to answer questions about his cargo. At that point, the Navy man picked up the *Manual of Navy Regulations* and, waving it in McNamara's face, shouted, "It's all in there." To which McNamara replied, "I don't give a damn what John Paul Jones would have done. I want to know what you are going to do, now." The encounter ended on Anderson's remark: "Now, Mr. Secretary, if you and your Deputy will go back to your offices, the Navy will run the blockade." (Allison, pp. 131–132)

The President of the United States, operating through the most powerful Secretary of Defense in history, at the moment in history when the world was the closest it had ever been to nuclear catastrophe, found his hierarchical authority challenged by the authority of expertise.

This authority of expertise is a fact in today's organizations, keeping them from being characterized as dictatorial hierarchies. The social choice theory approach taken in this section suggests that, as long as hierarchies have more than one subordinate unit in the organization, each capable of determining some aspect of the organization's behavior, then hierarchies may be subject to the same problems of inefficiency and intransitivity which have been more extensively studied in voting, committee, and legislative contexts. Nondictatorship, efficiency, and transitivity can be reconciled, but only by making unrealistic assumptions regarding restrictions on individual preferences. As long as individuals value leisure or have their own policy preferences, shirking or "deviationism" will have the potential to produce inefficiencies or instabilities in otherwise homogeneous teams or in simple hierarchies. Multiple specialized subordinates and expertise further compound the problem by building in additional pluralism of values within the organization and by reinforcing the decentralized decision rules that give subordinate units the ability to determine aspects of the organization's over-all behavior. The traditional Weberian elements of bureaucracy—hierarchy, specialization, and expertise—each present new faces for the Sen paradox.

CONCLUSIONS

One conclusion of this paper is that the new economics of organization is extraordinarily promising. For decades, the study of public bureaucracy has been heavily influenced by sociological organization theory and the prescriptive, nuts-and-bolts concerns of traditional public administration. It is no accident that this is one of the most underdeveloped areas in all political science. The work of Simon, March, and others in the behavioral tradition has, to this point, been far and away the most promising source of creativity and theoretical progress; but despite the high regard in which it is held by political scientists, it has yet to generate the amounts and kinds of theoretical work its proponents had hoped for and probably would have predicted many years back. The economics of organization may turn out to be different. It sheds interesting new light on bureaucratic behavior by focusing on hierarchical control—an elegant, beautifully suitable focus that points to the essence of organizational relationships and offers a coherent framework for integrating both the bureaucratic and the political dimensions of administrative performance. Largely because it maintains the optimizing model of choice, moreover, it offers virtually the full range of powerful analytical methods characteristic of neoclassical economics, and it overlaps in useful and important ways with better-developed areas of economics, information economics in particular. For these reasons, among others, many students of politics are likely to find the new economics of organization an especially attractive line of inquiry.

Another basic conclusion is that contributors to the new economics of organization can greatly extend our understanding of hierarchy through systematic application of social choice theory. We have tried to illustrate the point by focusing on an important theoretical issue: hierarchy is a setting for manifestations of the Sen paradox. Superior-subordinate relationships, as we have seen, are subject to inefficient, stable outcomes. The problem is enhanced when superiors must supervise multiple, specialized subordinates, as specialization tends to build in the preconditions for the Sen paradox: pluralism of values supported by multiplicity of decision centers. The more the specialist-subordinates monopolize expertise in the organization, the greater the tension between hierarchy and expertise. The inefficiencies and instabilities noted in organizations where hierarchy conflicts with expertise can themselves be viewed as manifestations of the Sen paradox.

It has been customary for authors of papers on theory in public administration to close with the hope for more rigorous theoretical development in the field. This hope already seems to have been fulfilled, for the rigorous theoretical analysis of hierarchy is a full-blown fact in the new economics of organization. We hope instead that political scientists will make their contribution to this field, helping this new literature to steer clear of its potential for creating theory that is more and more sterile. Once again, past developments in the positive theory provide a model; for when economists were creating elegant but arcane models of decision-making processes, it was political scientists who kept asking, "What does this mean for real-world institutions like Congress?" It was this interplay of rigor from economic theorists and substantive concerns from political scientists that has given rise to the blossoming of legislative analysis in the last few decades, as political scientists grappled with questions of rational choice, stability, and the Arrow Paradox in the legislative setting (for example, see Shepsle, 1979; Weingast, 1983; Weingast and Moran, forthcoming; Fiorina, 1977). We hope that, by promoting a positive theory of hierarchies, we can provide—for public administration—the framework for the kind of useful interchange of economists and political scientists that has proved so beneficial in other fields of institutional analysis.

NOTES

1. The ideas of Simon (1947) and March and Simon (1958) overlap in crucial ways with those being discussed here. See Moe (1984).
2. Matthew McCubbins and Thomas Schwartz, personal communication, 1983.

REFERENCES

Alchian, Armen A., and Demsetz, Harold (1972). Production, information costs, and economic organization. *American Economic Review* 62: 777–795.
Allison, Graham T. (1972). *Essence of Decision*. Boston: Little-Brown.
Arrow, Kenneth J. (1963). *Social Choice and Individual Values*. 2nd ed. New Haven: Yale University Press.
Baiman, Stanley (1982). Agency research in managerial accounting. *Journal of Accounting Literature* 20: 154–213.
Coase, Ronald (1937). The nature of the firm. *Economica* 4: 386–405.
Coase, Ronald (1972). Industrial organization: a proposal for research. In V. R. Fuchs (ed.), *Policy Issues and Research Opportunities in Industrial Organization*, pp. 59–73. New York: National Bureau of Economic Research.
Commons, John R. (1934). *Institutional Economics*. New York: Macmillan.
Cyert, Richard M., and March, James G. (1963). *A Behavioral Theory of the Firm*. Englewood Cliffs, N.J.: Prentice-Hall.
Demsetz, Harold (1982). *Economic, Legal, and Political Dimensions of Competition*. New York: Elsevier North-Holland.
Downs, Anthony (1966). *Inside Bureaucracy*. Boston: Little-Brown.
Fiorina, Morris (1977). *Congress: Keystone of the Washington Establishment*. New Haven: Yale University Press.
Gouldner, Alvin (1954). *Patterns of Industrial Bureaucracy*. New York: Free Press.
Hammond, Thomas, and Miller, Gary (1985). Expertise and authority in decentralized organization. *American Journal of Political Science*, 29: 1–28.
Hess, James D. (1983). *The Economics of Organization*. New York: Elsevier North-Holland.
Holmstrom, B.R. (1979). Moral hazard and observability. *Bell Journal of Economics* (Spring): 74–91.
Jensen, Michael C. (1983). Organization theory and methodology. *The Accounting Review* 8: 319–337.
Jensen, Michael C., and Meckling, William (1976). Theory of the firm: managerial behavior, agency costs, and ownership structure. *Journal of Financial Economics* 3: 305–360.
Latane, Bibb, et al. (1979). Social loafing. *Psychology Today*, October, 1979.
March, James G., and Simon, Herbert (1958). *Organizations*. New York: Wiley.
Moe, Terry M. (1984). The new economics of organization. *American Journal of Political Science*. 28: 739–777.
Myerson, R.B. (1979). Incentive compatibility and the bargaining problem. *Econometrica* 47: 61–73.
Niskanen, William A. (1971). *Bureaucracy and Representative Government*. Chicago: Aldine-Atherton.
Roethlisberger, F. J., and Dickson, William J. (1939). *Management and the Worker*. Cambridge, Mass.: Harvard University Press.
Ross, Stephen A. (1973). The economic theory of agency: the principal's problem. *American Economic Review* 12: 134–139.
Sen, A. K. (1970). The impossibility of a Paretian liberal. *Journal of Political Economy* (Jan./Feb.): 152–157.
Shafritz, Jay M., and Hyde, Albert C., eds. (1978). *Classics of Public Administration*. Oak Park, Ill.: Moore Publishing Co.

Shavell, S. (1979). Risk sharing and incentives in the principal and agent relationship. *Bell Journal of Economics* 10: 55–73.

Shepsle, Kenneth (1979). Institutional arrangements and equilibrium in multidimensional voting models. *American Journal of Political Science* (February): 27–59.

Simon, Herbert A. (1947). *Administrative Behavior*. New York: Macmillan, 1947.

Spence, Michael (1974). *Market Signaling*. Cambridge, Mass.: Harvard University Press.

Spence, Michael, and Zeckhauser, Richard (1971). Insurance, information, and individual action. *American Economic Review* 61: 380–387.

Taylor, Frederick W. (1947). *Scientific Management*. New York: Harper.

Tullock, Gordon. (1965). *The Politics of Bureaucracy*. Washington, D.C.: Public Affairs Press.

Weber, Max (1947). *The Theory of Social and Economic Organizations*, Talcott Parsons, ed. New York: Oxford University Press.

Weingast, Barry R. (1983). A principal-agent perspective on congressional-bureaucratic relations, delivered at Fifth Carnegie Conference on Political Economy, Carnegie Mellon University.

Weingast, Barry R., and Moran, Mark. Bureaucratic discretion or congressional control: regulatory policy-making by the Federal Trade Commission. *Journal of Political Economy*, forthcoming.

Wilson, Woodrow. The study of administration. Reprinted in Shafritz and Hyde, *Classics of Public Administration*.

Part III
The Science of Political Behavior

CHAPTER 9

STRUCTURAL ESTIMATION WITH LIMITED VARIABLES

Charles H. Franklin and John E. Jackson

Political scientists have increasingly turned to complex multiequation models to represent and test theories of political behavior. The most common is the linear structural equation system,

$$Y^*C + X^*B = U$$

where Y^* and X^* are endogenous and exogenous variables respectively, C and B are matrices of parameters, and U is a vector of stochastic disturbances. This set of equations expresses our theory about the causal relations underlying the behavior, and we refer to this as the "behavioral" structure. If our theory is correct, and if our statistical method is appropriate for the data used to observe and measure Y^* and X^*, the estimates we get for B and C will be good estimates of the hypothesized causal relations in the behavioral structure.

As the parameters in C and B represent our hypotheses regarding the behavioral structure, it is natural that most attention has been devoted to their specification and estimation, and to developing various nonlinear extensions to the structure. Nevertheless, recent research has begun to recognize that data, and political science data in particular, are generated both by a behavioral structure and by an observational structure. The nature of the observational process, its implications for the observed data, and its statistical consequences substantially affect our ability to estimate B and C accurately. For example, survey interviewers ask respondents if they feel "much," "some," "little," or "no" interest in politics. As degree of interest is a continuous concept, our observational structure cuts this scale into ordinal categories. Consequently, we do not actually observe the person's level of interest, but only data which are related in some way to that continuous variable. Furthermore, this categorization induces errors in our observations, in that some people with different underlying interest levels are treated identically, while some others with nearly similar amounts of interest are assessed as being different. Such observational errors may seriously impede empirical efforts.

The simplest observational structure assumes that all variables are measured directly and without error, i.e., $X = X^*$ and $Y = Y^*$. Under these conditions, the classical linear estimator, e.g., generalized least squares (GLS) or instrumental variables, gives consistent and asymptotically efficient estimates of the parameters in the behavioral structure, including estimates of the variances and covariances of the stochastic terms, denoted by Σ_u.

The classical econometrics literature expands the observational model so that endogenous variables include an additive, purely random component, i.e., $Y = Y^* + e$, with $E(e) = 0$. In this case, the above statistical properties hold, except we cannot separately estimate Σ_u and Σ_e. (The stochastic term in the statistical estimation adds U and e to form a single term.) It is important to note the special restrictions in this observational structure, its wide and robust application in spite of the assumptions, and the fact that the behavioral and observational models are combined in a way that makes neither identifiable.

The desirable properties of our estimators vanish, however, when we further loosen the restrictions on the observational model. If the exogenous variables contain error, we lose the purchase on estimation of B and C which was gained by the standard estimators. (For a discussion and an illustration of the consequences of observing X^* with error, see Hanushek and Jackson, 1977, pp. 286–298.) The result is that we can no longer estimate the behavioral model which our theory implies unless we take into consideration the structure which relates our observations to the terms which appear in the behavioral model.

This loss of desirable statistical properties, and the growing recognition of the potential complexity of the observational structure, has lead to considerable recent interest in models which explicitly specify and estimate both the behavioral and observational structures. These approaches reflect the recognition that neither model can be properly estimated without consideration of the other.

Previous work on the observational structure has taken two largely separate paths. Probit and logit models have concentrated on the difficulties of coarse measurements which produce only ordinal and nominal variables but have assumed very limited behavioral models. The other, referred to generically as LISREL, permits complex linear behavioral and observational structures, but is generally limited to the case of continuous measures. (The work by Muthén, 1979, is an important exception.) We will briefly consider the characteristics of each of these approaches.

LIMITED ENDOGENOUS VARIABLES

The categorical nature of most survey data, as represented by the previously mentioned interest measure, and by choices in multicandidate elections, provides considerable incentive to develop and use procedures for limited endogenous variables. These procedures require a model of the observational structure that gives predicted probabilities for each possible value of the observed variable, conditioned on the value of the latent behavioral structure, $Y^* = X^*B$. Several possible functions are used to represent this stochastic relationship. (See Amemiya, 1981, for a review of several approaches.) The functions differ in how they expect the observed outcomes to be distributed among the possible categories.

The first class of models assumes an ordered grouping of the observed variable's categories, such as with the interest variable and with Guttman scales. These procedures specify exogenous variables observed without error, $X = X^*$, and a reduced form model relating observed exogenous variables to the latent continuous endogenous variable, $Y^* = X^*B$. The estimation procedure then "assigns" predicted outcomes for the observed Y for each case based on a series of thresholds,

$$Y = 1 \text{ for all } Y^* < t_1 \qquad\qquad \text{Category 1}$$

$$Y = 2 \text{ for all } t_1 \leq Y^* < t_2 \qquad\qquad \text{Category 2}$$

$$\cdot$$
$$\cdot$$
$$\cdot$$

$$Y = m \text{ for all } t_{m-1} \leq Y^* < t_m \qquad\qquad \text{Category } m$$

$$\cdot$$
$$\cdot$$
$$\cdot$$

$$Y = M \text{ for all } t_{M-1} \leq Y^* \qquad\qquad \text{Category } M$$

where Y^* is the latent continuous endogenous variable, and Y is the observed, ordinal indicator of Y^*.

Procedures vary in the cumulative distribution assumed for the observed outcomes. Probit models are based on the standard cumulative normal distribution $[\text{Prob}(Y = m) = F(m) - F(m-1)]$, and logit models assume a logistic distribution, $[\text{Prob}(Y = m) = L(m) - L(m-1)]$, where $L(m) = \exp(a_m + Y^*)/(1 + \exp(a_m + Y^*))$.[1] With these models it is possible to estimate the behavioral model, represented by X^*B, and the observational structure consisting of the set of thresholds.[2]

A major limitation of these models is their very simple behavioral and observational structures. According to the model, values for any observed variable arise only from a single latent variable, which is related only to X^*. There is no allowance for structural behavioral equations, for multiple influences on observations, or for multiple indicators of latent variables. Thus the process implicit in these models is a direct, one-to-one linking of latent and observed variables.

The probit and logit models combine behaviorally and observationally derived stochastic terms, as do conventional linear models. Larger deviations from $X^{\cdot}B$ *and* more frequent "misclassification" of outcomes both imply that the predicted probabilities for each observed category, conditioned on $X^{\cdot}$, will approach the observed sample frequencies regardless of the values of $X^{\cdot}$.[3]

Recent work has extended the probit model to include ordered endogenous variables within a structural equation framework for the behavioral model. (Lee, 1981, presents an extensive discussion of these models.) This two stage procedure, analogous to the instrumental variables linear model, greatly enhances our ability to estimate the behavioral parameters, and several applications appear in the political science literature (Fiorina, 1981; Franklin and Jackson, 1983; and Franklin, 1984).

Muthén (1979) has extended the probit model to the case of multiple observed indicators of latent behavioral variables. He derives maximum likelihood estimators for this model and provides an empirical example for two dichotomous indicators of a single latent variable. Muthén suggests that the computational requirements of the maximum likelihood estimation are too extensive for the model to be applied in the general case. Avery and Hotz (1981), however, have recently suggested an alternative estimator which is computationally tractable and consistent, although not efficient. Applications of these multiple indicator multiple cause (dubbed MIMC) models have yet to appear.

A second class of limited dependent variable models is designed for multiple (more than two) unordered outcomes, as found, for example, in a three candidate election. The limited variables work here has turned to the logit model, which is well suited to nominal dependent variables, as the probability of each categorical outcome can be modeled without imposing a cumulative ordering on the groups.

The logit procedure assumes a behavioral model with a latent endogenous variable corresponding to each outcome category, $Y^{\cdot}_m = X^{\cdot}B_m$. The observational structure assumes that the probability of each outcome follows a logistic distribution based on the values of the $Y^{\cdot}_m$. The expressions are normalized to insure the sum of all probabilities equals one. The specification means that the log of the odds of observing Y_m relative to Y_j is $(Y_m - Y_j) = X^{\cdot}(B_m - B_j)$. The relevant point is that a particular structure for the relationships between behavior and the generation of observed outcomes is specified and estimated as part of the statistical method to get more accurate estimates of the behavioral model.[4]

The multinomial logit model has been extended to cover the multivariate case. A single observed endogenous variable is constructed where each joint, or conditional, outcome in the multivariate structure defines one of the unordered categories. The log-odds of each joint outcome are modeled as the sum of a series of main effects terms, defined by each marginal outcome, and of possible interaction terms. This structure is similar to that underlying the ANOVA or dummy variable regression models. Early work assumed these terms to be constant for all observed cases. Later work expanded this structure to make the various terms conditional upon values of exogenous variables. This extension effectively converts the main and interaction effects into latent endogenous variables. This latent structure is defined by the construction of the observed variables, and not by a latent behavioral structure. The specification of the multivariate-multinomial logit model does not permit inclusion of the constraints on the coefficients in the behavioral structure required by many applications, nor does it permit the constraints required by the multiple indicator (MIMC) models.

All of the limited variable models just described allow specifications of the observational structure that will accommodate many types of commonly observed data. Unfortunately, these models do not permit very sophisticated specifications of the behavioral structure. With the exception of Muthén's MIMC probit model and the two-stage probit approach, the behavioral structures are limited to single equation, reduced form specifications, and the observational structures are limited to a one-to-one mapping of latent to observed variables (or to categories of observed variables). The challenge from this perspective then is to develop a model for limited endogenous variables that can accommodate the constraints and specifications of more complex behavioral and observational structures.

THE LISREL MODEL

By far the most general and flexible approach to estimation of both behavioral and observational structures is the LISREL model and statistical program (Jöreskog, 1973). This approach incorporates the general structural equation behavioral model with a general specification of a linear observational model.

The LISREL behavior structure is

$$Y^{\cdot}C + X^{\cdot}B = U$$

and the observational model is

$$Y = L_y Y^{\cdot} + e_y$$
$$X = L_x X^{\cdot} + e_x$$

where $Y^{\cdot}$ and $X^{\cdot}$ are latent endogenous and exogenous variables, respectively, Y and X are the observations arising from them, and L_y and L_x are the matrices of coefficients relating observed to latent variables. U is a vector of stochastic terms in the behavioral model, and e_x and e_y represent deviations from the hypothesized observation model. Some authors interpret e_y and e_x as measurement error. This they may be, but they also include *any* and *all* deviations from the explicitly specified linear observation model. These deviations can arise from many sources, such as nonlinearities in the functional form, variations among observations in the "true" values of L_y and L_x, and in the case of survey work, respondent error, as well as from having unreliable measures.

The statistical procedure assumes that U, e_x, and e_y are distributed multivariate normal and are independent of each other. With these assumptions, we can estimate values for the unknown parameters by maximum likelihood methods. The only restrictions on the unknown parameter matrices are those required for identification. This amounts to a very powerful system with potentially wide application in political science (Dalton, 1980; Jackson, 1983).

The primary limitation of the LISREL model is the requirement that all observed variables be continuous and that all stochastic terms be drawn from a multivariate normal density function with mean zero. For much political science data, and especially for survey data, these assumptions are frequently not satisfied. The discrete nature of the observed variables is a more serious problem, in that it leads to strong violations of the assumption of a linear observational structure, and may yield severely biased estimates. Thus the most powerful and general approach to estimation of models containing erroneous observations requires assumptions political science data usually will not support. What is to be done?

One possible method of circumventing these problems is to attempt to estimate the variances and covariances of the implicit continuous variables underlying the limited, observed variables. This has been done by estimating the correlations among these implicit variables using the tetrachoric or polyserial family of estimators. (Olsson, Drasgow, and Dorans, 1982, discuss estimation of these coefficients. Mebane, 1982, discusses their application to LISREL estimation.) This approach assumes that each observed variable arises from a single normally distributed latent variable, which itself is a function of the latent variables in the behavioral structure. A second set of latent variables, denoted as X^{**} and Y^{**}, are assumed, where $Y^{**} = Y^*L_y + e_y$ and $X^{**} = X^*L_x + e_x$, from which the observed Y and X arise, $Y = F_y(Y^{**})$ and $X = F_x(X^{**})$. The joint outcomes among the Y's and the X's are used to estimate the correlations among the X^{**} and Y^{**}. This estimated correlation matrix becomes the input to LISREL and forms the basis for the estimation of both the behavioral and observational models.

One difficulty with the approach is that it confounds efforts to systematically model and estimate the observational structure by effectively creating a two step structure. One conforms to the basic LISREL model in relating Y^{**} and X^{**} to Y^* and X^*, and the other relates Y^{**} to Y and X^{**} to X. Unfortunately, these two steps are not integrated into a single model, and estimation proceeds piecemeal. It is unclear what the assumptions and calculations at one stage imply for the next, or what the consequences of violation of assumptions are likely to be.

NEW DIRECTIONS

The obvious solution to the dilemma we have sketched is to develop a statistical model that includes both a behavioral structure that matches current theoretical work and an observational structure that relates this structure to limited endogenous variables. The remainder of the paper outlines such a statistical method.

As with all applied statistical work, this model is based on explicit decisions creating a set of maintained hypotheses that permit the development of the statistical and computational procedures. The first of these is the positing of a linear, structural behavioral model identical to that in the LISREL procedure. Obviously an approximation to most social, political, and economic behavior, this model has proved to be quite robust and insightful in many different settings.

The second explicit decision is to base the observational structure on the multinomial logit model, adapted to the multivariate case. Thus we assume that the observed joint outcomes among the observed limited endogenous variables are generated by a multinomial logistic process, conditioned on the values of the behavioral structure. Some of the implications and trade-offs inherent in this decision are discussed in the concluding section. It is important for the reader to grasp that there are two parts to the statistical model's structure, to see how the two structures used here are rooted in existing work, and to comprehend how they are combined to give a single statistical model capable of estimating the parameters in each structure.

THE STATISTICAL MODEL

The method developed here consists of two parts, a latent structural behavioral model and a stochastic model relating the observed endogenous variables to the latent structure.

Behavioral Model

The latent systematic relationships describing expected behavior are summarized in traditional linear structural equation form,

$$Y^{*}C + X^{*}B = 0 \tag{1}$$

and in reduced form,

$$Y^{*} = -X^{*}BC^{-1} = X^{*}\Pi \tag{1a}$$

We consider the case with T individual observations and M endogenous and K exogenous variables (Y^{*} and X^{*}, respectively). This gives the appropriate dimensions for X^*, Y^*, B, and C. Any number of restrictions in the elements of B and C, consistent with maintaining identification, can be applied to give a variety of structural models.

The exogenous variables, denoted by X, are treated as directly observable and measured without error, i.e., $X = X^*$, and as fixed for successive replications. Alternatively, the results developed here are conditional on the observed values of X in any given data. We do not observe Y^*, but assume that the latent structure in equation (1a) generates a set of observable variables systematically related to Y^*, and thus to the observable exogenous variables, X. In the case of traditional linear models (e.g., LISREL), it is assumed that observed values are normally distributed about linear functions of the unobserved values of Y^*. In our case, we assume that the unobserved values of Y^* generate a set of J categorical or ordinal variables, Z. We next specify a model of the stochastic process relating the observed values of Z to Y^*, and thus to X, that will facilitate estimation of the parameters in the behavioral model, defined by the matrices B and C, and in the stochastic observational model. As with the single equation limited dependent variable models, behavioral and observational deviations are combined and appear in the observational part of the model.

Notation and Definition

Before deriving the statistical model, we must establish some notation and define some terms for describing the observed measures. Thus we have

Z_j the jth observed endogenous variable, $j = 1, 2,. . .,J$;

N_j the number of categories in Z_j, denoted as $1, 2,. . .,N_j$;

W categorical variable that includes all possible combinations of Z;

H the number of categories in $W = \prod_{j=1}^{J} N_j$;

P_h the probability of being in category h of variable W.

The variable W is used to define all possible patterns of the observed variables Z, and we want to develop a model for predicting the probability that an observation falls into each category. The appropriate value of W for given values of $Z = (Z_1, Z_2,. . .,Z_J)$ is

$$W = h = [\sum_{j=1}^{J-1} (\prod_{i=j+1}^{J} N_i)*(Z_j-1)] + Z_J$$

with $h = 1,. . .,H$. This is simply an expression for uniquely numbering and ordering each category in the set of possible outcomes.

The Observational Model

The second part of the model describes the stochastic relationships producing the observed endogenous variables, Z, given the hypothesized structural model and the values for X. Once we specify this precise stochastic relationship, we can pick the values for the parameters in the behavioral and the observational models that are most consistent with the observed data.

We assume a multinomial logistic form for the stochastic equations, which is then constrained to fit various hypotheses about the relations between Z and Y, and among the various individual variables in Z. This model has been extensively developed and described by McFadden (1973, 1981), and is consistent with a double exponential, or Weibull, choice distribution. The logistic form for the process generating the observed endogenous variables is selected for mathematical and computational convenience. The multiequation models cited above use variations on the probit model because of the more general applicability of the assumption of a cumulative normal distribution producing Z. However, as Avery and Hotz argue, this leads to nearly intractable analytical and computational problems and necessitates a series of still expensive numerical approximations. We hope to avoid these difficulties by the choice of the logistic function.

The assumption of a logistic function relating the probability of being in a given category to a linear function of Y^* gives the expression for P_h as

$$P_h = \exp(A_{0h} + Y^*A_h) / \sum_{i=1}^{H} \exp(A_{0i} + Y^*A_i) \tag{2}$$

(We delete the observation subscript as a matter of convenience.) Y^* is the $1 \times M$ vector of implicit observed values of the latent endogenous variables, given by $Y^* = X^*BC^{-1}$, for any observation, and A_h is an $M \times 1$ vector of parameters determining the linear combination of values of the Y_m^*'s relating the observed values of Z to Y^*, and thus to X. (We discuss the question of normalization and identification in a later section.)

The A_{0i} terms are appropriate constants for each category. The larger these constants, the more the predicted probability of each categorical outcome approximates its sample frequency, regardless of the values for X^* (and implicitly for Y^*). These constants reflect, among other things, the size of the behavioral and observational stochastic terms. Increased stochastic components, from either source, obscure any relationship between X^* and the observed values, Z, and raise the values of A_{0i}, relative to Y^*A_i, for each category. For example, X^*BC^{-1} may accurately predict the behavior represented by Y^*. However, if the particular measures used, the Z's, are very unreliable, there will be little systematic variation in the outcomes observed for different values of X^*. Similarly, the true but implicit and unobserved endogenous behavior may deviate substantially and randomly from the model $-X^*BC^{-1}$, i.e., $Y^* = -X^*BC^{-1} + V$. In this case, we will also see very little pattern to the observed outcomes for different values of X^*, even if Z measures Y^* very well. As just suggested, both cases lead to relatively large constant terms. This model will not discriminate between these situations, but can handle the presence of either one, or both.

We slightly modify the model at this point to simplify the mathematical derivations. The vector X is expanded to include a constant value, e.g., $X_0 = 1$, and the B and C coefficient matrices are augmented so that $Y_0^* = X_0 = 1$. The matrix A is then expanded so that its first row is now the appropriate element A_{0h}. (This means that the order of all matrices previously defined by M, the number of endogenous variables, is expanded by one, $M^* = M + 1$.) This alteration leaves the model unchanged, but greatly facilitates its description, because now

$$P_h = \exp(Y^*A_h)/\sum_{i=1}^{H} \exp(Y^*A_i)$$

Given that we have H possible categories for W, we have H different column vectors denoted by A_h. We can write these vectors as A, which is an $M^* \times H$ matrix of parameters in the multinomial logistic function for each category. We also create an $H \times 1$ vector D_i, defined so that the elements equal zero except that $d_j = 1$ for $i = j$. Thus D_i is a zero vector except for the ith element. With these definitions for A and D_i, we can rewrite equation (2) in matrix form as

$$P_h = \exp(Y^*AD_h)/\sum_{i=1}^{H} \exp(Y^*AD_i) \tag{3}$$

Equation (3) implicitly assumes that the observed values for the different endogenous variables in Z are generated independently of each other for given values of the Y^*'s. Yet there is every reason to believe that the observed values of Z may not be independently distributed, even after we account for the latent structure and that there are stochastic elements that likely lead to further systematic interactions among the Z's. If, for example, Z_1 and Z_2 are complementary policies in a study of political preferences or attitudes and are being used to measure the same underlying preference function, knowing how the value of Z_1 deviates from that predicted by the values of Y^* may provide information about how the observed value for Z_2 is likely to deviate from its predicted value. Thus we must include terms to reflect these possible interactions and to allow for nonindependence among the categories of the observed variables.

We define a vector of interaction terms, Q, to represent these possible interdependencies. Since we have J observed variables, there are $J^*(J-1)/2$ possible elements in Q, making it a $1 \times J^*(J-1)/2$ vector. The elements of Q are zero only if we specify that the distributions of the observed values for the respective variables in Z are independent of each other, given the values of the Y^*'s. We also define a $J^*(J-1)/2 \times 1$ vector, F_h, of coefficients that relate the elements in Q to the specific categories of each Z that constitute the category W_h. In many instances, such as with Z's that are dichotomous, the values of F_h will either be plus or minus one, depending upon whether we expect positive or negative dependencies between the relevant categories. In Table 1 we show the pattern of

TABLE 1. Interaction Pattern Among Two Ordered Trichotomies[a]

		Z_2		
		1	2	3
	1	q_{12}	$f_2 q_{12}$	$-q_{12}$
Z_1	2	$f_2 q_{12}$	$f_5 q_{12}$	$f_6 q_{12}$
	3	$-q_{12}$	$f_6 q_{12}$	q_{12}

[a] Entries are the interaction terms that are included in the logit expression for the probability of observing $Z_1 = i$ and $Z_2 = j$.

interactions that might exist between the joint responses to a set of two trichotomous, ordered variables.

When these interaction terms are added to the model in equation (3), we have the full form of the relationship between the latent structure and the observed values of Z, given by

$$P_h = \exp(Y^*A_h + QF_h) / \sum_{i=1}^{H} \exp(Y^*A_i + QF_i)$$

$$= \exp[(Y^*A + QF)D_h] / \sum_{i=1}^{H} \exp[(Y^*A + QF)D_i] \qquad (4)$$

where F is the $J^*(J-1)/2 \times H$ matrix composed of the different column vectors, F_h. An interpretation of equation (4) is that we estimate the log of the odds of observing $W_t = h$ rather than $W_t = g$ for the tth observation as

$$\log(P_{th}/P_{tg}) = (Y^*_t A_h + QF_h) - (Y^*_t A_g + QF_g)$$

$$= Y^*_t(A_h - A_g) + Q(F_h - F_g)$$

NORMALIZATION, IDENTIFICATION, AND SPECIFICATION

The model in equation (4) is incomplete. First, it is unidentified, in that there are too many unknown parameters, relative to available information, so that many structural models are consistent with what we observe; and second, normalizations for the parameters in the probability equations and to scale the underlying structure are required.[5] We cannot, in this section, "solve" the identification problem, as that must be determined by the appropriate structure for the problem at hand. What we can do here is indicate how the model can be constrained to achieve identification for a wide variety of problems. We also present two simple normalizations of the model to permit estimation of the parameters in the probability equations.

The easiest normalization for the probabilities is to set the first column in A (including A_{01}) to zero. This normalization is needed to identify the parameters in the stochastic structure. Thus, for the first category in W, the numerator in equation (4) is only the exponential of any stochastic terms, given by QF_1.[6] We also set one value in each row of A equal to 1 in order to give an implicit scale to the unobserved latent endogenous variables, Y^*.

The more difficult constraints to develop and to describe are those dictated by the structure of the model and the data generation process and that identify the model. As formulated in equation (4), we have many more coefficients than we have information with which to estimate those coefficients, the classic case of underidentification. This problem can only be solved by placing restrictions on various coefficients. The easiest set of restrictions to outline are those on B and C, so that the reduced form coefficients, Π in equation (1a), are identified. This problem is discussed routinely in all statistical textbooks (See, for example, Hanushek and Jackson, 1977; Johnston, 1972; Wonnacott and Wonnacott, 1979) and is given a full treatment in Fisher (1966). We will simply assume that this part of the model is identified, and concentrate our discussion on the parts of the model relating this structure to the observed values of Z, e.g., the parameters represented by A, Q, and F.

The majority of the constraints needed to estimate the model in equation (4) are in the form of equalities and linear relationships, rather than the zero restrictions found in most econometric work. For example, for the categories of W with the same values of Z_j, we may want the coefficients on Y^*_m to be equal. This constraint is represented by equating certain elements in the mth row of A. In other situations, we may want to specify that the coefficients on Y^*_m for several of the categories of W satisfy a linear constraint, denoted by $\Sigma_{h=1}^{H} g_h a_{mh} = 0$, where the g_h's are given. We will have similar linear constraints on the entries in F, the matrix denoting the potential interactions among the stochastic parts of the responses. (The entries in Table 1 show several equalities, for example.) The parts of the model introduced here incorporate these linear constraints on the A and F matrices. We will not discuss restrictions that set elements of A and F to constants, as they can be incorporated directly into the model.

Constraints, other than fixing values of A and F as constants, are incorporated through two matrices G_A and G_F. The columns of these two matrices contain the necessary coefficients for any one linear constraint. For example, an equality of coefficients is represented by values of $+1$ and -1 for appropriate elements in a column of G_A. If there are R_A linear constraints among the values of A, and R_F among the values of F, this means that G_A is H by R_A while G_F is H by R_F.

In order to mathematically express these constraints in matrix form, we define the following arbitrary matrices L_A and L_F. The elements of these matrices indicate which rows of A and F, respectively, are constrained by a given column of G_A and G_F. Thus $LA_{ij} \neq 0$ if the constraint in column i of G_A applies to the jth row of A and is zero otherwise. The elements of L_A and L_F are either zero, if the appropriate constraint does not apply to the corresponding row of A or F, or any arbitrary nonzero value if the constraint does apply.

L_A and L_F allow us to express the constraints in the following manner:

$$\text{tr}(AG_AL_A) = 0, \quad \text{for } L_A \neq 0 \tag{5}$$

and

$$\text{tr}(FG_FL_F) = 0, \quad \text{for } L_F \neq 0 \tag{6}$$

These equalities must hold for any and all values that the nonzero elements of L_A and L_F may take. We shall use the information implied by the entries in L_A and L_F subsequently when we come to determine the best values for the parameters in the model. At this point, we simply use these matrices to facilitate the writing of the constraints.

ESTIMATION

To begin estimation of this model, we must have a set of T observations, where each observation has the requisite values for X_t and Z_t. Based on the values of the Z_t, we determine the appropriate category of W and classify and organize the sample by their respective values of W_t. We define D_t analogously to D_h, so that D_t indicates the category of the tth observation. From equation (4) we can define the probability of each observation being in its observed category and write the log of the likelihood of that observation as

$$L_t = \log P_t = (Y_t^*A + QF)D_t - \log \left[\sum_{i=1}^{H} \exp(Y_t^*A + QF)D_i \right] \tag{7}$$

We now write the log likelihood function for the sample as

$$L = \sum_{t=1}^{T} L_t = \sum_{t=1}^{T} (Y_t^*A + QF)D_t - \sum_{t=1}^{T} \left[\log \sum_{i=1}^{H} \exp(Y_t^*A + QF)D_i \right] \tag{8}$$

Expressed as a function of the observed exogenous variables, we have

$$L = \sum_{t=1}^{T} (X_tBC^{-1}A + QF)D_t - \sum_{t=1}^{T} \left[\log \sum_{i=1}^{H} \exp(X_tBC^{-1}A + QF)D_i \right] \tag{8a}$$

To estimate the model's parameters, we want to pick the values for the unknown elements in A, B, C, Q, and F that maximize this likelihood function, e.g., that are most likely to have produced the observed data, subject to the constraints given by equations (5) and (6). To incorporate the constraints, we interpret L_A and L_F as matrices of Lagrangian multipliers in a constrained maximization problem. We then maximize the function,

$$L = \sum_{t=1}^{T} (X_t BC^{-1}A + QF)D_t - \sum_{t=1}^{T} [\log \sum_{h=1}^{H} \exp(X_t BC^{-1}A + QF)D_h] \quad (9)$$
$$+ \ tr(AG_A L_A) + tr(FG_F L_F)$$

with respect to the elements of A, B, C, Q, F, L_A, and L_F.

To keep the exposition tractable, we first present some additional notation:

T_H $H \times 1$ vector of category sample sizes, i.e., T_h is the number of observations in category h;

S_X the $H \times K$ matrix of sums of the values of X for each category, i.e., $S_{x,hk} = \sum_{t=1}^{T_h} X_{tk}$;

S_{PX} the $H \times K$ matrix of sums of cross-products of estimated probabilities and values of X for each category, i.e., $S_{PX,hk} = \sum_{t=1}^{T_h} P_{th} X_{tk}$;

S_p the $H \times 1$ vector of summed estimated probabilities for each category, i.e., $S_{P_h} = \sum_{t=1}^{T_h} P_{th}$.

The first two terms permit us to write

$$\sum_{t=1}^{T} (X_t BC^{-1}A + QF)D_t = tr (BC^{-1}AS_X) + QFT_H$$

and the third and fourth simplify the writing of first order conditions.

The necessary first order conditions are the partial derivatives of L with respect to the unknown elements in the parameter matrices. In deriving expressions for these partial derivatives, we make extensive use of Dwyer (1967) on matrix derivatives.[7] These derivatives are:

$$\left(\frac{\partial L}{\partial B}\right)' = C^{-1}A \ S_X - C^{-1}A \ S_{PX} \tag{10a}$$

$$\left(\frac{\partial L}{\partial C}\right)' = -C^{-1}A \ S_X \ BC^{-1} + C^{-1}A \ S_{PX}BC^{-1} \tag{10b}$$

$$\left(\frac{\partial L}{\partial A}\right)' = S_X BC^{-1} - S_{PX}BC^{-1} + G_A L_A \tag{10c}$$

$$\left(\frac{\partial L}{\partial Q}\right)' = F(T_H - S_P) \tag{10d}$$

$$\left(\frac{\partial L}{\partial F}\right)' = (T_H - S_P)Q + G_F L_F \tag{10e}$$

$$\left(\frac{\partial L}{\partial L_A}\right)' = AG_A \tag{10f}$$

$$\left(\frac{\partial L}{\partial L_F}\right)' = FG_F \tag{10g}$$

The left-hand sides of these expressions are matrices, where individual elements are partial derivatives of L with respect to specific elements of the matrix in the denominator. For example, $(\partial L/\partial b)_{ij}$ is the partial derivative of L with respect to B_{ij}. The right-hand side of each equation gives the expression for these first partial derivatives in terms of the matrices computed with observational data—T_H, S_X, S_{PX}, and S_P—and the matrices of unknown parameters, A, B, C, Q, F, L_A, and L_F. These, then, constitute the first order conditions for the maximization of the likelihood function in equation (9). Specifically, we locate the expressions on the right-hand side of equations (10a)–(10g) that correspond to the first partial derivatives of the unknown elements of the parameter matrices, shown on the left-hand side, and search for the estimated parameter values that equate these expressions to zero. For example, if B_{ij} is an unknown parameter whose value we hope to estimate, we take the expression from the (i,j)th element of equation (10a) as one of the equations defining the first order conditions. To find the estimates of the unknown parameters in the model, we collect all these right hand-side expressions corresponding to the unknown parameters and equate all of them to zero.

The procedure just outlined gives us a set of simultaneous, nonlinear equations which must be solved by numerical analysis methods. These methods rely on the matrix of estimated second partial derivatives of L with respect to each parameter.

SOME APPLICATIONS

Current research has identified several substantively interesting models that can only be estimated with limited endogenous variables and where a full information treatment is either required or will greatly improve the parameter estimates. This section outlines one example of such a model, and gives a brief description of how the estimation problem can be cast to fit the statistical model proposed here. We do not give elaborate details of the specification, as this example is offered primarily to give the reader an appreciation for the types of applications in political science.

Models of Party Identification

There is considerable skepticism about whether the traditional seven point party identification scale used in the National Election Study surveys reflects a single ordered dimension of partisanship, as originally intended. Several authors (Weisberg, 1980; Van Wingen and Valentine, 1979; Brody, 1977; Dennis, 1981) present evidence suggesting at least one, and at times more, additional dimensions that underlie a respondent's classification on the party identification variable.

The first of the additional hypothesized dimensions is based on the idea that the concept of "independent" has an attraction for some individuals irrespective of their partisanship. Some of these people may be quite partisan in their voting behavior and in their party evaluations, but prefer to classify themselves as independents, or leaning independents. This situation clearly illustrates the problem created when one tries to use the party identification variable to assess partisanship. People with strong partisan preferences, but who prefer to be classed as independents, are treated the same as people who are independents (or leaners) because they are close to being indifferent in their evaluations of the two major parties, thus confounding the two groups of people. Another possible dimension is the distinction between weak and strong partisans. Brody (1977) and Weisberg (1980) for example, see this choice, among those who have stated a partisan preference, as being qualitatively different and subject to different influences than the party preference.

If these arguments are correct, to conceptualize and measure party identification accurately, we need to consider the possibility that three different underlying dimensions exist, that individuals implicitly locate themselves at different places along these three dimensions, and that the responses to the party identification questions are influenced by each of these separate placements. The obvious empirical questions are: How much variation is there among individuals on each dimension, and what weight is given to each dimension in the response to the party identification question?

In order to address these questions, we pose an underlying latent model that represents all three dimensions and that relates individual positions on these dimensions to measurable exogenous characteristics of the individual, such as their parents' identifications, their education, religion, race, region and place of residence, etc. We represent these exogenous variables by the vector X. The three latent dimensions are:

$$Y_1^* = XB_1 \qquad \text{partisanship}$$
$$Y_2^* = XB_2 \qquad \text{independence}$$
$$Y_3^* = XB_3 \qquad \text{strength}$$

Although we have expressed each of the underlying dimensions as functions of the same set of exogenous variables, we can specify that certain elements of B_1, B_2, and B_3 are zero to account for different hypotheses. For example, if independent parents predispose one towards independence, but not towards either of the major parties, the coefficient on the "independent parents" variable will be specified as zero in B_1.

TABLE 2. Party Identification Model

Category	Probability Expression
Strong Democrat	$\exp(a_{01} + \quad Y_1^* \quad + Y_3^* + \quad \sigma_{12} + \sigma_{23})$
Weak Democrat	$\exp(a_{02} + a_{12}Y_1^* \quad\quad + \quad \sigma_{12} - \sigma_{23})$
Ind. Democrat	$\exp(a_{03} + a_{13}Y_1^* + Y_2^* \quad - \quad \sigma_{12} \quad\quad)$
Ind. Independent	$\exp(\quad\quad\quad\quad + Y_2^* \quad + f_1\sigma_{12} \quad\quad)$
Ind. Republican	$\exp(a_{05} + a_{15}Y_1^* + Y_2^* \quad + \quad \sigma_{12} \quad\quad)$
Weak Republican	$\exp(a_{06} + a_{16}Y_1^* \quad\quad - \quad \sigma_{12} + \sigma_{23})$
Strong Republican	$\exp(a_{07} + a_{17}Y_1^* \quad + Y_3^* - \quad \sigma_{12} - \sigma_{23})$

We next hypothesize that respondents' probabilities of being in each of the seven categories of the party identification variable are a function of their positions on these underlying variables, and that this function follows the logistic form. Table 2 gives the expressions for the numerators in the respective probability terms. (The denominator is the sum of these seven numerators.) We have incorporated normalizations for each latent component by setting a number of coefficients to zero. Expressions can be compared to give the odds of being a particular partisan or independent, relative to another category. We also fix certain coefficients on Y_1^*, Y_2^*, and Y_3^* to 1.0 in order to scale the underlying equations. The σ_{12} interaction term estimates the lack of independence between being a partisan and being a Democrat. (A positive value for σ_{12} indicates that people who are partisans, rather than independents, are more likely to be Democrats, other things equal.) The σ_{23} term estimates the dependence between strength and partisan preference. (A positive σ_{23} indicates that irrespective of the latent structure, strong rather than weak partisans are more likely to be Democrats.)

The specification in Table 2 incorporates all the above hypotheses about the dimensionality of party identification. The inclusion of Y_2^* in the three independent expressions and the values for B_2 measure whether independence is an attribute separate from partisan preferences, i.e., from neutral values for Y_1^*. For example, the odds of being a Democrat leaning toward independence rather than a weak Democrat, are

$$\exp[(a_{03} - a_{02}) + (a_{13} - a_{12})Y_1^* + Y_2^* - 2\sigma_{12} + \sigma_{23}]$$

If the probability of being a weak Democrat, relative to that of being an independent Democrat, does not vary with partisanship, a_{13} will equal a_{12}. The only way, then, to systematically discriminate between independent and partisan Democrats is by their score on Y_2^*, the independence dimension. A comparable interpretation applies to the presence of Y_3^* in the expression for strong Democrats and Republicans. For example, the odds of being a strong Republican, rather than a weak Republican, are $\exp[(a_{07} - a_{06}) + (a_{17} - a_{16})Y_1^* + Y_3^* - 2\sigma_{23}]$. If partisanship does not differentiate weak and strong Republicans (i.e., a_{16} and a_{17} are similar), then Y_3^* is the only systematic explanation for why people are strong partisans.[8] We expect Y_2^* only to distinguish independents from partisans, hence its omission from the strong and weak partisan expression. Similarly, Y_3^* enters the strong partisan expressions, as it is expected to differentiate strong partisans, but not others.

The size and statistical significance of different coefficients and components constitute tests of the various propositions about the dimensionality of the current (and past) party identification measures. Omitting Y_2^* and Y_3^* reduces the model to the one dimensional partisanship structure. The addition of Y_2^* makes the model two dimensional, adding the Independence concept. Similarly, the addition of Y_3^* adds the strength concept to the structure. The tests of these different models are done by statistical comparisons of how well the different structures fit the observed data.

CONCLUSIONS

Applied statistical work requires choices, either about what aspects of a problem to address and which to assume away or about what specifications and approximations to use. These choices all imply a risk that the consequences of an unfortunate decision may be sufficiently large to affect the empirical results and the conclusions developed from them. The problems ignored may be more consequential than the problems addressed and/or the maintained structure may be a poor approximation to the actual process underlying behavior and the generation of the observations. The decisions required in empirical research, and the implied risks, cannot be avoided and can only be improved by more sophisticated and elaborate statistical procedures. In this concluding section, we want to discuss some of the assumptions, and their likely consequences, in the specification of the logit observation model.

The key assumption made in the observation model is that the probability of an observation being in any one of the possible categories created by the measured variables follows the multinomial logit form. There is no strong theoretical justification for this assumption, unless one is partial to Weibull choice distributions. It was made for mathematical and computational convenience. The model then permits constraints on the logistic form to reflect various hypotheses about the structure of the observational model. Other choices "could" have been made, such as treating the likelihood of observing a particular outcome as a function of a multivariate normal distribution rather than the logistic function. We want to point out some of these decisions and discuss their possible implications for the model's results.

Distribution Assumptions

We have assumed that the distribution of observed values follows a multinomial logistic function. Thus one difference between our model and the "true" nature of the world lies in deviations from this assumption. We have no way of knowing the "true" distribution, nor even whether the observed variables are generated by any known distribution. In the absence of this information, we can only ask what are likely alternatives, and what consequences ensue from our assumption, if one of the alternatives is a better approximation.

An alternative assumption is that the observed marginal values of each limited variable are cumulatively normally distributed (Ashford and Sowden, 1970). This assumption underlies the probit and n-chotomous probit models and is applicable to ordered variables. The joint, or conditional, probabilities describing possible outcomes in the multivariate case are developed to be consistent with these marginal distributions. The multinomial logit model, on the other hand, starts with a description of the conditional probabilities, and then deduces the cumulative marginal distributions. For dichotomies, there is very little difference between the normal and logistic distributions (Hanushek and Jackson, 1977, pp. 187–189). Differences do appear in the multivariate-multinomial case, however. Multivariate distributions with logistic conditional probabilities have logistic marginal distributions (Nerlove and Press, 1973, pp. 26–32), but if the marginal categories are ordered, the cumulative distribution is not logistic. Thus, the similarities between the normal and logistic distributions in the binary case do not extend to multivariate-multinomial applications. We are then left with the question of whether the logistic (conditional) or cumulative normal (marginal) model fits best. The logistic function has the advantage of having a relatively simple form for the conditional probabilities, which are the heart of this exercise.

The logistic function used here is more expensive statistically than the normal distribution if one has ordered variables. The logistic probability function requires estimation of a greater number of parameters, and is most appropriate for unordered variables. This method will appropriately fit an ordered variable. However, as in all statistical applications, any use of a priori information to reduce the number of parameters estimated gives more precise estimates for the unknown terms. Thus, use of the multivariate-multinomial logit model when the observed variables are known to have ordered categories gives less precise (larger variance) estimates than a comparable probit model. Restructuring the model to incorporate this restriction is a major undertaking.

Logistic Choice Models and Irrelevant Alternatives

A frequently cited difficulty with the multinomial logistic model is the effect on predicted choice probabilities of the addition of an "irrelevant" alternative. The frequently given example of this situation is McFadden's car/red bus and car/red bus/blue bus choice problem. In essence, the paradox is that the predicted odds of a person choosing a car relative to bus differs between the first and the second case because of the addition of the third alternative. Yet, why should the predicted car/bus choice be dependent upon whether one also has the choice of a red or blue bus in the second case? We contend that the paradox is primarily the consequence of not fully specifying the observational structure and not taking full advantage of the multivariate logit model.

In the common presentation of the problem, the probability that a person chooses the car in the first case is given by

$$\text{Prob}(Z = \text{car}) = e^{Y1^*}/(1 + e^{Y1^*})$$

and the probability that he or she chooses a red bus is

$$\text{Prob}(Z = \text{red bus}) = 1/(1 + e^{Y1^*})$$

so that the odds of choosing "car" are e^{Y1^*}. (We suppress the subscript for person i for notational convenience.) In numeric terms, if the odds of choosing car over red bus are 2:1, then the probability of choosing the car is 0.667. In the second case, the probabilities are

$$\text{Prob}(Z = \text{car}) = e^{Y1^*}/(1 + e^{Y1^*} + e^{Y2^*})$$

$$\text{Prob}(Z = \text{blue bus}) = e^{Y2^*}/(1 + e^{Y1^*} + e^{Y2^*})$$

and

$$\text{Prob}(Z = \text{red bus}) = 1/(1 + e^{Y1^*} + e^{Y2^*})$$

$Y1^*$ again indicates the relative preference for car over red bus, and $Y2^*$ indicates the relative preference for blue over red busses. The odds of choosing car over red bus remain e^{Y1^*}. However, the odds of choosing car over blue bus are $e^{(Y1^* - Y2^*)}$, and of choosing car over "bus" are $e^{Y1^*}/(1 + e^{Y2^*})$. This latter expression indicates that the odds of choosing car over bus are predicted to be different in the two cases. In the numeric example, we cannot continue to maintain odds of 2:1 for car over red bus and for car over any bus, and have relatively even odds for choosing red or blue busses. The obvious inconsistency here is that the odds of choosing car rather than bus should not change simply because we introduce the option of different colored buses. This characteristic of the multinomial logit model, developed by McFadden (1974), makes estimation of the behavioral structure describing people's relative preference for car versus bus transportation difficult and the results dependent upon the choices presented in particular situations.

The model developed here restructures the car/red bus/blue bus example in a way that skirts the importance of the irrelevant alternatives problem. The behavioral model here is a two equation structure, describing preferences for car relative to bus (denoted by $Y1^* = XB_1$) and for blue relative to red (denoted by

$Y2^* = XB_2$). Implicit in the observed outcomes is an observational structure that presents individuals a set of two dichotomous choices, which combine to give a set of four possible outcomes; blue car, red car, blue bus, and red bus. The observational model relating choices to the behavioral structure describing preferences is now assumed to follow the multivariate logit model developed in this paper. The expected probability of each possible outcome is:

Color	*Mode*	
	Car	Bus
Blue	$e^{Y1^* + Y2^*}/D$	e^{Y2^*}/D
Red	e^{Y1^*}/D	$1/D$

where $D = (e^{Y1^* + Y2^*} + e^{Y2^*} + e^{Y1^*} + 1)$. Now, the expected odds of choosing car over bus are

$$(e^{Y1^* + Y2^*} + e^{Y1^*})/(e^{Y2^*} + 1)$$
$$= e^{Y1^*}(e^{Y2^*} + 1)/(e^{Y2^*} + 1)$$
$$= e^{Y1^*}$$

We thus have the same expression for the odds of choosing car whether we use the conditional probabilities in the table or the marginals created by disregarding the color option.

The model presented here indicates that the trouble with the red bus/blue bus example is in the observational structure, where the options of red car/blue car are not observed, thus complicating the appropriate model for the process generating observations. This situation requires respecification of the observational model, not a recasting of the behavioral model. Our model also makes the expression for the odds of choosing car over red bus (or blue bus) more complicated, in that the log-odds does not reduce to a linear expression, as does the traditional formulation. We contend, however, that ours may be a more accurate description of the choice process, in that it recognizes the two dimensional nature of the choices being presented, as reflected in the two equation behavioral model.

The model just described is simplified, in that it assumes that preferences for mode and color are additive and linear in the log-odds and that the observed dichotomous choices are independent. Neither assumption is tenable in all cases. The observed choice of mode may not be independent of the observed color choices, and preferences may interact, so that preference for color is more (or less) important when the selected mode is car than when bus is selected. Both situations can be incorporated in the model developed here.

If there is interaction between observed mode and color choice, so that either red car or blue bus is more likely to be observed for all individuals than predicted by the model above, we can incorporate this with the elements in the Q matrix. In this case, with only two dichotomous choices, Q is a scalar, and the coefficients in F are either plus or minus one, depending upon the cell. If there is systematic interaction among individuals' preferences, so that color assumes a greater influence among car choosers, an additional behavioral equation denoted as $Y3^* = XB_3$ is required. This equation models how the magnitude of the interaction term varies among individuals (it may be a constant). In the observational structure, $Y3^*$ enters the expressions for the blue car choice (the entry in the upper left corner of the choice table).

These examples discuss points where the structure of the model has to be assessed against expectations about how particular observations are generated. To the extent there is empirical or theoretical evidence to indicate that the maintained hypothesis of a multivariate logistic process is a poor approximation to how the observations were generated, one must then consider the magnitude of the estimation errors introduced and the gains to be had by using an alternative estimation technique. This paper has, however, embarked in the direction pointed to in the full structural equation behavioral model and an observational structure that relates this behavioral model to the broad range of limited variables encountered frequently in social science research.

Acknowledgments. This work was supported by a grant to The University of Michigan from the National Science Foundation, SES-8218814.

NOTES

1. The terms $F(m)$ and $L(m)$ represent the standard cumulative normal and logistic distributions, respectively.
2. Because the scale of the latent variable is known only up to a linear transformation, the coefficients and thresholds may be scaled by any convenient restrictions of the model parameters, which are usually that of the standard normal and the specification that $t_1 = 0$.
3. In the probit model, this stochastic element is summarized in the variance of the cumulative normal distribution relative to the variance of the systematic component, Y^*. In the logit model, the magnitude of the combined stochastic element is implicit in the size of the constant term coefficients for each category, denoted by a_m, relative to the variation in values of Y^*.
4. The coefficients in the latent models are adjusted to give an implied scale to the model. (See Nerlove and Press, 1973).
5. Normalization of the parameters in the probability equations is required because it is possible to add a constant to every element in row m of A (the coefficients relating Y_m^* to each category's probability) without changing the probabilities assigned to each category. Without the normalization to scale the model, it is possible to multiply the reduced form coefficients in the equation (1a) for Y_m^* by a

constant and divide the corresponding coefficients for Y^*_m in the logistic equations for each category (the values in the mth row of A) by the same constant and leave the probabilities unchanged. The normalizations discussed here eliminate these identification problems.

6. Others have used the normalization that the sum of each row of A equals one (Nerlove and Press, 1973), but the choice is arbitrary and does not alter the predicted probabilities of an observation falling into a particular category. We choose our normalization because it is mathematically and notationally simpler.

7. The important formulas and their application to the problem are available separately from the authors.

8. The distribution of voters along the independence and strength dimensions is assessed by the size of the coefficients in B_2 and B_3. Large values for these coefficients imply substantial variation among citizens on the independence and strength dimensions. Coefficients close to zero indicate slight variation and suggest that the behavioral model cannot systematically distinguish citizens on these dimensions.

REFERENCES

Amemiya, T. (1981). Qualitative response models: a survey. *Journal of Economic Literature* 19: 1483–1536.

Ashford, J. R., and Sowden, R. R. (1970). Multivariate probit analysis. *Biometrics* 26: 535–546.

Avery, P. B., and Hotz, V. J. (1981). Estimation of multiple indicator multiple cause (MIMIC) models with dichotomous indicators. W. P. #60-80-81, Graduate School of Industrial Administration, Carnegie-Mellon University, Pittsburgh, Pa.

Brody, R. A. (1977). Stability and change in party identification: presidential to off-years. Paper presented to the 1977 Annual Meeting of the American Political Science Association, September 1977, Washington, D.C.

Dalton, R. J. (1980). Reassessing parental socialization: indicator unreliability versus generational transfer. *American Political Science Review* 74: 421–431.

Dennis, J. (1981). On being an independent party supporter. Paper presented at the 1981 Annual Meeting of the Midwest Political Science Association, April 1981, Cincinnati, Ohio.

Dwyer, P. S. (1967). Some applications of matrix derivatives in multivariate analysis. *American Statistical Association Journal* 62: 607–625.

Fiorina, M. P. (1981). *Retrospective Voting in American National Elections.* New Haven: Yale University Press.

Fisher, F. M. (1966). *The Identification Problem in Econometrics.* New York: McGraw-Hill.

Franklin, C. H. (1984). Issue preferences, socialization and the evolution of party identification. *American Journal of Political Science* 28: 459–478.

Franklin, C. H., and Jackson, J. E. (1983). The dynamics of party identification. *American Political Science Review* 77: 957–973.

Goldberger, A. S., and Duncan, O. D. (1972). *Structural Equation Models in the Social Sciences.* New York: Academic Press.

Hanushek, E. A., and Jackson, J. E. (1977). *Statistical Methods for Social Scientists.* New York: Academic Press.

Jackson, J. E. (1983). The systematic beliefs of the mass public: estimating policy preferences with survey data. *Journal of Politics* 45: 840–865.

Johnston, J. (1972). *Econometric Methods* (2nd ed.). New York: McGraw-Hill.

Joreskog, K. G. (1973). A general model for estimating a linear structural equation system. In A. S. Goldberger and O. D. Duncan (eds.), *Structural Equation Models in the Social Sciences,* pp. 85–112. New York: Academic Press.

Lee, L. F. (1981). Simultaneous equation models with discrete and censored dependent variables. In Manski and McFadden, *Structural Analysis of Discrete Data with Econometric Applications*, pp. 346–364.

Manski, C. F., and McFadden, D. (1981). *Structural Analysis of Discrete Data with Econometric Applications*. Cambridge, Mass.: MIT Press.

McFadden, D. (1973). Conditional logit analysis of qualitative choice behavior. In P. Zarembka (ed.), *Frontiers in Econometrics*, pp. 105–142. New York: Academic Press.

McFadden, D. (1981). Econometric models of probabilistic choice. In Manski and McFadden, *Structural Analysis of Discrete Data with Econometric Applications*, pp. 198–272.

Mebane, W. R., Jr. (1982). Measuring covariance and noncentrality for few-category variables in maximum likelihood estimation of linear structures. Paper presented at the 1982 Annual Meeting of the American Political Science Association, Denver, Colo.

Muthén, B. (1979). A structural probit model with latent variables. *Journal of the American Statistical Association* 74: 807–811.

Nerlove, M., and Press, S. J. (1973). Univariate and multivariate log-linear and logistic models. R-1306-EDA/NIH, Rand Corp., Santa Monica, Calif.

Olsson, U., Drasgow, F., and Dorans, N. J. (1982). The polyserial correlation coefficient. *Psychometrika* 47: 337–347.

Van Wingen, J. R., and Valentine, D. C. (1979). Biases in the partisan identification index as a measure of partisanship. Paper presented at the 1979 Annual Meeting of the Midwest Political Science Association, Chicago, Ill.

Weisberg, H. F. (1980). A multidimensional conceptualization of party identification. *Political Behavior* 2(1): 33–60.

Wonnacott, R. J., and Wonnacott, T. H. (1979). *Econometrics* (2nd ed.). New York: Wiley.

CHAPTER 10

THE DYNAMICS OF PUBLIC OPINION

Richard G. Niemi

Public opinion is so broad a topic as to defy simple summarization. Often included under this heading are what at other times are thought of as entire fields of study: political socialization, political psychology, parts of the study of mass media, much of electoral behavior, and small parts of several other fields. Add to this the nonacademic study of public opinion, and one finds a truly staggering volume of literature.

Faced with this situation, I have not tried to write a bibliographic essay, as a glance at the short list of references would indicate. Rather, I have tried to address current shortcomings in the study of public opinion. But this raises a problem for me, since I usually find such essays to be long on platitudes (not to mention just plain long) and short on specifics. In order to avoid that pitfall, I address only what I consider the most pressing needs—most especially the need for more dynamic studies. Yet even such a narrow focus leads to a number of important methodological points about the kinds of surveys needed, questions used in those surveys, dissemination of the results, and reporting of surveys in academic and other outlets. Encyclopedic reviews (e.g., Kinder and Sears, 1983) exist and serve a genuine purpose. With the approach taken here, I am instead trying to influence some aspects of future surveys and analyses of them.

THE NEED FOR MORE DYNAMIC STUDIES

Most of our theorizing about public opinion is not very dynamic, and when it is, it is even less precise than most of our theorizing. That is, even when we deal with subject matter over time, we rarely make specific, and especially testable, generalizations about change. An analogy that comes to mind is a complaint frequently made about so-called comparative studies. Most are not really comparative but simply study a country other than the one the researcher is in.

In similar fashion, we have studies that compare opinions at different times, but rarely are there any linkages drawn to explain why opinion is not identical at the two points in time.

Political scientists may be more guilty of this than others. Matters of public opinion are often tied to presidential elections. Since to some degree every presidential election is different from every other one, it is easy to use that fact as the reason for not modeling changes more explicitly over time. Not that candidates should be ignored. I am much taken, in fact, by Petrocik's (1980) analysis of the effect of pairs of candidates on voter reactions. Instead, the point is that we have to become more explicit about the ways in which candidates and other changeable factors alter public opinion. Instead of simply marveling at the fact that coefficients in a prediction equation vary over time, we have to begin to explain why those coefficients change, and to do so in a way that allows us to predict future changes rather than append explanations after the fact.

Opinions may change over the short run as well as the long run. My own view, however, is that the most useful dynamic theories will come from taking a much longer run perspective than we typically do. I come to this conclusion after having thought about a number of interesting theories that are dynamic, four of which I will briefly describe. All of these take what I would call a very-long-term perspective. They address changes that can be properly tested only with data over a period of decades if not generations.

The first example I cite is Inglehart's (1977 and elsewhere) theory of materialist/postmaterialist changes in political ideology. Inglehart argues that formerly in industrialized societies, politics revolved around materialist goals: satisfying basic needs for physical and economic security in a context of scarcity of food, shelter, clothing, and safety. Who would benefit most from industrialization, and related questions such as ownership of the means of production and the distribution of income, were the basis for political conflict. As "advanced" industrial societies developed—ones in which basic material wants of most individuals were satisfied—the basis of political conflict began to change. Arguments developed over nuclear power, women's liberation, and numerous issues related to the family, the peace movement, the environment, and so on, which were of a fundamentally different character from those about materialist goals. These "postmaterialist" issues are replacing the older, more strictly economic issues as the major dimension of poltical conflict.

Surely one can find fault with this as an example of theorizing about changes over time. Perhaps more importantly, the change from industrial to postindustrial society is not an experience that is likely to be repeated—at least in western societies. Therefore, it might be viewed as an ad hoc explanation of observed changes. However, we are still undergoing this change, and with the 1973-74 oil crisis and other energy concerns, the recent worldwide recession, and the enormous north-south differences in economic security along with greater interdependence among the world economies, it is not at all certain that the change will ever be completely consummated. Therefore, it stands as a predictor of future change as well as an explanation for the recent past. In any case, if we can understand and to some small degree predict changes in the entire basis on which political arguments are formed, we will perhaps achieve a meaningful science of public opinion. As noted, however, this is not a change that can be confidently detected with surveys a few years or even a few presidential elections apart.

My second example has some of the same characteristics as the first one, but it speaks of a repeated phenomenon, and we should be able to test it by the turn of the next century. I am thinking of Paul Allen Beck's (1974) "socialization" theory of realigning elections. The essence of Beck's theory is that both those who experience a realignment directly, and their children, who experience it indirectly through their parents, will be so affected by the realigning events and ideas that they will be the focus of their political thinking for the rest of their lives. Such individuals can alter their opinions, and they will naturally be forced to take positions on new issues that arise later on. Nonetheless, they will focus primarily on issues arising out of the realignment. The dynamic element comes from Beck's argument that a new realignment will occur only when there is a generation of individuals who themselves have not experienced the previous realignment *and* whose parents have not experienced it directly.

We can, of course, go backward in time with this theory, and the regular pace of past realignments—in about 1860, 1896, and 1932—lend a degree of support to it. But the theory also makes a specific prediction about the future. Let me illustrate with some numbers. Let us think of the New Deal realignment as having occurred between 1930 and 1940. We might now wonder why another realignment did not occur in the 1940s or surely in the 1950s. Individuals grew to adulthood during those decades who did not directly experience the New Deal period (except perhaps as children). They, like myself, would not have been deeply moved by the events of the Great Depression. But these are precisely the individuals who are strongly influenced by their parents, or in my case by an eighth grade math teacher who taught us little about numbers but a lot about how fortunate we were to be growing up in the 1950s. If we think of a generation as being 25 years long (a number pretty commonly used and not picked to make this calculation work out correctly), it is not until 1965 that a generation comes of age whose parents came of age after 1940. As we all know, 1965 was a watershed year with regard to party identification, a major element in realignments. The exact correspondence of these numbers is perhaps a coincidence, but the occurrence of a change in partisanship (in this case a decline in the number of identifiers) around that time is much more than coincidental if Beck is correct.

But we can go one step further. If we can identify the end of the realignment period, we can predict the next realignment. Thus if we again think of the realignment (or dealignment if you wish) as taking ten years to 1975, then the next realignment should occur as we go into the 21st century. On this basis, I will boldly assert that APSA conventions around that time will be regaled with papers on "A new alignment for a new century?" and similar topics. But my main point is not to set the agenda for Association meetings that far in advance. Rather the point is that Beck's theory suggests an important, relatively specific and testable, dynamic element in one aspect of public opinion.[1] Perhaps also of significance is the fact that Beck's theory, like Inglehart's, deals not with the specific distribution of opinions but rather with the agenda of politics.

My third and fourth examples of dynamic theories of public opinion are less ambitious but perhaps more frequently obtainable. They are models of opinion formation and change that are highly specified—that usually means mathematical—and that can be used to probe the consequences of change in some of their parameters. Philip Converse (1969) created a model that expresses the level of partisanship of a cohort of individuals as a function of personal partisan experience (number of years eligible to vote multiplied by a turnout factor and a factor intended to measure resistance to new learning among cohorts that were first able to vote sometime beyond the normal age of adulthood) and inherited partisan experience (essentially the father's personal partisan experience). Frankly, my own recent work has shown that this model is in some respects a flawed one. In new electorates it predicts that partisan strength is greatest among the youngest adults and declines monotonically as age increases (since in a new electorate all have had the same—i.e., no—experience, and the older one is at the time of enfranchisement, the more resistance there is to learning a new behavior or attitude). Yet evidence from new electorates does not support this conclusion (Niemi et al., forthcoming).

Whatever the correctness or incorrectness of this aspect of the model, however, I very much like the fact that it yields specific predictions about the relationship between age, time of enfranchisement, turnout, and partisan strength. Considering the small number of variables in the model, it is surprisingly rich with implications, the shape of the age by partisan strength curve in new electorates being one of them. And while it is best tested with a long series of observations of a new electorate, some tests can be made with cross-sectional data. Finally, it is also useful to note that Converse's model is unusual in that it relates in a precise and relatively straightforward fashion the impact of an institutional change, enfranchisement, on one aspect of public opinion.

The other example of a narrow but precise model of public opinion is in many ways very similar to Converse's. Carlsson and Karlsson (1970) assume, like Converse, that individuals are less likely to change as they got older. Thus a new stimulus is most likely to be reflected in the attitudes of young adults and is decreasingly likely to alter the aggregate outlook of older cohorts. Unlike Converse's model, however, older individuals may have strong opinions prior to the stimulus change. By assuming a specific form of the age-change relationship, Carlsson and Karlsson are able to model how the population reflects changing stimuli. One of the interesting implications of their model is a smoothing effect in the overall population for what in the young are abrupt changes. Another is the blurring of adjacent cohorts, especially among the elderly. An elderly cohort will reflect a whole series of past stimuli, and a slightly younger cohort will reflect these same stimuli in almost the same way. Thus, the distinctiveness of older cohorts will be very difficult to detect. While this feature may make the model a good description of attitudinal change, it also makes it extremely difficult to test, and I have not seen any good examination of it. Nevertheless, it is striking in the precision and substance of its predictions.

If more of our theories were as dynamic as the four that I have described, we would be closer than we are to a science of public opinion. For the most part we deal with static relationships; alternatively, we observe and describe changes over time, but with little theoretical explanation and attempts at modeling why those changes occurred. Fortunately, change in public opinion itself sometimes forces us to think dynamically, as changes in voting behavior in the 1960s forced many of us to reevaluate our ideas about voting behavior. Yet this does not happen often enough. Therefore, it behooves all of us to recognize how much less we know about the dynamics than about the statics of public opinion and to begin to rectify that situation. In what follows I suggest three ways in which we might do that.

STUDIES OF THE LIFE CYCLE

Despite all of the recent attention to life cycle, generational and period effects on party identification, I believe that we have only begun to scratch the surface in our knowledge of the relationship of the adult life cycle to political opinions and behavior. Admittedly, this is a controversial point. Markus (1983, p. 734), for example, has recently said that even with respect to the development of partisan strength, "age as a variable has no direct theoretical meaning." And apart from the well known relationship between age and voting turnout,[2] there are relatively few instances in which age-related differences appear to be genuinely caused by a person's position in the life cycle.

The lack of many significant findings to date may be attributable to at least two factors. First, the biggest changes may occur at the time in the life cycle that is most difficult to study. Because of their considerable mobility and lack of social ties, 18- to 24-year-olds are especially difficult to sample properly (Converse, 1976, pp. 49–51), so much so that it has become commonplace to set this group aside in looking at the development of partisanship. While this may be prudent given the apparent biases in most samples, it avoids rather than overcomes the problem. If the greatest amount of change occurs very early in adulthood—and the Jennings-Niemi (1981) and Jennings-Markus (1984) panel results suggest that that might be the case—then we need to overcome the sampling problem if we are properly to understand life cycle changes.

A second reason for the sparse findings in regard to the life cycle may be that we have looked for the wrong thing. It may be that few attitudes ever show a systematic relationship to age, much less being directly attributable to age or life-cycle position. The salience of issues, however, may to some degree be a direct function of the life cycle. This is especially true if we look at the salience of topics as reflected in behavior. How many 25-year-olds and how many 60-year-olds, for example, are heavily involved in school politics? Some, to be sure, but for obvious reasons the greatest attention to schools occurs among the middle-aged. And more generally, attention to local politics, as opposed to the more glamorous world of international politics, seems to be a concern of the middle-aged (Jennings and Niemi, 1981, pp. 127–128). The way in which opinions are translated into action also varies by age. Once again, it may be the very youngest adults who stand out in this regard. It is hard not to observe the youthfulness of most protesters, whether the civil rights protesters of the 1960s or the environmentalist protesters of the 1980s, and it is hard not to attribute this to stages in the life cycle.

It will not be easy to develop and test theories of life cycle phenomena because they are hard to distinguish from generational and period effects, are sometimes disrupted by these same effects, and because their principal impact may be on less prominent aspects of public opinion. But we must make the attempt to understand the adult life cycle if we are to more fully understand the dynamics of public opinion.

HISTORICAL STUDIES

A second way in which studies of public opinion can become more dynamic is to extend them backwards into history. An immediate objection, of course, is that we lack relevant data. Pushed to its extreme, this objection is surely correct. Scientifically drawn sample surveys do not go back far enough for us to examine public opinion, say, about the Revolutionary War or even about World War I. As time marches on, however, the objection that we cannot do historical studies becomes less and less significant. There are now over 30 years worth of academic surveys of the general public, and commercial public opinion polls go back almost another two decades. Fifty years represents almost a quarter of our history as a nation, and hardly anyone would regard the decades of the 1950s and earlier as identical to the 1980s. While we may not yet think of studies of the 1950s as "historical," it is becoming increasingly insightful and important to test our ideas on the entire scope of available survey data.

There are also creative ways in which some aspects of public opinion can be studied for earlier periods. Some 19th century data on individual partisanship have been found (Hammarberg, 1977), and personal journals, town and city records, church records, contracts, and other such material are being used to give us at least a glimpse or two into public attitudes in earlier times. Such sources are not equivalent to random samples, of course, but knowing the kinds of biases in such material sometimes allows us to make tentative but useful inferences in spite of their selectiveness. To date, most of this work has been done by historians. Political scientists should join them on this bandwagon lest they be left behind. But more importantly, attention to history—whether of the last several decades or of the last several centuries—should stimulate a far more dynamic view of public opinion than exists now.

A RELATED NEED: COMPARATIVE ANALYSES

One of the themes of recent work in social choice theory is the rediscovery of institutions. Riker (1980), for example, argues that studies of attitudes and institutions went their separate ways two decades or more ago, and that only now is social choice theory beginning to incorporate institutions into studies of the way in which attitudes are aggregated. The same lack of attention to institutions characterizes public opinion research. The question is how to alter this situation.

Dynamic theories, especially those covering long historical periods, are one way of bringing institutions into our work. But in emphasizing dynamics, we should not overlook the need for more comparative analyses, especially when they are dynamic as well. Comparative studies of voting behavior are now legion. And insofar as voting studies overlap with public opinion more generically, there have been some efforts at studying public opinion in a variety of countries. But attention has seldom focused on the study of public opinion per se. This is most unfortunate since a lesson well learned in voting studies is that concepts and measurements do not always travel well. Yet understanding why they do not travel often leads to new insights.

As an example of the possiblities, I offer some work that I recently completed with a Swedish collaborator on the stability of attitudes in Sweden and the United States (Niemi and Westholm, 1984). Following Converse's work on attitudes and nonattitudes, we first used panel studies from the two countries to determine overall stability levels of political attitudes. Leaving aside an array of methodological problems, the results demonstrated to our satisfaction that there was substantially more stability of expressed opinions in Sweden than in the United States. In the U.S., the average over-time correlation was .43; in Sweden it was .55. Moreover, there were abstract issues in Sweden on which the correlations were .65 and above, and among highly interested respondents the correlations reached .75–.80. More important than simply determining this fact, however, was that we offered an explanation for the results and successfully tested the explanation. Is the Swedish electorate better informed than that in the United States? Probably not, at least in most senses of the word. What is the case is that the Swedish political parties tend to take clearer, more consistent stands on issues, more consistent across political leaders and across time. As a consequence, there is typically a stronger relationship between partisanship and respondent opinion. This in turn leads to more stable attitudes, often, we conjecture, even in the absence of any real understanding of the issues. The point here, of course, is that the effect of an institution (parties) on attitude stability would probably not have been discovered in the absence of comparative work.

One other set of analyses is particularly worthy of note because they incorporate data over a couple of decades or more and are reasonably well developed theoretically. Studies of the impact of the economy on the popularity of executives, having begun with studies of presidential popularity, are now a genuinely comparative enterprise (see Hibbs, 1982, among others). The results of these studies are mixed in the sense that somewhat different formulations are often found significant, but they are rather consistent in finding that fluctuations in the economy alter evaluations of presidents and prime ministers. The important point here, however, is that differences between countries have had to be taken into account, both in formulating equations and in interpreting results. The consequence has been increased insight into the way in which public opinion relates to both economic events and party platforms. Interestingly, the two examples that came most immediately to mind again call attention to events and opinions over a long period of time. Madsen (1981) suggests that the reason for a different relationship between macroeconomic policy and party strength in Norway than in the U.S. is that attitudes in the Norwegian public, even more so than among Americans, were fundamentally shaped by the Depression of the 1930s. Similarly, Baker, Dalton, and Hildebrandt (1981) interpret German results in light of attitudes developed as a result of rapid recovery of the German economy following World War II.

Other examples, of course, could be cited. Many studies in voting behavior, for example, at least touch on public opinion more generally. Yet it is significant that the major examples of collaborative work that I can think of grow specifically out of voting research, studies of socialization, and so on. When I think of public opinion abroad, I think primarily of Gallup affiliates in other countries. While these affiliates provide a useful set of data that should be exploited much more than currently, they are most unlikely to provide the kind of theoretical understanding that is needed if we are to develop a science of public opinion. Comparative studies should contribute a lot to our understanding of public opinion. At present they do not.

METHODS

Question Wording and Questionnaire Content

If we make the study of public opinion more dynamic, how will this affect the methods that we use? First, an emphasis on models of change will lead us away from the close scrutiny of single, cross-sectional surveys. Longitudinal studies will become more frequent, whether that means panel designs, cohort analyses, or examination of repeated cross-sections. If my examples above are any indication, analyses will increasingly cover long periods of time, sometimes a generation or more. But if all of this is correct, it should convey an important message:

Don't change question wording

and, insofar as possible,

Don't change questionnaire content

One's immediate reaction to this prescription, I suspect, is to think of all of the reasons why questions and questionnaire content sometimes have to be changed: the subject matter changes, outdating old wordings; better methods of asking questions are devised; new issues arise and squeeze out those that are outdated. If this were not enough, we know that constant question wording and content do not guarantee constant meaning. And if our theories, as in the case of Inglehart and Beck, deal with changes in the focus of discussion, new questions and topics are imperative.

Yet we are constantly plagued by changing question wording and by the absence of key variables. Changes in question wording are the most obvious. Probably all of us know the example of the apparent changes in attitudinal constraint that began in 1964 (Nie and Andersen, 1974), which have since been identified to my satisfaction as having come from changes in the wording of attitude questions (see, e.g., Sullivan et al., 1978). More important though less visible are the volumes of over-time studies that have never been written because changes in question wording invalidated the desired comparisons.

A similar though also low visibility problem occurs because of changes in questionnaire content. Herbert Hyman (I have forgotten where) once lamented the fact that it was difficult to trace the origins of attitudes on current issues because no one asks about them until they become highly salient, and by that time the major changes have occurred. Similarly, the ebb and flow of attitudes cannot be traced. In the area of tolerance of nonconformity, for example, there is apparently an absence throughout the 1960s of "Stouffer"-type questions on civil liberties. At the time no one felt any loss. But their absence is now felt since interest in the topic has revived. A more mundane example occurs in an article I recently coauthored on perceptions of presidential candidates (Wright and Niemi, 1983). The theory we used is a general one, having been taken in large part from earlier work by Shively. It would have been sensible to test this theory on data across a number of election years. Yet in the end we tested it only for 1976. The reason? Even in 1972, one of the variables we used (and we had only a small number of them) was absent. While we could have substituted something "similar," we felt that it would not have been adequate. I suspect that we are far from the only ones to have faced this predicament in recent years.[3]

Another closely related implication of my discussion is the following:

> *As much as possible, surveys should include questions*
> *that can be used over a long period of time*

If at least some of our theories are best tested over periods as long as a generation or more, we will necessarily encounter the problem of questions becoming outdated. Newcomb, for example, when he interviewed Bennington College graduates in the early 1960s (Newcomb et al., 1967), could hardly ask about the Spanish Civil War as he had when he first interviewed them as undergraduates in the mid-1930s. To some degree this problem can be overcome by using current items that measure (we hope) similar concepts. A much better solution is to have available questions about relatively permanent topics. Questions about parties, presidents (the role more so than the incumbent), and groups come to mind. These should be emphasized at the expense of questions about more transitory individuals and issues. Another solution is to emphasize generic rather than specific issues (e.g., aid to the poor rather than food stamps). These steps represent a tradeoff, of course, and other things being equal, I would like to have numerous questions about contemporary issues. But other things are not equal, and when forced to choose, I would go for the long-term and generic terms. It is also the case that data on attitudes on contemporary issues are more likely to be available—and on a repeated basis—from commercial pollsters.

Won't all of this stifle creativity? Will we, for example, still be using old question formats when better ones are available? Not if we adopt another suggestion:

> *Conduct more frequent research and development studies*

All too often we alter question wordings on the basis of weak evidence—often just a feeling that a different wording would be better or would clear up some ambiguity in the existing question. We require empirical evidence for our theories. Why not require it for methodological innovations? In fact, I would require that

> *Changes in question wording be adopted only upon proof*
> *of improvement based on R & D or similar studies*

This would surely reduce the number of changes, but it would also mean having a firm basis for the changes that were made. Moreover, it would very likely mean that we would have some baseline for assessing changes that were adopted. R & D studies that included both the new and the old versions of a question (perhaps necessarily in a split-half sample) could tell us directly how the two measures compared, both in the sense of obtaining different marginals and different relationships with other variables. Since even a bias toward constancy will not eliminate all question changes, this information would facilitate the kind of long-term studies that I think are necessary.

Good studies need not be conducted on a large scale, and in general, I think we need to make more use of local, state, and other such research facilities. Nonetheless, even small-scale survey studies are difficult to mount. Therefore, I suggest:

More studies like the 1979 national election
pilot study be conducted

The existence of that study created a lot of interest in methodological innovations and experimentation. A continuing series of such studies—even if conducted infrequently and irregularly—would more than make up for the lack of facile changes to existing questionnaires. However, it follows from my reasoning that they must be conducted well in advance of the studies they will modify. To conduct a pilot study in 1979 that strongly influences the 1980 election study, or one in 1983 to affect the 1984 study, is not a good practice.

Testing Theories on Multiple Data Sets

Currently when I read manuscripts or journals, I ask myself whether or not the theory should have been tested on more data sets. Yet I also wonder, both as a researcher and as a reader, whether every theory needs to be tested on every available data set, such as every election study since 1952. As more and more studies are archived, this problem looms even larger. Moreover, if my earlier suggestions are adopted, fewer and fewer authors can use the excuse that key variables were missing from alternative data sets.

Rather than adopt an arbitrary rule about the number of tests required, I suggest that

More journal space be devoted to replications
of previous research

Such replications could take the form of updates, as currently published by the *American Journal of Political Science*. These generally extend previous research to data sets that have become available since the original study was done, e.g., a new election study. But this concept can be extended to any kind of replication. Thus, an author would not be compelled to use more than one data set, but he would be forewarned that others could readily publish retests. As my colleague, David Weimer (1983), has noted, such a practice might also yield a less biased sample of research results. Knowing that their work would undergo this form of rechecking, researchers might be less inclined to search in an atheoretical fashion for any results that survive conventional tests for statistical significance.

Such replications would require a different manner of writing than is presently customary. Most importantly, reports would be considerably shorter, sometimes possibly only a page. New standards of evaluation would probably have to be developed as well. For example, would a replication of a result from a nationally representative sample be worth publishing if performed on an ad hoc sample of college students? So my proposal raises problems, but I think it creates opportunities as well. It is possible, for example, that one journal would choose to specialize in this kind of report, accepting replications of work done throughout the profession, including that published in book form. In any event, a publishing outlet of this sort is necessary now and will become increasingly valuable as our data base becomes bigger and bigger.

Source Books, Especially Over-Time and Cross-National

Long term, comparative, and historical studies would be easier if public opinion data were more readily available. Of course the Consortium (ICPSR) and European data archives have helped enormously in this regard. Yet as more and more data accumulate, and especially if our theories call for long-term and cross-national assessments, it becomes increasingly cumbersome to manipulate the amounts of potentially relevant data. Thus, in addition to preservation of data for secondary analysis, I suggest that

> *More public opinion resource books are needed,*
> *especially with over-time and cross-national information*

A start has been made in this direction. Gallup data are now published in yearly volumes. Summaries of the Michigan studies (Miller et al., 1980; Converse et al., 1980) are now available, and a cumulative code book exists for the General Social Surveys (NORC, 1982). *Public Opinion* and *Public Opinion Quarterly* regularly provide overviews of public opinion of specific topics. Abroad there are two volumes on Germany (Noelle and Neumann, 1967; Noelle-Neumann, 1981), Gallup's international volumes, and the brief *World Opinion Update*. However, many more volumes of this sort are needed. What will be especially useful are volumes that give results over time, provide data for a variety of groups in the population, give some details about sampling procedures, and are well indexed.[4]

As such publications become more numerous, it also becomes important to update them regularly. Unless there is enough material to justify an annual volume, however, as in Gallup's case, publishers have found this prohibitively expensive. With new techniques for data storage, updating, and processing, I cannot see why this should be so. Means must be found to keep over-time data current. As with replications, a journal might find it in its interest to update data, as the *European Journal of Political Research* currently updates election information. My guess, however, is that other means will be found to update reference works inexpensively.

CONCLUSIONS

In order to make this paper as sharply focused as possible, I have concentrated exclusively on survey data, and a narrow aspect of it at that. Lest I convey an incorrect impression, let me conclude by joining in a call recently made by Margolis (1984a,b) not to equate public opinion with survey data. Survey researchers all know, but frequently need to be reminded, of discrepancies between attitudes as expressed in surveys and behavioral manifestations of attitudes.

Learning this lesson well is important if we are to make maximum use of what we learn about public opinion, i.e., if our knowledge of public opinion is to be anything other than an end in itself. Margolis (1984b, p. 6) notes that studies beginning with public opinion data generally assume that public opinion is causally related to the development of public policies. Yet there are serious questions about that assumption, often related to discrepancies between poll responses and actual behavior. To be sure, there are examples of theories that use public opinion in a more sophisticated way, linking it to some behavior. An excellent recent example is Jacobson and Kernell's (1983) theory about the strategic calculations of prospective congressional candidates and the way these calculations interact with voters' opinions and behavior. Yet such theories are much less common than they should be.

Kent Jennings struck the right note in his comments on this paper at the APSA meetings. He noted that "another way in which the methods of opinion research need to be improved is by relating mass distributions of public opinion to behavioral manifestations of these opinions. Can we model these dynamics to specify and understand these processes? Is it possible to calibrate the visible outcroppings of opinion in the form of unconventional behavior with the underlying opinion distribution in mass publics?"

Attempting to answer these questions brings us back to the need for more dynamic theories of public opinion, but it adds an important dimension. We very much need theories to explain the dynamics of public opinion. But we also need theories that link public opinion to mass political behavior, elite behavior, and to public policy. There will not be a science of public opinion if we cannot explain changes in attitudes. But a science of public opinion—at least as it relates to political science—will only be meaningful if we can use it to understand and explain important elements in the political process.

Acknowledgments. I would like to thank Larry Bartels, Paul Allen Beck, M. Kent Jennings, Warren Miller, David Sears, and James Stimson for their comments on previous versions of this essay.

NOTES

1. Recently, the first direct test of Beck's theory (Clubb, Flanigan, and Zingale, 1984) found no support for it. However, other implications of the theory should also be tested before it is modified greatly or rejected.

2. Even here some of the relationship with age is spurious. That is, the decline in voting among the elderly can be attributed to other factors, such as their lower education (Wolfinger and Rosenstone, 1980, chap. 3).

3. Another case in which new questionnaire content made comparisons impossible is found in the 1978 National Election Study. Fiorina (1981) tried to investigate changes in voters' knowledge, perceptions, and behavior in the 1958 and 1978 congressional elections. Most of the writing about 1978 suggested that voters had become more knowledgeable, but Fiorina wanted to test this assertion by actual comparison with the 1958 data. It appears from his analysis that the difference between the two electorates may be much smaller than one would have thought. That Fiorina cannot draw a firm conclusion is due precisely to changes in the questions. Eubank and Gow (1983) indicate that question changes also led to a strong proincumbency bias in 1978. Thus we are left with somewhat circular results. We were convinced in 1978 that changes in congressional voting demanded changes in question wording. Now we are finding that the question changes may be what is prompting the discovery of the anticipated vote changes.

4. An example of exclusive reliance on published data is the long series of studies on the economy and presidential popularity. It would be extremely tedious as well as pointless for each researcher to derive the data directly from the surveys.

REFERENCES

Baker, Kendall L., Dalton, Russell J., and Hildebrandt, Kai (1981). *Germany Transformed.* Cambridge: Harvard University Press.

Beck, Paul Allen (1974). A socialization theory of partisan realignment. In Richard G. Niemi (ed.), *The Politics of Future Citizens.* San Francisco: Jossey-Bass.

Carlsson, Gosta, and Karlsson, Katharina (1970). Age, cohorts, and the generation of generations. *American Sociological Review* 35: 710–18.

Clubb, Jerome M., Flanigan, William H., and Zingale, Nancy H. (1984). Family socialization by the New Deal generation: a test of Beck's thesis. Presented at the annual meeting of the Midwest Political Science Association, Chicago.

Converse, Philip E. (1969). Of time and partisan stability. *Comparative Political Studies* 2: 139–171.

Converse, Philip E. (1976). *The Dynamics of Party Support.* Beverly Hills, Calif.: Sage.

Converse, Philip E., Dotson, Jean D., Hoag, Wendy J., and McGee, William H. (1980). *American Social Attitudes Data Source Book.* Cambridge: Harvard University Press.

Eubank, Robert B., and Gow, David John (1983). The pro-incumbent bias in the 1978 and 1980 National Election Studies. *American Journal of Political Science* 27: 122-139.

Fiorina, Morris P. (1981). Congressmen and their constituents: 1958 and 1978. In Dennis Hale (ed.), *The United States Congress, Proceedings of the Thomas P. O'Neill, Jr. Symposium on the U.S. Congress*. Boston College.

Gallup, George. *The Gallup Poll*. Now published yearly by Scholarly Resources, Inc.

Hammarberg, Melvyn (1977). *The Indiana Voter: The Historical Dynamics of Party Allegiance During the 1870s*. Chicago: University of Chicago Press.

Hibbs, Douglas A., Jr. (1982). On the demand for economic outcomes: macroeconomic performance and mass political support in the United States, Great Britain, and Germany. *Journal of Politics* 44: 426-462.

Inglehart, Ronald (1977). *The Silent Revolution: Changing Values and Political Styles Among Western Publics*. Princeton: Princeton University Press.

Jacobson, Gary C., and Kernell, Samuel (1983). *Strategy and Choice in Congressional Elections* (2nd ed.). New Haven: Yale University Press.

Jennings, M. Kent, and Markus, Gregory B. (1984). Political socialization over the long haul: results from the three-wave political socialization panel study. *American Political Science Review* 78: 1000-1118.

Jennings, M. Kent, and Niemi, Richard G. (1981). *Generations and Politics*. Princeton, N.J.: Princeton University Press.

Kinder, Donald R., and Sears, David O. (1983). Public opinion and political action. In Gardner Lindzey and Elliot Aronson (eds.), *The Handbook of Social Psychology* (3rd ed.). Reading, Mass.: Addison-Wesley.

Madsen, Henrik Jess (1981). Partisanship and macroeconomic outcomes: a reconsideration. In Douglas A. Hibbs, Jr., and Heino Fassbender (eds.), *Contemporary Political Economy*. Amsterdam: North-Holland, 1981.

Margolis, Michael (1984a). Public opinion, polling, and political behavior. *The Annals* 472: 61-71.

Margolis, Michael (1984b). Public opinion and public policy: in search of a genuine linkage. Presented at the annual meeting of the Midwest Political Science Association, Chicago.

Markus, Gregory B. (1983). Dynamic modeling of cohort change: the case of political partisanship. *American Journal of Political Science* 27: 17-39.

Miller, Warren E., Miller, Arthur H., and Schneider, Edward J. (1980). *American National Election Studies Source Book, 1952-1978*. Cambridge: Harvard University Press.

National Opinion Research Center (1982). *General Social Surveys, 1972-82: Cumulative Codebook*. Chicago: NORC.

Newcomb, Theodore, Koenig, Katharine, Flacks, Richard, and Warwick, Donald (1967). *Persistence and Change*. New York: Wiley.

Nie, Norman H., and Andersen, Kristi (1974). Mass belief systems revisited: political change and attitude structure. *Journal of Politics* 36: 540-591.

Niemi, Richard G., and Westholm, Anders (1984). Issues, parties, and attitudinal stability: a comparative study of Sweden and the United States. *Electoral Studies* 3: 65-83.

Niemi, Richard G., Powell, G. Bingham, Stanley, Harold W., and Evans, C. Lawrence (forthcoming). Testing the Converse partisanship model with new electorates. *Comparative Political Studies*.

Noelle, Elisabeth, and Neumann, Erich Peter (1976). *The Germans: Public Opinion Polls, 1947-1966* Bonn: Verlag Fur Demoskopie.

Noelle-Neumann, Elisabeth (1981). *The Germans: Public Opinion Polls, 1967-1980*. Westport, Conn.: Greenwood Press.

Petrocik, John R. (1980). Contextual sources of voting behavior: the changeable American voter. In John C. Pierce and John L. Sullivan (eds.), *The Electorate Reconsidered*. Beverly Hills, Calif.: Sage.

Riker, William H. (1980). Implications from the disequilibrium of majority rule for the study of institutions. *American Political Science Review* 74: 432–446.

Sullivan, John L., Piereson, James E., and Marcus, George E. (1978). Ideological constraint in the mass public. *American Journal of Political Science* 22: 233–249.

Weimer, David L. (1983). Collective delusion in the social sciences: publishing incentives for empirical abuse. Department of Political Science, University of Rochester.

Wolfinger, Raymond E., and Rosenstone, Steven J. (1980). *Who Votes?* New Haven: Yale University Press.

Wright, John R., and Niemi, Richard G. (1983). The perception of candidates' issue positions. *Political Behavior* 5: 209–223.

CHAPTER 11

CHOICE, CONTEXT, AND CONSEQUENCE:
Beaten and Unbeaten Paths toward a Science of Electoral Behavior

Paul Allen Beck

The progress of a scientific field typically is gauged by the "accumulation of knowledge in the form of more or less verifiable propositions" (Riker, 1982, p. 753). Yet achievement by this standard alone is not sufficient for scientific progress. The intrinsic importance of the questions the field addresses also is crucial, especially in the social sciences, where research questions often are imposed externally. Neither the accumulation of scientific knowledge on small matters nor the consideration of large questions without reaching any authoritative answers will bring distinction to a scientific field in the eyes of scholars or the broader community. The most successful scientific fields are those which have accumulated scientific knowledge on weighty research questions.

The electoral behavior field usually receives high marks in terms of the scientific quality of its research. Considerable knowledge in the form of verifiable propositions has been gained over the last several decades regarding the factors determining voter choices in specific elections. This focus seems natural, for commentary on elections is full of speculation about why voters decided as they did. The field also has been blessed with rich sources of data for answering questions about vote choice. These data have been mined extensively using theoretically based hypotheses and strong methodologies. With good reason, electoral behavior often is referred to as the most scientific field in political science.

The matter of vote choice in specific elections, though, is not the only question of significance to the study of electoral behavior. Scholars must seek to explain the context that transcends a single election, that is, the patterns of electoral behavior over time and space. Additionally, scholars must concern themselves with the consequences of elections for politics and policy, for this question too dominates political commentary in democratic societies.

These three questions of choice, context, and consequence comprise the agenda for electoral behavior research. This agenda has been defined by the broad community of political analysts as much as by researchers in the field. Only by building a base of scientific knowledge to address each of these three questions can the field become truly successful in the eyes of both electoral behavior scholars and this wider community.

This chapter evaluates the electoral behavior field as a scientific enterprise from the perspective of these three research questions. Much of the distinction the field already has earned comes from its study of vote choice. Considerable scientific knowledge has been built up around voting choice especially in presidential elections. It is the proverbial "path well beaten." Vote choice research was directed early on by researchers at the University of Michigan, and they deserve principal credit for its accomplishments. This chapter reviews the study of choice from the vantage point of the Michigan Model, which emerged principally with *The American Voter* (Campbell et al., 1960). We consider its initial structure and impact as well as the cumulative effect of recent research seeking to refine and replace the basic components of the model.

The paths towards answering the questions of context and consequence have been "unbeaten" by comparison. The study of electoral context was moribund until slightly more than a decade ago and remains scientifically immature in spite of tremendous progress in the last few years. The question of consequence has received even less study. Only recently have scholars begun to wrestle with the thorny issues of the impact of elections, and considerable ground-clearing conceptual work remains to be done. Theoretical perspectives drawn from the study of electoral realignments can lead the way in research on both context, where they naturally applied, and consequence.

CHOICE: THE BEATEN PATH

Considering the widespread attention paid to the "horse race" aspect of elections in the U.S., it is little wonder that explanation of election outcomes has been the principal focus of the electoral behavior field. Yet intrinsic interest in elections cannot account fully for the attention that researchers have paid to the question of vote choice. Voluminous data on elections and powerful theories for bringing order to these data also have figured prominently in the development of the field.

Official election returns have always provided a treasure trove of information to analysts of politics. Dependence on aggregate data, though, greatly limits the kinds of explanations that can be invoked validly to account for vote choice. Since the 1930s, sample surveys increasingly have become *the* data of voting behavior specialists, allowing explanation to extend to attitudinal factors. The comprehensive Michigan studies of course are the major source of these materials. As evidenced by the involvement of the television networks and major national newspapers in their own polling activities, the survey focus has diffused well beyond the academic community. Today analysts of voting decisions, especially at the presidential level, have access to a rich array of individual-level materials. Few scientific fields enjoy such an abundance of data.

Of even greater significance in the development of the scientific study of electoral behavior has been the theoretical framework outlined in the early and mid 1960s by Angus Campbell, Philip E. Converse, Warren E. Miller, and Donald E. Stokes of the University of Michigan. Their Michigan Model has dominated the study of elections, shaping inquiry in its field more than any other framework in political science. It has become fashionable to describe scientific fields in terms of the establishment, hegemony, then replacement of dominant paradigms (Kuhn, 1962). While it is debatable whether it qualifies as a paradigm in the strict Kuhnian mould, the Michigan Model nonetheless has performed many paradigmatic functions in the study of voter choice. An assessment of the science of electoral behavior must begin by evaluating this model.

The Michigan Model

Discussion of the Michigan Model seems to be a growth industry these days. Several excellent analyses have appeared in recent years (Prewitt and Nie, 1971; King and O'Connor, 1981; Asher, 1983; Rusk, 1982), and one hesitates to add to the list. It is difficult to identify an explicit model of voting behavior in the Michigan studies. This leaves room for disagreement about the components of the model and for yet another attempt to outline it.

What we shall refer to as the Michigan Model is the conceptualization specified in *The American Voter* (Campbell et al., 1960) and subsequent publications through *Elections and the Political Order* (Campbell et al., 1966) six years later. While earlier works were instrumental in developing the framework, the initial synthesis appeared in the 1960 volume. These prolific scholars continued to make major contributions to the study of voting behavior after 1966, but some of this work diverged from the basic framework set by 1966. The pre-1966 works all contributed to the same loose framework, elaborating and specifying where the need arose. Subsequent research, especially since 1972 (Miller et al., 1976), sometimes exhibits a revisionary character and so does not involve the building or even extending of the basic model.

The American Voter employs virtually all of the concepts conventionally drawn upon in analyzing voter choice: attitudes toward parties, candidates, and issues; party loyalties; ideology; election laws; social group membership; social class; economic outlooks; farm conditions; geographical mobility; education; occupation; sex; age; personality; party performance in managing government;

and turnout. Even some factors that appear to be missing (e.g., ethnicity, region, campaign activity) are handled under the rubric of a more general concept. What is often forgotten is that the most distinctive feature of *The American Voter* itself is its comprehensiveness.

What turns the Michigan Model into a theory of vote choice rather than simply a catalogue of factors involved in such decisions is its differentiation among the concepts in terms of their utility in accounting for electoral behavior. Two ordering devices are used to accomplish this task. The first employs the metaphor of the funnel of causality to array explanatory factors by their proximity to the vote decision. The distinction between short-term and long-term forces, best articulated in Converse (1966a), captures this conceptual ordering. Short-term forces are specific to a particular election. Since the configuration of issues and candidates in the campaign is most proximate to a particular vote choice, the model assigns them priority in explaining the vote. That perceptions of parties and candidates in the election context are analyzed first in *The American Voter* indicates their causal priority in the Michigan Model. Out of this initial focus flow the familiar six components of the electoral decision (Stokes, Campbell, and Miller, 1958; Campbell et al., 1960, p. 67; Stokes, 1966): voter perceptions of the personal attributes of each candidate, the group interests they represent, domestic issues, foreign policy issues, and performance of the parties as managers of government. They are the model's *short*-term forces, lying in the part of the funnel of causality closest to the vote.

In most respects, *The American Voter* is organized so that successive chapters move progressively further from the vote decision towards the rim of the funnel of causality. After dealing with the immediate perceptions of candidates and parties, and detouring briefly to examine voter turnout, the authors turn to what later (Converse, 1966a) would be referred to as the long-term forces. Relegation of potential short-term forces (e. g., issues) to these later chapters reflects the view that all short-run forces of importance are captured by the six components of the electoral decision.

The second important decision in developing the Michigan Model involves theoretical differentiation among the long-term forces. Both theory and empirical results inform this important step. A number of candidates vie for supremacy as the long-term forces motivating voting choices most, e.g., party, social class, religion, ideology, issues. *The American Voter* is comprehensive in its identification of these enduring factors. The Michigan Model establishes an ordering among them. Some are distinguished on theoretical grounds, while empirical analysis is relied upon to assess the explanatory power of contenders which share the same conceptual order.

Long-term forces are ordered theoretically by the extent to which they are translated into political terms. Political party loyalties are considered more proximate to the vote than social class or religious grouping (the short-term influence of which will be picked up by the likes/dislikes questions) because they have explicit political meaning. In this treatment, party loyalties are viewed implicitly as an expression of the major political cleavages in the society. A social class cleavage will be expressed in the contrasting party ties of the social classes. That is, party loyalties encapsulate the sociological factors so often ceded importance in explaining the vote—*if these factors are relevant to politics.* By building enduring party loyalties directly into the model, there is no need to incorporate the more distal factors contained in party as independent influences.

Party loyalties, ideology, and issues all qualify as long-term forces of equal conceptual status, because each has been translated into political terms. Yet, due to different empirical relationships to the vote in the 1950s and 1960, they are not accorded equal status in the Michigan Model. It is in distinguishing among these three competing explanatory factors that the Michigan researchers make their most crucial theoretical contribution.

Political ideology stands in potential rivalry to party identification as a long-term force of the same conceptual order. Given the emphasis placed on the ideologies of voters, candidates, and parties in popular treatments of presidential elections, it is crucial to test the hypothesis of a strong linkage between ideology and the vote in formulating a model of vote choice.

To test this hypothesis, the Michigan team (in *The American Voter* and Converse, 1964) have provided conceptualizations and operationalizations of ideology that remain dominant to this day. Ideology is conceived of in several ways in the Michigan studies, two of which are of interest in understanding how ideology figures in explanations of vote choice. One meaning of ideology is the abstract conceptualization of politics along liberal-conservative lines that are applied to concrete political objects. Here ideology is a belief system in which political evaluations are deduced from overarching liberal or conservative principles. The second meaning of ideology is more operational in nature. Here attitudes are bound together in packages without the requirement that the source of binding be abstract principles. Converse (1964) refers to the former type of ideology as conceptualization, the latter as constraint. A focus on conceptualization and constraint is necessary to understand how the Michigan studies treat the role of ideology in voting behavior.

The importance of conceptualization for voting behavior can be determined quite simply. For conceptualization to account for vote choices, voters must possess abstract ideologies. Yet preciously few Americans employed abstract ideologies in thinking about the candidates and the parties in the 1950s and early 1960s (Campbell et al., 1960, p. 249). In fact, ideological conceptualization was too rare to explain more than a trivial portion of the vote in the elections upon which the Michigan Model was developed. This finding supported the conclusion that conventional treatments of elections as struggles among alternative ideologies, consciously rooted in voter minds, are vastly overdrawn. As the authors of *The American Voter* put it: "the concepts important to ideological analysis are useful only for that small segment of the population that is equipped to approach political decisions at a rarefied level" (p. 250).

The other type of ideological thinking, constraint among issue positions, seems a far more likely source of guidance in voting behavior. Unfortunately, the Michigan researchers never estimated the relationships between operational ideologies and the vote. Perhaps such analysis was judged unnecessary because of the narrow scope of attitude constraint on policy issues found in the early studies. While some constraint existed among domestic issues and among foreign policy issues, the weak associations between foreign and domestic policy attitudes precluded their treatment as derivatives of a single liberal-conservative continuum (Converse, 1964, p. 50). For whatever reason, a simple unidimensional ideological explanation of voting behavior was not deemed appropriate in the 1950s or early 1960s.

If ideology per se is not an important factor in voting choice, what about single issues? Voting on the issues (or policy voting) long has been a cherished ideal of democratic theory. Early voting research challenged this ideal as a realistic description of voter behavior (Berelson, Lazarsfeld, and McPhee, 1954, pp. 305–323) although not without important dissent (Key, 1966). So central a place has it held in democratic theory that *The American Voter* had to address the question of issue voting. The requisites the Michigan researchers identified for issue voting are: cognition of the issue, intensity of feeling about it, and a perception that one party better represents the individual's position than another. At most 36% of the sample fulfilled all three of these conditions on any single issue. The amount of single policy voting on any particular issue cannot exceed this threshold and, given the imperfect links between issue position and vote, must be much lower.

The case against widespread policy voting was reinforced by subsequent findings on the stability of issue positions over time. Between 1958 and 1960, attitudes on the principal issues of the day were considerably less stable than political party identifications (Converse, 1964). While such instability could reflect changing opinions over time, Converse attributed it in a work first published years after its presentation mostly to the absence of true attitudes among many respondents who nonetheless responded to the issue questions (Converse, 1970). While there is sufficient stability in these items to qualify many respondents as long-term issue voters, the Michigan researchers eschew this interpretation, preferring to view the "glass as half empty rather than half full." They leave the impression that the quest for issue voters had reached an empirical dead end.

The dismissal of ideological and issue voting leaves party identification as the key long-term force of direct political relevance in the Michigan Model. Further support for this position comes from the significant relationships in the early studies between party and both issue positions and ideology. Assuming that party identifications are formed for the most part during childhood long before cognitions of issues or ideology develop, these relationships are attributed to the causal influence of party on issue positions and ideology.

The essence of the Michigan Model is captured by the elegantly simple normal vote formulation (Converse, 1966a). Operating as a long-term force from election to election is party identification. The absence of any other long-term forces in the normal vote conceptualization reflects the view that party identification encapsulates everything that goes before it in the funnel as well as the temporally equivalent factors of ideology and issues. By representing more distal influences through party identification, the model exposes the inadequacy of sociological explanations of political behavior, which are based on remote causes, often too remote to be cognized by the actor. Deflecting voters from this long-term baseline are a series of immediate stimuli in the election campaign. The six components of the electoral decision primarily are designed to contain these short-term forces, but some residue of long-term factors appears in them as well. And of course party identification itself has a direct impact on the vote, especially when the short-term forces are balanced between the candidates.

The Michigan Model imposes a tight cause-effect framework on the factors involved in the voting decision. The funnel of causality orders these factors by proximity to the vote decision. Equally proximal factors are differentiated further in terms of their political relevance. Taken together, these ordering devices produce a model of unidirectional causal flows without feedback and with minimal simultaneous influences. This kind of model could be estimated at the time by "state of the art" techniques for recursive modelling. The advent of nonrecursive techniques in recent years eliminates the need for simple unidirectional paths. It is easy to forget how much technical capabilities shape theory, but this fact is central to an understanding of the original development of the Michigan Model.

It is unfair to the Michigan researchers to reduce their rich analysis of voting behavior to a handful of concepts and key relationships. They never presented their work so parsimoniously, and it is questionable whether they even conceptualized their research in such explicit terms. Nonetheless, the outlines of a definite model of voter choice can be gleaned from various writings of the Michigan team from 1960 to 1966. This model is distinguished as much by what is excluded as included, what is emphasized rather than deemphasized. But it is no less a theoretical model for this. In spite of its comprehensiveness and cautiousness, the Michigan work is hardly formless. Followers and critics alike have seen it in fairly bold relief. If members of the Michigan team do not rush forward to claim paternity for what I have called the Michigan Model, then I gladly accept the burden.[1]

The Diffusion of the Michigan Model

The explanatory power of the Michigan Model accounts in part for the influence it has exerted on the field of voting behavior, but it does not tell the whole story. A crucial chapter in the full story is a classic illustration of how a "paradigm" can come to dominate a field of study. Any full evaluation of the science of electoral behavior must examine how the Michigan Model diffused through the scholarly community.

The discipline of political science in the early 1960s was especially fertile ground for a new model of voting behavior. While elections long had been a subject of study in the discipline, there was little to distinguish political science treatments of elections from less scholarly accounts. A sophisticated theory of vote choice provided the means through which scholars could place their own stamp upon the study of elections. So influential has this "stamp" become that it now permeates even popular accounts. The Michigan Model also appeared at a time when the behavioral revolution—with its emphases on individual political behavior, scientific inquiry, and the utility of the other social sciences —was taking root in political science. The emphases of the Michigan researchers dovetailed nicely with this revolution, both helping to spread it and being carried by it.

As if the ground were not fertile enough already, the Michigan researchers actively developed a community of scholars whose principal research focussed on the Michigan election surveys. The Michigan Model has virtually monopolized data collection efforts in the electoral behavior field. Since 1952 the Michigan surveys have provided the primary data for the academic study of electoral behavior. Particularly in more recent years, other surveys have been available for scholarly analysis, but they have lacked the richness of the Michigan data and consequently have not been nearly as attractive to researchers. The early Michigan surveys were designed to reflect the emphases of the Michigan Model. Perhaps no better example exists of the influence of theory upon data collection activities, for what the Michigan Model dictated the Michigan surveys implemented.

This data monopoly was reinforced by the intensive professional socialization of many of the new generation of political scientists. From the beginning, the research activities at Michigan were team efforts in which developing scholars, sometimes as graduate students, were encouraged to participate almost as equals with the senior researchers. As a result of the creative leadership of Warren Miller, this arrangement was broadened and institutionalized through the Inter-University Consortium for Political Research (ICPR), founded in 1962. Soon after their collection each election year, the Michigan data were deposited in this central archive, drawing rights to which were in the hands of scholars at a number of member universities. This archive, now the Inter-University Consortium for Political and Social Research (ICPSR), has expanded well beyond its original foundation on the Michigan surveys. Yet the election surveys remain the most widely used of all ICPSR holdings.

As if making the surveys available to scholars were not enough inducement to stimulate electoral behavior research, the Consortium undertook the task of providing methodological training to social scientists through a summer program at the University of Michigan. Since its inception thousands of social scientists—from all disciplines and most nations where the social sciences exist—have received methodological instruction at Michigan. While the training was formally methodological, because the Michigan researchers and election studies were its centerpiece, students were also imbued, however unconsciously, with the framework reflected in the Michigan Model, especially in the early years when instruction was dominated by the Michigan researchers and their graduate students. And of course a large number of active researchers in the field received all, not just one summer, of their professional training at the University of Michigan. Most active researchers in the field surely are alumni of at least one of these Michigan programs.

It is easy to underestimate the influence of the Michigan Model in the professional socialization of a generation of electoral behavior researchers, for much of its contribution was subtle. The work of the Michigan team, especially *The American Voter*, was intellectually powerful and exciting. For training at the frontiers of quantitative methodology, Michigan was the place to be—if not as a full-time student, at least in the ICPSR summer program. And through the Consortium young researchers were provided with a rich data set ready to be used for dissertations and professional publications. The lures of the Michigan Model to bright young scholars were overwhelming.

Given these forces, it is little wonder that attachments to the Michigan Model have been so strong and lasting. So pervasive was its influence that scholars often failed to appreciate the assumptions of the framework and their own acceptance of them. As is the case with any theoretical model of paradigmatic force, the Michigan Model has not been without challenge. But in the field of electoral behavior, where they must take root to be really effective, the most serious challenges did not come right away and even then were at least partially fueled by movement away from the original model by the Michigan researchers themselves. The hegemony of the Michigan Model perhaps is best illustrated by the fact that its principal critique in recent years, *The Changing American Voter* (Nie, Verba, and Petrocik, 1979), is developed largely within the theoretical framework laid out in *The American Voter.*

Revising, Refining, and Replacing the Michigan Model

The Michigan Model does not dominate the field of electoral behavior as it once did. The political context has changed. New theoretical perspectives have emerged. More sophisticated methodologies have been developed to allow estimation of highly complex relationships. It was inevitable that the hegemony enjoyed by the Michigan Model would not last. What is striking is not its decline but rather how much the original formulations continue to shape the study of electoral behavior. The model has been renovated, although so much reconstruction has been done at certain places as to create quite a new theoretical structure for the explanation of electoral behavior. The following pages review more recent research in the electoral field from the perspective of its relationship to the Michigan Model.

The model has been refined substantially with respect to treatment of the short-term factors modelled as the components of the electoral decision. As originally formulated, these components were broad coding categories for spontaneously mentioned likes and dislikes. While maximizing the applicability of the components to changing election conditions, such an approach fostered ad hoc explanations of vote choice (Prewitt and Nie, 1971). As emphasis shifts across elections from one short-term force to another, without any specification of how or why, the Michigan model seems unsatisfyingly ad hoc and atheoretical. Refinement of the six components of the electoral decision has been long overdue.

The greatest problems have appeared with the candidate factors: what respondents like and dislike about the major party candidates. Fortunately most of the refinements are concentrated here. Candidate evaluations may represent "bottom line" decisions about the overall attractiveness of each candidate (Page and Jones, 1979; Markus and Converse, 1979). If the candidate likes/dislikes merely contain summary judgments that mirror the vote, it is little wonder that they do so well in accounting for vote choice (Stokes et al., 1958; Stokes, 1966). But if they are simply surrogates for the vote, then they warrant no separate conceptual standing in a model explaining the vote decision.

One way to move away from the "summary judgment" quality of candidate evaluations is to differentiate them in advance by thematic content. Several different dimensions of candidate evaluation have emerged. Competence was identified as a key element in candidate evaluations in 1972 (Popkin et al., 1976). Markus (1982) discovered separate competence and integrity dimensions in his analysis of the 1980 campaign. Lawrence (1978) emphasized personal attributes and experience as important predictors of vote. Davidson (1982) distinguished three different general components of candidate evaluation: experience, qualifications, and image or personality. These studies share a commitment to breaking down the broad candidate component into substantively meaningful and measurable dimensions. Such enrichment of candidate evaluations is a very promising research development. Not only does it provide an opportunity to treat candidates in a less ad hoc manner, but it can also shed some light on the traits voters most value in presidents and reduce the temptation to regard candidate evaluations as noninstrumental "fluff" (Davidson, 1982).

The use of specific traits as stimuli for voter evaluations of candidates in the 1980 National Election Studies (NES) survey constitutes an important step towards making candidate evaluations more theoretically discriminating. In the 1979 pilot study of these "presidential prototypes" (Kinder at al., 1980), competence and trust emerged as most related to candidate preferences, with likeability and personal morality becoming more important for respondents with low education. These evaluations foreshadowed the dominant motifs of the 1980 presidential campaign a year later. Further research on candidate evaluation promises to clarify disputes over which dimensions are important and thereby improve our understanding of how candidate evaluations influence the vote.

A second important refinement in the candidate component is the increased theoretical importance attached to retrospective evaluations of the incumbent as a manager of government. Judgments of past performance always have played a role in the Michigan Model, but they were submerged in the broader assessment of the parties as managers of government. When an incumbent president runs for reelection (the situation in six of nine contests covered by the Michigan surveys), attention is likely to be focussed more on presidential performance than general party performance. Following the tradition of Key (1966), Page (1978) and Fiorina (1981) emphasize retrospective voting as punishment or reward for past performance of incumbents.

The need for a separate short-run factor reflecting judgments of incumbent performance never was clearer than in the 1980 presidential contest. The consensus of scholarly opinion attributes Carter's defeat to his failure to win a referendum on his performance as president in the previous four years rather than the attractiveness of Reagan's policy promises. (See Ladd, 1981; Miller and Wattenberg, 1981; Petrocik and Verba with Schultz, 1981; Abramson, Aldrich, and Rohde, 1982; Hibbs, 1982. But for the dissenting view that prospective policy voting was important, see Miller and Shanks, 1982). Retrospective voting is handled clumsily by the Michigan model, turning up in both the party performance and candidate evaluations. A more straightforward treatment is necessary for analysts to incorporate retrospective incumbent evaluations into a theoretical framework that will serve from election to election.

Over the years the most persistent assaults on the Michigan Model have come from scholars who were unwilling to accept its relegation of issues to a secondary place in voting behavior. Attacks on the Michigan Model from this perspective have been somewhat, but only somewhat, overdrawn. The Michigan researchers presented a mixed picture regarding the role of issues in voting behavior (Kessel, 1972). Issues were dealt with as both long- and short-term forces. Foreign and domestic issues were treated as important short-term components of the electoral decision. Issue constraint was regarded as ideology, implicitly a long-term force but one of little significance. Issue voting also can be examined from a third perspective: how attitudes on the dominant issues of the day affect the vote. Without completing the necessary analysis, the Michigan Model assumes implicitly that such policy voting is rare—that "the glass is half empty."

Subsequent research has clarified the role of issues to some extent, by concentrating on the short-run force of single issue voting. Key (1966) contended that issue orientations underlay vote switches in presidential elections, but his study could not distinguish issue voting from rationalization, persuasion, and projection (Brody and Page, 1972; Markus and Converse, 1979). For all its methodological frailties, Key's work stands as an important intellectual precursor to recent studies of retrospective voting. Taking issue salience into account, RePass (1971) showed that issue voting on matters of prime importance to the individual was common—and strong enough to overcome party. Carmines and Stimson's (1980) distinction between easy and hard issues in terms of the cognitive demands they placed on voters provides another useful clarification, for it shows that policy voting does not require high levels of sophistication, and therefore may be more widespread than previously thought.

One of Key's (1966) principal contributions to the study of issue voting was his appreciation that candidate differences on an issue were a necessary prerequisite to voting on it. From this perspective, Page and Brody (1972) explained why widespread issue voting on Vietnam did not occur in 1968. Nixon and Humphrey differed so little on Vietnam policy during the 1968 campaign that there was little room for policy voting on the war. But a "mock election" between Wallace and McCarthy, whom the electorate perceived as supporting very different policies, showed that policy preferences on Vietnam were strongly linked to candidate evaluations where choice existed. More recent studies concur with this view in finding that Wallace was an issue candidate in 1968 (Converse et al., 1969) and that 1972 was an election in which issue voting was important (Miller et al., 1976).

Other research has investigated the extent to which vote choices in presidential and congressional elections are based on economic evaluations. The evidence now seems clear, after considerable initial confusion on the matter, that economic issue voting has been common in recent years (Kramer, 1983; Weatherford, 1983). Increasingly it is viewed as based on respondent perceptions of general economic conditions, what Kinder and Kiewiet (1981) call sociotropic voting, rather than personal economic situations (Tufte, 1978, pp. 105–136).

That economic issue voting may be linked more to evaluations of general economic conditions than personal pocket book concerns calls into question the common assumption that issue voters act solely out of narrow personal interest. This notion has been challenged even more directly by Sears and his colleagues (Sears, Hensler, and Speer, 1979; Sears et al., 1980). On a variety of issues, these researchers found that pure self-interest explanations for policy positions were less satisfactory than accounts focussed on such symbolic orientations as ideology, party, or prejudice. The notion of rational political man, always calculating gains and losses based on the information at hand, may be extended to cover symbolic orientations. But this approach taken to its logical extreme views all behavior as necessarily rational, thus robbing the rational choice approach of its theoretical distinctiveness. It seems fair to say that narrow self-interest is not as powerful a force in voting as commonly assumed.

Considerable attention has been paid to issue voting since the original Michigan formulations. It is now apparent that single issue voting occupies a more prominent position in explanations of the vote than is permitted in the Michigan Model. We now understand that the prerequisites for issue voting are satisfied with varying degrees of success from election to election. Furthermore, while issues may be no more influential than before, scholars have been less inclined to deemphasize the role of issues as the need to debunk the idealistic view of widespread issue voting has declined. Just as the Michigan Model's treatment may have been dominated by the desire to refute the conventional wisdom of the fifties, more recent treatments have been shaped by reactions to the new conventional wisdom of the Michigan Model. In short, while the role of issues may be little different from previous years, we now are more cognizant of it than was the Michigan Model.

Recent studies of long-term forces challenge the basic foundations of the Michigan Model even more directly. That this is so provides an important insight into the nature of the model. The model is comprehensive in its identification of relevant short-term forces, even if treatment of any single force is imprecise and somewhat *ad hoc*. Further research here can only flesh out the nature of particular factors and thereby can be accommodated by the model without large scale changes. In its treatment of long-term forces, on the other hand, the model is selective—explicitly emphasizing some (e.g., partisanship) to the exclusion of others (e.g., ideology). It is the greater specificity here that turns the Michigan work into a model, because theoretical choices have been made. Yet the more choice is exercised, the more the model is subject to theoretical and empirical challenge. These challenges have become especially compelling in recent years.

The most serious challenges focus on the role of partisanship. Partisanship is the keystone of the Michigan "arch." It encapsulates other long-term considerations and translates them into short-term vote choice. Successful assaults on partisanship threaten the very foundations of the model.

The most familiar problem arises from the measurement of partisanship using the party identification index. The concept of partisanship as an enduring psychological identification with a party seems meaningful. Since the Democratic and Republican parties compete with one another in the American system, it also makes sense that identification with one might detract from identification with the other. More problematic is the placement of a third object of identification—political independence—on this same continuum. Nonpartisanship may be the deserving occupant of the middle of a continuum anchored by Democrat and Republican at either pole. But "independent," the choice presented to respondents, is not synonymous with nonpartisanship in American politics. Independence is valued, even revered, in American political life. Americans like to think they vote for the candidate, not the party, even if they are unyielding party loyalists. Independent is an attractive stimulus, not a residual category for those who lack partisanship. In short, considerable measurement error is introduced by modelling a complex phenomenon using a single dimension.

Because the party identification index is loaded with the burden of representing several different concepts, it is little wonder that it seems plagued with problems. These problems become apparent in attempts to validate the index using criterion variables. Petrocik (1974) found intransitivities in the expected linear relationship between partisan intensity and involvement; independent leaners typically were more involved in politics than weak partisans. Other studies (Keith et al., 1977; Van Wingen and Valentine, 1978; Asher, 1980, pp. 91–94) reported intransitivities in the relationship between partisanship and vote, especially presidential vote. Again independent leaners often exhibited more partisan behavior than weak partisans.

For all their sound and fury, these challenges to the party identification index do not undermine its validity or that of the Michigan Model. Much of their case rests upon criterion variables that do not reflect enduring partisanship. An intransitive relationship between partisan intensity and involvement undermines some conclusions of Campbell et al. in *The American Voter* (pp. 142–145) regarding participation, but it does not affect the Michigan Model of vote choice. More troubling are intransitivities in the relationship between partisanship and party affect or vote. But even they are not entirely anomalous, for both party affect and vote choice are influenced heavily by short-term forces.

Vote regularity over time and votes for lower level offices are the most appropriate criterion variables for party identification because they are least influenced by powerful but temporary election-specific factors. When one examines the relationship between partisanship and these variables over the 1952 to 1980 period, quite a different picture of the predictive validity of the index emerges. No intransitivities appear for vote regularity, probably the best available criterion variable. Voting for the House and in state and local contests, the decisions probably guided most by long-term forces, exhibit some intransitivities, but they are neither large nor frequent enough to be troublesome. Based on this evidence, it appears that the measurement error challenges to the Michigan measure of partisanship are overdrawn.

Dissatisfaction with the party identification index fueled attempts in the 1979 NES pilot study and later in the 1980 NES presidential election survey to develop alternative measures of partisanship (Dennis, 1981). These alternatives—the partisan supporter typology (PST) and party thermometers—do not tap long-term identification as well as the party identification index but do a better job of capturing immediate partisan affect. The best of them, the PST, though, is highly complex, and its multiple categories require ordering by the very party identification index it seeks to displace. The traditional party identification index remains the preferable measure of enduring partisan loyalties.

A more serious challenge to the role of partisanship assigned by the Michigan Model is empirically based. Since 1964 the share of the American electorate with partisan loyalties has declined (Nie et al., 1979; Ladd, 1981). Operationally, this decline is handled easily by the Michigan measure of party identification because respondents simply shift towards the center of the Democrat-Republican continuum. The problem is that the center is theoretically hollow. According to the model, independence provides no partisan predispositions to guide voting behavior. Pure independents are motivated solely by short-term forces, while leaners are influenced heavily by them. Because relatively more Americans have positioned themselves in the center of the partisanship scale, disclaiming enduring loyalties to either major party, the long-term partisan component of voting perforce declines and the Michigan Model loses much of its distinctiveness. Many independents seem to be sophisticated voters, who do not need party loyalties to bring order to politics (Shively, 1979). They may rely upon enduring issue and ideological considerations instead.

The Michigan researchers did not foresee the possibility of partisan *de*alignment (Inglehart and Hochstein, 1972; Beck, 1977). They anticipated times when the party system would be realigned and elections in which there might be temporary deviations from the normal vote due to strong and one-sided short-term forces (Campbell, 1966). But a presidential electorate without strong party ties was never envisaged. New political conditions have magnified a long-standing theoretical weakness—the model's dependence on a highly partisan electorate.

A third and related threat to the Michigan Model involves the sources of partisanship. In the model, partisanship is formed by forces located even farther back toward the rim of the funnel of causality. Chief among these forces is childhood socialization, through which parents inculcate partisan allegiances in offspring long before the children can make independent evaluations of political objects (Campbell et al., 1960, pp. 146-148).

Recent research challenges this socialization view of partisan development. The picture of great partisan continuity from one generation to the next is clouded by the flight from inherited partisanship among young Americans since 1964 (Jennings and Niemi, 1981, pp. 89-93). At the same time, the relationships between background sociological characteristics and partisanship too have weakened (Petrocik, 1981).

If early socialization is less influential in forming partisan orientations, then what has taken its place? Fiorina (1977, 1981) sees party indentifications as a "moving" summary judgment based on past party identification, retrospective evaluations of performance, and future expectations. Short-term evaluations "feed back" on partisanship in a manner not permitted in the Michigan Model. This squares with earlier findings by Dobson and St. Angelo (1975) and Brody (1977) that partisanship is responsive to short-term forces. In light of this evidence, partisanship no longer can be considered the *fixed* long-term force that it was in the Michigan Model. It now must be modelled as both a cause and an effect of short-term evaluations. In most times, the preponderant weight may fall on the cause side. In an era of considerable electoral change, though, the possibility that partisanship is as much "moved" as "mover" must be entertained.

The extent to which party identifications are formed from forces even more distal in the Michigan Model also surely varies over time. During a period when the party coalitions are closely knit and electoral politics centers on the dominant cleavage line, the Michigan Model conception of partisan development may be appropriate. Only minimal discordant feedback should flow from contemporary forces to party, largely because short and long-term forces are reinforcing. Since the present is a replicate of the past, this also is a time of strong influence from family and social group. As the old cleavages age and the political agenda changes, short-term forces are more likely to carry the individual into votes that contravene partisan loyalties, thus straining these loyalties. This strain may be resolved by resort to nonpartisanship if no clear partisan alternative is available. Or, if such an alternative appears, new partisan loyalties may form in conflict with the partisan shadings of more distal factors. It surely is not coincidental that the Michigan Model was formulated near the end of the period when the New Deal agenda dominated politics and the party coalitions were stable, nor that the challenges to the model have come in a time when the New Deal system is in decay. Major revisions are required in the Michigan formulations for it to handle these new realities.

Serious challenges have also been raised on behalf of an alternative long-term force to party—ideology—that was relegated to a secondary position in the Michigan Model. Ideological conceptualization has been more common in recent years than in the 1952-1960 period. Initial analyses showed that ideological evaluations of candidates and parties increased dramatically in the 1964 election (Field and Anderson, 1969) and continued to grow until 1976, when they declined somewhat without returning to the pre-1964 levels (Nie et al., 1979). These results are based on a measure of conceptualization developed from the broad master code categories in the Michigan survey code books, not the direct content analysis of interview protocols in Converse's (1964) original analysis. Analysis based on replicates of the Converse measure shows parallel but more modest changes. The percentage of ideologues and near-ideologues by this measure increased steadily from 1956 to 1964, then declined after 1964 through 1976 (Klingemann, 1979; Pierce and Hagner, 1982), but the number of pure ideologues at any time was very small.

These results show that abstract ideological thinking plays a larger role in voting behavior now than ceded by the Michigan Model. Whether this justifies its inclusion in the model as a long-term force, though, is questionable. Ideological conceptualization is unstable over time (Smith, 1980), even more so than most issue orientations. Even pure ideologues, who exhibited more stability than any other group, were less likely than not to qualify as ideologues four years later (Pierce and Hagner, 1982). Overall, the number of ideologues remains low: less than half the number of partisans even using the most generous coding for ideology (Converse, 1975). Ideology as abstract conceptualization about politics can only be of minor importance in accounting for vote choice, however much ideology guides the few who possess it. The Michigan Model does not need major overhaul where abstract ideology is concerned.

Probably no topic has stimulated more scholarly controversy in recent years than the matter of issue constraint within the mass public. A strong challenge to the Michigan Model's conclusion that constrained issue thinking, especially across domains, is not characteristic of the American electorate has been mounted by Nie and his colleagues (Nie with Andersen, 1974; Nie et al., 1979). They reported higher levels of constraint among both domestic issues and all issues in the 1960s and 1970s than in the 1950s.

The principal inference drawn from these results is that consistency in issue thinking is largely a function of elite political discourse. The ideological 1960s, so the revisionist argument goes, increased coherence in mass issue thinking. That issue constraint has fallen off a bit in recent years is taken as further evidence of the responsiveness of mass thinking to the prevailing political context (Nie et al., 1979). Where the Michigan Model erred, the revisionists contend, was in generalizing from the quiescent 1950s. In this view, ideology in the form of issue constraint deserves a place in a model of voting behavior.

This revisionist position in turn has been challenged by a series of studies beginning with Bishop, Tuchfarber, and Oldendick (1978) and Sullivan, Piereson, and Marcus (1978), which attribute the rise in issue consistency to better measurement of issue positions in the Michigan surveys. The effect of these changes is to improve the reliability of the issue questions and thereby decrease attenuation in intercorrelations among them. Seen in this light, the increase in issue constraint beginning in 1964 may be largely artifactual. Variations in the level of constraint using equivalent questions across recent years, on the other hand, show that there nonetheless is some merit in the revisionist notion that issue thinking is a function of the electoral context (Nie and Rabjohn, 1979).

Because important matters remain at issue in this debate, it is easy to over-look the fact that consensus has emerged on one crucial point. Everyone, in-cluding by implication the Michigan researchers since they revised their issue questions, agrees that the newer issue question formats yield more reliable mea-sures of issue positions. This means that the pre-1964 Michigan survey data un-derestimated the amount of constraint in mass policy thinking. Operational thinking in terms of issue constraint was rejected on empirical grounds from in-clusion in the Michigan Model. It is now clear that a reassessment of this con-clusion is required.

Abstract liberal-conservative principles and operational constraint, the two kinds of ideology employed in the Michigan Model, do not exhaust the possible forms of ideological expression. An attractive alternative is to conceive of ideol-ogy as a symbolic psychological identification much like party identification. In this construction, ideological labels do not need either issue content or abstract bases. All that is required is that they trigger symbolic political associations for the individual.

Levitin and Miller (1979) developed such a measure of symbolic ideology from self-locations on the liberal-conservative continuum, perceptions of closeness to liberals and conservatives, and thermometer ratings of the two ide-ological groups. They found symbolic ideology to be consistent over time—more stable than issues and almost as stable as party identifications—and to in-fluence the vote independently of party identification. Measuring symbolic ide-ology by liberal-conservative self-identification, Conover and Feldman (1981) traced its roots to the association of particular groups with ideological positions and issues. These results suggest that ideology conceptualized in symbolic terms also warrants inclusion as a long-term force in models of vote choice.

Probably the most dramatic illustration of the power of the Michigan Model is the fading away of social group explanations of American electoral behavior since the early 1960s. While social group interpretations of electoral politics continued to be popular in comparative studies (e. g., Lipset, 1960; Alford, 1963; Rose and Urwin, 1969; Inglehart, 1977; Lijphart, 1979), they were rarely employed in the study of American electoral behavior while the Michigan Mod-el dominated. To some degree, this can be accounted for by different realities. Class voting is more pronounced in European polities, and party identifications do not achieve a life of their own. But the most important reason for this ne-glect of social groups is theoretical: their treatment in the Michigan Model as wholly mediated distal forces.

Yet ignoring social groups defies reality even in America. Conspicuous exam-ples exist of voting patterns which only can be explained by recourse to group-related concepts. Virtually unanimous black support of Democratic presiden-tial candidates since 1964 cannot be accounted for fully without emphasizing racial group identifications. Nor can block voting by religious groups for president (Converse, 1966b) or in local elections (Parenti, 1967) be squared with the Michigan Model approach. Interestingly, relegation of social groups to a secondary role in the model is accompanied by the extensive treatment of social group identifications in relation to the vote in *The American Voter* (pp. 295–380).

From this perspective, the recent revival in the use of social group variables in voting analysis is highly promising. Research that places the voter in a social network where interpersonal influences are powerful has been on the upswing (Eulau and Siegel, 1981; Weatherford, 1982). This work draws upon a long tradition of contextual analysis that is largely ignored in the Michigan Model. Also heartening has been the resurgence of interest in the impact of group identifications on political behavior, as represented in recent NES surveys.

The impact of all this revisionary research is reflected in recent attempts to model the vote decision employing methodologies, measures, and conceptualizations not present in the original Michigan studies. Using two-stage least squares procedures, Jackson (1975) estimated the feedback of candidate and party evaluations on party identifications, foreshadowing Fiorina's (1977, 1981) theory of partisan formation. The Michigan Model was developed at a time when techniques for nonrecursive modelling were unknown in the social sciences, so even had the Michigan researchers conceptualized causal flows as bidirectional, estimation of the relationships would not have been possible. Methodological advances since the early 1960s have opened up new opportunities for empirical theory building.

These opportunities were capitalized upon more fully by Page and Jones (1979) in a study of the relationships among issues, party, candidate evaluations, and the vote in 1972 and 1976. Building upon spatial theory (Downs, 1957), issue orientations were measured as comparative policy differences between individual and candidate positions. Candidate evaluations were indicated by differences in placement of candidates on the feeling thermometers and then used as surrogates for vote. These measures were made possible by new questions adopted first in the 1968 Michigan survey. These questions paved the way for serious challenges to the Michigan Model and show that the Michigan researchers themselves have played a revisionist role.

The results of the Page and Jones study directly challenge the assumption of unidirectional causal influences in the Michigan Model. When modelled nonrecursively, long-term forces such as party are found to affect short-term forces and in turn be affected by them. In the 1970s at least, party identifications were more effects than causes. Additionally, the Page-Jones formulation ignores the neat ordering of variables along the funnel of causality in treating social background variables as direct effects on both short- and long-term forces. Education, for example, is modelled as a direct influence on both comparative policy distances and current party attachment.

Issue effects varied greatly across the three different issue variables in the Page-Jones model. The new comparative policy distances variable exhibited the strongest relationship to vote. In both 1972 and 1976, this issue variable had a stronger influence on candidate evaluations than either party or candidate personal qualities. Yet, it in turn was highly sensitive to candidate evaluations—influenced more *by* them than affecting them. Given these findings, treatment of issues as unimportant or wholly endogenous forces is unwarranted.

The foundations of the Michigan Model clearly are shaken by these results, even if some of them could have been anticipated from earlier research. This revised view of the vote decision, though, comes at the expense of the considerable parsimony and theoretical strength of the Michigan formulation. The Page-Jones "model" is much more complicated and constitutes in initial form a congeries of theoretical propositions rather than an integrated theory of vote choice.

Another study, by Markus and Converse (1979), models the vote choice non-recursively as well but also takes advantage of the panel embedded in the 1972–1976 data to add a dynamic quality. This effort reinforces the Page-Jones conclusion that candidate evaluations are of prime importance in presidential voting. Candidate evaluations are seen as "bottom line" judgments, carrying the effects of all other variables in explaining the vote. The single most important direct prior influence on candidate evaluations is perceived candidate personality, not issues as in the Page-Jones study. While issues play an important role, their independent effect is compromised by evidence of widespread projection and persuasion.

The Markus and Converse model also revives the role of party identification. The direct effects of party identification on candidate evaluations are the smallest among the issue-candidate personality-party trilogy, although they are not significantly different from the estimates for issues. What is significant about party, though, is its strong association with other components of the model. The overall impact (direct plus indirect) of party on candidate evaluations exceeds that of any other term. As Markus and Converse conclude:

> Partisan predispositions may be outweighed by other model terms at particular stages . . . but these loyalties *keep coming back* as determinants while the vote decision process unrolls . . . (W)hile partisan predispositions are unlikely to dominate the process completely at given stages where the candidates are being assessed, these loyalties appear to make repeated inputs of substantial magnitude throughout the process. (1979, p. 1069, emphasis mine)

Conceptualization of the vote decision as a dynamic process, unfolding over a considerable period, is necessary to portray accurately the contributions of enduring party attachments.

The Markus-Converse model also incorporates revisionist insights into its treatment of the formation of party attachments. Both issues and past vote are seen as shaping party identification; but this feedback, while significant, is small. A single deviating vote slightly weakens partisan attachments, but were these deviations to cumulate over time considerable changes would occur. In short, this model shows that while Fiorina (1979) is correct in viewing partisanship as endogenous to the electoral process, partisanship was not nearly as responsive to short-term influences in the 1972–1976 period as were other leading variables. In the Markus-Converse model, partisan predispositions remain enduring orientations of considerable power.

These recent modelling efforts have advanced considerably our understanding of voting behavior. They address a major weakness of the Michigan Model: the omission of simultaneity and feedback. By conceptualizing net candidate evaluations as the crucial electoral decision, to be converted directly into a vote, these models also avoid the specification problems of the Michigan Model, in which candidate evaluations and vote are treated separately. These efforts are good signs of progress towards a more realistic theory of voting choice that could potentially replace the Michigan Model.

Yet these models are only the first step in this direction. The points of disagreement between them, especially involving partisanship and the role of issues, must be reconciled. As these disagreements show, the empirical estimates are extremely sensitive to changes in the posited structure of the model and the indicators employed. Another serious problem arises from the need to find exogenous variables for the two and three stage least squares procedures used in nonrecursive modelling. Demand exceeds supply of qualified variables, and even the most statistically sophisticated modelling efforts often are compromised by the questionable validity of key variables. Finally, these models have yet to achieve the theoretical integration and parsimony of the Michigan Model, factors which contributed mightily to its power.

Conclusions

The study of electoral choice has borrowed substantially from other social science disciplines for its theoretical frameworks. Early research on voting was shaped primarily by sociology. Its dependence on demographic data to measure both the vote and the characteristics of voters placed a heavier burden on group-based explanations of vote choice than they could bear, and they fell into disfavor. The rise of the Michigan Model, drawing upon measures of attitudes through survey research techniques, and its ensuing hegemony imposed a social psychological framework on explanations of the vote decision, pushing the sociological approach to the background. Attitudes became the primary explanatory variables at the expense of social groups. Social groups were dealt with, if at all, through group identification (an attitude) rather than ascribed group membership.

In recent years, the major challenges to the Michigan Model have come from yet a third disciplinary perspective. Drawing heavily upon rational choice formulations in economics, the vote has come to be seen by some as the result of a strict benefit-cost calculus based primarily on issue and candidate evaluations. Ignoring the caution of some economists that individuals are an unreliable source of information about their perceived benefits and costs because they have an incentive to strategically misrepresent, analysts of vote choice using a rational choice perspective too have come to rely upon surveys.

One of the most promising developments in the voting behavior field has been the recent integration of sociological, psychological, and rational choice perspectives in models of vote choice. This integration has been fostered by the expanded theoretical framework of the Michigan election studies. Rational choice hypotheses about voter behavior now can be subjected to empirical examination, and a new generation of rational choice theorists have exhibited skill in leavening their deductive theories with inductive reasoning from real world applications. Recent years even have witnessed a resurgence in emphasis on social group antecedents to voting. A major attraction of the Markus-Converse and Page-Jones models is that they combine several different disciplinary approaches.

In passing it is important to acknowledge the critical role an institutional change has played in these recent developments. Just as the institutionalization of a research community around the election studies helped to establish the Michigan Model, recent changes in the organizational guidance of the presidential election surveys have nourished the new approaches to the study of vote choice. Since 1978, involvement in the design of the Michigan surveys has been broadened greatly through the National Election Studies Board and its working committees. Any widening of the circle of participants in the planning of research threatens to compromise the theoretical integrity of a project because of the need to reconcile many competing viewpoints. While successfully minimizing this risk, the NES Board has stimulated an infusion of new perspectives and ideas to enrich the presidential election studies. NES efforts deserve much of the credit for rekindling intellectual excitement in the study of vote choice.

Recent years have witnessed a decline in the hegemony of the Michigan Model. While the model has not been totally discarded, in a social science imitation of the Kuhnian scientific revolution, it now is seen as an incomplete and misleading account of voting behavior. Ideology, issues, social groups, and party loyalties adjusted in response to short-run factors are now integral parts of the conceptual lexicon of the student of voter behavior. There is an increased tendency to view the voter as a rational decision maker weighing present promises against past peformance rather than as the committed partisan of the Michigan Model. Our theories of voter behavior have become more verisimilitudinous but also less parsimonious.

Before any new integrated formulation becomes enshrined as *the* model of vote choice, though, it must pass the hard test of changing electoral contexts. Electoral choice in any particular election is shaped by a set of forces that are exogenous to the voter. Such changes in the "times" created many of the anomalies that weakened the hold of the Michigan Model. Current theoretical efforts must avoid being tailored exclusively to fit ephemeral contemporary phenomena. A truly comprehensive theory of vote choice must internalize the troublesome externalities of context. Further progress along the well beaten path to vote choice depends upon developments in the study on context, heretofore a largely unbeaten path.

CONTEXT AND CONSEQUENCE: THE UNBEATEN PATHS

For good reason the study of presidential vote choice has received extensive attention. However, while it may be a satisfactory focus when one is concerned only with the individual, concentration on choice alone is not sufficient for a discipline whose primary focus is the study of politics. The context and consequences of elections are also of great importance, yet they remain largely unbeaten paths of electoral research.

As more elections are added to our observational base through the passage of time and with historical and comparative studies, scholars have become increasingly aware of contextual variation. Context sets the boundaries of the choice situation, encompassing such diverse parameters as the rules of the electoral system, the predispositions of voters, the lines of electoral cleavage, and the agenda around which competition is organized. Most voting theory is based on elections conducted in the last thirty years in the United States—only a thin slice of experience with democratic elections. A better understanding of context is required to determine how much can be generalized from this experience.

A fundamental premise of most voting studies is that elections enhance citizen influence in the conduct of government. Most scholars see them as key mechanisms of citizen influence, while others (Ginsberg, 1982) maintain that elections function more to contain than increase popular pressures. The question of the role of elections in a democratic order is trivialized when the debate is couched in terms of either they are or are not influential. It is more important to study the conditions under which democratic elections have more or less influence. We shall refer to this inquiry as the study of consequence.

The Study of Context

The study of context is essentially concerned with systematic variations in electoral settings. An unavoidable conclusion from research on vote choice is that every election is different. Candidates and issues change. Since World War II, for example, the candidate pairings have been repeated in only one presidential contest, and the dominant issues were not identical in any two elections. Voter predispositions shift. Even the structural and legal context rarely remains constant. The composition of the American electorate has varied significantly by age, race, and partisan affiliation during this century. Sometimes even the parties are different. Contextual differences among elections are magnified when one moves beyond recent U.S. presidential elections to state/local contests or to elections in other nations and other times.

The study of context in American electoral politics has come to be organized by "realignment theory," according to which American electoral history is demarcated by a succession of distinct party system eras (Ladd, 1970; Sundquist, 1973). The electoral coalitions, the balance of electoral power, and the agenda of partisan politics, key ingredients in the context for electoral choice, are set in various eras by realigning elections (Chambers and Burnham, 1967; Burnham, 1970; Clubb, Flanigan, and Zingale, 1980). Of the many possible lines of cleavage that may divide an electorate into partisan camps, realignment theory maintains that only a few are relevant at any time and that one typically dominates. Movement from one party system to another, through the process of realignment, reflects a shift of these dominant lines of cleavage and hence changes the issue agenda of politics. Such a change can have dramatic impact on political outcomes (Schattschneider, 1960, p. 62). Thus, one important aspect of context is which cleavage line dominates, for that determines the electoral alliances and the issue agenda of elections.

Party system context clearly affects the parameters of choice. Sectional cleavages may dominate one system; class cleavages another. Economic concerns might be ascendant at one time; racial concerns at another. Even the content and relevance of political ideologies is conditioned by the prevailing party system and the cleavages it represents. Because the research on vote choice has been confined to the New Deal party system, serious questions must be raised about its generalizability. The Michigan Model's increasing difficulties in recent years may be at least partly attributable to changing political realities.

Realignment theory introduces another fundamental variation in context by distinguishing realignments from other types of election. Realignments are "constituent acts" (Burnham, 1970) that mark the transitions between party systems as shifts in cleavage lines occur (Key, 1955; Sellers, 1965; Campbell, 1966; Campbell and Trilling, 1980) and define the party system which follows. Yet, realignment research is plagued by difficulties in determining when a realignment occurs. Shifts in aggregate vote outcomes are commonly employed to measure the alterations in mass party coalitions that constitute a realignment, because aggregate electoral statistics are the only data available for historical analysis. Yet, vote changes are blunt and sometimes misleading indicators of change in the "standing decision" to support a particular party over the long run because of their sensitivity to short-term forces. A far superior measure of realignment is a shift in party identifications. When measures of party identification are not available, however, changes in long-term voting patterns must serve as a surrogate. But it is important to recognize that, because of their sensitivity to short-run influences, votes often play this surrogate role poorly.

There has been a tendency to require change in the net party balance for realignment to occur (Campbell, 1966). While past realignments typically have produced significant shifts in the partisan balance of power, with the major exception of 1896, such a net change is really not necessary. Significant shifts in the party loyalties of the electorate can occur without disturbing the balance of party power "on net." It is the changes in coalitions, not the displacement of party margins, that constitutes the realignment.

A more expansive conceptualization of realignment has appeared in recent years. Burnham, Clubb, and Flanigan (1978) and Clubb et al. (1980) argue that realignment requires change in both mass party loyalties and party control of government. This definition allows analysts to prevent situations from being classified as realignments in which mass voting patterns change but the agenda of politics remains the same. While this conceptualization handles an anomaly in aggregate vote results, it creates a far more troubling problem by confounding mass electoral change with its consequences. There is no doubt that the causes and consequences of realignment transcend mass politics. Nonetheless, it is preferable to treat realignments as "constituent acts" to avoid unnecessary complications in realignment theory and to be able to examine the impact of mass changes on elites.

Early studies of realignment identified single critical elections as the crucial times of change in electoral coalitions (Key, 1955; Burnham, 1970). Disagreement about which elections were critical inevitably produced reservations about the critical election concept. Emphasizing Key's later (Key, 1959) rather than earlier (Key, 1955) article, scholars now tend to view realignments as secular rather than critical (Sundquist, 1973; Carmines and Stimson, 1981), occurring over several years, not just one. Whether realignments are seen as critical or secular is influenced by how they are measured. Voting patterns change more sharply than underlying partisan loyalties. Therefore, realignments may look more secular the more they are defined in terms of partisan loyalties and the more information about voter party affiliations we have.

Scholarly debate also has raged over the sources of realignment. The initial position was that realignments are produced by conversion of voters from one party to another (Sundquist, 1973). This view, entirely consistent with the early conception of realignments as critical, has gradually given way to an emphasis on the mobilization of new voters (Beck, 1974; Salisbury and MacKuen, 1981). Considerable evidence has been marshalled to show that mobilization underlay the realignments of the 1930s (Andersen, 1979; Petrocik, 1981) and the 1890s (Wanat and Burke, 1982). The mobilization view is compatible with the Michigan Model assumption that partisanship is hardened against change among veteran voters, leaving only relatively new voters available for mobilization in new partisan directions (Converse, 1969).

The mobilization proposition in turn has been challenged. Erikson and Tedin (1981) found evidence in Literary Digest polls of more conversion than mobilization during the New Deal realignment. These results should be viewed with great caution, though, because the Literary Digest polls they rely upon are a frail data source for partisan change. For years they have been cited as the major example of the substantive dangers of sampling and response biases. The polls also recorded only vote reports, not partisanship, and evidence of vote change is based on the notoriously biased recall of previous votes. In spite of serious reservations about the data, the Erikson and Tedin study raises doubt about attributing all realignment change to mobilization.

Both mobilization and conversion surely occur during any realignment. The contribution of each probably depends upon the difference between old and new lines of cleavage and the extent to which the electorate already was mobilized. Contemporary data on partisan decay provide some insight into this mix, although it is dangerous to generalize from evidence on contemporary *dealignment* to past *realignments*. The recent aggregate decline in partisanship has been greatest among young voters—a mobilization phenomenon (Beck, 1977). But partisan declines have been registered among older voters as well (Norpoth and Rusk, 1982), making them available for conversion. The relative amounts of conversion and mobilization in the contemporary period depend to a substantial degree upon how partisan switches of active voters in their late twenties and thirties are coded, making a decisive resolution of the debate all the more unlikely.

Dealignment constitutes a second, more recently appreciated, type of election period. The concept of dealignment was developed to characterize declines in partisanship during the last two decades (Inglehart and Hochstein, 1972). A dealignment is a period during which the partisan share of the electorate actually shrinks. While declines in party identification reflect dealignment best, it may be inferred from other evidence of weakening partisanship—increases in third party voting, ticket splitting, interelection volatility in vote or turnout declines—when direct measures of partisanship are unavailable.

Dealignment may be viewed as the final phase in the cycle of American electoral politics (Beck, 1979). The cycle begins as a realignment defines new party coalitions. As realignment pressures subside, a stable alignment phase ensues, during which stable party groupings compete over the agenda defined by the realignment. For a variety of reasons, including generational replacement of the electorate and resolution of issues along the principal line of cleavage, this party system decays and ultimately dealignment sets in.

Beck (1979) found evidence of a recurrent realignment-stable alignment-de-alignment cycle since the 1830s, relying mostly on aggregate measures of partisan strength in the electorate. Previous dealignments were arrested by the confluence of new social, economic, and political pressures and skillful leadership to pull the system again into realignment. What is unique about the present dealignment is its longevity. The full electoral cycle for previous party systems lasted thirty to forty years. The New Deal party system, by contrast, has endured now for fifty years, although for the last twenty years in only a vestige of its original form.

A regular electoral cycle with distinct realignment, stable alignment, and dealignment phases provides a neat ordering to American electoral history. To the political scientist, this cyclical theory is more important for its implications for vote choice and the consequences of elections than it is in periodizing history. We postpone until later the discussion of consequences to consider now the possible impact of changing electoral context on vote choice.

The prominent factors in vote choice should vary systematically with the electoral cycle. A realignment period should result in more intense feelings about politics and heightened consistency among policy preferences, performance evaluations, partisan affiliations, and vote. Realignments are a time of maximum feedback to partisanship from short-term forces and vote, thus challenging partisan inheritances. Depending upon the nature of the emerging cleavage, furthermore, this may be a time of maximum articulation between social group identifications and party preference. Following the predictions of consistency theory, the high salience of electoral politics then should induce consistency in short- and long-term partisan orientations.

The stable alignment period represents an institutionalization, even a freezing, of the previous political conflicts. It is the time when party identifications should figure most prominently in the vote decision and other long-term forces are encapsulated in partisanship. Because the intensity of politics has subsided, there should be minimal feedback of short-term forces upon partisanship when they disagree. But such disagreement should be rare as parties typically will nominate centrist representatives of their coalition.

During the dealignment phase of the electoral cycle, partisanship is less widespread among the electorate and less determinative of vote even for partisans. This leaves more room for the other long-term forces and especially short-run factors to guide vote choice. Even issue voting may suffer during dealignment, as voter ambivalence about alternative positions grows. Dealignment electorates will be inclined to turn elections into presidential plebiscites (Ladd, 1981), voting on the basis of retrospective evaluations of presidential performance when an incumbent stands for reelection.

Because the Michigan Model was developed during a period of stable alignment, it should not be surprising that it accentuates the role of party and its origins in the socialization process, downplays the long-term role of issues and social groups, and permits no feedback from short-term forces to party. The most compelling challenges to the Michigan Model have been mounted as dealignment spread. While some of these challenges may have found fertile ground in the 1950s if an alternative theoretical perspective had been adopted, many were based on changes in "reality." This raises the possibility that, like the Michigan Model, the revisionist work may be a dealignment-period piece. Unfortunately, no model has been developed from electoral behavior during a realignment. The possibility remains that yet a third set of empirical patterns might emerge to justify one more model of electoral choice.

The American political experience is of course only one source of contextual variation in electoral behavior. The electoral experience of other democracies provides additional evidence for formulating general theories or frameworks of vote choice. While space limitations preclude review of the rich array of studies of electoral politics abroad, two important lessons that can be learned from these comparative studies warrant attention here.

The first is that the electoral system (e. g., the number of parties and elections, parliamentary versus presidential government) is a crucial contextual influence on electoral behavior. Different arrangements for electoral politics abroad reduce the utility of enduring partisan loyalties. The nature of the social structure also affects voting behavior. Muted social class differences and interclass mobility may limit the long-term influence of class in American voting. Expression of group identifications in electoral politics may also be limited in the United States because, in a heterogeneous nation without any dominant cohesive groups, the task of parties is to aggregate many interests rather than articulate the interests of one or two large factions (Burnham, 1974). For reasons of electoral system and social structure, then, models of voting behavior based on the American experience cannot be generalized well to other democracies.

The concepts of realignment theory have been exported to other democracies with greater success. Party systems appear to change throughout the democratic world in response to shifts in underlying mass political cleavages (Lipset and Rokkan, 1967). Evidence of electoral realignments abroad is widespread, although the search for historical patterns of change has not progressed as far as in the United States. The concepts of realignment and dealignment can be employed usefully to explain recent electoral changes in many of the industrialized democracies as the old electoral order seems to be eroding (Dalton, Flanagan, and Beck, 1984).

That the old political order is crumbling simultaneously in many democratic polities provides another important lesson for the study of American electoral behavior. Nationally unique explanations for recent electoral change are unsatisfactory. While contributing to the dealignment, the racial and antiwar turmoil of the 1960s and early 1970s, the Watergate affair, or even changes in candidate nomination processes (Polsby, 1983) may not account fully for the decline of party in the United States, for these events were largely absent from other nations undergoing similar changes. Cross-national growth in post-industrial values (Inglehart, 1977), the shared feeling among young people everywhere that party systems established decades before are irrelevant to modern-day concerns, or even the greater relative number of young voters may be more promising sources of common electoral changes.

No theory of vote choice is complete without specification of the impact of context. The Michigan Model and its revisionist competitors have identified almost every conceivable component of the electoral decision. Both the ordering of these components and their empirically based weights undoubtedly vary with contextual factors. Scholars analyzing particular elections have become increasingly conscious of how the factors that enter a voter's decision calculus depend upon the amount and nature of choice among the candidates. Other contextual factors can be identified only through historical and comparative analysis. Full understanding of the influence of context upon choice awaits more experience and grander theorizing. The prospect of expanding our theory of electoral behavior so that it can encompass conditioning influences opens an attractive research agenda for the electoral behavior field. Until this research path is beaten by many scholars, though, our understanding of the effects of context will be woefully incomplete.

The Study of Consequence

Virtually all students of electoral politics would concur that democratic governments are responsive to mass opinion, that elections guarantee that public opinion will be heeded, and that demonstrating these points analytically is difficult. That elections matter is the underlying rationale for most studies of electoral behavior, and considerable attention has been paid to the consequences of elections. Nonetheless, as Key (1964, pp. 411–412) observed some years ago, in specifying the consequences of elections in democratic politics, "the forest is more visible than the trees."

Aside from referenda, in which public policy is enacted directly by voters, one can distinguish three different ways in which the impact of elections may be conceptualized. The most obvious is that the presence of democratic elections alters the environment for political elites so fundamentally that it qualitatively transforms the system. A second conceptual approach is the study of representation as a means through which elected leaders translate mass wishes into governmental decisions. Finally, since elections endow democratic citizens with the ability to change leaders, consequence can be studied in terms of the effects of elections on leadership composition and turnover. Each of these approaches warrants review, although we must broaden our focus beyond presidential elections to do so satisfactorily.

Opponents of democracy have feared that selection of political leaders through elections will forever transform political systems. They assume that democratic elections open leadership roles to a new group of people who do not possess the desired values and that even the same leaders will act differently under democratic pressures. In short, it is presumed that polities with democratic elections will be more responsive to mass concerns than polities without them.

Empirical testing of this proposition seems almost hopelessly difficult. One approach, the diachronic analysis of interventions in historical time series, is confounded by several factors. Transformation of western nations into democracies has been a slow and continuous process. Sharp interventions are hard to identify, although expansions of the franchise were key turning points. The important changes also antedate the availability of reliable data on mass publics. Nonetheless, as Dahl (1961) has shown in his study of New Haven's political history, the consequences of the democratization of political systems is fertile ground for historical inquiry.

The alternative analytic approach, synchronic comparison among modern day nations, is equally unyielding because the symbolic trappings of democracy appear in even the least democratic of regimes, and nations differ in so many ways beyond their electoral institutions. Nonetheless, some understanding of the consequences of elections may be gained from comparative studies of governmental outputs in the American states and western nations, although variance in the key exogenous variable, the presence of democratic elections, is restricted to differences in the nature of elections—not whether or not they exist. Potentially more useful information can come from comparisons between democratic and nondemocratic industrialized nations, although the impact of elections may lie less in the realm of programmatic expenditures than in the less quantifiable areas, such as civil liberties and equality. Further mining of this considerable research agenda awaits an identification of the key values polities should allocate and collaboration between students of mass democratic politics and students of public policy.

Evidence of the effects of elections also may be found in studies of representation. From the assumption that members of Congress are motivated solely by a desire to be reelected, Mayhew (1974) has constructed a compelling explanation of both the behavior of individual representatives and the operations of the institution itself. If reelection were not in question or were not determined by a mass electorate, Mayhew's work suggests, congressional behavior would change markedly. Fenno's (1978) study of congressmen in their constituencies is an excellent empirical illustration of how reelection needs dominate their lives.

The fidelity of representatives seems to be linked closely to electoral competition. Representation of mass opinion was shown to increase with the proximity of the election in California (Kuklinski, 1978). The votes of state assembly members, elected every two years, consistently corresponded with the issue positions of their constituents. On the other hand, state senators, whose four-year terms insulated them more from electoral pressures, exhibited higher agreement with constituents during their reelection year than in other years. The framers' assumption, articulated by Madison in Federalist 52, that frequent elections would instill a greater sensitivity to popular wishes among elected leaders seems valid.

The ambition to hold office serves as a crucial linchpin of democratic control. Just as the absence of elections may reduce the need to serve public wishes, indifference or downright reluctance to holding office should dull the linkage between citizen and leader. Prewitt (1970) demonstrated how accountability is attenuated by absence of the drive for reelection among "volunteers" pressed into service at the local level. In the same vein, "lame-duck" officials are thought to be released from what Mayhew (1974) calls "the electoral connection."

Representation has been measured by Miller and Stokes (1966) according to the relationship between the actions of the representative and constituent views on important policy issues. They found district opinion to be strongly correlated with roll call votes on civil rights issues, less well related on social welfare issues, and poorly connected with congressional voting on foreign policy issues. Representatives' perceptions of constituent opinion were credited as the predominant influence in the civil rights area, illustrating the role of representative as a neutral delegate for transmitting strong district views. Representatives' own views were more influential on social welfare policy, showing how representation also may be achieved through the selection of leaders who share district orientations.

Like so many Michigan study results, the Miller-Stokes findings quickly became the conventional wisdom about representation. In recent years, however, this research has been seriously challenged. Achen (1977) questioned the correlational methodology for measuring constituency-representative agreement, because it reflects variance in district opinion as well as congruence. Erikson (1978) charged that the Miller-Stokes study underestimated the extent of representation by failing to correct adequately for attenuation due to measurement error in constituency opinions. When he simulated district opinion from district demographic characteristics and their known relationship to issue positions, representative-constituent agreement was heightened across all three issue policy areas. The empirial evidence cited to characterize constituent-representative agreement at the national level comes from a single election setting, 1958, and replications of the Miller-Stokes study would seem to be in order. There has been so much criticism of the measures of representative, constituent congruence and of the relationship of congruence to representation in general, however, that strict replication—without considerable reconceptualization of the problem—is probably unlikely.

Looking for agreement on policy positions constitutes only one approach to the study of representation. Also important is convergence in perceived priorities for public action. In their study of local leaders and citizens of sixty-four small communities, Verba and Nie (1972) examined the concurrence in identification of important problems. Leaders concurred more with politically active than inactive citizens, and concurrence was higher in communities characterized by high levels of overall activity. Using the same data, Hansen (1975) reported that concurrence between constituents and leaders was heightened as well by active parties, widespread partisanship, and competition for local office. Robust interparty competition and citizen participation do, as is often hypothesized, seem to be highly important for the representation process.

These various studies of citizen-leader agreement in policy preferences and priorities suggest that elections have important consequences for representation, but only some of the evidence directly links elections to the representation process. Considerably more research is necessary to specify the nature of these linkages.

The consequences of elections can be studied from yet another promising perspective. Competitive elections provide voters with the opportunity to determine who shall govern. In America's nonparliamentary system, voters may also determine whether the reins of government should be concentrated in the hands of a single party. The most noticeable impact of elections may be found in those surprisingly rare periods when the electorate through a realignment has vested control of all popular branches of government in one party for a lengthy period. Divided and alternating party control, the far more common features of American government, may attenuate the representation process where broad policies are concerned.

It is here that context and consequence join. The view that American electoral history has been punctuated regularly by partisan realignments also suggests that these mass changes have materially changed the governmental process. In recent years, largely due to the influence of Burnham's (1970) classic work, realignment theory has stimulated considerable research on the consequences of realignment for the operation of government and the making of public policy.

Of course the primary force of partisan realignment is felt by the popular institutions of government. Previous American realignments have been characterized by the election of a new president with unusually strong electoral support, a mandate to enact new policies, and congressional party majorities responsive to his leadership. Continuation of this unified control of the popular institutions gives the new majority time to implement comprehensive policy changes. Only five times in American history has one party controlled the presidency and both houses of Congress for more than a decade. Significantly, this control began just after the elections of 1800, 1828, 1860, 1896, and 1932—the five elections usually cited as beginning a new realigned party system.

In a system where separate institutions share governmental power, the elections providing the greatest opportunity for changing governmental policy directions are those which vest the full power to govern in the presidential party. Landslide presidents can wield considerable power, but if they lack congressional majorities this power is diluted by the constant necessity to bargain with opposing forces in Congress. In a system with multiple veto points to stymie change, enactment and implementation of bold new programs also require time. Time for a new majority to work its will is purchased with an electoral realignment.

With Wildavsky's (1964) study of the budgetary process in the postwar period, it has become fashionable to describe policy making in the United States as incremental. But incrementalism cannot characterize the bursts of comprehensive policy change that have emerged when a strong president has been able to count on widespread legislative support (Clubb, Flanigan, and Zingale, 1980). With rare exception, these times of policy change have coincided with realignments (Beck, 1979; Ginsberg, 1976; Hansen, 1980).[2]

Recent research has also studied the effects of realignment on specific institutions of government. Due to the short terms of its members, the House of Representatives is probably the most vulnerable to electoral pressures. Through greater than normal turnover in congressional seats and increased party voting, majority party strength in realignment periods has grown dramatically (Brady, 1980; Brady with Stewart, 1982). Incumbents have been especially vulnerable to defeat during realignment periods, often by insurgents within their own parties. This turnover paves the way for a new generation (carried into office by realignment) to place its particular stamp upon the Congress (Seligman and King, 1980).

Once the secular trend towards less party voting since the 1820s is removed, it is obvious that local maxima for party-line voting in the House were attained during periods of realignment (Clubb and Traugott, 1977; Beck, 1979). One reason for a surge in party voting is membership turnover. The replacements for defeated incumbents have been more likely to support their party's legislative program (King and Seligman, 1974). Even changes in the internal operations of Congress, such as the institutionalization of the House (Polsby, 1968), may be attributable to realignment (Burnham, 1970, pp. 100–106). Finally, realignment periods set a new political agenda for the Congress, evidence of which is found in the transformation of the dimensions of roll call voting (Sinclair, 1977, 1983; Brady and Stewart, 1982).

Even the national institution most insulated from popular pressures, the Supreme Court, seems to be affected by partisan realignments. Dahl (1957) viewed the Supreme Court as an integral part of the national policy-making majority and found that it rarely confronted live legislative majorities. Although the president and Congress determine membership on the Court through the appointment process, the lifetime tenure of justices creates a lag between the establishment of a new ruling coalition and its representation on the bench. During this lag period, acting as the last bastion of the old majority, the Supreme Court sometimes has opposed the new majority (Adamany, 1980). In the New Deal period especially, this opposition was expressed through the use of judicial review to overturn actions of the popular branches of government (Funston, 1975). But even the Supreme Court ultimately follows the election returns. Changes in the composition of the Court gradually convert it to the new majority. Even before these changes have run their course, the Court usually succumbs to the new realities.

In a review of how realignments have affected the major institutions of American politics, it is easy to miss the transcending importance of the realignment—to overlook the forest for the trees. Realignments are constituent acts, reorganizations of party coalitions at the mass level. Vestiges of the past remain after any realignment (Lipset and Rokkan, 1967), as is exemplified by the loyalty of white southerners to the Democratic party for a century, but the dominant cleavage lines of the past always are submerged in the new issue agenda. The political system faces new priorities with new arrangements of power. Only a few, realigning elections have such disproportionate impact upon the operations of the American political system. In short, consequence varies with context.

Only feeble attempts have been made to date in generalizing this approach to the full electoral cycle. American politics seems to show different patterns in stable alignment and dealignment periods as well as realignments (Beck, 1979). Governmental politics during a dealignment may be the antithesis of that during a realignment. The coordination of policy-making activities that can on occasion be provided by strong party control is absent during a dealignment because of divided and (over time) alternating control of the major governing institutions. Without party clarification of policy alternatives, voters are ambivalent about what they want (Ladd, 1981) and appear to be fickle. In this environment, policy changes are hard to initiate and sustain. With the paralysis of popular institutions, nonpopular forces become more powerful.

A stable alignment period may produce yet another political environment. The antecedent realignment provides the majority party adequate powers to work through a political agenda, but the major changes associated with that agenda have already been implemented by the time of stable alignment. The minority party during stable alignment picks at soft spots in the agenda, waiting in the wings to assume power briefly should the majority party falter. Interparty bargaining and incrementalism are probably the dominant characteristics of stable alignment politics.

In short, American politics follows three different operating models, depending upon the phase of the electoral cycle. During stable alignment, when pulling and hauling among separate institutions sharing power is most common, the

American system fits most closely the *Madisonian model*. In a period of re-alignment, when strong mass party loyalties endow the majority party with sufficient power to control all institutions of government, American politics approximates the *responsible party model* of a cohesive-party parliamentary system.

Perhaps because we have such limited experience with extended dealignment, no model comes to mind that captures its essential features. Two prominent characteristics of the contemporary dealignment, though, provide some clues as to what characterization might be appropriate. Without the glue of party, politics becomes much more individualistic, narrow interests prevail more frequently over diffuse interests, and the capabilities of government for sustained policy change and coordination are weakened. Lowi's (1967) pejorative term "interest group liberalism" may be borrowed to describe this situation. Perhaps this new public philosophy, as Lowi identifies it, has its primary roots in dealignment.

Contemporary American politics also seems unusually concentrated on the president. Voters look to him for solutions to public problems and judge him harshly when his leadership is ineffective—as it almost inevitably must be when he lacks broad powers to govern and party control is weak. If this characteristic predominates during all dealignments, then a plebiscitary model (Lubell, 1971; Ladd, 1981) may be applied. Clearly research on earlier dealignment periods is warranted, so that their common characteristics may be identified.

The realignment perspective in recent years has provided important new insights into American politics and has greatly expanded the focus of the study of electoral behavior. Yet realignments are not the only periods which yield distinctive patterns of American politics. To view the American political system as in reality containing quite different arrangements for political power, depending upon conditions of electoral politics, may provide the necessary first step towards a theory of consequences.

Conclusions

As we have seen, the so-called "realignment perspective" provides a theoretical framework conducive to the study of both context and consequence. For all of its promise, though, realignment theory has not yet brought our understanding of these phenomena nearly as far as the Michigan Model and its competitors have in explaining vote choice. One limitation is its immaturity. The study of realignment contexts and consequences has flourished only in the last decade. While scholars have discovered the theoretical path to context and consequence, it remains relatively unbeaten.

Two other limitations of the realignment perspective are more fundamental and cannot be overcome by the sheer weight of research activity. The study of electoral choice focusses on micro-level individual behavior. Context and consequence are macro-level concerns, intrinsically less amenable to explanation because they are more complex and offer only a limited number of cases for analysis. Systematic analysis of party system change at the state level, pioneered by Clubb, Flanigan, and Zingale (1980), holds some promise for alleviating this problem of insufficient observations, but state forces may be so interdependent with national forces that they fail to constitute a separate domain of analysis. Some potential perhaps lies in comparative analysis, but this approach is plagued by the inherent problem of excessive variation and the sheer complexity of macro-level phenomena.

Beyond these empirical problems, a major shortcoming of realignment theory itself is that it lacks an adequate explanation for the dynamics of the electoral cycle. The causes of realignments typically are treated as exogenous to the electoral system. Some scholars attribute them to major crises or traumas in the social-cultural-economic order (Burnham, 1970). Others emphasize the role of leadership in capitalizing upon rare opportunities for building a new majority coalition (Sundquist, 1973; Beck, 1982). The causes of dealignment are regarded more as endogenous, usually the by-product of inexorable generational replacement processes (Beck, 1974), yet the possibility remains that dealignment too may be influenced from outside the electoral system (e.g., period effects influenced partisanship after 1964).

This shortcoming has become transparent in recent years, for the thirty to forty year periodicity of realignments has been upset. The New Deal party system has outlived its predecessors by at least a decade. To expect realignments at this regular interval may simply signify our inadequate understanding of the realignment process. Or the absence of realignment might indicate that American politics has entered a new era, when the old regularities and theories developed to explain them no longer apply. The danger of theories founded upon historical patterns is that there is no compelling reason for the future to repeat the past.

We should not allow these shortcomings, though, to obscure the importance of realignment theory for the study of electoral behavior. By emphasizing the effect of different party systems and election periods, realignment theory integrates intensive analysis of immediate events into a broader mosaic of electoral politics. Appreciation of differences in context inevitably must precede understanding of how changes in context may fundamentally refashion the ingredients of electoral choice or the consequences of those choices for the political system.

TOWARDS AN AGENDA FOR ELECTORAL BEHAVIOR RESEARCH

The science of electoral behavior today stands at a crossroad. One path just ahead is very familiar. It is the path to the study of vote choice that has been traveled heavily for well over twenty years. By taking this path in the past, scholars have advanced significantly our understanding of voting behavior, particularly in presidential elections. The other paths ahead are much less familiar, having been blazed only recently. For all its success in treating the question of vote choice, the field's progress has been retarded because it has shed little light on the important questions of context and consequence.

Continued progress of the science of electoral behavior requires advances along all the paths that stretch out before us. Scholarly attention and resources must be distributed more evenly among key research questions. The choice path undoubtedly will continue to be well beaten. The primary task for research continues to be what it always has been—to integrate various influences on the vote into a model that can apply across electoral contexts, including those at the subpresidential level. But the study of vote choice is still too much wedded to analysis of individual elections, although the importance and integrity of that activity must not be discounted. The bulk of new research investments should be made along the paths to context and consequence, for greater scholarly attention to these long-neglected research questions is necessary for the field to make significant progress.

Given these prescriptions, recent directions of research activity are heartening. The accumulation of presidential election surveys since 1952 inevitably has drawn scholarly attention to questions of changing context. These surveys themselves in recent years have benefitted greatly from the infusion of new ideas and perspectives. Except for lamentable inattention to state and local voting behavior, a result doubtlessly of unwarranted devaluation of subnational surveys when national data are available, the study of vote choice thrives. Thanks to recent developments in realignment theory, the study of context and consequence too has become a productive research area. With heavy travel along all important paths of electoral behavior research in the future, electoral behavior can remain a paragon of success among social science fields.

Acknowledgments. I am grateful to Gregory Markus, James A. Stimson, and Herbert Weisberg for their constructive comments on the original version of this paper.

NOTES

1. Because the works expressing what I have called the Michigan Model were written by different scholars at different times on somewhat different subjects, there is a danger that the only unity in thinking is what I have reconstructed. Yet, I perceive a unifying conceptualization of the voting decision underlying the works in the 1960–1966 period, although this conceptualization may not have attained the consciousness or formality of a true model. Since 1966, the unity of conceptualization even among the original research team has broken down, and the conceptualization itself has changed.
2. The Great Society policies enacted in the 1965–1968 period seem a major exception

to this rule. Johnson's successes in carrying out major policy changes may be attributable to an unusual "rallying around the flag" after the Kennedy assassination. Whatever the cause, one thing that differentiates the comprehensive Great Society policy changes from their realignment-era predecessors is public dissatisfaction with them shortly after their enactment. Beginning in 1969, successive presidents have attacked and whittled down Great Society programs. Without an electoral realignment to support it, the Great Society in the long run may lack the staying power of previous bursts of policy change.

REFERENCES

Abramson, Paul R., Aldrich, John H., and Rohde, David W. (1982). *Change and Continuity in the 1980 Elections*. Washington, D.C.: Congressional Quarterly Press.

Achen, Christopher H. (1977). Measuring representation: perils of the correlation coefficient. *American Journal of Political Science* 4: 805–815.

Adamany, David (1980). The Supreme Court's role in critical elections. In Campbell and Trilling, *Realignment in American Politics*, pp. 229–259.

Alford, Robert (1963). *Party and Society*. Chicago: Rand McNally.

Andersen, Kristi (1979). *The Creation of a Democratic Majority 1928–1936*. Chicago: University of Chicago Press.

Asher, Herbert (1980). *Presidential Elections and American Politics*. Homewood, Ill.: The Dorsey Press.

Asher, Herbert (1983). Voting behavior research in the 1980s: an examination of some old and new problem areas. In Ada W. Finifter (ed.), *Political Science: The State of the Discipline*. Washington, D.C.: American Political Science Association.

Beck, Paul Allen (1974). A socialization theory of partisan realignment. In Richard G. Niemi (ed.), *The Politics of Future Citizens*, pp. 199–219. San Francisco: Jossey Bass.

Beck, Paul Allen (1977). Partisan dealignment in the postwar south. *American Political Science Review* 71: 477–496.

Beck, Paul Allen (1979). The electoral cycle and patterns of American politics. *British Journal of Political Science* 9: 129–156.

Beck, Paul Allen (1982). Realignment begins? The Republican surge in Florida. *American Politics Quarterly* 10: 421–438.

Berelson, Bernard R., Lazarsfeld, Paul F., and McPhee, William N. (1954). *Voting*. Chicago: University of Chicago Press.

Bishop, George F., Tuchfarber, Alfred J., and Oldendick, Robert W. (1978). Change in the structure of American political attitudes: the nagging question of question wording. *American Journal of Political Science* 22: 250–269.

Brady, David (1980). Elections, Congress, and public policy changes: 1886–1960. In Campbell and Trilling, *Realignment in American Politics*, pp. 176–201.

Brady, David, with Stewart, Joseph, Jr. (1982). Congressional party realignment and transformations of public policy in three realignment eras. *American Journal of Political Science* 26: 333–360.

Brody, Richard A. (1977). Stability and change in party identification: presidential to off-years. Presented at 1977 American Political Science Association Convention, Washington, D.C.

Brody, Richard, and Page, Benjamin I. (1972). Comment: the assessment of policy voting. *American Political Science Review* 66: 450–458.

Burnham, Walter Dean (1970). *Critical Elections and the Mainsprings of American Politics*. New York: Norton.

Burnham, Walter Dean (1974). The United States: the politics of heterogeneity. In Richard Rose (ed.), *Electoral Behavior*, pp. 653–725. New York: The Free Press.

Burnham, Walter Dean, Clubb, Jerome M., and Flanigan, William H. (1978). Partisan realignment: a systemic perspective. In Joel Silbey, Allan Bogue, and William Flanigan (eds.), *The History of American Electoral Behavior*, pp. 45–77. Princeton, N.J.: Princeton University Press.

Campbell, Angus (1966). A classification of the presidential elections. In Campbell et al., *Elections and the Political Order*, pp. 63–77.

Campbell, Angus, Converse, Philip E., Miller, Warren E., and Stokes, Donald E., (1960). *The merican Voter*. New York: Wiley.

Campbell, Angus, Converse, Philip E., Miller, Warren E., and Stokes, Donald E., eds. (1966). *Elections and the Political Order*. New York: Wiley.

Campbell, Bruce A., and Trilling, Richard J., eds. (1980). *Realignment in American Politics*. Austin: University of Texas Press.

Carmines, Edward G., and Stimson, James A. (1980). The two faces of issue voting. *American Political Science Review* 74: 78–91.

Carmines, Edward G., and Stimson, James A. (1981). Issue evolution, population replacement, and normal partisan change. *American Political Science Review* 75: 107–118.

Chambers, William Nisbet, and Burnham, Walter Dean, eds. (1967). *The American Party Systems*. New York: Oxford University Press.

Clubb, Jerome M., and Traugott, Santa A. (1977). Partisan cleavage and cohesion in the House of Representatives, 1861–1974. *Journal of Interdisciplinary History* 7: 375–401.

Clubb, Jerome, Flanigan, William, and Zingale, Nancy (1980). *Partisan Realignment: Voters, Parties, and Government in American History*. Beverly Hills., Calif.: Sage.

Conover, Pamela Johnson, and Feldman, Stanley (1981). The origins and meaning of Liberal/Conservative self-identifications. *American Journal of Political Science* 25: 617–645.

Converse, Philip E. (1964). The nature of belief systems in mass publics. In David Apter (ed.), *Ideology and Discontent*, pp. 206–261. New York: Free Press.

Converse, Philip E. (1966a). The concept of a normal vote. In Campbell et al., *Elections and the Political Order*, pp. 9–39.

Converse, Philip E. (1966b). Religion and politics: The 1960 elections. In Campbell et al., *Elections and the Political Order*, pp. 96–124.

Converse, Philip E. (1969). Of time and partisan stability. *Comparative Political Studies* 2: 139–171.

Converse, Philip E. (1970). Attitudes and non-attitudes: continuation of a dialogue. In Edward Tufte (ed.), *The Quantitative Analysis of Social Problems*, pp. 168–189. Reading, Mass.: Addison-Wesley.

Converse, Philip E. (1975). Public opinion and voting behavior. In Fred E. Greenstein and Nelson W. Polsby (eds.), *Handbook of Political Science*, Vol. 4, pp. 75–169. Reading, Mass.: Addison-Wesley.

Converse, Philip E., Miller, Warren E., Rusk, Jerrold, and Wolfe, Arthur (1969). Continuity and change in American politics: parties and issues in the 1968 election. *American Political Science Review* 63: 1083–1105.

Converse, Philip E., and Markus, Gregory B. (1979). "Plus ca change . . .": The new CPS Election Study Panel. *American Political Science Review* 73: 32–49.

Dahl, Robert A. (1957). Decision-making in a democracy: The Supreme Court as a national policy-maker. *Journal of Public Law* 6: 229–295.

Dahl, Robert A. (1961). *Who Governs?* New Haven: Yale University Press.

Dalton, Russell, Flanagan, Scott, and Beck, Paul Allen, eds. (1984). *Electoral Change in Advanced Industrial Democracies: Realignment or Dealignment?* Princeton, N.J.: Princeton University Press.

Davidson, Dorothy K. (1982). Candidate evaluation: rational instrument or affective response. Presented at Midwest Political Science Association Convention, Chicago.

Dennis, Jack (1981). Some properties of measures of partisanship. Presented at 1981 American Political Science Association Convention, New York.

Dobson, Douglas, and St. Angelo, Douglas (1975). Party identification and the floating vote: some dynamics. *American Political Science Review* 69: 481–490.

Downs, Anthony (1957). *An Economic Theory of Democracy*. New York: Harper & Row.

Erikson, Robert S. (1978). Constituency opinion and congressional behavior: a reexamination of the Miller-Stokes representation data. *American Journal of Political Science* 22: 511-535.

Erikson, Robert S., and Tedin, Kent L. (1981). The 1928-1936 partisan realignment: the case for the conversion hypothesis. *American Political Science Review* 75: 951-963.

Eulau, Heinz, and Jonathan W. Siegel (1981). Social network analysis and political behavior: a feasibility study. *Western Political Quarterly* 34: 499-509.

Fenno, Richard F., Jr. (1978). *Home Style: House Members in Their Districts.* Boston: Little, Brown.

Field, John Osgood, and Anderson, Ronald (1969). Ideology in the public's conceptualization of the 1964 election. *Public Opinion Quarterly* 33: 380-398.

Fiorina, Morris P. (1977). An outline for a model of party choice. *American Journal of Political Science* 21: 601-626.

Fiorina, Morris P. (1981). *Retrospective Voting in American National Elections.* New Haven: Yale University Press.

Funston, Richard (1975). The Supreme Court and critical elections. *American Political Science Review* 69: 795-811.

Ginsberg, Benjamin (1976). Elections and public policy. *American Political Science Review* 70: 41-49.

Ginsberg, Benjamin (1982). *The Consequences of Consent: Elections, Citizen Control, and Popular Acquiescence.* Reading, Mass.: Addison-Wesley.

Hansen, Susan B. (1975). Participation, political structure, and concurrence. *American Political Science Review* 59: 1181-1199.

Hansen, Susan B. (1980). Partisan realignment and tax policy: 1789-1976. In Campbell and Trilling, *Realignment in American Politics,* pp. 288-323.

Hibbs, Douglas A., Jr. (1982). President Reagan's mandate from the 1980 elections: a shift to the right? *American Politics Quarterly* 10: 387-420.

Inglehart, Ronald (1977). *The Silent Revolution.* Princeton, N.J.: Princeton University Press.

Inglehart, Ronald, and Hochstein, Avram (1972). Alignment and dealignment of the electorate in France and the United States. *Comparative Political Studies* 5: 343-372.

Jackson, John E. (1975). Issues, party choices, and presidential votes. *American Journal of Political Science* 19: 161-185.

Jennings, M. Kent, and Niemi, Richard G. (1981). *Generations and Politics.* Princeton, N.J.: Princeton University Press.

Keith, Bruce E., Magleby, David B., Nelson, Candice J., Orr, Elizabeth, Westley, Mark, and Wolfinger, Raymond (1977). The myth of the independent voter. Presented at the 1977 American Political Science Association Convention, Washington, D.C.

Kessel, John H. (1972). Comment: the issues in issue voting. *American Political Science Review* 66: 459-465.

Key, V.O., Jr. (1955). A theory of critical elections. *Journal of Politics* 17: 3-18.

Key, V.O., Jr. (1959). Secular realignment and the party system. *Journal of Politics* 21: 198-210.

Key, V.O., Jr. (1964). *Public Opinion and American Democracy.* New York: Knopf.

Key, V.O., Jr. (1966). *The Responsible Electorate.* Cambridge, Mass.: Belknap Press.

Kinder, Donald R., Peters, Mark D., Abelson, Robert P., and Fiske, Susan T. (1980). Presidential prototypes. *Political Behavior* 2: 315-337.

Kinder, Donald R., and Kiewiet, Roderick (1981). Sociotropic politics: the American case. *British Journal of Political Science* 11: 129-161.

King, Michael B., and Seligman, Lester (1974). Critical elections, congressional recruitment, and public policy. Presented at the Midwest Political Science Association Convention, Chicago.

King, Michael B., and O'Connor, Robert E. (1981). The contribution of the ISR voting studies: review and critique. Presented at the American Political Science Association Convention, New York.

Klingemann, Hans D. (1979). Measuring ideological conceptualizations. In Samuel H. Barnes and Max Kaase (eds.), *Political Action,* pp. 215-254. Beverly Hills, Calif.: Sage.

Kramer, Gerald H. (1983). The ecological fallacy revisited: aggregate versus individual-level findings on economics and elections, and sociotropic voting. *American Political Science Review* 77: 92-111.

Kuhn, Thomas S. (1962). *The Structure of Scientific Revolutions.* Chicago: University of Chicago Press.

Kuklinski, James H. (1978). Representatives and elections: a policy analysis. *American Political Science Review* 72: 165-177.

Ladd, Everett Carll, Jr. (1970). *American Political Parties*. New York: Norton.

Ladd, Everett Carll, Jr. (1981). The brittle mandate: electoral dealignment and the 1980 presidential election. *Political Science Quarterly* 96: 1-25.

Lawrence, David G. (1978). Candidate orientation, vote choice, and the quality of the American electorate. *Polity* 11: 229-246.

Levitin, Teresa E., and Miller, Warren E. (1979). Ideological interpretations of presidential elections. *American Political Science Review* 73: 751-771.

Lijphart, Arend (1979). Religious vs. linguistic vs. class voting: the 'crucial experiment' of comparing Belgium, Canada, South Africa, and Switzerland. *American Political Science Review* 73: 442-458.

Lipset, Seymour Martin (1960). *Political Man*. New York: Doubleday.

Lipset, Seymour Martin, and Rokkan, Stein (1967). Cleavage structures, party systems, and voter alignments. In Seymour Martin Lipset and Stein Rokkan (eds.), *Party Systems and Voter Alignments*, pp. 1-64. New York: Free Press.

Lowi, Theodore (1967). The public philosophy: interest-group liberalism. *American Political Science Review* 61: 5-24.

Lubell, Samuel (1971). *The Hidden Crisis in American Politics*. New York: Norton.

Markus, Gregory B. (1982). Political attitudes during an election year: a report on the 1980 NES Panel Study. *American Political Science Review* 76: 538-560.

Markus, Gregory B., and Converse, Philip E. (1979). A dynamic simultaneous equation model of electoral choice. *American Political Science Review* 73: 1055-1070.

Mayhew, David R. (1974). *Congress: The Electoral Connection*. New Haven: Yale University Press.

Miller, Arthur H., Miller, Warren E., Raine, Alden, and Brown, Thad (1976). A majority party in disarray: policy polarization in the 1972 election. *American Political Science Review* 70: 753-778.

Miller, Arthur H., and Wattenberg, Martin P. (1981). Policy and performance voting in the 1980 election. Presented at American Political Science Association Convention, New York.

Miller, Warren E., and Stokes, Donald E. (1966). Constituency influence in Congress. In Campbell et al., *Elections and the Political Order*, pp. 351-372.

Miller, Warren E., and Shanks, J. Merrill (1982). Policy directions and presidential leadership: alternative interpretations of the 1980 presidential election. *British Journal of Political Science* 12: 299-356.

Nie, Norman H., with Andersen, Kristi (1974). Mass belief systems revisited: political change and attitude structure. *Journal of Politics* 36: 540-591.

Nie, Norman H., Verba, Sidney, and Petrocik, John R. (1979). *The Changing American Voter*. Cambridge, Mass.: Harvard University Press.

Nie, Norman H., and Rabjohn, James N. (1979). Revisiting mass belief systems revisited. *American Journal of Political Science* 23: 139-175.

Norpoth, Helmut, and Rusk, Jerrold G. (1982). Partisan dealignment in the American electorate: itemizing the deductions since 1964. *American Political Science Review* 76: 522-537.

Page, Benjamin I., and Brody, Richard (1972). Policy voting and the electoral process: the Vietnam War issue. *American Political Science Review* 66: 979-995.

Page, Benjamin I. (1978). *Choices and Echoes in Presidential Elections*. Chicago: The University of Chicago Press.

Page, Benjamin I., and Jones, Calvin C. (1979). Reciprocal effects of policy preferences, party loyalties and the vote. *American Political Science Review* 73: 1071-1089.

Parenti, Michael (1967). Ethnic politics and the persistence of ethnic identification. *American Political Science Review* 61: 717-726.

Petrocik, John R. (1974). An analysis of intransitivities in the index of party identification. *Political Methodology* 1: 31-47.

Petrocik, John R. (1981). *Party Coalitions: Realignment and the Decline of the New Deal Party System*. Chicago: University of Chicago Press.

Petrocik, John R., and Verba, Sidney, with Schultz, Christine (1981). Choosing the choice and not the echo: a funny thing happened to *The Changing American Voter* on the way to the 1980 election. Presented at the American Political Science Association Convention, New York.

Pierce, John C., and Hagner, Paul R. (1982). Conceptualization and party identification: 1956–1976. *American Journal of Political Science* 26: 377–387.

Polsby, Nelson W. (1968). The institutionalization of the U.S. House of Representatives. *American Political Science Review* 62: 144–168.

Polsby, Nelson W. (1983). *Consequences of Party Reform.* Oxford: Oxford University Press.

Popkin, Samuel, Gorman, John W., Phillips, Charles, and Smith, Jeffrey A. (1976). Comment: what have you done for me lately? Toward an investment theory of voting. *American Political Science Review* 70: 779–805.

Prewitt, Kenneth (1970). Political ambitions, volunteerism, and electoral accountability. *American Political Science Review* 64: 5–17.

Prewitt, Kenneth, and Nie, Norman (1971). Review article: election studies of the Survey Research Center. *British Journal of Political Science* 1: 479–502.

RePass, David E. (1971) Issue salience and party choice. *American Political Science Review* 65: 389–400.

Riker, William H. (1982). The two-party system and Duverger's Law: an essay on the history of political science. *American Political Science Review* 76: 752–766.

Rose, Richard, and Urwin, Derek (1969). Social cohesion, political parties and strains in regimes. *Comparative Political Studies* 2: 7–67.

Rusk, Jerrold G. (1982). The Michigan election studies: a critical evaluation. *Micropolitics* 2: 82–109.

Salisbury, Robert H., and Michael MacKuen (1981). On the study of party realignment. *Journal of Politics* 43: 523–530.

Schattschneider, E. E. (1960). *The Semi-Sovereign People.* New York: Holt, Rinehart, and Winston.

Sears, David O., Hensler, Carl P., and Speer, Leslie K. (1979). Whites' opposition to busing: self-interest or symbolic politics? *American Political Science Review* 73: 369–384.

Sears, David O., Lau, Richard R., Tyler, Tom R., and Allen, Harris M., Jr. (1980). Self-interest vs. symbolic politics in policy attitudes and presidential voting. *American Political Science Review* 74: 670–684.

Seligman, Lester G., and King, Michael R. (1980). Political realignments and recruitment to the U.S. Congress, 1870–1970. In Campbell and Trilling, *Realignment in American Politics*, pp. 157–175.

Sellers, Charles (1965). The equilibrium cycle in two-party politics. *Public Opinion Quarterly* 30: 16–38.

Shively, W. Phillips (1979). The development of party identification among adults: exploration of a functional model. *American Political Science Review* 73: 1039–1054.

Sinclair, Barbara (1977). Party realignment and the transformation of the political agenda: the House of Representatives, 1925–1938. *American Political Science Review* 71: 940–953.

Sinclair, Barbara (1983). *Congressional Realignment, 1925–1978.* Austin: University of Texas Press.

Smith, Eric R. A. N. (1980). The levels of conceptualization: false measures of ideological sophistication. *American Political Science Review* 74: 685–696.

Stokes, Donald E. (1966). Some dynamic elements of contests for the presidency. *American Political Science Review* 60: 19–28.

Stokes, Donald E., Campbell, Angus, and Miller, Warren E. (1958). Components of electoral decision. *American Political Science Review* 52: 367–387.

Sullivan, John L., Piereson, James E., and Marcus, George E. (1978). Ideological constraint in the mass public: a methodological critique and some new findings. *American Journal of Political Science* 22: 233–249.

Sundquist, James L. (1973). *Dynamics of the Party System.* Washington, D.C.: The Brookings Institution.

Tufte, Edward R. (1978). *Political Control of the Economy.* Princeton, N.J.: Princeton University Press.

VanWingen, John R., and Valentine, David C. (1978). Partisanship, independence, and the partisan identification index. Presented at the Midwest Political Science Association Convention, Chicago.

Verba, Sidney, and Nie, Norman H. (1972). *Participation in America*. New York: Harper & Row.

Wanat, John, and Burke, Karen (1982). Estimating the degree of mobilization and conversion in the 1890s: an inquiry into the nature of electoral change. *American Political Science Review* 76: 360–370.

Weatherford, M. Stephen (1982). Interpersonal networks and political behavior. *American Journal of Political Science* 26: 117–143.

Weatherford, M. Stephen (1983). Economic voting and the 'symbolic politics' argument: a reinterpretation and synthesis. *American Political Science Review* 77: 158–174.

Wildavsky, Aaron (1964). *The Politics of the Budgetary Process*. Boston: Little, Brown.

CHAPTER 12

MODEL CHOICE IN POLITICAL SCIENCE:
The Case of Voting Behavior Research, 1946-1975

Herbert F. Weisberg

The continuing theme of this book has been the choice of models for the scientific enterprise in political science. Some authors have chosen to emphasize the importance of the inductive approach in their subfields while others have stressed deductive approaches. This runs contrary to the usual way of thinking about scientific models in which one approach would predominate in a discipline. The purpose of this concluding chapter is to demonstrate how competitive models can coexist in the scientific inquiry through a case study of the field of voting behavior. This is a good area for a case study since many would view it as one of the most scientific areas of the discipline, though not all who view it in that way would agree as to which elements of that study are the most scientific.

This examination of model selection will adapt Paul Beck's focus in chapter 11 on "Choice, Context, and Consequence" in our study of voting behavior. These "3 C's" provide an especially useful framework for reflecting about the scientific status of a field. After all, we do make *choices* when we decide to approach a field from the perspective of one model rather than another. These choices are made within particular *contexts* for the study of the field. And these choices have *consequences* for our further understanding of the field. Thus, Beck's 3 C's are important to consider as we reflect about the scientific status of a subfield. To these 3 C's I will add two more: change and criteria. How well our models deal with the inevitable political *change* is critical if they are to have continuing value, and more generally we must select *criteria* for assessing the success of our scientific treatment of an area. We shall consider these 5 C's as we review the history of science in voting behavior research.

THE CHOICE OF A MODEL, 1946–1965:
A FIELD BECOMES SCIENTIFIC

Beck contends in chapter 11 that in the study of voting behavior we have made the choice of adopting the "Michigan Model." While accepting his description of the elements of the model, we shall not accept any claim for that being our exclusive model for the study of voting. Instead, we can recall that several models of voting have been proposed over the years, and we shall examine what was involved in the discipline's choice among these models.

The Michigan Model was put into place by four researchers writing about the elections of the 1950s in their classic work, *The American Voter* (Campbell et al., 1960). But what if that book had not been written? What if Warren Miller had stayed at Berkeley when he visited there in the mid 1950s, if Donald Stokes had not visited Ann Arbor while working on his graduate degree at Yale, if Philip Converse had decided to continue his research on Chaucer rather than switch to social psychology, and if Angus Campbell had not been able to keep the election studies going after the 1948 or 1952 surveys? After all, the Michigan Model is largely due to the choices of these four scholars in the 1950s, and what if they had made different choices themselves?

This excursion into the history of science requires us to look back at how voting behavior was studied in the formative post-World War II period. It immediately leads to the question of what were the other models that could have served as choices?

Part of the story is very familiar. Before Michigan there was Columbia. The research team from the Bureau of Applied Social Research at Columbia University had conducted single county panel studies of the 1940 and 1948 elections. Their reports on those studies employed a sociological model of the vote decision, with emphasis on the Index of Political Predispositions, based on a person's religion, social economic status, and urban or rural residence. The University of Michigan researchers took the Columbia Model so seriously that one of their first journal reports on their own national surveys was devoted to a disconfirmation of the Index of Political Predispositions.

But how was voting being understood in the political science treatments of the day? If we are to understand how the subfield has chosen models to understand voting, we must be able to recall more vividly how political scientists were studying voting during the crucial choice years of 1946 through 1975. Specifically, I shall focus on the question of how American political behavior was being understood in the pages of the political science journals of that period.

For the purposes of this chapter I have scanned the 1946–1975 volumes of three leading journals: the *American Political Science Review, The Journal of Politics,* and the *American* (originally *Midwest*) *Journal of Political Science* (starting with its inception in 1957). All articles related to mass voting were examined; most public opinion pieces were included since there was little differentiation between the two areas in the early years. As a result the inclusion of articles is probably too expansive rather than insufficiently so. Still this search misses research trends in books, other journals, and papers not accepted by these journals, but a reasonable argument can be made that during this period these three journals would have reflected the dominant trends in voting research. Tables 1 and 2 use a rough categorization to show the trends in data employed and topics studied across these decades.

The 1946–1955 Decade

Only thirteen articles on political behavior appeared from 1946 to 1951, but the flow increased from 1952 to 1955. As might be expected, aggregate (and official) data were the most common data base for the articles in this period (two-fifths of the articles). As might not be expected, surveys were the next most common data base (one-third), including eight studies using Michigan Survey Research Center data and five using other surveys. The remaining quarter of the articles did not employ empirical data; these pieces ranged from treatments of legal matters related to voting to more theoretical discussions. None of the pieces were mathematical studies of voting.

There are not enough articles in particular categories to make strong conclusions about trends in this decade, but there are some suggestions of patterns. The aggregate data studies and those using non-SRC surveys tended to be state or local studies. The non-SRC surveys also tended to emphasize participation, broadly defined.

The largest category of articles in the first decade involves social groups, with particular attention to the South and blacks (particularly when the articles on black suffrage in the South are included). The sociological emphasis inherent in the Columbia Model affected the political science journals, but the emphasis was not on the class, religion, and residence variables that the Columbia re-

TABLE 1. Data Sources for Voting Behavior Articles in Leading Journals, by Decade

	1946–55	1956–65	1966–75
Nondata	26%	13%	4%
Aggregate	41	52	34
Surveys			
Non-Michigan	13	23	22
Michigan	21	11	25
Formal theory	0	1	11
Experiments and			
simulations	0	1	3
Total	101%	101%	99%
N=	39	91	242

TABLE 2. Topics Studied in Voting Behavior Articles in Leading Journals, by Decade

Topic	1946–55	1956–65	1966–75
Groups			
General	1	0	1
Region	3	4	2
Race	1	3	5
Class	1	4	3.5
Cities	1	2	0
Religion	1	2	1
Ethnic	1	1	2
Suburbs	0	1	1
Primary groups	0	1	1
Farmers	0	1	0
Interest Groups	1	0	0
Age	0	0	2
Gender	0	0	1
Total	10	19	19.5
Institutional			
Legal	3	5	7
Suffrage	3	5	7
Legislative	1	5	21
Nonpartisan	1	2	0
Primaries	1	3	8
Referenda	0	3	13
Total	9	23	56
Partisanship			
General	4	7	17
Independence	2	0	1
Realignment	1	7	4
Competition	0	1	4
Total	7	15	26
Participation	3	3	39
Personality	3	7.5	15.5
Issues	2	4	14
Communications	1	0	1
Ideology	1	1.5	10
Candidates	1	5	9
Theory			
General	1	1	0
Formal	0	0	7
Spatial	0	1	8

Continued

TABLE 2. *(Continued)*

Topic	1946–55	1956–65	1966–75
Total	1	2	15
Vote determinants	0	4	12
General	1	7	25
Total	39	91	242

searchers employed. Their choice of Erie County, Ohio, and Elmira County, New York, for their research efforts meant that the Columbia team was skipping the regional and racial foci that were of greater interest to the political scientists of the day.

An institutional direction is evident in several of the early pieces, covering such topics as voting procedures. A few papers also focused on partisanship, including independence and realignment.

The 1946–55 decade was when the Michigan Model was just beginning to be developed. Table 2 suggests that the sociological model was influential in political science, with some further attention to institutional and partisanship factors.

The 1956–1965 Decade

The second postwar decade was marked by a considerable increase in the number of relevant articles. This decade coincides exactly with Harvey Mansfield's editorship of the *APSR*. Also, the *Midwest Journal of Political Science* began publishing in the second year of this period. The growth in articles on voting turns out to be limited to two categories. Aggregate studies tripled in number while survey studies not using SRC data quadrupled. Meanwhile nondata studies and studies employing SRC data did not change in number.

While this period is one which we associate with a growth in survey research, aggregate studies predominated. Half of the articles involved analysis of aggregate data, a third of the studies involved surveys, and there was one experimental study and one on formal theory, with the remaining articles being nondata papers. As in the previous decade, a large number of the aggregate studies were state or local studies. Many of these aggregate studies focused on partisanship, legislative elections, and participation. The surveys using non-SRC data include many articles emphasizing psychological variables, especially personality effects.

The themes mentioned for the 1946–55 period remained important: groups, institutions, and partisanship. Region and race continued to define the groups studied most, now along with class. There was also a considerable increase in the focus on legislative elections, though often in the context of studying presidential coattails. Legal factors and suffrage matters commanded much attention. And the largest increase in these categories was in the study of realignment.

Additionally, a new theme became important: personality. Personality studies were based on a psychological model for voting that we have now nearly forgotten. *The Authoritarian Personality* (Adorno et al., 1950) was an important book at that time, and it was reflected in several articles. The interest in personality variables is well illustrated by the March 1958 issue of the *American Political Science Review* with its opening debate between M. Brewster Smith and Alexander George on "Opinions, Personality, and Political Behavior," followed by Herbert McClosky's study of "Conservatism and Personality." The importance of personality in this period is underscored by the fact that *The American Voter* devoted a chapter to countering the emphasis that other work at the time was giving to the topic.

In the 1956–65 decade, the Michigan researchers were publishing their work in the mainline political science journals. Yet the major themes in the journals were groups, institutions, and personality, elements that were not emphasized in the Michigan Model. This was still a formative period, before the Michigan Model was diffused through the field.

Model Choice

As the study of voting behavior became scientific during this period, the question of which variables would be emphasized in our understanding of voting became important. Through the first postwar decade, the emphasis was clearly on more sociological and institutional variables. The Michigan Model was presented in the next decade, but the journal literature suggests that personality variables were an important possible choice for the field. Indeed, a model could have been formed around groups, institutions, and personality, individually or taken together. By contrast the Michigan Model emphasizes three different aspects of elections: the parties, the candidates, and the issues, generally in that order of importance. The choice inherent in the choice of the Michigan Model is the emphasis on those variables rather than the others mentioned above. Yet the Michigan Model became important in the mid-60s rather than a triumvirate of groups, institutions, and personality. What accounts for this model choice?

Part of the explanation may be that it would have been more difficult to mold groups, institutions, and personality into a single coherent theory. Their proponents did come from different disciplinary backgrounds. It would have been difficult to merge the sociology focus on groups, the legal (and sometimes historical) focus on institutions, and the psychology focus on personality into a single model of voting. Of equal importance is that the early voting studies often obtained negative conclusions about the importance of these factors. The Michigan researchers showed that Columbia's Index of Political Predispositions was not very useful nationally and that personality variables were relatively unimportant. They did devote a chapter of *The American Voter* to institutional factors and found them to be of some importance, but their effects were limited. A third important point is that the theory of the vote decision presented in *The American Voter* was unusually comprehensive. It simultaneously took the previous factors into account and relegated many of them to minor positions in the overall model. The comprehensiveness of the model appealed immediately to other researchers who were favorable to developing a science of voting behavior. Each of these three explanations undoubtedly accounts to some extent for the dominance of the Michigan Model, but a further explanation is probably more important.

As Beck emphasizes in the preceding chapter, the formation of the Inter-University Consortium for Political Research (ICPR; now the Inter-University Consortium for Political and Social Research, or ICPSR) was critical in the diffusion of the Michigan Model. The diffusion of the model was in very large part due to the distribution of their data through the Consortium. In a real sense this allowed the Michigan world view to predominate because it suddenly was easier for researchers to analyze a common set of data than to collect their own data based on different theories of the vote. Additionally, the summer training programs of the ICPSR further allowed faculty and graduate students to journey to Ann Arbor for a summer to learn the methods on which the Michigan Model was based, leading to a much faster diffusion of a model through a discipline than would occur if a model were being taught at only a single graduate school. All of this helped foster the Michigan Model over possible alternative models of groups, institutions, and/or personality.

THE CHOICE OF A MODEL, 1966–1975:
AN INCOMPLETE REVOLUTION?

This chapter has so far implied that by 1965 the field of voting behavior was ready for the dominance of the Michigan Model. However, two related developments of importance occurred about this time. Several revisionist studies began to question the world according to Michigan, and a new rational choice model of voting was being developed. The result was to forestall complete dominance of the Michigan Model.

The revisionist work did not accept the Michigan claim that party, candidates, and issues are the most important factors in elections with the issue factor being a distant third. The motto of this movement became V. O. Key's (1966) line in his posthumously published *The Responsible Electorate*: "voters are not fools." The revisionist work found that issues and ideology were both more important than the Michigan studies had claimed. At least when given issue choices, voters would vote on the basis of those issues.

The rational choice model is based on the premise that political man and wo-man are rational actors, in the same sense that economic man and woman are considered rational actors in economics. If certain assumptions are made about how individuals behave as a result of their political self-interest, deductions about the behavior of the political system can be derived. Prime examples are the spatial theory of voting and the rational calculus of electoral participation. Mathematical studies of the properties of different election systems also fit this rubric. If the Michigan Model generally downplays the role of issues in voting as opposed to that of party or candidates, this approach instead emphasizes the role of ideology and issues in individual vote decisions, thus fitting in well with the revisionists. Indeed, party loyalty and candidate personality factors general-ly must be reinterpreted to discover reasons for a rational actor to consider them in voting.

The beginnings of this approach can be traced back to Condorcet's discovery of the paradox of voting in the eighteenth century and to work on location the-ory in economics in the 1920s, but the more immediate beginning for the study of individual voting behavior was Anthony Downs's work *An Economic Theo-ry of Democracy* (1957). The development and transmission of this rational choice perspective in political science is largely due to the efforts of William Riker. When he moved in the early 1960s from Lawrence College to the Univer-sity of Rochester to chair its political science department, he built a lively young department committed to the formal theory perspective. They actively recruited bright graduate students, trained them well in positive theory, mathematics, and methods, and then placed them well across the discipline. These students have diffused this positive theory approach through their own work at such re-search centers as Carnegie Mellon University and the California Institute of Technology. While it would be oversimplistic to identify this approach with a single graduate school, it is convenient to refer to this as the Rochester Model.

The 1966–1975 Decade

At this point we can turn back to our historical review to compare the 1966–75 decade with the earlier two decades. ICPR was founded in 1963, so the impact of its distribution of SRC data and its methodological training of non-Michigan researchers were evidenced for the first time in the journal litera-ture of this decade. Simultaneously, Bill Riker had been at Rochester long enough for his department to begin to have its impact on the field.

There was a true explosion of journal literature in the field in this period. Ta-ble 1 shows that a growth in survey studies occurred at the expense of aggregate studies. Only a third of the articles employed aggregate data, compared to one-half using survey data. With the release of the SRC data to non-Michigan scholars through the Consortium, the growth was indeed in the use of the Michigan election surveys. Additionally, note from Table 1 that there was near-

ly as much growth in experimental and especially formal theory studies during
this decade. The figures in Table 1 actually understate the number of formal
studies in that several articles originating from a formal perspective are coded
as analyzing aggregate data (such as the fluctuation of the midterm congressional vote with the state of the economy) or survey data (for example the extent to which citizen turnout in an election varies with the different terms in the
formal calculus of participation).

A closer look at the third postwar decade indicates that the claimed ascen-
dancy of the Michigan Model is less complete than might casually be recalled.
True, secondary analysis of the Survey Research Center surveys now was possible and led to a proliferation of articles. However, this was also the time that re-
visionism appeared in the voting behavior literature. Also, the formal theory
papers reflected the Rochester Model of voting, a model with an emphasis on
issues that fits well with much of the revisionist work. Even some of the aggregate studies were actually attempts to show the importance of issues (generally
economic) from a revisionist perspective. If we would have expected the Michigan Model to dominate during the 1966–75 decade, in fact it was frequently the
target rather than the guide.

In this decade, aggregate studies primarily involved state and local research,
studies of participation, legislative elections, and to a lesser extent, partisanship, race, region, referenda, and issues. Non-SRC survey studies focused most
on participation, state and local research, and psychological and personality
variables. Articles based on the SRC election studies emphasized issues, partisanship, participation, vote determinants generally, psychological and personality variables, and ideology. Participation was also a frequent topic of the several
formal studies.

The large increase in publications in this decade compared to the earlier ones
is especially marked by increases in articles on participation, legislative elections, referenda, partisanship, party competitiveness, spatial modelling, formal
theory more generally, vote determinants generally, and issues. If there is evidence of the journal output shifting as the Michigan Model took hold, it appears not in the explicit numbers in Table 2 as much as in the coding process
that generated the table. In the 1966–75 decade, for the first time there are clear
sets of articles on issues, on candidates, on ideology, and on vote determinants
generally, and the coding of articles into these categories is a more clear-cut decision than in the earlier decades. In fact, many of these articles challenged the
Michigan Model, but they had to accept its demarcation of the field in order to
attack its specific findings.

Model Choice

The journal search reminds us that the Michigan Model did not fully dominate the field in the 1966–75 period. It is not that this was too early a period to

show the effects. If the Michigan Model dominated to the extent that a reading of Beck's chapter implies, then the effects should be visible soon after the data were available for secondary analysis. To the contrary, the availability of the data for secondary analysis permitted researchers from other approaches to attempt to counter the Michigan Model. This is an effect which is unusual in the history of science, as those who base new theories on data they have collected usually maintain exclusive access to those data long enough for their theories to dominate a field. This is a rare instance in which the generosity of the researchers permitted others to challenge their model using the original researchers' own data.

Another important development which prevented the Michigan Model from achieving full dominance was the development and transmission of the Rochester Model. The diffusion of this model was also aided by a series of institutional developments. Bill Riker helped form the Public Choice Society in the mid 1960s, and its annual meetings have grown in size with many excellent papers on rational choice and voting emerging from its sessions. That society founded the journal *Public Choice*, which provided an additional outlet for formal studies of social choice theory and voting. Additionally, in the late 1960s and early 1970s, the Mathematical Social Science Board sponsored several conferences which allowed formal theorists to exchange their views on political science concerns. The diffusion network for the Rochester Model was never as large as that of the Consortium, but it did allow the Rochester Model to have a greater impact than if it had been confined to a single graduate school.

The advocates of the Rochester Model not only were adept at developing formal theories, but they had the methodological abilities to probe the Michigan election studies for evidence in favor of a rational choice interpretation and against the social psychological approach of Michigan. The Rochester Model has never been more widely used than the Michigan Model, but at least the development of a separate model of voting coincident with that of the Michigan Model imposed limitations on the dominance of the latter.

The existence of two lively models in the same scientific field can have some advantages, and that has been the case in the voting behavior field. Empirical researchers had to reassess the role that issues and ideology play in voting, leading to some of the modifications of the Michigan Model that Beck describes in chapter 11. At the same time, the formal theorists were constantly prodded by emprical data results, and so their work has had to include more empirical testing than one might expect for a deductive approach. Thus this was a period of competition between inductive and deductive models, with both benefitting from the resulting creative tension. If the competition in this period was sometimes marked by antagonism, it was followed by more peaceful coexistence in the 1976–85 decade (which will not be analyzed in detail here) with several studies blending deductive theorizing with inductive insights, generalizing mathematical models of voting which previously had little fit with reality to better accomodate empirical facts, and incorporating rational choice based measures into the national election studies.

The discussion so far has focused on the choice of model in the field. Of course, a model choice occurs within a context, has consequences, must handle political change, and must satisfy criteria for the choice of a model. These are also important points, but our discussion of them will be briefer.

CONTEXT FOR MODEL SELECTION

Context considerations directly affect the choice of a scientific model, especially when one model is seen as being able to cover a broader domain than other models. In the voting behavior area, this translates to whether a model is restricted to one set of elections or can explain a broader set of elections.

When one looks at the voting behavior journal articles of the 1946–55 period, one is struck by their distinct local flavor. National surveys were beyond the resources of most researchers, and even collection of aggregate data for the entire nation was often not feasible. As a result, a large proportion of the early papers were based in a single city, state, or region. This local focus was, of course, often quite appropriate, but it could also be limiting, as in a 1950 *APSR* piece on "Voting Behavior in 1948 as Compared with 1924 in a Typical Ohio Community."

The context for the study of voting changed with the emergence of the Michigan Model. This model was based on results of a national sample of voters, and so the context became national. For the first time it was possible to study voting nationally, and many of the major articles now utilized national samples.

Yet, the context for the Michigan Model has proved somewhat confining. First, since it was based on a national sample, the SRC data could not be used to obtain representative samples for the study of state elections, including elections for Congress. Congressional elections were not irrelevant to the theory, but they could not easily be studied from this data base. Some researchers were able to secure funding for state studies, especially the Comparative State Elections Project in 1968. Eventually, the problem was seen to be serious by congressional researchers themselves, and they played an important role in the funding and study design for the 1978 election study. The result has been increasing attention in the National Election Studies to congressional elections (and they would add senate elections if they could get funding for such an effort), but these studies are still not as useful for the study of state elections as would be desirable.

If the context of the Michigan studies was limited, Table 2 reminds us that the journal literature of the time actually included a very large number of articles on state and local elections, legislative elections, and issue referenda as well as an extensive journal literature on participation, including turnout. Fortunately, many individual researchers still mounted their own local or state surveys, so there remains a lively literature at these levels. The problem with these studies is that they were often isolated and noncumulative in contrast to the presidential election studies.

The context of the Michigan Model was also confining in the sense that it was basically American. The model itself was stated in such general terms that it should have applied to other countries as well. Indeed, it was soon exported to other countries, often by the Michigan researchers themselves working in collaboration with foreign scholars. Unfortunately, the scholars from other countries often found that the Michigan concepts did not fit their own countries all that well. In particular, European voting seemed more ideological than party based. The context for the American studies of voting apparently limited the generality of the findings more than the most sophisticated researchers realized.

Context considerations have different implications for the Rochester Model. Since the development of this model is more based on abstract mathematics than empirical data, it has been less tied to any single context, which has been both a blessing and has caused difficulty. The advantage has been greater generality for the model. It can be applied as easily to voting for lower offices, to voting turnout, and to other countries as to vote direction in American presidential elections. Many of the more interesting applications are actually to voting in congressional elections, on issue referenda, and in other countries, besides the development of different explanations for nonvoting. The fact that it is based on a broader rational choice theory means, however, that much of the work in the field is not related to mass voting per se, thus diminishing some of the influence of the model in this field.

Most empirical applications of this model are based on secondary analysis of surveys which were designed from other perspectives. The formal theorists have had to accept the questions in the Michigan election studies, instead of being able to design studies fully reflecting their own approach. It is true that the Michigan studies adopted some new measurement strategies (such as the 7-point issue scales), which are particularly useful in testing some formal theories. And the active involvement of researchers from around the country in the study design and question writing for the Michigan studies since 1978 has allowed formal theorists to affect the content of the studies more directly. Still, the lack of a national data set explicitly based on the Rochester Model has made it somewhat less influential than it might otherwise have been. In other words, the dominance of the Michigan data has given the Michigan Model a built-in advantage.

CONSEQUENCES OF MODEL SELECTION

What are the consequences of the model choice in the voting behavior field? What classes of variables have received little attention because of the models that have been selected, and how serious are these omissions? In a sense, the consequence question directs us to choices not made, paths not taken. It is hard to see fully what would have been the consequences of a path not taken, but some speculation is possible.

First, the deemphasis on sociological groups probably made the research of less relevance to political managers who view campaigns as coalition building. That may not be a terrible consequence, but it has probably led to more separation of some voting researchers from the practical world of elections than might otherwise have been the case.

The deemphasis on psychological variables seems even more benign, at least to me. Indeed, an emphasis on personality might have been too conducive to manipulation of candidate appeals to satisfy innate psychological needs of voters. There are probably enough such efforts in campaign commercials already without a theory of voting in which personality effects become dominant.

The deemphasis on institutional considerations is more unfortunate. Voting occurs within the context of particular electoral institutions, and those institutions do matter in the voting. This has always been recognized, yet the effects of institutional variables on voting remain largely unstudied. Ideally one would collect large amounts of contextual data on elections and try to maximize the institutional variable included in surveys, but in practice these are difficult goals to achieve. The Rochester Model is at least able to study the formal implications of varying the institutional setting, though many critics feel that the institutions studied through formal analyses are too often pale shadows of the complex institutions that exist in the real world. Many of the early articles in the spatial modelling area, for example, manipulated minor assumptions of their models without caring that the more major assumptions have little relationship to political reality. The consequences in that instance are to limit the impact of the studies on the discipline. Fortunately, the newer work, such as that embodied in Enelow and Hinich's (1984) *The Spatial Theory of Voting*, does try harder to develop realistic assumptions and to confront empirical data.

As another example of the lack of attention to institutional considerations, the effects of the electoral college have received remarkably little examination even though the field of electoral behavior has devoted most of its attention to presidential elections. The Michigan studies were not well suited to studying the electoral college, since their representative national sample does not yield representative state samples. Not until Steven Rosenstone's (1983) *Forecasting Presidential Elections* has there been a systematic attempt to predict election outcomes in the states and thus focus on the electoral college.

The deemphasis on ideology in the Michigan Model is also consequential. *The American Voter* showed that certain senses of ideology were of limited importance in voting. That had the effect of removing ideology from the equation. Yet ideology is so critical to our understanding of politics that it formed

the basis of the revisionist work on voting in the late 1960s and early 1970s. Indeed, more recent work by Warren Miller with Teresa Levitin is largely a cor-
rective for the early playing down of ideology. Also, ideology came to take on
new meanings, with the increased emphasis on the rationality in voting. In particular, the Rochester Model has emphasized ideology embedded in a spatial
model. Finally, as pointed out in the discussion of context above, the lack of
emphasis on ideology limited the Michigan Model more to the American case
than even its developers desired.

This way of thinking about consequences may seem strange in that the usual
view of science is that researchers should not consider consequences in choosing
a model. However, it is too easy for the current generation to lose sight of the
context within which the Michigan Model was being developed. The elections
of the 1950s were being held in the immediate aftermath of the Second World
War and in the early days of the Cold War. This was a period in which people
were fascinated by ideologies—nazism, fascism, communism, socialism, au-
thoritarianism, totalitarianism, and democracy—though some writers were beginning to proclaim the end of ideology. There was indeed attention to the Nazi
case in some of the early Michigan work, including Converse's belief systems
paper, but the net effect of the Michigan Model was to impose a temporary end
to ideology in the study of voting behavior. What is remarkable is that this is
the one element which could not be dropped from the model.

These matters of ideology play through rather differently for the Rochester
Model. Much formal work on politics explicitly brings ideology into account,
but often in a manner that is different from classical treatments of the topic.
Voters and candidates might be arrayed, for example, on a left-right ideological continuum. This becomes a rather nonideological view of ideology. If the
Rochester Model has ideological connotations, they are often from a conservative perspective. Rational political man and woman are acting in their own self-
interests, which makes it hard to understand or justify such forms of altruism
as government social welfare programs other than as crass appeals by politicians for votes from the masses. Government actions which might otherwise be
justified on the basis of liberal ideology are instead criticized as inefficiencies resulting from the political marketplace. The logic is often more beyond reproach
than is the understanding of what it takes to govern a large democracy which is
not entirely middle class.

Finally, communications variables have received little emphasis in any of the
models discussed in this chapter. Clearly elections are much influenced by the
media. Yet the media effects play only a minor role in these models. A few of
the early studies focused on the media or communications, often in a propa-
ganda framework, but this was not an important theme in the political science
literature. The Michigan researchers certainly were aware of this gap by the early 1970s and tried to supplement their surveys with media studies. Still the total

attention to these variables remains very limited. The consequences here are that we know less about the dynamics of opinion formation and change during the election season, as well as less about the impact of political events, than we might otherwise know.

CHANGE AND MODEL SELECTION

Change plays a critical role in elections. The factors that are important in one election are not necessarily the same as those that were important in the previous election. After all, politicians try to change the political setting so that they can win the next election (or keep winning). Electoral change is handled quite differently in the different models.

Some of the early models of voting were deficient in that they did not incorporate change. Thus the Columbia Model's emphasis on long-term social factors that change very slowly (like a person's class, religion, or residence) meant that it had no chance of explaining the electoral volatility that is of so much interest to political scientists. Personality studies and an institutional focus have similar problems. It was not until the Michigan Model was advanced that electoral change could be explained. Even then the linchpin of the Michigan Model was the long-term party identification variable, which seemed fairly unchangeable, but the possibility of change was incorporated in the short-term issue and especially candidate factors.

There was still the question of how change would be studied in the Michigan survey design. The early Columbia studies had been panel studies across the election year. They found little change in vote intention across the election year, and so year-long studies seemed to be a needless luxury. The Michigan researchers instead chose a design with a single preelection interview in September or October and with a postelection interview in November or December. Intraelection change would not be examined, and interelection change would be studied only through longitudinal comparisons. Thus the design permitted comparing the marginal distribution of party identification in different election years, but the dynamics of individual change processes could only be inferred. Similarly, changes in the relative causal importance of different influences on the vote could be noticed, but the change processes could not be directly observed. The problem, as Niemi demonstrates in chapter 10, is that many of the most interesting questions in public opinion and voting behavior are inherently dynamic in nature, and intraelection year panels are insufficient souces of information on individual change.

A panel design is one classic approach to dynamic processes. When the Michigan researchers adopted a panel design in the late 1950s and again in the early 1970s, they chose an across-election-years panel, reinterviewing the same respondents in three successive election years. Even this design minimizes attention to the political dynamics of the election year. The political context becomes a missing feature of the studies. The impact of media and events, and especially their interactions, cannot be studied within these designs. Not until 1980 did the National Election Studies secure funding for a multiwave panel study through the entire presidential election year.

Unfortunately, panel studies inevitably suffer from some methodological problems. For one thing, it is hard to trace people in our mobile society across a long panel study. People who do not move are often unwilling to be interviewed repeatedly. As a result of such "mortality effects," the final panel wave is less representative of the population than was the original sample, and we do not know how much we can generalize from such panels to the population. At the same time, the people who are willing to participate in a multiwave panel study may change their attitudes and behaviors as a result of the repeated interviews. Clausen (1968) has shown that even the single preelection interview design increases the turnout of respondents as compared to the overall population, and presumably the lengthy interview also increases their interest in politics. This makes it even more hazardous to generalize from panel studies to the underlying population.

The 1984 National Election Study attempts to counter these problems with panel studies by switching to continuous monitoring of public opinion during the election year through a series of weekly cross-section samples. This is an exciting new approach to studying the dynamics of public opinion, though the number of interviews taken any single week will be sufficiently small as to require caution in analyzing changes. But the point is that the design of the election studies over the years has limited the results, removing some of the most important political variables from potential analysis.

Moving on to the Rochester Model, change is sometimes incorporated in formal models. Studies of electoral equilibria, for example, are intrinsically dynamic in character, as are studies of bandwagon effects in campaigns. In spatial modelling, candidates can change their positions on dimensions or, in some versions of the model, can change their emphasis on different dimensions. Models in which the support of the president's party in congressional elections changes with changes in the economy also keep our attention on political change. This is not to say that every positive theory incorporates change, but that formal theory can often help us understand change.

CRITERIA FOR MODEL SELECTION

How do we choose among the models in a field such as voting behavior? What are the appropriate criteria? And that leads us to ask yet again, What are the appropriate goals of our scientific enterprise?

The strength of the Michigan Model may be in explanation of the individual vote decision, particularly in a variance explanation sense. Yet this strength is achieved by incorporating so many factors into its model that the theoretical parsimony and simplicity that Kramer demands in chapter 2 are sacrificed. And the model provides more of a framework for understanding past elections than a scheme for predicting future elections as MacRae desires in chapter 3.

The Rochester Model has the greater parsimony and simplicity, but often moves too far away from the real world in its assumptions to provide an explanation that is very satisfactory. It can be very useful in explaining how a candidate like Goldwater or McGovern can lose in a landslide when he moves too far away from the center of the American electorate, but added terms such as perceived candidate competence must be factored in to explain other election years. Fiorina (1981) developed the concept of retrospective voting to show that rational voting does occur even if voters pay little attention to campaign platforms. The model thus has become more complex over the years and has become more useful in explaining elections, though there is some tension between such adjustments to the model and the underlying desire for theoretical simplicity.

This discussion will not conclude with a choice between the Michigan and Rochester Models. The original versions of both were oversimplistic, but both have been influential and both have furthered our understanding of voting. What may be most intriguing from a history of science standpoint is that the two models have coexisted for more than two decades, each providing a source of challenge to the other. Our models for the development of science are ones of scientific revolution and progressive problem shifts rather than of creative tension between coexisting competing models. The science of voting behavior has been marked by models not adopted, like the Columbia Model and the triumvirate of groups, institutions, and personality that did not emerge from the 1950s, but it has also been marked by two strong models which fulfill different conceptions of science even if they both fail to satisfy still other criteria.

REFERENCES

Adorno, T. W., Frenkel-Brunswik, Else, Levinson, Daniel J., and Sanford, R. Nevitt (1950). *The Authoritarian Personality*. New York: Harper.

Campbell, Angus, Converse, Philip E., Miller, Warren E., and Stokes, Donald E. (1960). *The American Voter*. New York: Wiley.

Clausen, Aage (1968). Response validity: vote report. *Public Opinion Quarterly* 32(1968-69): 588–606.

Downs, Anthony (1957). *An Economic Theory of Democracy*. New York: Harper & Row.

Enelow, James M., and Hinich, Melvin J. (1984). *The Spatial Theory of Voting*. Cambridge: Cambridge University Press.

Fiorina, Morris P. (1981). *Retrospective Voting in American Elections*. New Haven, Conn.: Yale University Press.

Key, V. O., Jr. (1966). *The Responsible Electorate*. New York: Vintage Books.

Rosenstone, Steven J. (1983). *Forecasting Presidential Elections*. New Haven, Conn.: Yale University Press.

Author Index